UNDERSTANDING FOREST BIOLOGY

UNDERSTANDING FOREST BIOLOGY

By

Dr. Shubhrata R. Mishra

Department of Botany
Vikram University
Ujjain (M.P.)
(India)

DISCOVERY PUBLISHING HOUSE PVT. LTD.
NEW DELHI-110 002

First Published-2009

ISBN 978-81-8356-460-1

Published by:

DISCOVERY PUBLISHING HOUSE PVT. LTD.
4831/24, Ansari Road, Prahlad Street,
Darya Ganj, New Delhi-110002 (India)
Phone: 23279245 • Fax: 91-11-23253475
E-mail: dphbooks@rediffmail.com
dphtemp@indiatimes.com
Website: www.discoverypublishinghouse.com

Printed at:

Sachin Printers
Delhi

Preface

The present title "Understanding Forest Biology" has been written for those students interested in careers in diverse fields of biological sciences. It provides a structured approach to learning by covering all the important topics in a uniform, systematic format. The book has been comprehensively designed incorporating recent advances in this fast moving field. It also provides accessible information on forest biology in compact form for undergraduate students in biology and related life' sciences. It is intelligible to the educated layman, though it deals with some complex ideas. It is an adequate text for all the requirements of students in this area. In addition, busy lecturers who require a quick reference compendium will find it useful, particularly for tuitional planning. Simple, yet hopefully clear figures and tables are provided throughout the book.

The over-riding goal of this book, and indeed of the whole *Understanding series,* is to present the essential information concerning forest biology in a compact, readily accessible form which leads itself to student learning and revision. The convergence of various approaches has generated a rich panorama of detail, the significance of which we are still attempting to unraval. The present text has been written as an introduction to this rapidly growing field.

To make the work more comprehensive and informative, the author has consulted many authoritative books, research journals, abstracts, monographs etc., so there can be no claim to originality except in the manner of treatment.

The author expresses his thanks to his friends and colleagues whose continue inspirations have initiated him to bring out this book.

The author expresses his gratitude to Mr. Wasan and staff of M/s Discovery Publishing House Pvt. Ltd. for their whole hearted cooperation in the publication of this book.

In the mean time, the author will remain sincerely responsible for any shortcomings of the book and be grateful to the readers for their suggestions and constructive criticism for the continuous betterment of the book. He takes this opportunity to appeal to the readers to send their suggestions straightaway to his Publisher.

Author

CONTENTS

1

Introduction

Forests are the climax vegetation over about 40 percent (4500 million hectares 11115 million acres) of the world's lane surface, although Man has substantially altered them or entirely removed there from vast areas – from much of Western Europe, for example. Different types of forest are found in different climates, and there are striking convergences in forest structure and general appearance between areas with the same climate in different continents where the same type of forest occurs although composed of different species. The explanation of this similarity of appearance, or epharmony as it is called is still largely unexplained, although physiological causes such as response to water stress or mineral deficiency are clearly involved.

Tropical Rain Forests

In the tropics and subtropics evergreen tropical rain forests occupy about 1000 million hectares (a 500 million acres) in the wettest climates. They occur in three great blocks centered on Amazonia, the Guinea-Congo region of Africa and the Malay archipelago, the latter extending from the Western Ghats of India to the wet, high islands of the Pacific. There is also an isolated small zone in east Madagascar and the Mascarenes. There are 13 major categories or formations of tropical rain forest. Three of these (lower montage, upper montane and sub-alpine forest) occur at progressively higher altitudes. Beach, mangrove forest and brackish water forest are coastal. Two formations, peatswamp and freshwater swamp forest occur on inundated ground inland, three on extreme substrata (limestone, ultrabasics and nutrient-poor sands) and two on dry lowland mesic sites in continuously humid and mildly seasonal climates respectively. These last two formations include the most complex and species-rich plant communities in the world. They occur in the best conditions for plant life, with no dry or cold season to interrupt growth. The biggest trees average 30-45 m (100-150 ft) in height, although some reach 60 m (200 ft) or more. Beneath them grows a dense profusion of smaller trees. The tallest trees commonly occur as isolated emergents standing head and shoulders above a continuous canopy. Shrubs and herbs are rare, the undergrowth plants consisting mostly of small trees. Different tree species reach different heights at maturity, and characterize different strata in the canopy. The emergent and tallest canopy trees usually have broad, sympodial crowns, composed of numerous small rather dense subcrowns. Smaller trees commonly have crowns taller than broad, and these are frequently of monopodial construction, that is having a single main axis. Buttresses, which may reach 10 m (33 ft) or more up the trunk, are an important feature of many types of rain forest, and in some types stilt roots are common. Leaves are principally of mesophyll size and may have the apex extended as a prolonged drip tip. Climbers (lianes) and epiphytes are common in a great diversity of form and species. Stranglers, which start life as epiphytes but send down roots and ultimately engulf and kill the host tree, are prominent. Saprophytes and parasites occur (including in the East *Rafflesia*, which produces the largest flower in the world). The trees provide a complex framework for these other plant forms, and an intricate set of niches for animals. Both flora and fauna are exceedingly rich. For example, the rain forests of the Malay peninsula occupy an area equal to England and Wales, containing some 2 500 tree species and a total flora of about 8000 species of vascular plants. Many botanists believe that flowering plants evolved in tropical rain forests. Today they certainly contain the greatest concentration of primitive groups. Small areas of forest in southeast Asia are richer than in Latin America. The African forests are much poorer, for example as many species of palm are found on Singapore island as on the entire continent of Africa.

Structure becomes simpler and species become fewer away from the optimum, northward and southward where tropical forests merge into equivalent subtropical formations, for instance in Indochina and south China. There is a similar trend to simplification within the tropics to the other rain forest formations listed above. One of the most strikingly distinctive lowland rain-forest types is so-called heath forest (caatinga and campos in South America) which is, however, virtually absent from Africa. This develops on soils which even by tropical standards are impoverished, are mostly coarse, freely draining siliceous sands, and become podozolized. Heath forest is of low stature, microphyllous and very dense, with a uniform canopy top of high albedo. Its physiognomy is an adaptation to periodic water stress and to mineral deficiency. In the eastern tropics this structure and physiognomy is also found in upper montane rain forest (cloud forest) and several species occur in both.

Upper Montane or Cloud Forest

Upper montane or *cloud forest* is rain forest which occurs above the cloud level on tropical mountains. Its lower limit is quite sharply at the cloud line. Cloud forest characteristically has a low, dense canopy of small trees with thick, gnarled crowns of tiny, leathery leaves and high reflective power. Trees and ground are thickly swathed in epiphytes, mainly filmy ferns, but including bryophytes and flowering plants. *Sphagnum* (bog moss) often occurs in open places. In very humid climates peat accumulates. The soil is waterlogged for all or much of the time. Much of the precipitation is derived by the fog (ground-level cloud) condensing on the vegetation. Cloud forest occurs as low as 600 m (1970 ft) in Malaysia, and at 3000-3300 m (9250-10830 ft) in the main cordillera of New Guinea.

On the very highest mountains subalpine forest occurs above cloud forest up to the tree line; it is of low stature with very tiny leaves of manophyll size. Lower montane rain forest occurs between upper montane and lowland forest. It has a general resemblance to the latter and merges through a broad ecotone but differs in species composition and several structural features which taken together are diagnostic, and include lower canopy with fewer, smaller emergents, smaller buttresses and absence of big woody climbers.

Mangrove

Mangrove is a type of forest associated with muddy shores of a belt surrounding the equator. This belt reaches latitude 32°N, and as far south as Auckland in New Zealand and South Australia. Mangroves develop on sheltered muddy shores of deltas and estuaries exposed to the tide. They vary in width, some reaching up to several kilometres. The trees are evergreen, with the thick leathery leaves frequently associated with plants of saline soils and other physiological adaptations to live in salt water. Many species have viviparous seeds, which develop into seedlings on the parent tree and on being shed stick into the mud, when roots develop very quickly. Various types of prop and aerial root are another characteristic of these trees. Breathing roots enable the root system to respire in the anaerobic mud. The vegetation is almost entirely woody, varying from low scrub to forest 30 m (100 ft) high.

Mangrove swamps are one of the most unpleasant types of vegetation for the human visitor: the aerial roots make progress very difficult, and the deep mud releases unpleasant fetid gases which accumulate in the anaerobic conditions. The myriad biting insects are yet another disincentive.

There is a zonation of vegetation in mangrove swamps associated with the degree of immersion. Different species have different competitive powers according to their tolerances of salinity.

Monsoon and Savanna Forests (Dry Tropical Forests)

Rain forests change with increasing length of dry season to semi-evergreen and deciduous types. Initially species composition alters although the genera and families present remain much the same and only the taller trees are deciduous. Leaf shedding and flowering become synchronized and correlated with climatic seasonality. In the strongly seasonal dry tropics, forests of much simpler structure and with fewer woody species occur and ultimately closed forest is replaced by open woodland any savanna. In all climates with a marked dry season fire is an important factor controlling structure and species composition of the vegetation. In progressively drier climates, total amount of moisture becomes more important than length of dry season. Characteristically these so-called monsoon and savanna forests form mosaic pattern.

Closed moisture-loving, more nearly evergreen, so-called gallery forests occur along water courses. These seasonally dry tropical forests are extensive in all three continents. The flora is rich, with many fire-resistant herbs (including bulbous types) and grasses in the drier and more open types. There is a rich fauna, notably the spectacular group of ungulates in east Africa.

Sclerophyllous Forests

Sclerophyllous forests, with winter rain, occur around the Mediterranean and in the other parts of the world with similar climate. The summers are hot and dry, the winters warm and wet due to – cyclonic rain Annual rainfall is 500-1000 mm (20-40 in) but irregular, and there are prolonged periods of low relative humidity. There is no really cold season. Spring is the main growing and flowering season.

The Mediterranean basin has been the center of civilizations from ancient time and deforestation, cultivation, grazing and soil erosion have destroyed most of the original forest so that only variously degraded communities now remain. The original zonal vegetation was forest dominated by a canopy of the Holm Oal (*Quercus ilex*), 15-18 m (50-60 ft) tall, with shrubs and herbs beneath. Where the tree are cut about every 20 years it is replaced by a dense shrub vegetation called maquis This is very rich in species including many geophytes, but is subject to periodic fire, and becomes degraded by excessive grazing and burning to form open garigue. All the best sites are now occupied by vineyards and other agriculture. Many species are adapted to Mediterranean climatic conditions by the possession of small, leathery evergreen leaves which minimize water loss in dry periods.

Similar vegetation occurs in central and southern California. Here evergreen forests occur to the north, but southward, with decreasing rainfall, are replaced by a scrub called chaparral which is comparable to maquis except that it is the natural zonal vegetation with lightning-induced fires as a natural controlling factor. In the Southern Hemisphere, sclerophyll forest occur in a tiny area of Chile (only relicts remain), the Cape of South Africa, where the flora is fantastically rich especially with members of the heath family (Ericaceae) and the southwest tip of Australia, where the general appearance differs due to the predominance of members of the families Epacridaceae and Proteaceae and the genus *Eucalyptus*. The area occupied by dry forest and woodlands of all kind: (Mediterranean sclerophyll type, plus th monsoon and savanna tropical and subtropical forests) is 1400 million hectare (3500 million acres).

Warm Temperate Evergreen Forests

There are two groups of warn temperate forests. They total 100 million hectares (247 million acres) in area. The first kind is an extension of sclerophyl forest in conditions where there is no summer drought. In California north of 36°, the coastal strip is moist from summer fogs which result from cool onshore ocean currents. Forests of the Giant Redwood (*Sequoia sempervirens*) occur. This is the tallest tree in the world, attaining 100 m (330 ft) and more. Farther north on the same coast there are magnificent temperate rain forests of *Tsuga heterophylla* (Western Hemlock), *Thuja plicata* (Western Red Cedar) and *Pseudotsuga menziesii* (Douglas Fir). There is a comparable forest in South America, the Valdivian forest of Chile, but none in Africa. In Australia, the Karri (*Eucalyptus diversicolor*) forest abuts the summer-dry sclerophyll forest zone. This also is a tall forest Like the North American examples it is an important timber resource. In the

Mediterranean region, this type of vegetation occurs around the Black Sea, east as far as the shores of the Caspian, and includes the species-rich Tertiary-relict Colchic forest of Transcaucasia, which lies in a region where the summers are mild and wet enough for tea cultivation to have replaced most of the zonal forest.

The main warm temperate forests are found on the eastern seaboards of the continents, exposed to monsoon or trade winds. Rainfall is plentiful, 150-300 cm (60-120 in), and well distributed throughout the year. In southeast Asia (Thailand, Indochina, China, Korea and southern Japan), eastern Australia and southern Brazil there is a continuous gradation with increasing latitude from wet tropical to subtropical to warm temperate conditions. It is very difficult to distinguish zones in these evergreen forests. Characteristically penetration is difficult; they are rich in tree species including some conifers, and in epiphytes and climbers, but less so than the tropics. Plank buttresses are absent. Some trees are deciduous, giving marked seasonal differences in appearance.

Mosses, liverworts and ferns are abundant on the ground and tree-trunks. Bamboos are common in some types, as are tree ferns. There are strong similarities in structure and physiognomy with montane tropical forests and at the family level also in the flora. The climate, however, has a marked annual rhythm, whereas the montane tropics have a greater diurnal than annual climatic range. General appearance varies with different regions and there is a complete change in flora from low to high latitudes. In Australia, it has been shown that tropical types extend farthest south on the best soils and moistest sites. The main temperate type is the *Nothofagus* forest of Tasmania and Victoria, whose boundaries are determined by frequency of fire. In Africa, only the Drakensburg mountains have suitably moist sites for this type of forest, and it is of limited extent.

In North America it is also poorly defined because cold air masses move south as far as the Gulf of Mexico, but it is found near the coast from Louisiana, Florida and Georgia to North Carolina. The tree flora is rich including evergreen oaks (*Quercus* spp), a few palms and some climbers. Bald Cypress (*Taxodium distichum*) swamps occur in wet areas and fireclimax pine (*Pinus* spp) forests are found on dry sands. Most of the forests of New Zealand fall into this class; dominant trees include *Nothofagus*, mixed conifers, and a kauri pine (*Agathis australis*) subtropical broad leaved species mixture, depending on locality, soil and past history.

Temperate Deciduous Forest

Temperate deciduous forests are perhaps the most familiar type in the world. The total area is 800 million hectares (2000 million acres). They formerly covered most of Western Europe and are still extensive in North America. They are virtually restricted to the Northern Hemisphere (apart from an area in Patagonia, southern Chile and Tierra del Fuego). Leaf fall is an adaptation to the marked but not very prolonged cold season when water is unavailable or restricted (by contrast with the tropics where it is simply an adaptation to drought). Annual rainfall is 70-150 cm (28-60 in). Evergreen broadleaved trees cannot withstand cold or winter drought and in Western Europe *Ivy* (*Hedera helix*) and Holly (*Ilex aquifolium*) are both Atlantic species absent farther east where winters are more severe. *Rhododendron* and *Vaccinium* species, also evergreen, by contrast, survive winter cold below a snow covering. These forests are found on the eastern coasts of North America and Asia between the warm temperate forests and cold or arid temperate regions. In North America, they extend north to the Great Lakes and upper reaches of the Gulf of St. Lawrence, and west of the Mississippi. In Asia, they occur in northern Japan and on the adjacent part of the continent. They are also found on the western edge of Eurasia in Europe, north of the Mediterranean zone, and where the Gulf Stream causes winter rains to be replaced by evenly distributed rainfall or rain with a summer maximum, and where the cold season is relatively short. Here they range east to the Urals as a wedge between the steppes and the boreal coniferous forests. Deciduous trees occur where there are four to six months with adequate rain and this forest is absent from extreme maritime climates of the western seaboard as well as extreme continental climates.

The temperate deciduous forest zone of Western Europe is one of the most populous regions of the world because the climatic conditions also favour prosperous agriculture and grazing, and only tiny fragments of the forest remain with virtually none in virgin condition. Floristically the Western-European forests are poorer than the others due to extinction in the Pleistocene ice ages. Beeches (*Fagus* spp), oaks (*Quercus* spp), limes (*Tilia* spp) and ashes (*Fraxinus* spp), are locally dominant in the single tree layer. In wet places alders (*Alnus* spp) and willows (*Salix* spp) become common. There is a single shrub layer in which hazels (*Corylus* spp), Field Maple (*Acer campestre*) and hawthorns (*Crataegus* spp) are common, and a herb layer. There are few climbers and only cryptogamic epiphytes. The trees flower early, commonly before the leaves open, and most are wind-pollinated; this allows a long period for fruits to form and ripen before the onset of winter. In early spring before the canopy becomes leafy the forest floor herbs flower, creating carpets of blossom; especially of Bluebell (*Endymion non-scriptus*), Primrose (*Primula vulgaris*) and Oxlip (*Primula elatior*), which are one of the glories of these forests, equalled only by the spectacular yellow, orange and red tints of the dying foliage in the fall. The early spring temporal niche is succeeded by a spring one, occupied by other herbs, for example Wood Sorrel (*Oxalis acetosella*), which flower at the time of leaf flush. In Asia and North America there are more genera and species in both tree and shrub layers, including magnolias, numerous maples (*Acer* spp), Tulip Tree (*Liriodendron tulipifera*), buckeyes (*Aesculus* spp) and hickories (*Carya* spp), as well as temperate outliers of mainly tropical families.

The *Boreal region* encircles the globe at and beyond the northern limit of forests and covers major portions of North America and Eurasia as well as the islands of Newfoundland, Sakhalin and Iceland. It abuts southward on the temperate deciduous forest but the winters are colder and longer. Part of the region, between 45° and 70°N is occupied by the very extensive boreal coniferous forest, which covers 1500 million hectares (3700 million acres). In addition there are big areas of bog, peatland and swamp, known as muskeg, and in oceanic regions, such as Iceland, dwarf shrub vegetation known as heath. The main forest dominants are conifers with xeromorphic needle leaves, more resistant to winter cold and drought than broadleaved trees. Such trees can commence photosynthesis immediately conditions permit in the spring, so are better adapted to exploit regions where the growing season is short. Deciduous trees need about 120 days per year with mean temperature over 10°C, conifers can manage with 30 days, though there are differences between species. The narrow, conical, monopodial tree form with drooping branches is adaptive to regions of high snow fall. These forests have only a poorly developed shrub and herb layer: shade is greater, decay of falling leaves is slow so that undecomposed litter covers much of the surface, and the climate is worse. Spruces (*Picea* spp) with Norway Spruce (*P. abies*) merging eastward with Siberian Spruce (*P. obovata*) in Eurasia and White Spruce (*P. glauca*) in the New World, firs (*Abies* spp), pines (*Pinus* spp) and larches (*Larix* spp) dominate in different places. At its northern limit the boreal conifer forest merges into open parkland with scattered groves of trees, taiga. The northernmost forest in the world is in eastern Siberia at 72° 50'N, 105°E and is dominated by a larch *Larix gmelinii* (*L. dahurica*), which is highly productive in the very short summer, but one of the few deciduous conifers, losing its needles each winter. The ground layer of boreal forests is predominantly of dwarf shrubs, for example bilberries and cranberries (*Vaccinium* spp), Leatherleaf (*Chamaedaphne calyculata*) and Labrador Tea (*Ledum palustre*), and is also richly mossy. Drier pine forests typically have herbs like *Linnaea borealis*, *Trientalis europaea* and the wintergreens (*Pyrola* spp) as well as saprophytes such as the orchids *Goodyera repens* and *Corallorhiza trifida*. There is no comparable belt of coniferous forest in the Southern Hemisphere, where indeed there is no land mass at the appropriate latitudes.

On north temperate mountains south of the boreal zone a conifer forest zone commonly occurs above the deciduous broadleaved forest, reaching up to the tree line. Resemblance extends to the herbs - several species are shared with boreal latitudes. Trees, though of the same genera, are mostly different species, for example the European Larch (*Larix decidua*) and in the Appalachians the Red Spruce (*Picea rubens*) and Fraser Fir (*Abies fraseri*).

Forest Dynamics

As we have seen, the species composition of a forest is dependent at the grossest scale on plant geography and within any region there is variation due to habitat, for example between swamp and dry land, and with different soil types. A further important variation arises from the complex structure of a forest community. At maturity a closed forest canopy casts dense shade. Plants can only grow up under the canopy which are able to succeed in conditions of low light and high root competition. In temperate deciduous forest many herbs to some extent avoid these limitations by making much or all of their growth (including flowering) before the trees come into leaf. Only certain tree species have seedlings which can grow up under a closed canopy. These are often called shade bearers. Sometimes gaps form in a closed forest canopy. A storm may blow down isolated trees or fell a swathe, fire may sweep through. A second group of tree species has seeds efficiently dispersed and (in the tropics) continually available, and these soon colonize such gaps. The seedlings are adapted to grow and succeed in the brightly lit, sometimes desiccating, conditions of gaps. These species are often known as light demanders. The seedlings cannot grow up in shade, so the trees cannot replace themselves *in situ*. They always colonize gaps and are also sometimes referred to as pioneer species. The forests of pioneers are always seral. Familiar English examples are Scots Pine and birch. In fact there is a spectrum of types from obligate shade bearers to strict pioneers, especially in regions with a rich flora, and most markedly in the humid tropics. In the temperate deciduous forest of North America the pioneers *Pinus strobus*, *Quercus* spp and *Castanea* spp tend to be replaced in the absence of catastrophic forest destruction by the shade bearers *Aces* spp, *Tsuga* spp and *Fagus* spp. The two oaks native to England (*Quercus petraea* and *Q. robur*) are also both light-demanding species. In West Africa present-day extensive tall speciesrich rain forest containing much valuable timber in the form of several species of Meliaceae (African mahogany) is being replaced by a lower forest with fewer species of less commercial value. The principal timber species of Malaysia, the Philippines and Indonesia, light-wooded meranti (*Shorea* spp), are near-pioneers, favoured by mild but not total forest disturbance. This dynamic aspect of forest composition, with different species adapted to different temporal niches in the canopy growth cycle, therefore has important ecological and commercial implications. The science of silviculture is based on understanding and manipulating it. Trees have long lives, and rare catastrophes leave their mark on forest composition for a century or more. Pioneers come up in large gaps as even-age stands and a rather coarse mosaic of large patches of different age develops. Shade bearers succeed the pioneers, replacing each other or themselves on smaller areas so that ultimately a mixed-age stand develops with a fine-scale mosaic pattern of gap, building phase and high mature forest. But it is doubtful if there is ever an equilibrium state, or constant species composition; a catastrophe, or indeed secular climatic change, sooner or later intervenes to cause gross alteration. In Western Europe Man's interference with the forests has been prolonged and profound and influences present-day structure and species composition. The dominance of light-demanding oak over much of England reflects its conscious selection by silviculture not its ecology.

2

Climate in the Forest

Most people imagine the rainforest to be hot, sticky and swarming with insects Indeed, many missionaries died of yellow fever during colonial times, a fact which led their fellow Europeans to decry West Africa's shore the "Fever Coast" Today still, a glance at the obligatory innoculations listed on an international vaccination card tends to reassure travellers disembarking from an airconditioned plane in Monrovia or Accra. Tropical disease comes to the minds of many as they find themselves drenched with sweat merely waiting to pass through customs. Surely, no one should forego preventive medication against malaria nor the usual vaccinations but the stories of the "Fever Coast" originated at a time when the rainforest was still considered "green hell" by most non-Africans. Admittedly, it can be uncomfortably hot and humid in West African cities, in areas cleared of forest cover and where plantations have been established.

A Comfortable Climate – in the Forest

Although the relative humidity in closed rainforest is usually around 90% both day and night, temperatures are moderate and quite stable. West Africa's mean annual temperature is 26°-27°C whereas the monthly average ranges from 24°-28°C. The seasonal fluctuation of the mean temperature is therefore considerably less than the day to day fluctuations. Daily temperatures vary greatly, however, depending on where they are recorded: closed forest shows a very different temperature curve than a clearing or plantation area. It can be unpleasantly hot and humid beneath the noon day sun without the shelter of trees above. Microclimatic differences exist not only between closed forest and cleared areas. The same temperature span can be recorded

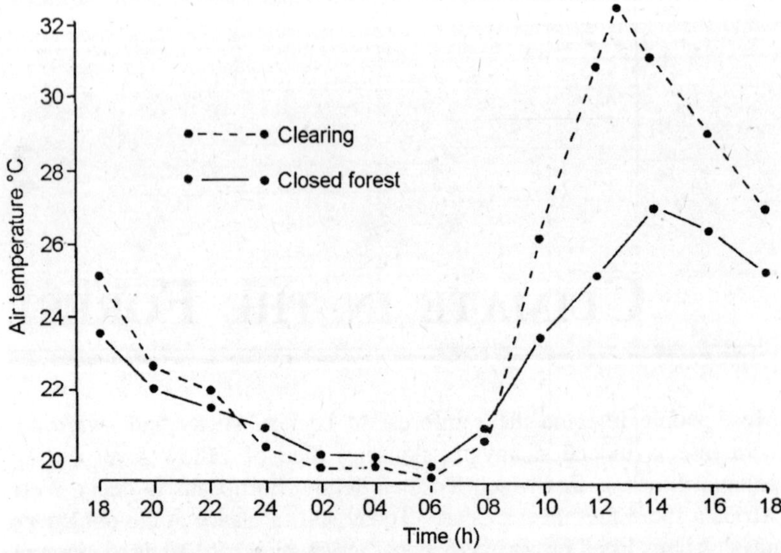

Fig. 2.1. Daily march of air temperature within a rain forest in S.W. Ghana, compared with a large clearing. Both at 10 cm above the ground.

between the floor and the canopy within the forest. Temperatures recorded at canopy level are similar to those measured in clearings at 15 meters above ground. Forest vegetation thus greatly influences temperatures near ground level. Consequently, extensive cleared areas show a generally different temperature pattern.

Contrary to popular belief, the climate of the rainforest is quite comfortable for humans. Lowland rainforest is seldom too cold, nor is it ever too hot, so seasonal clothing is unnecessary. It is quite conceivable that human physiology adapted to a rainforest environment at some past time although archeological findings have not as yet proven this. Temperatures above 35°C in the rainforest are rare and even that is still far below the maximum temperatures reached in subtropical regions or even in temperate climates.

Not only do closed forests in West Africa show steady daily and annual temperatures, their temperature characteristics also show little difference when compared with rainforests at similar altitudes on other continents. This fact strongly indicates the self-regulatory nature of temperature patterns in tropical moist forest ecosystems. The stable temperatures within the forest, however, should not lead to the conclusion that rainforest cannot exist under other conditions Montane rainforests, in which generally colder temperatures prevail, prove the

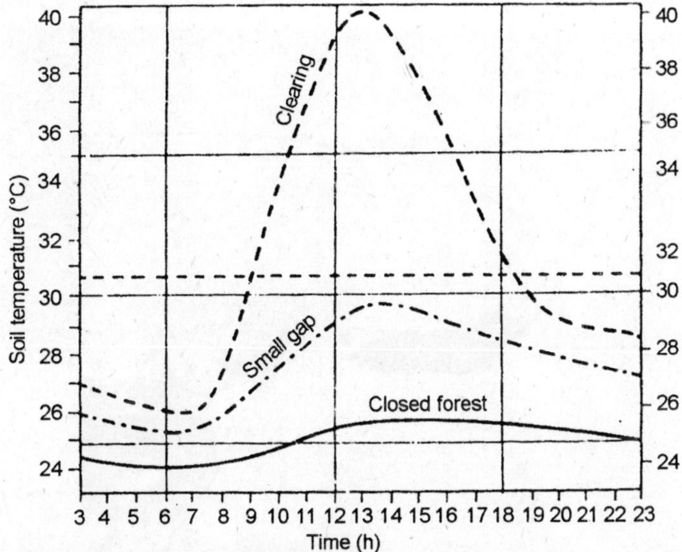

Fig. 2.2. Daily march of soil temperature in a rain forest in Surinam, in closed forest, a small gap and a large clearing.

point. A sufficient level of precipitation is apparently the more important factor for the development of rainforests.

A Lot of Rain – Unevenly Distributed

The forests along the Gulf of Guinea are sandwiched between a maritime and a continental climate. Land air masses meet with oceanic air masses thereby causing more seasonal fluctuations in climate than is the case in other rainforest areas. The line along which these two air masses converge corresponds to the equatorial trough of low pressure encircling the earth near the equator. Over the ocean, it typically runs north of the equator, Scientists have termed this line the *intertropical convergence* zone (ITC).

In the first half of the year, the ITC moves inland with the overhead sun and parallel to the West African coast. At its southern most position, the ITC lies just behind the coast between 5°N and 7°N. It moves inland at an approximate speed of 160 kilometers a month, reaching its most northern position by July or August at some 20°N far into the Sahara.

The northern displacement of the ITC allows warm, moist air to move in from the ocean and spread across West Africa pushing the dry and dusty desert air out of the lower atmosphere. This does not

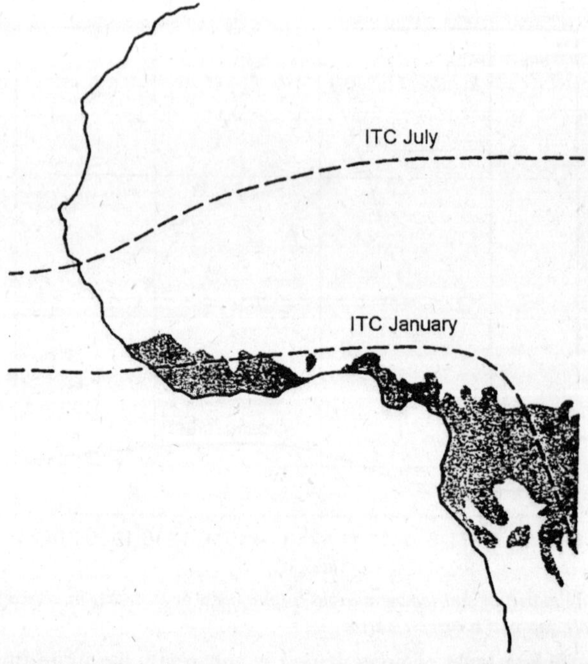

Fig. 2.3. Position of the intertropical convergence zone (ITC) in January and July.

necessarily produce rainfall in all areas under the influence of maritime air masses. Rainfall generally occurs behind the front where maritime air masses are at least 1500 meters thick. This explains why there is hardly any rainfall over the southern parts of the Sahara although moist air reaches the desert. During the second half of the year, the ITC moves back south much more rapidly and dry desert winds blow across West Africa clouding the air with dust and sand particles. Throughout West Africa, desert winds are known as *Harmatan*. They pass through the rainforests the of West Africa around the turn of the year, reaching almost down to the coast and causing a number of smaller forest streams to dry up for some time The Harmattan cause the relative humidity within the forest to drop from its normal level of 90% to about 70%. At the northern edge of the rainforest, humidity can even sink to desert-like levels. Thus, the climate of West Africa consists of two major seasons: a wet Season and a drier season depending on the type of air mass present in the atmosphere.

These circumstances explain why coastal regions receive more precipitation than areas further inland. Rain can be expected to fall more frequently where maritime air masses are present for a longer period of time. It is more difficult, however, to explain the varying levels of precipitation from place to place along the coast itself: 3000 mm or more rain fall annually near the coast in Guinea, Sierra Leone and Liberia as well as further east along a narrow stretch of the Niger Delta in Nigeria and in Cameroon. Africa's highest levels of rainfall have been recorded at the foot of Mount Cameroon where some places show impressing levels of 10000 mm and more.

Situated between the two wettest areas along the West African coast is the Dahomey Gap, a dry region where less than 1200 mm of rain fall annually. And even this minimal precipitation occurs rather seasonally which means that the climate is even drier for a good part of the year. Rainforest vegetation cannot survive under such conditions. But how did this abnormality of climate come to be? Beginning near Axim in western Ghana, the West African coastline runs southeast. Annual rainfall here measures 2032 mm. The coast then turns northeastward at Cape Three Points and in Takoradi - a mere 60 kilometers from Axim - only 1194 mm of rainfall are recorded annually. Takoradi marks the beginning of the Dahomey Gap on the coastline. Since the moist air masses originate from the southwest, they move parallel to the coast from eastern Ghana to Benin producing an effect similar to the rain shadow which often occurs on the lee side of mountains. Although the land behind the coast is flat, little rain falls along this part of West Africa. That is perhaps the most plau-sible explanation for the arid climate of the Dahomey Gap although there are a number of other theories.

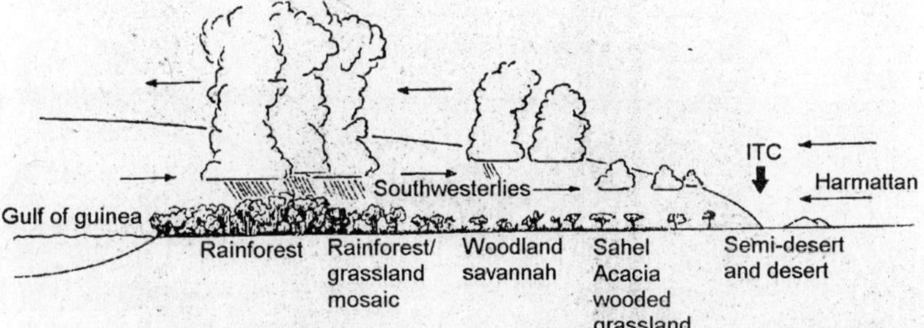

Fig. 2.4. In July, the intertropical convergence zone lies well over the interior of the continent. But heavy precipitation only occurs much further behind the front, in the rainforest zone.

Wet and Dry Seasons

Most African rain-forests receive an annual precipitation of between 1600 and 2000 mm. As a general rule, levels lower that 1600 mm are typical for transition areas to Guinea savannah vege-tation The quantity of precipitation is an impor-tant but not the only determining factor for rainforest growth. Just as important is the seasonal distribution No less than 100 mm of rain should fall during at least nine months of the year. Thus, if rainforest is to thrive, rainfall should be as evenly distributed as possible over 12 months. West Africa's climate, however, is relatively seasonal. Two extreme examples show what this can mean for rainforest vegetation:

1. Although the coast of the Republic of Guinea receives an annual rainfall of more than 4000 mm in certain places, there is practically no rainfall during the four months from December to March. The long dry season does not allow rainforest to establish itself here in spite of the high level of annual precipitation.
2. Only 1230 mm of rain fall in Ibadan (Nigeria) per year and yet the city lies within the rainforest zone. The dry season is shorter than three months and the high relative humidity remains constant throughout the year.

It is peculiar to note that the West African rainforest zone shows two distinct periods of high rainfall separated by a short dry season.

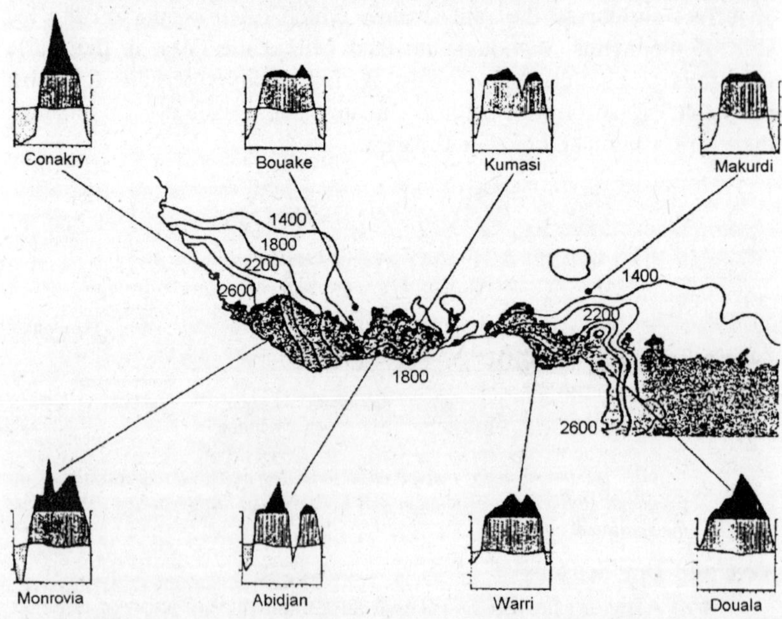

Fig. 2.5. Geographical and seasonal distribution of mean annual precipitation in West Africa's rainforest zone.

Surprisingly, during July and August when the ITC is at its furthest inland position and the moist air masses over the coast are at their largest, very little rain actually falls. This drop in rainfall lasts about six weeks and is known as the "little dry season". The reasons for this phenomenon are not easily explained. Climatologists have found that in July and August the ocean winds change direction from southwest to west and thus blow more or less parallel to the coast. So the winds approach the rainforests east of Sierra Leone from the continent and not from the sea thus producing a rain shadow effect similar to that in the Dahomey Gap West Africa's coastal geography could therefore be responsible for the twofold wet season. But climatologists do not hesitate to cite other theories for this unusual phenomenon. For example, behind a maritime front cooler air is often trapped near the ground under warmer air above. Such inversions tend to calm weather conditions.

In addition to the level of precipitation and its seasonal distribution, the relative humidity of the air and the ability of the soil to retain moisture are also probable factors in determining rainforest cover. There is still too little known about their precise effects, but they, in turn, are also dependent upon rainfall.

Yellow and Red Soil upon Ancient Rock

Northern and western Africa consists of a low-lying plain of immense size reaching far into the center of the continent. Except for the Atlas, the Hoggar and Tibesti massifs, few summits rise more than 1000 meters above sea level. Only the Nimba mountains rising up to 1700 meters stand out in an otherwise flat or undulating landscape where the borders of Liberia, the Cote d'ivoire and the Republic of Guinea meet. In the east, the West African plateau jutts against the volcanic high lands of western Cameroon, which end with Mount Cameroon directly on the coast and surface again to form the islands Fernando Po, Principe and Sao Tome.

Although the land rises gradually from the lowlands along the Gulf of Guinea, only in very few places does it reach 300 meters above sea level. West African rainforests are thus almost exclusively lowland rainforests with only slightly hilly areas.

The ancient crystalline shield underlying most of the African continent is exposed at various places in the rainforest. Granites, gneisses, quartz and schists are the basis from which rainforest soils develop by intensive weathering processes. Although the soil is deep, nutrients are stored only in the thin topsoil layer. In some places, outcrops of granite protrude from beneath the surface creating peculiar rock formations at times reaching far above the surrounding forest canopy.

In the wettest areas along the coast, weathering of the basement rock has produced ferralitic soils of a yellowish hue. They are quite acidic and leached out especially in areas of maximum precipitation. Few minerals remain. Aside from kaolinitic minerals with iron and aluminium oxides, the soil is extremely poor in nutrients. Rainforest soils of this kind, also known as oxysols, are particularly unsuitable for agriculture. Further inland where precipitation measures about 1500-1750 mm annually, ferralitic soils are of a reddish colour and less acidic or even neutral. These are the forest ochrosols. They are richer in nutrients especially in less washed out places, in depressions and at the bottom of valleys. In transitional forest areas bordering on savannah and in savannah regions, ochrosols are of a reddish brown colour. Soils of this type are also known as savannah-ochrosols. The term "laterite" and to some extent also the term "latosol" words earlier used to describe tropical soils in general sense, have led to considerable confusion and are now often replaced by the above terminology.

Not only does the underlying rock influence the soil type formed above, but the amount of precipitation obviously also plays a role by determining the soil's nutrient content. Rainfall thus has a twofold effect on forest vegetation: Directly, by determining the amount of water available to the plants, and indirectly, by leaching the soil of its nutrients and so influencing its fertility. Relatively fertile forest soils are found on late tertiary volcanic rock formations. The soils which have developed from these basalts have a fine, claylike texture and are well-known among farmers as an ideal basis for agriculture. This type of soil is common in the highlands of western Cameroon but otherwise quite rare in West African rainforests.

In general, the rainforest has never been more wrongly judged than concerning its soil, The lush and immensely diverse vegetation of tropical rainforests was long thought to be partly due to fertile soils, It seemed difficult to believe that tropical rainforests could exist on surfaces almost bare of nutrients, Consequently, many a well-meaning development project based on the false assumption of fertile soil has led to failed harvests, fallow land and erosion. Only recently has increased public concern for the fate of the rainforests led to more careful planning of development projects and a better understanding of soil conditions.

The Result: Different Types of Rainforest

The complex interaction of various environmental factors determine the distribution and characteristics of the rainforest Climate, geology and soil are the most important although no single factor shows a perfect correlation with the distribution area of one specific type of forest. The level of precipitation, however, is of central importance in determining the various forest types. Since rainfall decreases as we move inland from the very wet coastal areas, the structure of the forest changes accordingly. It is commonly believed that the tallest trees grow in those rainforests where the most rain falls. But that is neither the case in the Amazon region nor in Africa. Both the biomass as well as the girth and height of individual trees are less in the wettest tropical rainforests than in evergreen and semi-deciduous forests with more seasonal climates This could be due to leached soils and an accordingly low level of nutrients Increased cloud cover leading to a generally lower light intensity could also be responsible for the lower growth potential. Thus, the giant trees for which the rainforest is famous do not characterize the wettest evergreen forests but rather a drier, more seasonal forest type.

Unfortunately, the Unesco/AETFAT/UNSO Vegetation Map of Africa does not distinguish between rainforest types The map shows only the approximate distribution of "wetter" and "drier" types and an undefined mosaic of both. Although quite valuable 'otherwise, this factor has led to the map being declared useless by some. While it is a genuine vegetation' map for savannah and dry woody areas, it does not merit the term concerning vegetation within the distribution area of rainforest. It is no wonder that the task was difficult. The Gulf of Guinea is lined with a number of relatively small countries, a fact which has not encouraged a uniform classification of local vegetation and climatic conditions. Not only is communication hampered by poor road connections but the language barriers, too, pose quite a problem. From, the Republic of Guinea to Nigeria, the national language alternates between English and French from country to country on an almost regular basis.

Rainforest Types in Ghana

The best analysis of West African rainforest types is undoubtedly that conducted by John B. Hall and Michael D. Swaine in Ghana. These two British scientists, Hall in particular, spent many years at the University of Ghana in Legon, near Accra, carrying out plant sociological studies. Their classification is based on 155 sample plots

(25 × 25 meters) distributed throughout Ghana's rainforest. Among other information, they listed all vascular plant species occurring in the plots (i.e. omitting algae, fungi and mosses). Tree seedlings - a common form of vegetation in the undergrowth of rainforests - were also recorded. In order to achieve as complete a picture as possible of the forest in its original state despite the existing degree of forest destruction, most of the plots were chosen within forest reserves and "Juju" places, sacred patches of forest reserved for religious ceremonies.

Of the 1248 vascular plants observed, only the 749 species occurring in at least three different plots were used for classification. For obvious reasons less common species are not as helpful in determining similarities between plots. A computer data analysis technique called "ordination" resulted in a classification of sample. Areas on the basis of similar characteristics. The groups so classified" have ultimately been defined as forest types. Environmental factor such as precipitation and geological criteria were taken into consideration in the analysis.

Hall and Swaine drew up a vegetation map of the rainforest zone in Ghana. It shows four main types of forest according to decreasing levels of precipitation from the coast moving inland. Since Ghana's rainforests are interrupted by the savannah of the Dahomey Gap, the forests towards the east also become increasingly drier. In this area directly on the coast; Hall and Swaine recognized a special "southern marginal" forest type which only exists in small patches today. In addition, they defined an "upland evergreen" type and the structure of certain isolated forest patches. Hall and Swaine's description of forest vegetation in Ghana explains all the forest types in detail. Although types of forest were defined according to floristic analysis, the authors used climatic and physiognomical terms in their definitions. For our purposes, a presentation of the four main types comparable with those occurring in other West African countries will suffice.

Comparable Types of Rainforest Elsewhere

Hall and Swaine may indeed have used a complex methodology to classify the rainforests in Ghana, but the complexity of the rainforest demands an accordingly detailed analysis. The commonly applied method of choosing more or less arbitrarily one or two characteristic species to classify forests is not adequate when 100 or more species of trees occur in a relatively small area. Clearly, dominant species according to which a type classification can be made are rare in rainforests. One exception in West Africa are the upland forests of the Nimba massif and the Foula Djalon plateau in the western Cote d'ivoire, where the Guinea plum tree (*Parinari excelsa*) occurs in high densities. Some experts today refuse to accept a classification of rainforests according to purely floristic principles. Most needs are better served by a classification according to a variety of factors such as forest structure, degree of humidity and soil conditions.

Table 2.1. Comparison of different rainforest classification in Ghana and the Cote d'Ivoire

Rainforest types in Ghana according to Taylor (1952)	*Rainforest types in Ghana according to hall and Swaine(1981) with annual precipitation*	*Rainforest types in the Cote d'love according to Guillaument and Adjanohoun (1971)*
Cynometra-Lophira-Tarretia "Rainforest"	Wet Evergreen (> 1750 mm)	– Foret sempervirente a *Diospyros* spp. et *Mapania* spp.
		– Foret sempervirente a *Eremospatha macrocarpa* et *Diospyros mannii* (partly)
Lophira-Triplochiton Association	Moist Evergreen (1500-1700 mm)	– Foret sempervirente a *Eremospatha macrocarpa* et *Diospyros manii* (partly)
		– Foret sempervirente a *Turraeanthus africanus* at *Heisteria parviflora.*
		– Variante a *Nesogordonia papaverifera* et *Khaya ivorensis*
Celtis-Triplochiton Association	Moist Semi-deciduous (1250-1750 mm)	– Foret semi-decidue a *Celtis* spp. et *Triplochiton scleroxylon* (partly)
Antiaris-Chlorophora Association	Dry Semi-deciduous (1000-1500 mm)	– Foret semi-decidue a *Celtis* spp. et. *Triplochiton scleroxylon* (partly)
	Fire Zone Subtype	– Foret semi-decidue a *Aubrevillea kerstingii* et *Khaya grandifolia*

Before Hall and Swaine's findings were published in 1976. Other more standard methods of plant sociology had been used to classify forest types in West Africa. Attempts to identify types according to characteristic species had already been made in "Ghana early this century. Taylor's classification became especially well known. Taylor used species of commercial timber to indicate forest type. At the time his work was published in 1952, timber exploitation was the main factor of interest regarding tropical forests, a fact which explains his selection of criteria. Despite the elementary nature of Taylor's plant sociology, a comparison with Hall and Swaine's precisely defined forest types shows a close correspondence with the main types.

A very detailed vegetation map for the Cote d'lvoire was published in 1971. This marvelously colourful map probably has no equal in all of Africa. Although the map also uses characteristic species to classify forest types within the rainforest zone, it has an important advantage: Not only does the map depict the distribution areas of forest types, it also shows the extent of actually forested areas - areas which were as yet undisturbed in 1971. The majority of the Cote d'ivoire's rainforests had already been sacrificed to both plantations and small-scale agriculture. Forest destruction has since continued and the lovely vegetation map may soon be nothing more than an historical document reminding us of what the Cote d'ivoire once was.

Rainforests in other West African countries have not nearly been as carefully studied and classified as in Ghana or the Cote d'ivoire. Liberia and Sierra Leone are but two examples. Not only have computer-aided methods of vegetation analysis just recently been developed, but many West African rainforests were destroyed before they could be classified At the Forestry Department of the University of Ibadan a classification of Nigeria's forests was made in the 1970s on the basis of data which had been collected around 1930. More recent data were not available because Nigeria has since lost most of its rainforests. A method of data analysis similar to the "ordination" technique used by Hall and Swaine was applied Strangely enough the Nigerian study was also conducted by a man named John B. Hall. Ibadan's John B. Hall, however, was not the John B. Hall who had worked at the University of Legon in Ghana and died in 1984. In Nigeria, too, forest types in the southern part of the rainforest zone proved to be characteristically moister than in the north. Soil quality was also shown to have an influence on forest type. Unfortunately, the data collected before World War II were not done so in a sufficiently consistent manner to, allow for a precise classification of Nigeria's rainforests.

A consistent study of the rainforests along the Gulf of Guinea, which would allow the use of a uniform terminology for forest types, has never been made. It is thus difficult to compare the forests from country to country. Identical criteria were not even applied for the classification of the Upper Guinea forest block between Sierra Leone and Ghana. And in Liberia, plant sociological studies have never ever been conducted surprisingly, however, the first botanical collections in Ghana were made in 1697, in Sierra Leone in 1772, in Liberia in 1841 and, finally, in the Cote d'Ivoire in 1882. Despite this early interest, the specimens collected were never used to classify the rainforest but shipped to Europe to satisfy taxonomic interests. Until recently, botanists have apparently not been interested in the forest as a plant community. But aside from that, French-speaking scientists did not, or could not communicate with their English-speaking colleagues and vice versa: Today, it is no longer likely that a sound classification of West African rainforests can be made on a uniform basis. Too much forest has been disturbed or destroyed over the past decades.

3

RAINFOREST

The thunder of drumbeats can be heard far and near, the smell of roasting meat permeates the air, palm wine and schnaps are passed around. Why has the Chief called to celebrate the yam festival? Nobody really knows, Nevertheless, drumbeats spread the news through out the forest with mounting excitement, the ornamental stools are removed from storage. The people of Debiso in Western Ghana seldom actually see their ancestral inheritance. The chairs are usually kept by the village chief, locked away in his personal storeroom. With the aid of his medicine men, the Chief is capable of speaking with the spirits of the forest, During three days of festivities, ceremonies will be held at specially chosen sites outside the village to appease the invisible beings.

The rainforest rises like a great fortress, behind the small village, in the clearing, simple tin-roofed huts stand unsheltered in these scorching sun. Even the chickens appear to be the smallest of birds against the backdrop of the rainforest. Few villagers have ever seen the end of the forest although the "Trotro" – an old Bedford truck – makes daily trips on the, timber transport route from Kumasi to the border of the Cote d'lvoire. Until a few years ago, the village could only be reached on foot via winding paths through the deep forest.

The Chief wears a heavy gold-plated crown for the ceremony. The same ponderous headdress had been born by his forefathers in leading the Sefwi tribe into battle against the Ashantis in brutal jungle wars of the past. That was before the hunting camp which once stood at this site had evolved into a permanent settlement. Only the name "Debiso" remains to remind one of the place where two forest elephants killed by Sefwi hunters came to fall upon each other. Sacrifices are made to the forest and its spirits every three years at the Yam festival. But the dwarfs must be appeased more often. Many West African tribes believe strongly in the lore of the little people. The dwarfs, invisible creatures who live at secret places in the 'forest, must be given due respect. Otherwise, their playful pranks may easily become evil tricks. They have even' been known to kill on occasion.

Natural clearings are rare in the deep forest, occurring only where the granite base of the African continent rises to the surface: The Sefwis call the clearings "Apaso"– the dwarfs' gardens. The "gardens" are magical places where sacrifices are made with great care according to the wishes of the village chief and his medicine men. It is also they who determine which of the village elders may accompany them along the twisting forest path leading to the secret site.

A stagnant pool of greenish water awaits the visitors. According to tradition they do not speak and have entered from one direction only. The medicine man now summons the dwarfs in a loud voice and invites them to hear his humble words. After a long sermon, the sheep which has been brought from the villages sacrificed - its throat slit allowing its blood to flow upon the colourful gifts of fruits" nuts, eggs and magical objects spread upon the bare rock. Bottles of schnaps are poured onto the ground as an offering to the dwarfs, no less is drunken by the Chief and his companions themselves for they are fearful and alcohol relieves their fear. It is said in Debiso that some men have never returned from the clearing because they were unable to appease the "little people" The dwarfs are the keepers of the forest and of the animals and do not hesitate to punish wrongdoers. The people strongly believe in this tradition and take care not to anger the little sentries. Thus, the responsibility of protecting the forest so vital to the Sefwi tribe is in the hands of these small creatures. But the dwarfs never reckoned with the Europeans.

A Source of Raw Materials for 500 Years

The sea-route from the major harbors at southern England, Germany or Holland to the coast of the Gulf of Guinea extends over 600 kilometers. Neither the rainforests in Latin America nor, the forests of Southeast Asia are, closer. West Africa's proximity to Europe has influenced its trade relations for centuries and left its mark on the rainforest.

Europe's first trade relations with the West African coast date back to the 15th century. The first trade agencies consisted of nothing more than storage houses and fortifications along the coast. A small" strip of land sufficed to develop trade from the coast famed for its rich natural resources. The rest of the African continent was still a mystery to the Europeans. Nevertheless, trade boomed: gold, ivory, cola nuts and slaves were shipped from the coast, of western Ghana in 1700, British, Dutch and Danish trading posts vied for the best ports. Not every trade settlement have been founded at an ideal location and the sailors had to battle against rough waters.

The Europeans did business with Arab slave dealers from the north and certain tribes of rainforest people who delivered goods and slaves from the interior of the continent to the coast. Slavery was not a European custom alone. The Ashanti tribe, for example, kept slaves for their own use. Entire villages in the savanna north of the West African rainforests were taken into bondage if they did not succeed in fleeing their captors. This led to a depopulation of large areas which still remain thinly populated today. The poor uprooted people from the north were considered nothing more than a good to be traded - even by the West Africans. Slaves were a cheap commodity in contrast to salt which was quite expensive. It was imported from the north in caravans and traded like gold. In the interior of Benin, Togo and in the Volta region of Ghana, a handful of salt was known to be worth one to two slaves.

The Danes were more liberal than other Europeans active in West Africa at the time, abolishing slavery in 1802. The British Government followed suit five years later with a ban on slave export which they applied to a number of other trading countries as well. The British confiscated foreign slave ships and freed their unfortunate passengers. The Europeans' new respect for other races however, posed a problem for some forest peoples; the Ashantis were, left with no takers for their wares and opted to settle their captives as planters. The slave trade was replaced by the export of palm oil. Inadvertently, the British were therefore actually responsible for creating export-oriented agriculture in West Africa. In 1850, they began to expand their influence.

Beginning of Commercial Exploitation

In 1879 following 400 years of trade with the West African coast the Europeans only ruled over large segments of the population in French -Senegal and on the British "Gold Coast" (Ghana) Except in Senegal. European administrations never controlled land more than a few miles inland. The British Colonies of Gambia, Sierra, Leone and Lagos were nothing more than small enclaves in a region still largely under African rule. Within but a few years, however, the situation was to change drastically. In 1870, gum copal from trees of the genus *Daniellia* found in closed rainforests was being exported for the manufacture of varnish in increasing quantities. The European demand for rubber tapped from *Funtumia* trees also rose steadily after 1883. Following a number of unsuccessful attempts, the export of agricultural products rapidly increased. The first successful oil palm plantations in southern Ghana exported up to 30000 tons of oil by 1884. In 1985, Ghaba also exported 63 tons of coffee.

During the last quarter of the 19th century, rainforest in Ghana, and Nigera increasingly gave way to cocoa plantations. In contrast, cocoa was not brought to the Cote d'lvoire until 1912 when, it was introduced from Ghana. Lowland rainforests in the southern part of the rainforest belt suffered most from the cocoa boom. Cocoa cultivation was especially successful in the rural areas of Ghana near Accra and in the forest region near Kumasi. In 1911 after only 26 years of profitable production, Ghana rose to become the top exporter worldwide and managed to hold its position for a number of decades while continuingly increasing production.

First attempts at logging in Ghana had been undertaken near Axim in 1800. They were abandoned, however, due to technical difficulties. It was not until 1887 that logging operations were again established on an '"experimental basis". The British, who now ruled the larger, part of southern Ghana, eliminated the political barriers to allow timber to be floated freely to the coast on the major rivers Tano, Ankobra and Pra. The "experiment" was to have serious consequences: Seven years later, the export of tropical timber had reached 450000 cubic feet (approx. 285 m^3) and the colonial government had begun to distribute timber concessions to European investors. By the year 1913, Ghana's exports had gradually risen to three million cubic feel (approx, 85000 m^3), World War I, however, brought difficult times and the export volume fell back to a much lower level. Nigeria was exporting similar quantities of tropical timber and earlier In the 19th century the country established its own forest service. Only African mahogany (*Khaya ivorensis*) and smaller quantities of sapele (*Entandrophragma cylindricum*) were actually in demand then for European furniture production.

Until World War I, the British largely controlled the export of tropical timber from the Cote d'lvoire as well. Mahogany was felled near the Bia river and the logs were floated to the Abi Lagoon near Assinie. The consequent depletion of the forest along the shore led to trees being felled further inside the forest. The logs were hauled to the nearest rivers along corduroy roads. In time, other African hardwoods such as makore and iroko gained popularity in Europe. Nevertheless, export statistics showed African mahogany to be at the top of the list until 1951. But until after World War II, timber exports, from West Africa showed slow growth. The fluctuating market demand was not the only reason. Transporting logs from distant locations to the coast posed nearly insurmountable technical problems. The interior rainforests were thus spared from large scale exploitation until the 1950s when the mechanization of forest operations changed the situation dramatically. Bulldozers were brought in to push their way through the forest and trucks were able to haul entire trunks from deep within the forest to the coast.

The European demand for tropical timber increased steadily throughout the 1950s. In the Cote d'lvoire, roundwood production sky-rocketed from 400000 cubic meters in 1958 to more than 5000000 cubic meters in the 1970s. Nowhere, along the Gulf of Guinea did the exploitation of the rainforest proceed at such a fast pace as in the Cote d'lvoire. Neighbouring Liberia was not similarly affected until the mid-1960s. While the export of timber from the West African coast drastically increased after World War II, the export of other forest products came to a near standstill. Artificial resin had long since replaced natural gum copal in the production of varnish and the rubber grown in, West Africa today is actually caoutchouc from Brazilian Hevea rubber trees grown on large plantations. Just as for the cultivation of cocoa, wide areas of rainforest were also cleared for Hevea and oil palm Plantations.

Early Attempts at Conservation: Theory

It would be unfair to assume that the Europeans were interested only in exploiting the natural resources of their African colonies with no consideration for their future. Early in the history of commercial timber exploitation, the colonial government in Ghana adopted the Timber Protection Ordinance of 1907 which banned felling commercial species of a lesser diameter.

In Togo, a German protectorate from 1884-1919, forest conservation had been a concern from the start of colonial rule. The country was endowed with a far smaller area of rainforest than other West African nations. In 1907, just as forestry regulations were adopted the Ghana, a conference was held in Berlin on the reforestation of Togo. The Germans decided to invest mainly in teak, an exotic species well adapted to the drier climate In addition, indigenous hardwoods were also chosen: doussie, sasswood, African mahogany and iroko, the kapok-tree (*Ceiba pentandra*) and "chew-stick" (*Anogeissus leiocarpus*). The bark and leaves of "chew-stick" are of medicinal value, only the roots are used as chewing sticks. Thirteen million trees are said to have been planted in Togo early this century.

In Nigeria, the British had begun with reforestation in the Benin District even before the forestry administration was established. Tens of thousands of African mahogany trees were planted It annually. Between 1901 and 1910, trees of several species native to Nigeria were planted: iroko, obeche, limba and mahogany. A few exotic species were also introduced: teak, cedrela and eucalyptus, In 1920, the Senior Conservator of Forests of Nigeria, A.H. Unwin stated, "Despite many failures owing to experiments on bad soil and seasons of extreme drought, the growth of the trees gives the greatest promise of mature trees, or at any rate merchantable trees being grown in a comparatively short period".

Soon after, the British realized that protecting the forest as a whole was even more important than planting individual trees. With the establishment of the forest service, the administration began to demarcate forest reserves, henceforth to provide a source for permanent and controlled timber exploitation. In order to preserve the steady flow of rivers to lower lying regions, watershed areas were especially given reserve status to protect against flooding, erosion and drought. Shelterbelt forest reserves bordering on savannah territory marking the transition to the Sahel were established to keep back the hot desert winds from the north.

In Ghana, the Forest Ordinance of 1911 allowed the colonial governor to give all uninhabited forest territory forest reserve status, a measure which stripped the surrounding inhabitants of their traditional user rights. The people protested strongly since their livelihood depended on just that which was thus prohibited by the ordinance, namely shifting cultivation and gathering forest products such as essences, fibers, fruits and nuts. The Aborigines' Rights Protection Society lodged a complaint with the Governor for disrespecting the traditional land tenure system.

Reality: Forest Inhabitants Resist

West African tradition holds land to be common property belonging to one or more communities. The members of the community are entitled to use as, much land as they need to clear and cultivate. Should land no, longer be needed, it falls back to the community. Sale of property is not allowed since it does not belong solely to the living users but also to their ancestors buried on the land and to future generations. For Akan tribes in the eastern Cote d'lvoire and in Ghana, the earthly resting place of their forefathers souls is symbolized by the "stools". The stools, each cut from a single block of wood and richly embellished with ornamental carvings, represent the common property, also termed "stool land". During rituals held at regular intervals, offerings of food are placed about the stools. Sacred wine and schnaps are used to douse the precious inheritance. The British were well aware of the importance of the stools in regard to property rights. In 1900, upon the conquest of the mightiest Akan group, the Ashanti tribe, British governor Sir Frederic Hodgson demanded possession of the "Golden Stool". In a storm of protest led by the mother of their imprisoned King Kwaku Dua III, the Ashantis attacked the British fortress in Kumasi. The remembrance of that event probably played a role in their reluctance to strictly enforce the new forest regulations. Local chiefs were still quite influential. The legislation was in fact temporarily withdrawn until the newly established forest service published long lists of forest reserves between 1922 and 1926. As one may expect, the forest reservation program was not at all popular with the local inhabitants, who felt they were being denied their traditional rights. By the year 1939, an area of 14800 square kilometers of Ghanaian rainforest had been declared forest reserves, which totalled 19% of the country's rainforest cover.

In 1926, the French colonial power began similar attempt at forest conservation in the Cote d'lvoire. By 1956, 43 000 square, kilometers of forest had been declared protected areas (forests classees). The local reaction was, no more favourable than in Ghana. Many of the Ivorian forest reserves, were so heavily damaged by illegal slash-and-burn clearing that redefinement was necessary in 1966. Unfortunately, the problem was not easy to solve. Illegal farming on reserved land continued largely uncontrolled.

Consequences of Centralization

Throughout the century, West African peoples have increasingly lost authority over their vast areas of forest. Colonial regulations withdrawing their self-responsibility within the newly established forest reserves were not the only reason. Logging activities made the forest more accessible. Transport routes, although crude, not only allowed timber to be carried out of the forest, but also let new settlers come in. Immigrant farmers came from other parts of Africa, especially from the north where the dry climate forced many to look elsewhere for their livelihood. The new settlers, however, were not familiar with the rainforest. In contrast to West African forest peoples who had lived and worked for generations in the forest, they did not know how to deal with the sensitive soil. Traditional West African forest farmers never do long-term damage to the land. The area surrounding a village is cultivated on a rotational basis and only small areas are cleared and planted for a few years before the next ones are cleared. Once a plot of land has been depleted of its nutrients, it is left under fallow for natural regeneration to occur and the rotation continues around the village allowing several years to pass before the same plot is replanted. This form of shifting cultivation is still practiced today in less populated areas in the western Cote d'lvoire in parts of Liberia and in western Cameroon.

The opening up of the forest for logging activities and increased population led to the collapse of traditional land tenure and, land-use systems in most West African forests. Coffee and cocoa plantations contributed in no lesser sense to the disintegration of the traditional systems. Although land is, considered to be community property, many tribes believe that which grows on the land to be the sole property of the planter. Coffee trees, cocoa trees and oil palm trees thus belong to the farmer and not to the community. Should the community wish to reclaim its land, the farmers must be compensated for their fruit trees. Many villages therefore do not allow immigrant farmers to plant fruit trees on the land for which they have received cultivation rights. The result is that the settlers then plant only corn, plantain and cassava, all of which quickly deplete the soil of its nutrients. After only a few years, the planters find themselves forced to move on to a new plot of land. Those who are determined to remain at one location for a longer period usually choose to plant coffee and cocoa. They do their best to gain possession of land against the traditional rules. These circumstances have led to a wider distribution of plantations and villages throughout the forests of West Africa.

West African tribes thus had good reason to resist the centralization of the forest administration at the turn of the century. They tried to defined their culture and their ancestors - without success. But neither did the West African forest services achieve their goals. Forest legislation based on European principles was inadequate in the light of African reality. In trying to encourage the sustainable development of the rainforest, the forest services lost control over the consequences of their ordinances. Even today, West African forestry departments lack the necessary foresight, control and overview to deal effectively with the situation. Law and regulations aimed at protecting the forest often lead to just the opposite.

Large-scale Exploitation and the Consequences

It was not until the 1970s that the inadequate implementation of forest regulations became apparent Following World War II, commercial exploitation had increased to such an extent that no West African forestry department was capable of enforcing the law. In comparison with rainforests in other parts of the world in 1973, Africa showed the greatest area encroached upon by logging activities although African timber production measured only one third that of Asia. This fact signalized very extensive exploitation practices in African rainforests which were continually opening up new areas.

In 1985, the U. N. Food and Agricultural Organization (FAO) estimated 72% of West African rainforests to be fallow land: destroyed forest, plantations or secondary bush. Between 1981 and 1985, the remaining areas of undisturbed forest on the Gulf of Guinea were being opened up at the rate of 1640 square kilometers annually. Many timber companies adopted highly selective logging practices to meet specific demands or merely for reasons of profit. Only the best specimens of mahogany, utile, sapele and makore were extracted from the forest. With few exceptions, however, such selective timber exploitation foresaw a one-time use only and did not aim at long-term sustainable use.

Table 3.1 The status of closed broadleaved forests ("rainforests") in West Africa from Sierra Leone to, Nigeria.

Status of forest	*km^2*	%
Undisturbed, productive	21260	4.1
Undisturbed, unproductive	64460	12.5
Logged	45870	8.9
Managed	11670	2.3
Forest fallow	370820	72.1
Total West Africa	514080	100.0

During the past decade, each year has seen an average loss of 7200 square kilometers of West African forest. The major cause is burning and clearing by migrant farmers. But over 90% of the areas destroyed were forests previously opened up by timber companies.

Logging roads 'not only serve to carry timber out of the forest but also pave the way for settlers to come in. What timber companies leave standing is devastated by slash-and-burn farming Unfortunately, the resulting increase in agricultural area is minimal: since the soil quality of the land thus gained affords only a few harvests, the process of burning and clearing continues. The planters follow the timber exploiters further into the rainforest leaving unproductive land behind.

Table 3.2. Annual decrease in area of closed broadleaved forests ("rainforests").

Forest Type	*km²*	%
Untouched, productive	210	2.9
Untouched, unproductive	340	4.7
Logged	6650	92.4
Total West Africa	7200	100.0

Today, we look back upon a half a millenium of trade relations with Europe - relations which were rarely in favour of West Africa. European demand dictated West Africa's export of natural resources. During times of war or upon the discovery of an alternative product, Europeans lost interest in trade, Whether dealing in slaves or hardwood, Africa's fate was typical for a deliverer of raw materials. Unlike the eastern and southern parts of the continent at higher altitudes, West Africa did not attract many white settlers, its climate being unpleasantly hot and humid. The whites were interested only in what could be exported. West Africa became Europe's major source of raw materials and remained a loyal trader even in less profitable times. But West Africa was poorly paid for her loyalty. What began as a sustainable use of forest products developed into a timber export economy nothing short of all out exploitation, In the words of tropical forest expert Professor H. Steinlin, "The exploitation can be compared to that of a mine, a natural resource is being excavated without guarantee of a sustainable production". This attitude has had serious consequences for the forest and last but not least for the local people.

4

Forest as Human Habitat

Although mankind's earliest origins may be traced back to African rainforests, our Stone Age ancestors had long ceased to favour the rainforest as a place to live. The climate fluctuations from cool, dry periods to warm wet spans and the resulting retreat and expansion of the rainforest zone during the Pleistocene also affected human settlement. Dry periods led to migration from the Sahara to the bend of the Niger River and from the savannah zone into the rainforest. Supported by archeological finding such migrations lead us to assume that prehistoric man was better suited to life in the savannah than in the desert or in closed rain forest. During the Middle Stone Age there were a number of migrations from the Niger Valley, not far from today's Niamey, to the Volta region of Ghana up to the Accra plains and to the edge of the rainforest zone but no further at least not at that time.

It was not until the, Late Stone Age, after 900 B.C., that two groups of settlers pushed into the rainforest zone from the east and northeast. They reached the area of Conakry in the Republic of Guinea, Somewhat later the Kintampo culture introduced the art of pottery from the Niger Valley; stone axes, picks, arrowheads and other stone tools found more and more use inside the rainforest. But the population density was low, settlements were scattered along the rivers, Even then, these Neolithic settlers already cultivated the soil. Yams (*Dioscorea* spp.) of which there are many wild species in the savannah and in the rainforest, were planted and harvested in crude plots of land. Agriculture, however, played a minor role for the early inhabitants of the rainforest. They did not yet know of slash- and-burn farming methods and lived mostly from hunting and gathering in the forest as the pygmies in Central Africa still do today.

There were no signs of shifting agriculture in the rainforest zone until 500-1000 A.D. when tribes that had knowledge of the art of working iron intruded from the north. The art stemmed from the Nile Valley. Iron however, did not completely replace stone in fabricating tools in the rainforest until just a few centuries ago. Settlements were not permanent but changed according to the principles of shifting agriculture and were usually located in the vicinity of rivers. It was then that basic tribal structures began to develop. Forest-dwelling people from the Cote d'lvoire, through Ghana, Togo, Benin, up to western Nigeria are related as is evident by their languages – they all belong to the linguistic group Kwa.

Around the 16th century, Portuguese travellers introduced new crops from Latin America and Asia to the west coast of Africa: Sugar cane, pineapples and bananas, sweet potatoes, oranges, limes and red peppers. Just when corn was introduced is uncertain. Plantains were possibly introduced much earlier from Southeast Asia. There is proof, however, that the Portuguese brought doves, chickens, pigs and sheep with them. Increased agriculture led to higher populations in certain areas of forest. While southwestern Nigeria was relatively heavily populated by the Yorubas from the 14th to the 17th century, wide areas of forest in West Africa remained practically uninhabited by man until this century. Hunters played an important role in forest settlement. Everywhere in West Africa, one hears stories of how hunting camps 10-30 kilometers from the nearest settlement often developed into settlements of their own. The name "Sunyani", today a small city in the Brong-Ahafo Region of Ghana, indicates a place where elephants were skinned.

Thus, agriculture is a relatively new tradition in West African rainforests. And should some forest peoples have used fire to clear land in pre-Christian times, the damage to the forest could not have been lasting. There is certainly no reason to believe that a few pre-Christian settlers could have caused the limited plant diversity of Africa's rainforests as has been suggested. In thinly populated areas, even land cleared by fire only a few hundred years ago has regenerated to such an extent that it is scarcely distinguishable from primary rainforest.

"Secondary" Forest Utilization

For centuries, forest-dwelling people have lived by hunting and gathering produce from the forest. Agriculture was a minor addition to their food supply. Today still, the culture and economy of forest-dwellers are a balance of hunting, gathering and agriculture. Knowledge of plants and animals, their uses for food medicine or for other purposes was passed by word of mouth from one generation to the next. Man had lived long enough in the forests of West Africa to develop intricate utilization patterns Local handicraft developed and raw material gathered from the forest was used in various ways. The Akan people, of whom the Ashantis in Ghana are the most dominant, actually made textiles from rainforest plants. Long pieces of bark were ripped off Kyenkyen trees (*Antiarts taxicaria*), soaked in water and beaten with wooden clubs The result was a soft piece of cloth much wider than the original piece of bark. The production of "bark cloth" was an important part of the local economy in the rainforest zone. In the mean time the Ashantis had introduced the art of Kente weaving. Kente cloth is sewn of narrow strips woven in traditional patterns. Kente cloth and European textiles eventually replaced "bark cloth". But until this century, hunters and poorer people in the Brong-Ahafo Region of Ghana still wore clothes made of Kyenkyen cloth.

Today, the forest continues to be a source of fruits, vegetables, nuts, oils, spices, tannins, fibers, resins, rubber and medicinal substances as well as bush meat, skins, honey, firewood and building materials. The official term used by for esters for all of the above is "secondary forest products", their use is categorized as secondary. The term also reveals their status. For some decades now the primary forest product - commercial timber - has been considered 'more important, usually at the cost of all other less damaging kinds of forest utilization. The socioeconomic value of hunting and gathering in intact rainforests has been grossly ignored in West Africa and elsewhere. Timber exploitation now opens up the forest to an invasion of farmers from the north. Age-old knowledge and traditional uses of the forest are likely to be lost. The new settlers, many of whom come from the overpopulated Sahel region, have no cultural ties to the forest and are not capable of dealing with its sensitive soil.

Old Knowledge - New Science

For some years now, worldwide efforts have been made to document the traditional knowledge held by many forest-dwelling people In the face of forest destruction around the globe, botanists and pharmacologists have begun to search for new organic substances before they are lost. The traditional knowledge of forest people is an invaluable aid and in the course of their work, it has become evident that the world's rainforests hold an incredible number of useful substances. A worldwide search is underway for plants containing substances capable of fighting cancer fighting number of African plants may also produce, new medicines. The economic value of new plant medicines should not be underestimated. Some years ago, more than a quarter of the 1.5 billion prescriptions written annually in, the United States were already based on substances gained from medicinal plants.

Ethnobotany the study of traditional knowledge concerning plants and their use by native peoples has become a popular branch of science. The majority of ethno botanical studies have been made among Mexican Indians and in Amazonia. A few studies have also been made in Asia. But the, new science has apparently not yet spread to Africa. A closer look, however, shows that some botanists had already done some very thorough ethnobotanical work in the years preceding World War II. J.M. Dalziel, a doctor and botanist who worked for many years in West African colonies, identified more than 900 genera of useful plants in West Africa, many of which included several species. His work of over 600 pages was based on notes made of West African traditions and included many of the ways in which the plants were used then and sometimes still today. Some of his sources dated back to 1905. But his information did not refer only to the rainforest, traditions in savannah areas were also found to be documented. In addition, F.R. Irvine published surprisingly detailed information on the traditional uses of woody plants in Ghana. Irvine worked at the Herbarium of the Achimota College in Ghana before World War II and later at the University of Edinburgh. According to his information, the leaves of 106 and the fruits of 326 woody plants were included in the local diet. Oils, fats and waxes were extracted from 84 species Parts of no less than 755 woody plants were used for medicinal purposes. The majority of the species listed are a part of rainforest flora.

A Pharmacy in the Forest

Today medicinal plants continue to play an enormous role in Africa. Local health care in many countries is still practiced mostly by traditional healers, medicine men and "barefoot doctors". Washes and pastes made from leaves, bark and roots are commonly used to treat 'Wounds' almost everywhere in Africa. But the treatment by natural remedies in Africa does not get the attention it deserves. Traditional healing is often accompanied by witchcraft. Medicine men also perform ritual ceremonies and recite magical incantations. Not only do they treat earthly ills, but they are also called upon to exorcise evil spirits. This obscure combination of magic and natural medicine has met with the scepticism of western civilization. And it is for this reason that western medicine considers traditional African medicine no more effective than a fairy tale when it comes to healing. Herbalists and medicine men are labeled charlatans. But such arrogance can have serious consequences for many developing countries. The low status of natural medicine has hindered traditional knowledge from being passed on as widely as in the past.

Africa suffers daily economic and cultural losses through the death of medicine men who have not passed on their secrets. The loss of traditional knowledge concerning the uses and effects of medicinal plants has been compared with the burning of entire medical libraries. Natural medicine is not only less expensive, it also includes substances effective against illnesses for which western medicine has not yet found a cure. One example are the leaves of the spreading shrub *Combretum mucronatum*; they can be used to expel the Guinea worm, a much-feared parasitic threadworm which embeds itself and eats away at skin tissue. Clinical tests at the Center for Scientific Plant Medicine in Ghana have only recently confirmed what traditional healers have long known. The effects of traditional medicinal plants against diabetes and bronchial asthma have also been confirmed.

African governments would at least be well advised to examine the medicinal plants used in their countries. Nationally, they could help save costs on health care. But there is also growing international interest in medicinal plants and the World Health Organization (WHO) has begun to study the topic. In Cameroon, the Centre for the Study of Medicinal Plants (CEPM) has started an inventory of the medicinal plants used in the country and is establishing a herbarium. Medical fluids, tablets and ointments are already being produced in larger quantities for commercial purposes; one example is an anti-bacterial ointment which contains an extract from a species of *Erythrina*.

Professor Edward Ayensu, former Director of the Species Conversation Program at the Smithsonian Institution in Washington, D.C. has examined the most commonly used medicinal plants in West Africa. A native Ghanaian, Ayensu is equally interested in both rainforest conservation and the link between traditional and modern medicine. He lists 187 medicinal plants used in one way or the other against more than 300 different pathological symptoms. Some of the plants are very popular and have a variety of uses. The Ashanti pepper (*Piper gwneensis*) is quite a versatile plant Soup made from its leaves is supposed to help women to conceive, soaked leaves are effective against coughs and used as warm compresses on wounds Pulverized twigs and bark are used against coughs, bronchitis, - and as an enema against intestinal infections The root relieves the pains of gonorrhea and is also effective against bronchitis. The small brownish-red fruit is similar to black pepper and used as a spice which is sold at local markets as "Bush Pepper". But aside from its culinary aspect, the fruit is supposedly effective against tumors and rheumatism. And finally, the pulverized seeds of the small fruit help relieve back pains, syphilis and rid clothes of insect pests. The healing properties of Ashanti pepper may be overestimated, but there is surely some truth to the mass of information passed on over the years concerning this humble climber found on the trunks of trees deep inside closed rainforests.

Trade in Secondary Forest Products

The inhabitants of West African forests were not the only ones interested in products gathered Gum Copal from the forest. During the last century, products from West African rainforests began to attract "Copal hunters" collected the gum in the wild much larger markets in Europe and North America. Long before rising industrialized countries discovered the forest's vital substance - tropical timber, major trade had developed with the West African coast in spite of strong fluctuations due to the political upheavals and the price offered for the commodities in Europe. The major export products gathered in the rainforest were gum copal, rubber and cola nuts.

Gum Copal

"Copal hunters" collected the gum in the wild from trees of the genus *Daniellia*. Lumps of gum copal were found buried at the base of the trunks and on wounded trees. In Ghana, copal production was concentrated in the forests surrounding Akropong where a branch of the basle Mission was located. The Basle missionaries were known for developing African trade with Europe. In 1850, gum copal was first exported to England for the production of varnish, veneer, paint and linoleum. The largest export volume of about 500 tons was reached in 1876, a quantity never again surpassed. Price fluctuations on the European market caused hardship for the exporters. Towards the end of the 1880s and just before World War I, the copal hunters again enjoyed an increased demand, this time from the United States as well as from Europe. In the following years, however, production sank until it eventually disappeared entirely in 1936. From 1920 onwards; Congo copal, found in the swamp forests along the courses of the

Congo tributaries, had begun to vie with the West African gum resin. Congo copal can be found buried up to one meter below ground at the base of *Copaifera demeusei*. But today, artificial resins have also replaced the demand for this gum copal.

Rubber

The West African rubber tree *Funtumia elastica* and the liana *Landolphia owariensis* exude a milky fluid (latex) which immediately hardens to a firm, robbery mass. This raw rubber is of comparable quality with *Hevea* rubber, tapped from a Brazilian tree (*Hevea brasiliensis*) widely cultivated throughout the tropical world today. The significance of West African rubber was first recognized in 1883 and the best quality was found in the Krepi area of southern Ghana. Rubber was exported from Accra under the term "Accra Biscuits" mostly from the production. But rubber tappers did not always treat the *Funtumia* trees with care. Instead of being tapped, the trees were often felled. The collectors then built a fire beneath one end of the trunk to increase the sap flow from the other end, a destructive practice which was forbidden by some village chiefs on their tribal land. Once the Ashantis became active in the rubber industry. Ghana rose to become the third most important rubber producer worldwide. Rubber was partly produced in plantations of West African rubber trees. After a last increased demand from England during World War I, production sank, however, and finally collapsed or made way for *Hevea* rubber plantations.

Cola Nuts

In Ghana, cola nuts did not become a popular export product until this century when their export volume surpassed that of all other forest products gathered from the wild. 13000 tons of cola nuts were exported in 1921. They were imported mainly by the Maghrib countries of North Africa. Cola nuts had been transported to the, north in much earlier times over the Sahara desert. The highest prices were paid for nuts of *Cola nitida*, which have a stimulating effect when chewed. Since 1870, the major market for cola nuts has been Lagos which Greated such a steady demand that cola plantations were established in some areas, notably in Ho and Kpandu in Ghana.

The Oil Palm Conquers the World

Gum copal, *Funtumia* and the cola nut are exports of the past. These products which can be extracted with little or no damage to the forest are no longer valuable on the export market. They have made way for other commercial products, the production of which causes much greater damage to the forest: cocoa, coffee, Hevea rubber and tropical timber extraction. Large areas of forest were also sacrified for plantations of oil palm (*Elaeis guineensis*), a tree native to West Africa. Earlier the fruit of the oil palm was gathered in the wild. The first plantations were established in Ghana around 1850 and led to a somewhat more steady export revenue. Palm oil is pressed from the red, fibrous pulp (pericarp) of the fruit and palm kernel oil is extracted from the oil-rich seeds- The export of both products provided foreign exchange income to West Africa Today, 14% of all plant oils worldwide is derived from the oil palm, which is nearly equal to the proportion covered by the soya bean and comparable to that of the sunflower. But since the oil palm grows throughout the year, the yield per hectare is much greater, from 1000 to 4000 kg and sometimes up to 6000 kg. Malaysia and Indonesia are responsible for more than half the current world production of palm oil. Other producers, including West African countries, suffer from the competition The situation was different not too long ago. Although the oil palm was introduced to Malaysia 75 years ago, production was not satisfactory. The trees needed to be pollinated manually, which was a tedious process and led to inefficient production. It was originally believed that oil palms were wind pollinated until Dr. R.A. Syed discovered the contrary. The Common wealth Institute for Biological Control assigned Syed to study the pollination of oil palms in a *Pamol* (Unilever) plantation in Cameroon. He found that the pollination was effected by insects and not by wind. The weevilbeetle *Elaeidobius kamerunicus* in particular plays an important role in the pollination process. After cautious tests, the release of the beetle in the Malaysian plantations increased the yield by 40 - 60%. The West African weevil-beetie proved to be a gold-bug for Malaysia, it raised the foreign exchange income by US$ 44 million in the first year. Today, biotechnological methods permit the cloning of oil palm tissue. Cloning allows the vegetative multiplication of the germs from especially productive plants. Thanks to biotechnology, production has sky-rocketed while prices have dropped – not to the advantage of the oil palm's native home: West African producers are losing out. The *Pamol* plantation in Cameroon, on which the valuable weevil was discovered, went bankrupt in 1987.

West Africa has given much to the world and received little in return. But there are products yet to be discovered in the rainforest which may someday be of commercial value, A shrub distributed from

Ghana through to Central Africa bears an incredibly sweet fruit: the "miraculous berry" (*Synsepalum duloficum*). In the Volta Region of Ghana, the local people eat this fruit which initially has a sweet-sour taste Surprisingly, the sweetness of the miraculous berry is retained in the mouth so long that even substances as bitter as quinine can be camouflaged up to an hour later. The miraculous berry is also used to sweeten palm wine. The British company Tate and Lyle is also interested in the super-sweeting agent. The sweetness is apparently not due to sugar content but to a protein complex. Nevertheless, one cannot assume that the commercial value of the miraculous berry or of any other secondary forest product would be reason enough to permanently protect the forest where these plants grow. West African rainforests have been and continue to be used commercially without thought to their future or to that of the people who depend on the forest for their livelihood.

The Economic Value of Traditional Hunting

On dark, moonless nights West African hunters leave their villages and venture into the forest despite their fear. Moonlight filtering through to the forest floor would hinder the hunt. The hunter sees his prey by its reflecting eyes in the light of his carbide headlamp. The blinded animal is not to see that a man stands behind the glaring light. Most of the nightly catch consists of duiker antelopes, usually the small blue duiker which seldoms weighs more than 10 kg. Not that hunters have a specific preference for the smallest of the duikers, they simply can never be sure of their prey until it lies at their feet in the light of the carbide lamp. In many areas the blue duiker is the most common hoofed animal. Occasionally, a hunter may bag a bongo the largest of the forest antelopes. This animal with its attractive colouring and massive spiral horns is usually very cautious and seldom seen by man. It is rarely listed under the catch of West African hunters. But should a hunter slay such a majestic animal on a dark night, he will think twice of how to deal with the unusual situation. In Ghana, forest-dwelling, people consider the bongo a sacred animal and the successful hunter will fear for his life. He may not bring his prey into the village at dawn. He must skin it outside the village and under: no circumstances should he carry the head of the bongo on his own head. Afterwards, the hunter must bath in "Sassandra", a spiritual medicine to prevent him, from either going mad or dying, Spirits may accompany him on his next hunt. The Gouro tribe, who live along the middle course of the Bandama River in the Cote d'Ivoire believe in the reincarnation of all men and animals. The same souls are born again and again. Whoever kills a man or an animal must reckon with the soul's revenge depending upon the strength of its "Bei". Bei, which more or less means "power", is not of equal strength in all animals. The leopard and the elephant have the most dangerous Bei. In order to prevent their Bei from attacking him while he sleeps, a hunter must make a sacrifice to the head of the slain animal immediately after the killing. The skulls are then piled at the base of a fetish tree outside the village.

Yoruba hunters also fear the revenge of an animal's soul. The Yorubas are native to southwestern Nigeria When a hunter kills a leopard, he binds its eyes because the animal "is a king and his gaze is too frightful for the people". It is, however, unlikely that there are many leopards left in the Yorubas native territory today The rainforest has given way to an increased human population density. But other West African tribes also believe in the special powers of the leopard. The fur of the animal must be presented to the tribal or village chief.

Hunting Taboos and Varied Prey

It is often forbidden to hunt or eat specific animals in West Africa. Such taboos usually pertain to individuals or families. As its name implies, only a chief may eat the meat of the royal antelope, Africa's tiniest ungulate. Hunting chimpanzees is often totally banned because of its similarity to man and the hunters fear of its soul. A village chief among the Sefwis in western Ghana admits, however, he would welcome a hunter's bringing him the skin of a chimpanzee for the great village drums. Drum skins from chimpanzees are said to be particularly resilient and can be beaten for four years, before having to be replaced. Along the West African coast and rivers, the python is often considered sacred. It symbolizes the spirits of the water and of war, fertility and wisdom. In today's Benin, it was once custom for traditional African priests to keep pythons.

There are few hunting taboos, however, which are exclusive and respected by all rainforest people or even by an entire tribe in West Africa. When the prey is worth more than the cartridge and the hunter is able to overcome his fear, practically no animal of the forest is spared. Monkeys active during the daylight hours are hunted at day In the Korup area of West Cameroon, as in other areas where the red colobus has not yet been wiped out, this monkey species is part of the most common catch. Drills (*Papio leucophaeus*) are also found in this scarcely accessible area of rainforest. The large groups of these ground-dwelling pavians are hunted with the aid of dogs. In order to prevent the powerful pavians from grabbing the dogs by the tail and killing them, the hunters dock the tails of their hunting companions. The dogs cut pavians off from their group and chase them up trees, where they are sitting prey for the hunters.

Wire snares are sometimes used to catch rodents, monkeys and duiker antelopes Reptiles are hunted with bush knives. The diets of some tribes in Ghana include squirrels, flying squirrels, pangolins and even fruit bats. The large maggot of the palm beetle, (*Phyncophorus* sp.) is also considered a delicacy by some forest people. Crocodiles, monitor lizards, snakes and the African giant snail in particular are also popular sources of meat; Europeans tend to poke fun at the omnivorous habits of many West Africans. A decent person supposedly eats beef and poultry. Consequently, the value of the rainforest as a source of protein is often greatly misjudged and underestimated. It is interesting, however, that bushmeat is in much higher demand and more expensive than domestic meat in most of West Africa. Even much of the urban population still prefers wild game.

Bushmeat - An Invaluable Resource

"One of the ironies of the age is the tendency of scientifically educated people to ignore or reject' whatever they cannot measure. Such is the case with the consumption of wildlife of all kinds for food in developing countries. The significance of this resource is largely ignored by nutritionists animal production experts and even some wildlife biologists because it is difficult to find statistics about the gathering, marketing and consumption of wildlife. In addition, these foods are mostly strange or even repugnant to the majority of specialists who are working so hard to increase food production and human nutrition levels among the peoples of developing countries. The specialists are inclined to think of the improvement of man's lot in terms of passing on what they are familiar with in their own lives, ideas and things which are often foreign, distant and unconnected to the lives of those whom they want to help." These words were written by the editor of "Unasylva", a 'periodical published by, the Food and Agriculture Organization (FAO) to introduce a series of articles dealing with the utilization of game as a source of food. The editor was apparently critical of his own organization. A survey of nutritional habits showed that in Africa, and particularly West Africa, a surprising variety of game continues to be a major source of protein. The FAO normally deals more with aspects of timber exploitation in tropical rainforests, a practice which in turn often considerably reduces the abundance of wild life.

Sunday S. Ajayi, from the University of Ibadan in Nigeria, and Emmanuel E.O. Asibey, former director of the, Ghana Forestry Commission, have both statistically proven that game or "bushmeat" as it is called in English-speaking parts of West Africa) is actually a very important factor for local economies. Game consumed in Nigeria during the early 1970s was worth £30 million and corresponded to 4% of the country's gross national product. In 1980, estimates of Nigerian trade in game fluctuated between 150 - 3600 million Naira (1 Naira = US$ 1.00). The range of these estimates mirrors the difficulty in judging a market which does not officially exist. Although the estimates point to several percent of the country's GNP and 95% of the population surveyed reported that they regularly or occasionally consume bushmeat, game scarcely appears in the statistics. Since it does not fall into a trade category, it is not considered a forest product of economical value. It is a non-product as are other "secondary forest products" as well. Emmanuel Asibey complains, "Unfortunately, the Africans themselves tend to fail to appreciate, and insist on, the inclusion of bush meat production in development plans". He has long pointed out the extreme importance of this kind of land-use, In Ghana, 75% of the population relies on traditional sources of protein: Game, fish, insects, maggots and snails.

Game is popular throughout West Africa and is not considered a substitute for better quality meat. In Nigeria, for example, bushmeat from indigenous forests commands a higher price than does any domestically produced meat. Only the best cuts of imported steak cost more than bushmeat in a Nigerian supermarket. Even the wealthier urban population prefers the meat of a cane rat or duiker to that of a goat or sheep. Urban eating habits still reveal the rural origins of the city's inhabitants much more than their other behaviour.

But the urban supply of game meat is not always sufficient. Nigeria's upper class does not consume as much bushmeat as does the rural population although the wealthier members of society would gladly pay the price. The majority of game meat is traded and consumed locally. Many hunters and trappers take their catch to the edge of the next cross-country road and hold it aloft. They are fairly certain to be relieved of their burden by one of the next passing vehicles. A survey in Bendel State in southern Nigeria disclosed the variety of the roadside market: Monkeys, genet cats, mongooses, bush-pigs, pangolins, flying squirrels, birds, tortoises and even snakes. Three quarters of the catch, however, consists of duiker antelopes, giant rats, brush-tailed porcupines and the much sought after cane rats. The abundance of the latter is due to the opening up of the forest and the increase of grassy areas: In Ghana, too, the large cane rat, locally known as "grasscutter", is the most popular form of bushmeat. At the Kantamanto market, one of the largest markets in the capital of Accra, same 24000 of these good sized rodents were said from December 1968 to June 1970 which corresponded to a live weight of 117 tans and a market value of US$ 125000. These figures led Emmanuel Asibey to test the domestic breeding of large cane rats as a source of meat in the 1970s. His experiments were quite successful and showed that cane rat breeding could supply extra income to farmers. The rodents are easy to keep and require only grass fodder. Unfortunately, large-scale cane rat breeding has never become popular although it would be an efficient method of meat production, especially aver wide expanses of West Africa where grassy areas are scattered throughout fallow forest.

Game Guarantees Local Income

Contrary to the prestigious sport hunter of the temperate zones, a West African hunter does not boast of his catch. Far him, hunting is a way of life and not a pastime for discussion. Neither does he dress far the occasion with a shooting jacket but wears the least valuable clothes he awns. Although hunting guarantees a respectable income, a hunter is not necessarily a respected man. Young people in the village consider the jab dangerous, difficult, dirty and old fashioned. Few strive to became hunters. At most, a hunter is admired far his weapon but not far his occupation. Fear of the animals and the invisible dwarfs, who can never be trusted; keep hunters modest and reluctant to speak of their actions. Many traditional hunters fear of breaking the law, knowingly or not, adds to their uneasiness. Indeed, many West African nations limit hunting to specific species, sea sans and: hunting methods. The use of arms usually requires a permit and in same areas such as, national parks, hunting is prohibited entirely. It is understandable that West African hunters remain silent when asked about their work. Mast earn their living as farmers and stalk animals only to supply their families with meat or to augment their agricultural income. It takes time to gain the trust of a hunter before he will tell of the tradition and his hunting habits.

At the suggestion of Emmanuel Asibey, the trust of several traditional hunters was slowly gained in order to study the importance of game-hunting for local economies. A considerable part of the population in Kwamebikrom, a small village north of Bia National Park in Western Ghana, lives wholly or in part from hunting. Allowing far uncertainties, one can assume that 50 wild animals are killed each month by the people of Kwamebikrom In 1978, the resulting market value corresponded to 8 or 9 minimal monthly salaries. The majority of the meat is said fresh or smoked to traders The people cover their own need for protein with other sources not included in the study: Fish, smaller animals caught in wire snares and especially giant snails. In relatively undisturbed forest areas, game thus probably provides 20-50% of the village cash income in addition to covering private nutritional needs.

Table 4.1. Game caught by inhabitants of the forest village kwamebikrom (ghana) from May to August 1978

	Number of Animals	*Local Market Value (Cedis)*
Blue duikers	50	1875.00
Campbell's mona monkeys	46	464.60
Royal antelopes	33	389.40
Lesser spot-nosed monkeys	11	115.60
Bay duikers	10	425.00
White-crowned mangabeys	9	135.00
Brush-tailed porcupines	9	108.00
Gaint rats	3	15.00
Olive colobus	3	30.00
Diana monkeys	2	30.00
Black-and-White colobus	2	24.00
African civets	2	80.00
Flying squirrels	2	14.00
West African dwarf crocodiles	2	40.00
Nile monitor lizard	1	20.00
Pangolin	1	10.00
Bush-pig	1	50.00
Large cane rat	1	12.00
Gaint forest squirrel	1	9.00
Total	189	3846.60

A close examination of hunting habits in the Korup area of West Cameroon showed that approximately 38% of a village's income is provided by hunting. Trapping provides an additional 18% of the income. Hundreds to thousands of traps are laid especially during the rainy seasons. The combined annual catch from hunting, and trapping amounts to at least 217 kg of meat per square kilometer.

Local restaurants in larger towns and in West African cities serve large quantities of bushmeat: In Ghana, such restaurants are called "chop bars". 'Tufu" a paste-like mass made by pounding cooked cassava, coco-yams and plantains, is served as an accompaniment to generous amounts of bush meat in a hot, spicy soup. At the chop bar "As Usual" in Sunyani, over 3000 wild animals were consumed during one year (1976). Since Sunyani lies in the transitional zone between rainforest and savannah, the menu at "As Usual" often lists savannah animals: bush bucks, Guinea-fowl and especially the popular large cane rats. A total of 123295 meals were prepared with 14630 kg of game meat and were sold for almost 78000 Cedis in the chop bar alone (78000 Cedis then corresponded to about US$ 68500.) About two thirds of the cash income went directly to the full or part-time hunters who sold their catch to the chop bar Close to 80 farmers in Sunyani earned as much money this way as does a government worker. For the farmers, however, this is a supplement to their income from subsistence and cash agriculture. According to Asibey, most small-scale farmers would not be able to continue cocoa production if it were not for the extra income. Since 90% of Ghanaian cocoa is grown on small-scale farms, the harvest would fall far below the present level without the additional income from wildlife utilization Thus, the rainforest's wild animals, which are usually overlooked in land-use planning or at best classified as secondary forest products, are not of such secondary value. Not only is game meat the most important source of protein and of local economic value which should not be underestimated - indirectly, game even subsidizes the export economy.

The Great Demand for Giant Snails

African giant snails are a kind of bushmeat which is easily gathered. Large quantities of snail meat are eaten in West Africa and it is incredibly popular with forest inhabitants in Nigeria, Ghana and the Cote d'lvoire. Plantation workers bake them in the shell over a campfire. Shelled, the snails can be roasted or cooked. Snail meat is often skewered and smoked to preserve for longer periods before it is prepared with okra (lady finger) or another vegetable and served with fufu. At first, the meat may seem somewhat rubbery, but one soon learns to appreciate its flavor Snail meat not only tastes good, its protein content is comparable to that of beef. It is even richer than chicken eggs in certain essential aminoacids, notably arginine and lysinel.

Snails do not only feed the poor; even in Abidjan, in many respects West Africa's most modern city, rainforest snails are eaten in large quantities. The city Likens a French metropolis with its silhouette of sky-scrapers, the department store chain "Uniprix" and an artificial ice rink located atop the luxury hotel "Ivoire". Abidjah is the major trade center of the Cote d'lvoire and provides a home to about 20 % ρf the nation's 10 million citizens. Eating habits, however, have remained traditionally rural. What may seem to appear a provocation in one of the city's elegant French restaurants is all the more appreciated at home. A survey by the Central Laboratory for Animal Production LACENA in Abidjan showed that in the city alone, one million kilograms of giant snails are eaten annually. The majority is consumed by people belonging to the forest tribes of the Baoule, Agni, Bete, Krou, Bakwe, Dida, Guere, Yakouba and Gouro. Although urbanized, these people have retained their preferences for forest delicacies. During the dry season when fresh snails are a rare commodity, these customers are prepared to pay more than double the price for beef. But even during the wetter months, snails are never cheaper than beef at Abidjan's eight marketplaces.

Approximately half of the giant snails consumed in Abidjan originate in the forests around Cechi, 140 kilometers inland They are gathered and packed live into bags which are then transported by truck to the capital. But snails are also delivered from all parts of the country's forest area to Abidjan. Allover the rainforest; snail gathering is a traditional pastime. Young and old take part in the gathering during the farming periods when families leave their villages to temporarily live in farming camps Soails collected in the forest surrounding plantations and not destined for private use are stored in the camps and head-carried to the weekly market.

Snails are abundant in relatively undisturbed forest areas where entire families can earn a living by gathering this sustainable product. Besides the gatherers, wholesale traders and retailers also profit from the snail business. Women are usually responsible for local trade and sale all over Weśt Africa. In the Cote d'lvoire, the total weight of snails sold in 1986 was estimated at 7.9 million kg and thus accounted for 10% of the trade in game meat. The proportion of snail meat in relation to the total game consumed in many regions of West Africa may be even higher.

Misunderstanding Forest Products

The fact that wildlife utilization and forest product gathering are still rated as being of minor importance is related to the unilateral export orientation of national economies. West African countries have remained export oriented and thus dependent on Europe as in past days of colonialism. Today, however, the income from timber export is dropping due to reduced supplies. Secondary forest products must all the more be given sufficient consideration in future land-use planning. "Team approach towards wildlife and forest management has to be accepted at the highest forestry decision-making levels and filtered through to the grassroots of both disciplines, particularly forestry whose staff have always looked to wildlife in their management unit as a fringe benefit of the service". This claim raised by Emmanuel Asibey of Ghana's forestry Commission, should be heeded. Future studies on the value of game and secondary forests products will be necessary.

In order to guarantee a sustainable use of wild life resources, the effects of hunting on the animal populations must also be examined. Although the potential for production of game meat from west African rainforests has been grossly underestimated, certain species react vulnerably and may be wiped out if hunting is not controlled. Top canopy monkey species, the red colobus in particular have already disappeared from much of west Africa's forest. If game populations are to be preserved, hunting and trapping doubtlessly need to be limited within most of Africa's remaining rainforests. Various recommendations have been made. The allocation of quotas for certain forest areas, the limitation of hunting licenses and even a total kill to be determined on the basis of wildlife population estimates. But how are hunting regulations to be enforced in a rainforest where the range of vision measures at most 15 meters and where the human population lives to a good deal from bushmeat? There are already a number of hunting regulations in West Africa: In Ghana, it is legally prohibited to hunt certain species and a general hunting ban extends from August to December. The ban goes unheeded – who is prepared to refrain from eating meat four months of the year? Or do the legislators expect the people to slaughter the country's entire population of chickens, goats and sheep during those four months? Unthinking conservationists even induced Liberia's head of state to declare a total hunting ban in 1988.

It was soon revoked, however, in favour of a shorter list of protected species.

Similar to the rest of West Africa, traditional hunting and trapping are of great importance in Cameroon. Hunting by means of traditional methods excluding firearms does not requires a license. This includes spears, bows and arrows, as well as traps fabricated from local materials. The pygmies, who live largely from hunting, do not require permits of any kind. But despite the liberal nature of Cameroon's hunting regulations, village income in West Cameroon would greatly suffer if they were strictly enforced.

"A law is only as good as its enforcement,". The truth to this statement can be found everywhere in West Africa, but it is of special importance in the rainforest. It would be an illusion to believe in the enforcement of laws imported from abroad and not in accordance with tradition. The best wildlife protection lies within the rainforest itself. If past decision-makers had sufficiently concerned gone by, hunting regulations would hardly be necessary today.

5

FOREST PRODUCTS

Plants have been used by man since the beginning of human culture for a great variety of purposes, including medicine. The earliest known record of a plant being used in medication is found on an Egyptian papyrus dated about 1550 BC. Since then, plants have provided nearly half of the world's successful drugs, ranging from anticancer drugs from the tiny periwinkle plant, to painkillers from willow bark, and even contraceptives from yams! Plants have provided modern medicine with more diverse and important drugs than any other natural source.

As technology and time progressed some of these natural drugs were synthesized and modified to improve or enhance their properties and as a result these natural products were largely supplanted by their synthetic counterparts. Successes in this field tended to overshadow the pharmaceutical industry's roots in natural products and it was generally thought that ultimately all the plant drugs would be obtained from synthetic sources. However, not all drugs can be commercially produced by synthesis and to this day pharmaceutical chemists still draw on plants when they search for new drug molecules. In the United States alone, pharmaceutical products originating from plants still make up some 25 per cent of prescription drugs.

BIOTIC RESOURCE

Estimates of the total number of higher plants species, both identified and unidentified, range from 250 000 to 5000 000 species and even to a higher figure of 750 000. However, most botanists would stick to a conservative figure of 250 000. Whatever the true figure is, one important factor is that only a small percentage of these plants have ever received any more than superficial screening. A great many of those screened comprise plants from the temperate and subtropical regions, due to the fact that phytochemical studies and medical advances in the temperate areas, involving temperate and subtropical plants, have taken place for a much longer period than those for the tropical regions.

The tropical rain forest is hailed to be the most biogenetically diverse of all the forested areas of the world. In a sample plot of 1 hectare of tropical rain forest, up to 100 tree species may be found, compared with only about 10-15, rarely up to 35, at the most, in a temperate forest. It covers only about 7 per cent of the earth's land surface, yet it is home to more than half the world's species of flowering plants. Undoubtedly, a vast storehouse of valuable new phytochemicals still awaits discovery. For example, nothing is known about 99 per cent of the flora of Brazil! Who knows what wonder drug still lies in wait within these dense and dark forest walls?

Role of Plants in Drug Discovery and Development

Plants produce a highly individual range of natural products which vary widely from species to species and are mostly structurally distinct from microbial metabolites. There are essentially four basic ways in which plants contribute to modern medicine. First, plants are sources of direct therapeutic agents. For example, the South American jungle liana *Chondodendron tomentosum* is the main source of d-tubocurarine, a muscle relaxant much used in surgery. Chemists so far have been unable to produce this drug synthetically in a form which has all the attributes of the natural product. Furthermore, there are incidences where, even when chemical synthesis is possible, it is less costly to harvest the drug from its natural sources. One such example is the hypotensive drug reserpine which is still commercially extracted from *Rauwolfia* species.

Plants are also a starting point for the elaboration of more complex semi-synthetic compounds. Among the most important therapeutic agents used in modern medicine today are steroidal drugs such as the corticosteroids, sex hormones, anabolic agents and oral contraceptives. Although these drugs can be obtained from a number of sources, including total synthesis, steroidal sapogenins obtained from plant species, for example diosgenin, which may be obtained from tubers of various species of *Dioscorea*, constitute one of the major raw materials for the partial syntheses of these drugs. At present the use of diosgenin has decreased by half or less due to the widescale use of stigmasterol and sitosterol which are also obtained from plant sources. Nevertheless diosgenin is still being used and *Dioscorea* species will continue to be an important source for steroidal drugs at least in the developing countries.

Plants are also a source of natural products which serve as models for new, pharmacologically active compounds in the field of drug synthesis. There are several reasons for this. It may be that the plant material is not present in abundance and large scale cultivation is not viable, precluding the direct use of the natural source. Another reason is that in some cases the side effects of a natural product often prevent its use in medicine and can be resolved only by preparation of a synthetic derivative; examples are cocaine, a template for other modern local anaesthetics, and modifications of podophyllotoxin to obtain other antitumour preparations. New and unusual chemical substances found in plants will continue to serve as models for novel synthetic substances and will prove to be increasingly important in the future.

Finally, plants may also act as a natural source of compounds whose side effects are too strong to permit their use as prescription drugs, but which are valuable in research such as in the investigation and characterization of biochemical process and their mechanisms. This is a very important, though obscure, use which assist in drug discovery and development. Many compounds with anticancer properties have been found to be toxic for use as clinical drugs but nevertheless are widely used and have proved to be very helpful in research.

Progress in Plant Drug Research

The 1950s coincided with a number of significant events such as the discovery of reserpine, the start of the investigation of the vinca alkaloids, and the development of refined chromatographic procedures and radioactive tracer techniques for biosynthetic studies. These provided considerable impetus to the investigation of drugs from plants. Apart from significant achievement in the field of drug synthesis, during the 40 years that followed, major advances were also continually being made in other areas related to plant drug research.

Much of the progress achieved in plant drug research today has been due to the analytical instrument and methods developed and employed during the last 40 years. Thin layer chromatography (TLC) and liquid chromatography techniques were widely used and remain of considerable importance to this day. Since such techniques were first developed they have undergone tremendous improvements and innovative modifications enabling better separations of mixtures of plant products. Advances in electronics brought more efficiency and sensitivity to spectroscopic techniques, especially nuclear magnetic resonance spectroscopy (NMR), mass spectrometry (MS) and X-ray crystallography. These analytical instruments are now more sophisticated and readily available; they are favoured as indispensable methods for structural determination. The spectral methods have been combined with chromatographic techniques, such as GC/MS, HPLC/MS and HPLC/NMR which permit the direct identification of separated compounds with remarkable ease.

The lack of simple bioassay procedures has been a continuing source of problems for natural products chemists in determining the physiological activity of plant materials, whether in the form of crude fractions or as purified chemical entities. Previously, fairly elaborate assays were used, for example the rat 'Hippocratic' screen. This was followed by the more successful brine shrimp (*Artemia salina*) toxicity assay, and the potato-disc assay which involves observation of the inhibition of crown-gall tumours induced on potato discs by *Agrobacterium tumefaciens* Conn. These methods were found to be rapid, reliable, inexpensive, and may be conveniently applied in-house by natural products chemists. In recent years major advances in bioassay techniques have taken place, in parallel with automated high-throughput screening technology based on the use of microelectronics, robotics and advanced spectroscopic instrumentation. The advent of modern biotechnology has led to the development of 'mode of action' bioassays including immunoassays capable of detecting picogram quantities of potentially useful compounds. Advances have also been made in areas of molecular and biochemical pharmacology which facilitated the development of assays for compounds which can selectively inhibit, or bind to, enzyme and receptors associated with known physiological events. Such integrated systems can screen thousands of samples daily and efficiently pinpoint those with pharmaceutical utility.

Another area relevant to plant drug research is the production of plant material for an adequate supply of the drug for clinical use. As civilization encroaches on forested areas, collection of plant material from the wild becomes less and less feasible. Drug producing plants do not often lend themselves to cultivation easily and agronomic research of drug producing plants has been somewhat limited because these plants were considered to be of relatively minor economic importance. Resorting to synthetic production of these drugs may not be as easy as it sounds as most often the structural complexity inherent in such natural products demands multi-step syntheses, which, although of distinct academic interest, are rarely of practical utility for large-scale industrial production. A solution to this question of increasing material availability and eliminating dependence on the living plant as the source is production using plant-tissue and cell culture techniques. As well as having great potential commercially, these techniques have been useful in the study of plant biosynthesis and regulation of plant secondary metabolite production. Although there are still limitations to such techniques such as slow growth, expensive media, and the tendency to store desired metabolites in the tissues rather than excrete them into the media, cell suspension cultures seem to be the most appropriate system for the production of secondary products on an economical scale, provided that strategies are developed to shorten fermentation times and increase yields. Currently, certain pharmaceutically important chemicals such as shikonin, digoxin, vinblastine and rosmarinic acid are being successfully produced commercially by cell culture in large bioreactors.

Some Significant Plant Drugs

Based on computerized information in the NAPRALERT database on natural products, there are currently about 125 clinically useful prescription drugs worldwide, derived from only 95 species of higher plants. A few of the more important drugs will therefore be briefly discussed in the following sections. At least 45 of the 125 drugs listed are derived from about 39 plants, originating in and around the tropical rain forests and almost half of these drug-yielding tropical species are Asian plants.

Drugs for Heart Diseases

The American foxglove (*Digitalis* species) has been used for medicinal purposes for hundred of years but it was only in the late eighteenth century that it was shown to be effective in the treatment of heart disease. It is the source of the digitalis drugs such as digitalin (1) digoxin, acetyldigitoxin, gitalin, lanatosides A, B, C, etc. These cardiac glycosides encompass compounds which contain a cardenolide linked to one or more glucose-like moieties and have a positive inotropic action on the heart. *D. purpurea* and *D. lanata* are two main sources of the digitalis drugs which are the treatment of choice for arrhythmias and heart failure. The major digitalis-producing countries are the USA, UK, The Netherlands, Switzerland and Germany.

A number of drugs used for cardiovascular disorder are drugs derived from tropical trees. The best example is probably the well-known alkaloids of *Rauwolfia serpentina*, used as antihypertensives and

Table 5.1. Clinically useful drugs obtained from plants.

Drug	*Action/clinical use*	*Species*	*Origin*
Acetyldigitoxin	Cardiotonic	*Digitalis lanata* Ehrh.	NT
Adoniside	Cardiotonic	*Adonis vernalis* L.	NT
Aescin	Anti-inflammatory	*Aesculus hippocastanum* L.	NT
Aesculetin	Antidysentery	*Fraxinus rhynchophylla* Hance	NT
Agrimophol	Anthelmintic	*Agrimonia eupatoria* L.	NT
Ajmalicine	Circulatory disorders	*Rauvolfia serpentina* (L.) Benth.ex Kurz	T, As
Allantoin	Vulnerary	A number of species	NT
Allyl isothiocyanate	Rubefacient	*Brassica nigra* (L.) Koch	NT
Anabasine	Skeletal muscle relaxant	*Anabasis aphylla* L.	NT
Andrographolide	Antibacillary dysentery	*Andrographis paniculata* Nees	T, As
Anisodamine	Anticholinergic	*Anisodus tanguticus* (Maxim.) Pascher	NT
Anisodine	Anticholinergic	*Anisodus tanguticus* (Maxim.) Pascher	NT
Arecoline	Anthelmintic	*Areca catechu* L.	T, As
Artemisinin	Antimalarial	*Artemisia annua* L.	NT
Asiaticoside	Vulnerary	*Centella asiatica* (L.) Urban	T, As, Am, Af
Atropine	Anticholinergic	*Atropa belladonna* L.	NT
		Hyoscyamus niger L.	NT

Table 5.1. Continued

Drug	*Action/clinical use*	*Species*	*Origin*
Azadirachtin	Insecticide	*Azadirachta indica* Juss.	T, As
Benzyl benzoate	Scabicide	A number of species	NT
Berberine	Antibacterial	*Berberis vulgaris* L.	NT
Bergenin	Antitussive	*Ardisia japinica* Bl.	T, As
Borneol	Antipyretic analgesic, anti-inflammatory	A number of species	NT
Bromelain	Anti-inflammatory proteolytic agent	*Ananas comosus* (L.) Mer.	T, Am
Caffeine	CNS stimulant	*Camellia sinensis* (L.) Kuntze	NT
Camphor	Rubefacient	*Cinnamomum camphora* (L.)	T, As
Castor oil	Laxative	*Ricinus communis* (L.)	T, Af
(+)-Catechin	Haemostatic	*Potentilla fragariodes* L.	NT
Chymopapain	Proteolytic, mucolytic	*Carica papaya* L.	T, Am
Ciassampeline	Skeletal muscle relaxant	*Cissampelos pareira* L.	T, As
Cocaine	Local anaesthetic	*Erythroxylum coca* Lamk.	T, Am
Codeine	Analgesic, antitussive	*Papaver somniferum* L.	NT
Colchicine amide	Anticancer	*Colchicum autumnale* L.	NT
Colchicine	Antigout	*Colchicum autummale* L.	NT
Convallatoxin	Cardiotonic	*Convallaria majalis* L.	NT
Curcumin	Choleretic	*Curcuma longa* L.	T, As
Cynarin	Choleretic	*Cynara scolymus* L.	NT

Table 5.1. Continued

Drug	*Action/clinical use*	*Species*	*Origin*
Danthron	Laxative	*Cassia* species	NT
Demecolcine	Anticancer	*Colchicum autumnale* L.	NT
Deserpidine	Antihypertensive; tranquilizer	*Raufolvia conescens* L.	T, Am
Deslanosides	Cardiotonic	*Digitalis lanata* Ehrh.	NT
Digitalin	Cardiotonic	*Digitalis purpurea* L.	NT
Digitoxin	Cardiotonic	*Digitalis lanata* Ehrh.	NT
		Digitalis purpurea L.	NT
Diosgenin	Contraceptive	*Dioscorea* spp	T, As, Am
L-Dopa	Antiparkinsonism	*Mucuna deeringiana* (Bort.) Merr.	T, As
Emetine	Amoebicide, emetic	*Cephaelis ipecacuanha* (Brot.) A. Richard	T, Am
Ephedrine	Bronchodilator	*Ephedra sinica* Stapf	NT
Etoposide	Antitumour agent	*Podophyllum peltatum* L.	NT
Galanthamine	Cholinesterase inhibitor	*Lycoris squamigera* Maxim.	NT
Gitalin	Cardiotonic	*Digitalis purpurea* L.	NT
Glaucarubin	Amoebicide	*Simarouba glauca* D.C.	T, Am
Glaucine	Antitussive	*Glaucium flavum* Crantz	NT
Glaziovine	Antidepressant	*Ocotea glaziovii* Mez	T, Am
Gossypol	Male contraceptive	*Gossypium* species	T, As, Am, Af
Glycyrrhizin	Anti-inflammatory, sweetener	*Glycyrrhiza glabra* L.	NT

Table 5.1. Continued

Drug	*Action/clinical use*	*Species*	*Origin*
Hemsleyadin	Antibacillary dysentery, antipyretic	*Hemsleya amabilis* Diels	NT
Hesperidin	Capillary, antihaemorrhagic	*Citrus* species	NT
Hydrastine	Haemostatic astringent	*Hydrastis canadensis* L.	NT
Hyoscyamine	Anticholinergic	*Atropa belladonna* L.	NT
		Hyoscyamus niger L.	NT
Kaninic acid	Ascaricide	*Digenia simplex* (Wulf.) Agardh	NT
Kawain	Tranquilizer	*Piper mythesticum* Forst.f	T, As
Khellin	Bronchodilator	*Ammi visnaga* (L.)	
Lanatosides A, B, C	Cardiotonic	*Digitalis lanata* Ehrh.	NT
α-Lobeline	Tobacco deterrent,	*Lobelia inflata* L.	NT
Menthol	Rubefacient	*Mentha* species	NT
Methyl salicylate	Rubefacient	*Gaultheria procumbens* L.	NT
Monocrotaline	Antitumour (topical)	*Crotalarïa sessiliflora* L.	T, As
Morphine	Analgesic, antitussive	*Papaver somniferum* L.	NT
Neoandrographolide	Antibacillary dysentery	*Andrographis paniculata* Nees	T, As
Nicotine	Insecticide	*Nicotiana tabacum* L.	T, Am
Nordihydroguaiaretic acid	Antioxidant	*Larrea divaricata* Cav.	NT
Norpseudoephedrine	Bronchodilator	*Ephedra sinica* Stapf	NT

Table 5.1. Continued

Drug	*Action/clinical use*	*Species*	*Origin*
Noscapine	Antitussive	*Papaver somniferum* L.	NT
Ouabain	Cardiotonic	*Strophanthus gratus* Baill.	T, Af
Pachycarpine	Ecbolic	*Sophora pachycarpa*	NT
Palmatine	Antipyretic, detoxicant	*Coptis japonica* Mokino	NT
Papaverin	Smooth muscle relaxant	*Papaver somniferum* L.	NT
Phyllodulcin	Sweetener	*Hydrangea macrophylla* (Thumb.) Seringe var. *thunbergii* (Siebold) Makino	NT
Physostigmine	Cholinesterase inhibitor	*Physostigma venemosum* Balf.	T, Af
Picrotoxin	Analeptic	*Anamiria cocculus* (L.) W. & A	T, As
Pilocarpine	Parasympathomimetic	*Pilocarpus jaborandi* Holmes	T, Am
Pinitol	Expectorant		NT
Podophyllotoxin	Antitumour agent	*Podophyllum peltatum* L.	NT
Protoveratrines A, B	Antihypertensive	*Veratrum album* L.	NT
Pseudoephedrine	Bronchodilator	*Digitalis purpurea* L.	NT
Quinidine	Antiarrhythmic	*Cinchona ledgeriana* Moens ex Trimen	T, Am
Quinine	Antimalarial, antipyretic	*Cinchona ledgeriana* Moens ex Trimen	T, Am
Quisqualic acid	Anthelmintic	*Quisqualis indica* L.	T, As
Rebaudioside A	Sweetener	*Stevia rebaudiana* Bertoni	T, As

Table 5.1. Continued

Drug	*Action/clinical use*	*Species*	*Origin*
Rescinnamine	Antihypertensive, tranquilizer	*Rauvolfia serpentina* (L.) Benth. ex Kurz	T, As
Reserpine	Antihypertensive, tranquilizer	*Rauvolfia serpentina* (L.) Benth. ex Kurz	T, As
Rhomitoxin	Antihypertensive	*Rhododendron molle* G. Don	NT
Rorifone	Antitussive	*Rorippa indica* (L.) Hochreut.	T, As
Rotenone	Piscicide	*Lonchocarpus nicou* (Aubl.) DC.	T, Am
Rotundine	Analgesic, sedative, tranquilizer	*Stephania sinica* Diels	NT
Rutin	Capillary antihaemorrhagic	*Citrus* species	NT
Salicine	Analgesic	*Salix alba* L.	NT
Sanguinarine	Dental plaque inhibitor	*Sanguinaria canadensis* L.	NT
Santonin	Anthelmintic	*Artemisia maritima* L.	NT
Scillarin A, B	Cardiotonic	*Urgenia maritima* (L.) Baker	NT
Scopolamine	Sedative	*Datura metel* L.	T, As
Sennosides A, B	Laxative	*Cassia acutifolia* Delile	NT
		Cassia senna L. var. *senna*	NT
Silymarin	Antihepatotoxic	*Silybum marianum* (L.) Gaertn.	NT
Sparteine	Oxytocic	*Cytisus scoparius* (L.) Link	NT
Stevioside	Sweetener	*Stevia rebaudiana* Bertoni	T, As
Strychnine	CNS stimulant	*Strychnos nux-vomica* L.	T, As
Taxol	Antitumour	*Taxus brevifolia* Nutt.	NT

Table 5.1. Continued

Drug	*Action/clinical use*	*Species*	*Origin*
Teniposide	Antitumour	*Podophyllum peltatum* L.	NT
Δ9-Tetrahydrocannabinol	Antiemetic decrease ocular tension	*Cannabis sativa* L.	NT
(±)-Tetrahydropalmatine	Analgesis, sedative, tranquilizer	*Corydalis ambigua* (Pallas) Cham. & Schlechtdl.	NT
Theobromine	Diuretic	*Theobroma cacao* L.	T, Am
Thymol	Antifungal (topical)	*Thymus vulgaris* L.	NT
Trichosanthin	Abortifacient	*Trichosanthes kirilowii* Maxim.	NT
Tubocurarine	Skeletal muscle relaxant	*Chondodendron tomentosum* R & P.	T, Am
Valepotriates	Sedative	*Valeriana officianalis* L.	NT
Vinblastine	Antitumour	*Catharanthus roseus* (L.) G. Don	T, Af
Vincamine	Cerebral stimulant	*Vinca minor* L.	NT
Vincristine	Antitumour	*Catharanthus roseus* (L.) G. Don	T, Af
Vasicine	Oxytocic	*Adhatoda vasica* Nees	T, As
Xanthotoxin	Leukoderma, vitiligo	*Ammi majus* L.	NT
Yohimbine	Aphrodisiac	*Pausynistalia yohimbi* (K Schum) Pierre ex Beille	T, Af
Yuanhuacine	Abortifacient	*Daphne genkwa* Sieb. & Zucc	NT
Yuanhuadine	Abortifacient	*Daphne genkwa* Sieb. & Zucc	NT

NT, non-tropical; T, tropical; As, Asia; Am, America; Af, Africa.

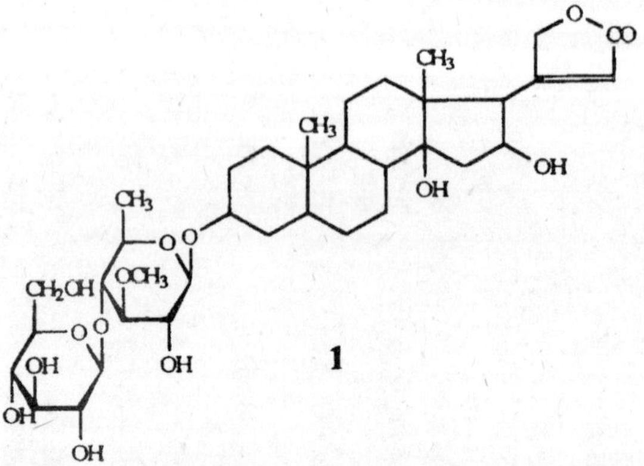

1

as tranquilizers. *R. serpentina* occurs throughout India, Malaysia and Thailand as small trees that grow wild in the humid forests. It is now cultivated in many tropical countries. Because of its highly toxic nature, use of *R. serpentina* has decreased considerably and a sister species, the African serpent wood *R. vomitoria* Afz., has been exploited much more for the world market.

Rauwolfia alkaloids used as drugs include reserpine (2) rescinnamine (3), deserpidine (4), ajmalcine (5) and ajmaline (6). Reserpine is used in combination with diuretics for controlling mild to moderate hypertension. It depletes peripheral nor-adrenaline stores, resulting in a fall in peripheral resistance and blood pressure as well as bradycardia and CNS depression. It was also formerly used to treat psychotic disorders. Rescinnamine and deserpidine have properties and uses similar to reserpine. Ajmalicine, also known as raubasine, has also been used in conjunction with other agents to treat hypertension and in peripheral and cerebral vascular disorders. Ajmaline has antiarrhythmic activity on the heart muscle and is used clinically as a therapeutic agent in cardiac arrhythmia, as well as being used as an antihypertensive and tranquilizer. This compound is found in very large quantities in *R. vomitoria* and has become much more popular as a hypotensive agent than reserpine. Other drugs for cardiovascular disorders derived from tropical species are the cardiotonic, ouabain (7) and the antiarrhythmic quinoline alkaloid, quinidine (8). Ouabain is an injectable cardiac glycoside, extracted from the seeds of *Strophanthus gratus*. It has a faster onset of action than the usual digitalis digoxin, hence its preferred use over the latter when rapid benefit is required and in emergency situations. Like digitalis, ouabain is used to treat atrial fribrillation (arrhythmia) with an uncontrolled ventricular rate, atrial

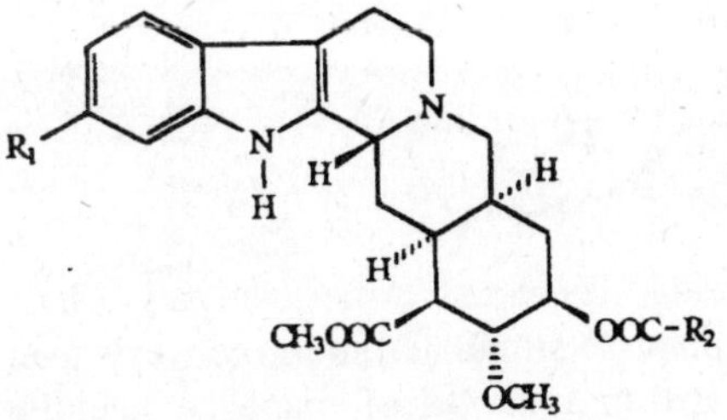

	R_1	R_2
2	OCH_3	$C_6H_2(OCH_3)_3$
3	OCH_3	$CH{=}CHC_6H_2(OCH_3)_3$
4	H	$C_6H_2(OCH_3)_3$

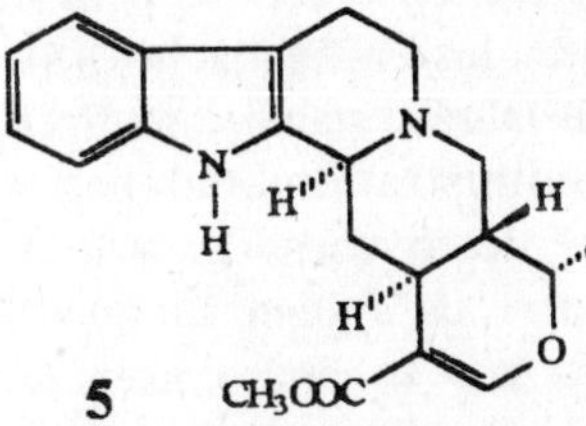

flutter, supraventricular tachycardia and acute left ventricular failure. Quinidine is extracted from the bark of *Cinchona ledgeriana* and used as a cardiac depressant or antiarrhythmic. Kawain (9) is a naturally occurring pyrone found in the rhizomes of *Piper mythesticum*, a shrub indigenous to islands of the South Pacific. Currently produced synthetically, it is used as a tranquilizer and to improve well-being in geriatric patients.

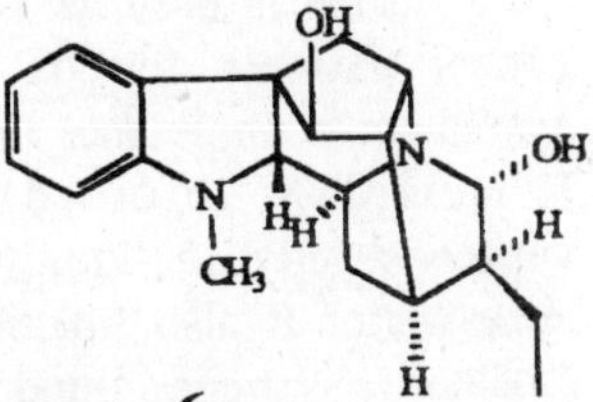

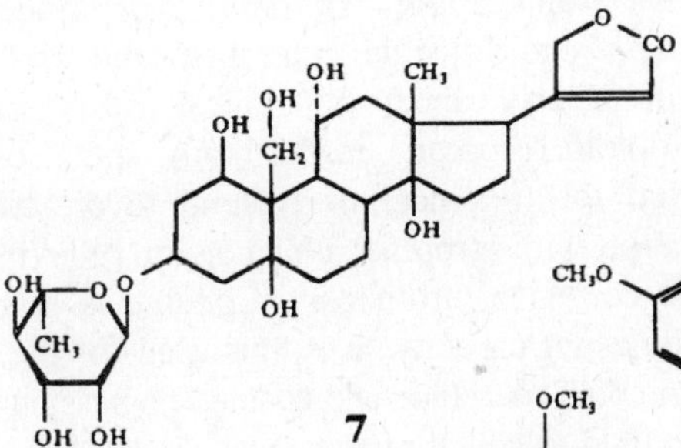

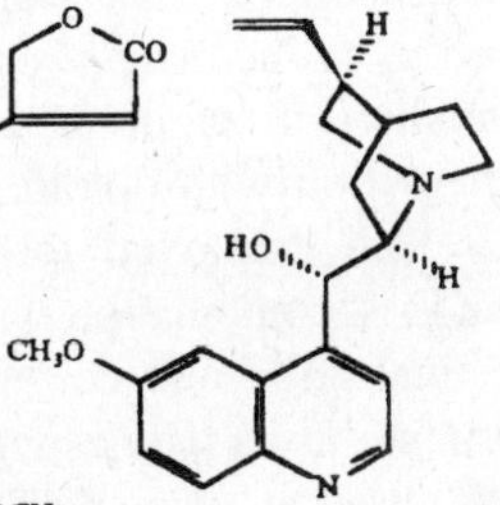

Local Anaesthetics

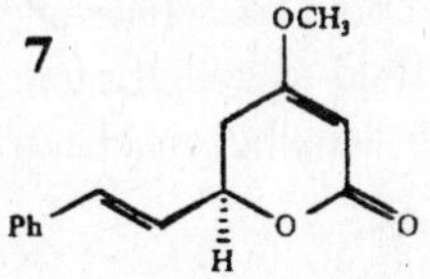

Cocaine or 2R-methoxycarbonyl-3S-benzoyltropine (10) is found in the leaves and barks of the South America shrub *Erythroxylon coca*. It is one of the major coca alkaloids. The South American native have been known to chew the coca plant to stimulate quick recovery from fatigue. The plant is now cultivated in a number of countries including Peru, Bolivia, Colombia, Indonesia and Sri Lanka.

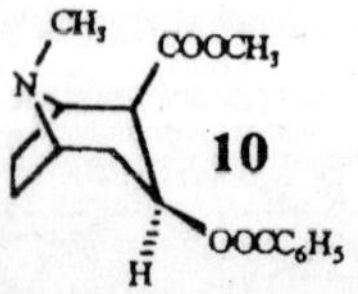

Cocaine is used as a topical local anaesthetic, to relieve pain in cancer patients and to relieve pain from cluster headaches. Its anaesthetic action comes from its reversible membrane stabilizing effect. It is rapidly absorbed after topical administration and has a vasoconstrictive action, thus enhancing its effectiveness as a local anaesthetic. It also functions as a central nervous system stimulant. Cocaine has been found to cause narcosis and its abuse leads to addiction.

Analgesics

Morphine (11) and codeine (12) are the two well-known opioid analgesic drugs. These alkaloids may be extracted from the dried sap obtained by lancing the unripe seed pods of the opium poppy (*Papaver somniferum*) or by solvent extraction of poppy straw. The most important opium-producing countries are India, turkey, Bulgaria, Yugoslavia, USSR, Australia, France and Spain. To date, morphine is still considered to be the drug of choice for the control of acute and chronic pain of malignant origin such as cancer. Its clinical use is dependent on its interaction with opioid receptors in the brain, spinal cord and gut. It is also employed for treatment of typhoid fever, traumatic shocks and, in combination with atropine sulphate, for relieving renal and intestinal colic and coronary thrombosis. Codeine is less potent than morphine in its pain relief capacity; it is thus used for the control of mild to moderate pain. Both morphine and codeine possess antitussive properties and have been used as cough suppressants. Codeine is however more acceptable for such uses because morphine tends to increase the

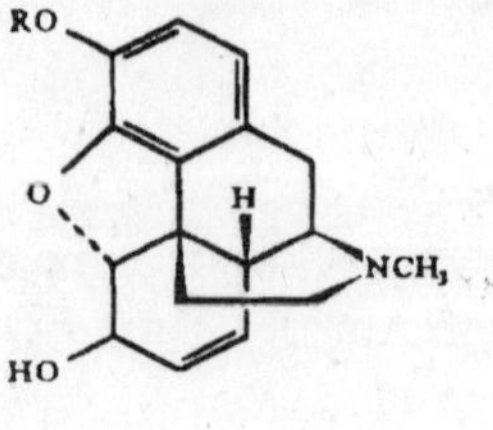

11 R = H

12 R = CH

incidence of post-operative chest complications by the suppression of a productive cough.

Antimuscarinics

Antimuscarinic agents are competitive inhibitors of the actions of acetylcholine at the muscarinic receptors of autonomic effector sites innervated by parasympathetic nerves. Plant drugs included in this class are the belladonna alkaloids atropine (13), hyosycamine and hyoscine (14). Atropine or DL-hyosycamine is the chief alkaloid extracted from the deadly nightshade, *Atropa belladonna*, *Datura stramonium* and several other Solanaceae plants. A belladonna is indigenous to Western Europe and cultivated in England, Germany, USSR, USA and India.

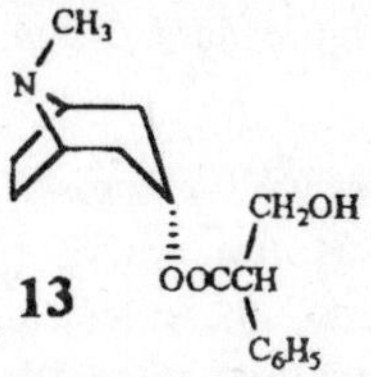

CH_3 N CH_2OH OOCCH C_6H_5 **13**

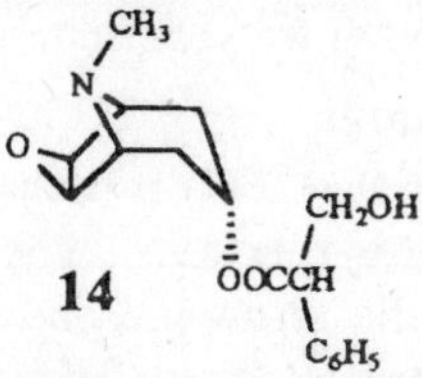

CH_3 N O CH_2OH OOCCH C_6H_5 **14**

Atropine may be prepared synthetically or by racemization of the naturally occurring L-hyosycamine. Atropine is the prototype and best known antimuscarinic agent although many of its uses are now superseded by other semi-synthetic antimuscarinic drugs. It is used primarily for the treatment of stomach spasm and also applied topically to the eye to produce dilatation during ophthalmic examinations. Hyoscine, also known as scopolamine, is a closely related ester of atropine. Although it can be produced synthetically, it is usually obtained by extraction from various members of the Solanaceae, including the well-known herb, *Datura metel*. The drug also has an anticholinergic effect but in contrast to atropine it also has a CNS depressant effect, hence its use as a sedative and to treat motion sickness.

Miotics

Pilocarpine (15) and physostigmine (16) are two well-known cholinergic drugs used as miotics in the treatment of glaucoma. Pilocarpine, an alkaloid obtained from the leaves of *Pilocarpus jaborandi*, is a direct-acting muscarinic parasympathomimetic agonist. Physostigmine, an alkaloidal constituent of the calabar bean of the woody vine, *Physostigma venemosum* is an indirect acting parasympathomimetic agent. Used as the hydrochloride or nitrate, pilocarpine is the first choice when miotics are required to reduce intraocular pressure in the treatment of open-angle glaucoma. This is

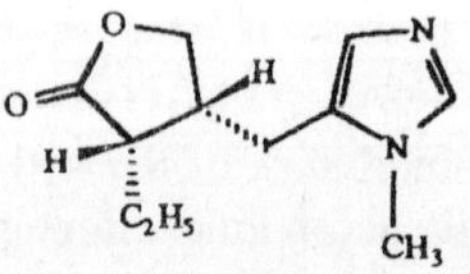

15 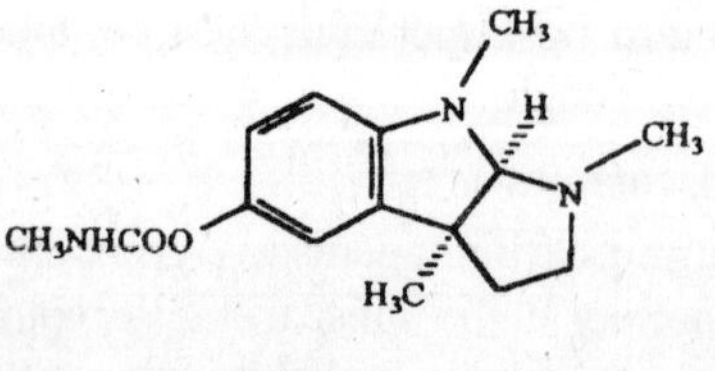 16

due to the fact that pilocarpine generally provides good control of intraocular pressure with relatively few adverse effects. Physostigmine is not as well tolerated as pilocarpine, hence is rarely used for long-term therapy. However physostigmine has been used for more than a hundred years as an antidote for atropine overdose and more recently in poisoning with tricyclic/tetracyclic antidepressant drugs.

Muscle Relaxants

d-Tubocurarine (17) is perhaps the most well-known of the natural skeletal muscle relaxants. The alkaloid is the active principle in 'tubocurate', the arrow poison used by the South American Indians in the Amazon-Orinoco basin. The compound can be obtained from extracts of the stems and bark of the liana *Chondodendron tomentosum* and several other species of this genus. Available pharmaceutically as the chloride, it is competitive neuromuscular blocker, primarily used intravenously to produce skeletal muscle relaxation during surgical procedures. It acts by competing with acetylcholine for receptors on the motor end-plate to produce neuromuscular blockade, seen as flaccid paralysis. A patient is given the drug to reduce the amount of general anaesthetic required to achieve total muscle relaxation, although the resultant paralysis of the respiratory muscle means that artificial ventilation of the patient is necessary.

Papaverine (18) is a smooth muscle relaxant and vasodilator. The alkaloid is also extractable from the opium poppy, *Papaver somniferum*,

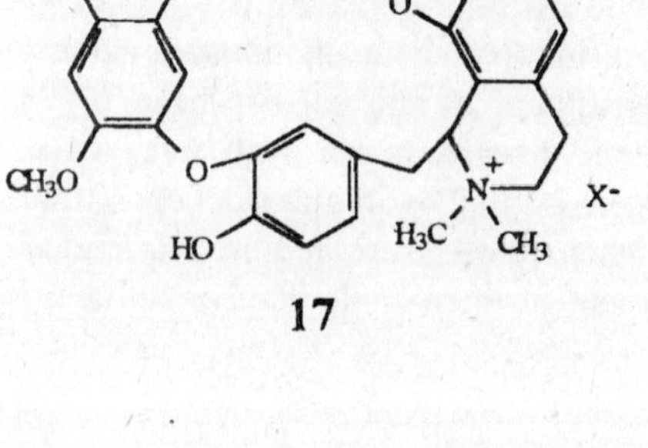

17 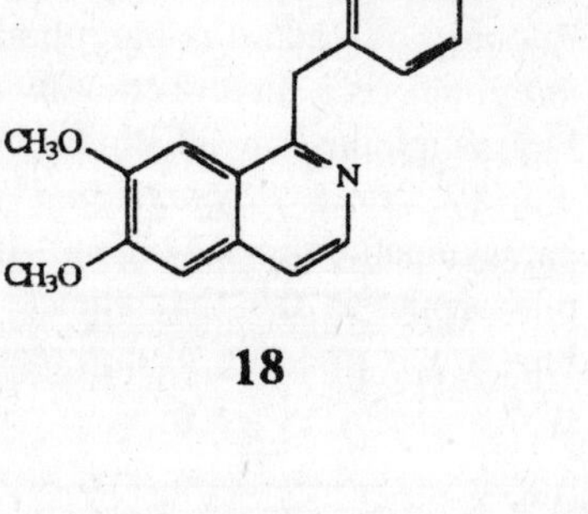 18

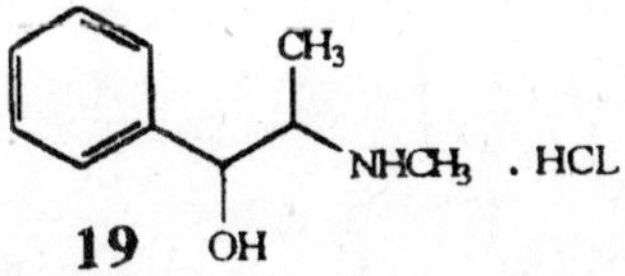

CH_3

$NHCH_3$. HCL

19 OH

but unlike the other opium derivatives, is not habit forming. Its use has been largely replaced by drugs with more specific actions such as α-adrenergic blockers and calcium slow channel antagonists but it may still have a place in the treatment of vascular spasms.

Bronchodilators

The ephedra alkaloids obtained from the Chinese plant 'Ma Huang' (*Ephedra sinica*), ephedrine (19), pseudoephedrine and norseudoephedrine, are sympathomimetic agents with direct and indirect effects on adrenergic receptors. These drugs are now produced synthetically. Ephedrine is used for the treatment of nasal congestion and as a bronchodilator for treating the symptoms of asthma. Pseudoephedrine, its naturally occurring stereoisomer, and nor-pseudoephedrine are also used for the same purpose but possess less potent pharmacological properties. The two drugs aer widely used as constituents in over-the-counter remedies for treating symptoms of the common cold. They have also been found to show significant CNS excitatory and pressor effects which makes them undesirable for use in hypertensive patients. Ephedrine is no longer a drug of choice in the treatment of asthma as more selective drugs with less cardiac and CNS stimulation effect are available.

Antineoplastic Agents

Cancer is a serious life-threatening disease for modern society today. Among the most prevalent forms of cancer are breast, colorectal, lung, ovarian, prostate and uterine. Many different structural classes of plant secondary metabolites have been found to be cytotoxic but only a few are used clinically. The most frequently used anticancer drugs are the dimeric indole alkaloids, vinblastine (20) and vincristine (21), which have been available since the 1960s. First discovered from the Madagascar periwinkle *Vinca rosea* (*Catharanthus roseus*), they have become the two most important clinically useful anticancer agents from any plant source. The durgs are still extracted from natural sources. Most of the *C. roseus* used for production of the two drugs is grown under cultivation in India, Madagascar, Israel and the USA.

Vinblastine and vincristine are used, either singly or in combination therapy, in the management of malignant diseases, particulary

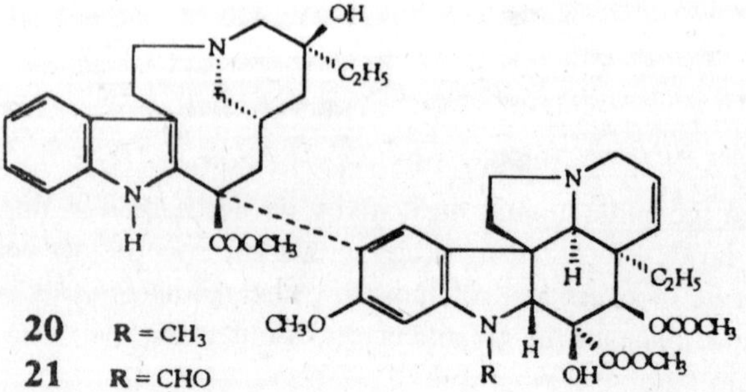

20 R = CH_3
21 R = CHO

lymphomas and sarcomas. Hodgkin's disease and the leukaemias. These vinca alkaloids exert their biological effects by binding specifically with the protein tubulin, inhibiting its assembly into microtubules with resultant dissolution of the mitotic spindle which eventually leads to cell death. Although not a first-line drug, vinblastine and vincristine have also been used in combination with other anticancer drugs for breast cancer.

Podophyllotoxin (22) is the active principle in podophyllin, the alcoholic extract of the dried rhizomes and root of the North American May apple, *Podophyllum peltatum*. The drug has applications in dermatology where it is an effective therapy for anogenital warts, and possibly nasal papillomas as well as psoriasis. Like the vinca alkaloids, podophyllotoxin is also a microtubule inhibitor. This compound and its congeners have however been found to attack both normal and cancerous cells. The toxic side-effects of these lignans have limited applications as drugs in cancer chemotherapy, except for etoposide and teniposide which are semisynthetic derivatives of podophyllotoxin. These two antitumour agents do not exhibit any effect on intracellular microtubules but induce breaks in single and double stranded DNA, through their interactions with topoisomerase II which is a critical enzyme in DAN replication.

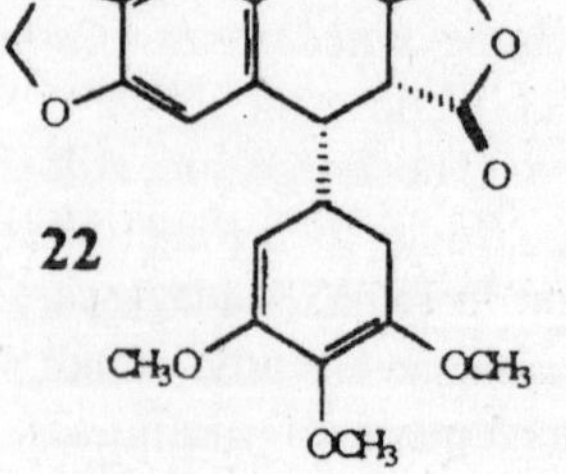

22

Antiprotozoals

Protozoal infections are responsible for a number of major diseases including malaria, amoebiasis, leishmaniasis, giardiasis and trypanosomiasis. These diseases affect millions of people worldwide, both in the developing and developed part of the world. The AIDS epidemic has resulted in an increase in infections due to *Cryptosporidium parvum* which causes severe diarrhoea and *Pneumocystis carinii* which results in pneumonia. In the last century there have been two major antiprotozoal drugs obtained from higher plants: the antimalarial drug, quinine (23), and the amoebicidal drug, emetine (24).

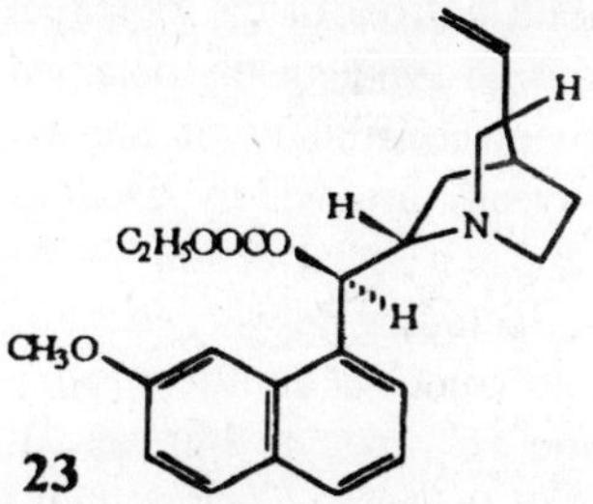

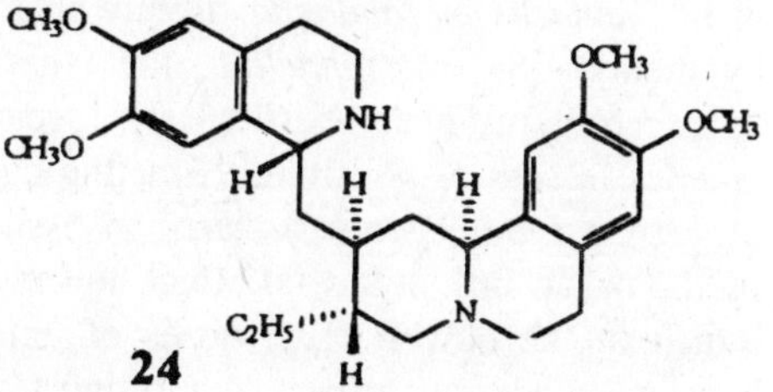

Quinine, a quinolinemethanol, was used in the treatment of malaria long before the malaria parasite was even discovered. It is extracted from the bark of various species of Cinchona, in particular *C. ledgeriana*, where it occurs together with its diextrorotaory stereoisomer quinidine and twop othe main alkaloids, cinchonidine and cinchonine. The main *Cinchona* producing countries are Indonesia, Zaire, Tanzania, Kenya, Rwanda, Sri Lanka, Bolivia, Colombia, Costa Rica and Indian.

Quinine is used primarily for the treatment of severe and complicated *Plasmodium falciparum* induced case of malaria, especially when the cases are resistant to synthetic chemotherapy. The chemical structure of quinine has also served as a template molecule for the design and development of several other antimalarial drugs including chloroquine. At one time quinine was superseded by synthetic antimalarials which have fewer side-effects. However resistance of *P. falciparum* to antimalarial chemotherapy favours the continued use of quinine.

The other three *Cinchona* alkaloids have also been shown to be effective in the treatment of falciparum malaria. Only quinidine however, which is actually superior to quinine in its antimalarial effect but more likely to cause cardiac toxicity and hypersensitivity, has been recommended for oral or parenteral use in the event of quinine unavailability.

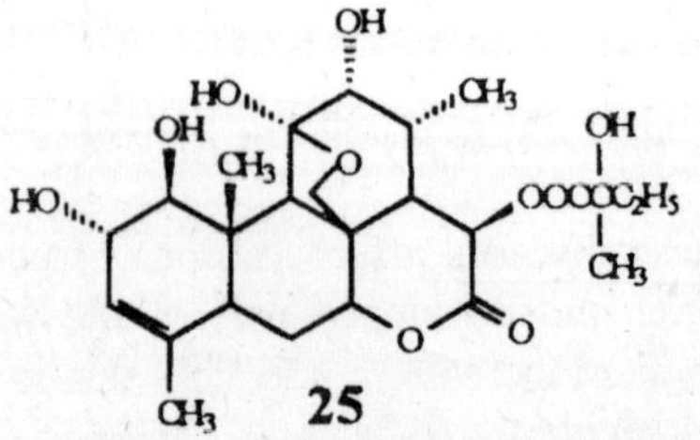

25

Emetine is a long recognized effective therapy for invasive amoebiasis, widely employed in developing countries for treating amoebic dysentery. Used in the form of the hydrochloride salt, the alkaloid is obtained from ipecac which is the dried root of the Brazilian plant *Cephaelis ipecahuanha*. It may also be semi-synthetically obtained by methylation of *cephaeline*, the othe rmain constituent of ipecac. Ipecac root products (particularly ipecac syrup) are widely used as emetics in cass of poisoning. Emetine has a direct lethal action on the protozoan *Entamoeba histolytica* in tissues, including bower, invaded by the organisms. It has no effect however an amoebae confined to the lumen of the bowel. High doses of emetine are toxic to humans. It has severe adverse effects, exhibiting toxicity to heart, liver, kidneys and gastrointestinal tract. It is currently superseded by the synthetic metronidazole and its use is restricted to initial treatment of severe amoebic abcesses. Another plant drug, glaucarbulin (25), which is a quassinoid-type degraded triterpene and is extracted form the American Simarouba glauca, has also been used in the oral treatment of amoebic dysentery.

Other Miscellaneous Drugs from Plants

There are a myriad of other diseases and medical conditions for which drugs derived from plants are prescribed. For example, berberine (26) is a widely used drug for the treatment of bacillary dysentery, a disease caused by bacteria of the genus *Shigella*. It is an abundant alkaloid extractable from *Berberis vulgaris* and many other plant sources of the families Annonaceae, Ranunculaceae (mostly herbaceous), Berberidaceae, Menispermaceae and Papaveraceae. It has good antibacterial activity and is poorly absorbed form the gastrointestinal tract when administered orally. Anisodamine (27) and anisodine (28), the atropine-like alkaloids isolated form the Chinese painkiller plant, *Anisodus tanguticus*, are anticholinergic agents. The quinolizidine sparteine (29) from *Cytisus scoparius* is employed as an oxytoxic in childbirth to initiate uterine contractions and to decrease post-partum haemorrhage. Vasicine (30), a quinazoline alkaloid form the Indian species *Adhatoda vasica*, has a similar use. The sennosides (31), derived from *Cassia angustifolia* and *C. acutifolia*, are used as laxatives. Sanguinarine (32) from *Sanguinaria canadensis*, is used in dental preparations due to its ability to prevent dental plaque formation.

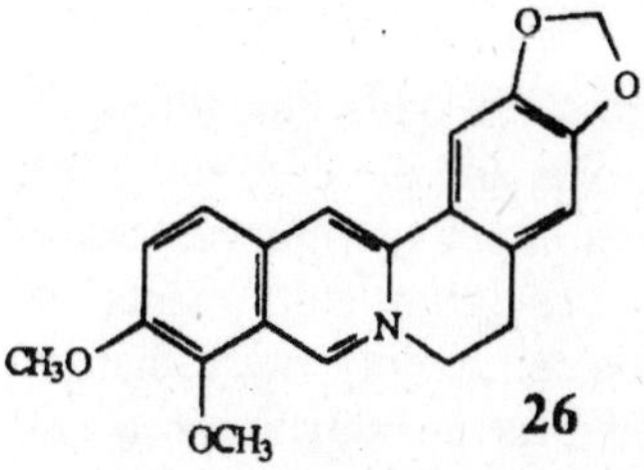

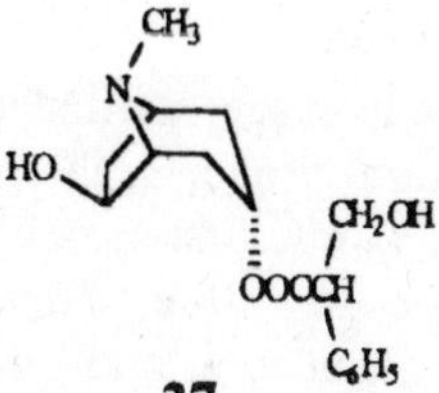

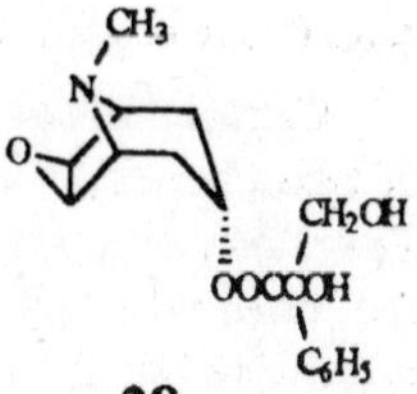

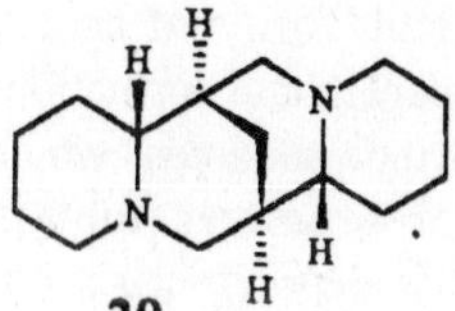

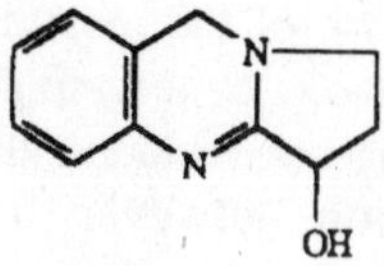

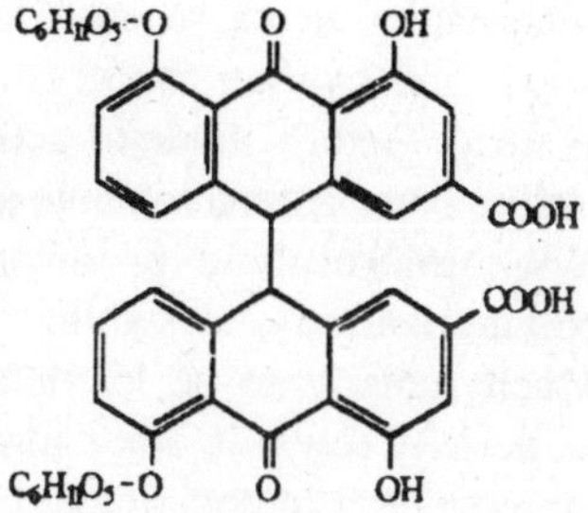

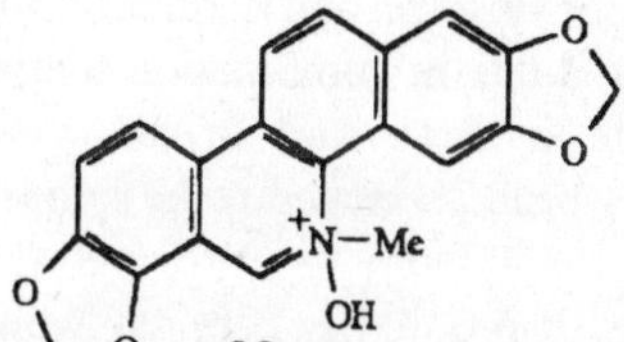

Recently Discovered Plant-based Drugs

Since the 1950s, spurred by the discoveries of the rauwolfia and vinca alkaloids, numerous plant species have been studied for their chemical constituents and biological properties. In 1985 NAPRALERT listed almost 200 000 compounds which have been identified from natural sources, 70 per cent of which were plants. This number may well have increased significantly since then. Success in the development of new, commercially viable drugs has however been modest. Since the last major breakthrough of vinblastine and vincristine, the only othe drug that the world has heralded with equal excitement has been taxol, which is also an antitumour agent. The discovery of the antimalarial, artemisinin, was also of particular importance, especially for tropical countries. Nevertheless many other potential drugs are still at their early stages of development and clinical trials and the outlook for the future of drugs from plants remains optimistic.

Taxol and Camptothecins

Current advances in cancer chemotherapy are due to the discovery of two classes of natural products, the taxoids and the camptothecins. Taxol or paclitaxel (33) was first discovered in 1971, from the bark of the northwest pacific yew tree, *Taxus brevifolia* Nutt. Since its discovery, structure elucidation and biological activity more than 20 years ago, taxol has finally been accepted as an anticancer agent, culminating in its recent FDA approval for use in the treatment of breast and ovarian cancers, two of the most difficult forms of cancer to treat. Taxol's mode of action is by targeting microtubule formation. Unlike other antimicrotubule agents, including the vinca alkaloids, which block microtubule production, however, taxol promotes tubulin polymerization and stabilizes microtubules against depolymerization. Much remains to be learned about the clinical use of taxol, such as its activity towards other forms of cancer dose-response relationships, effectiveness in combination with other drugs in combination therapy, etc. Nevertheless, based on just the ovarian and breast cancer utilization, worldwide need of taxol has been estimated to be hundreds of kilograms per year. The yield of taxol from its rare and slow-growing natural source is very low, less than 0.02 per cent dry weight. If the current trend of promising activities against other cancer forms, countinues larger supplies and alternative sources of taxol will be needed and many mature trees would have to be felled in order to supply sufficient drug for clinical use. Although the semi-synthesis of the compound has been achieved, it will be probably still not answer the supply problem. Efforts at solving this problem through tissue culture and microbial fermentation are currently underway and show great promise of success.

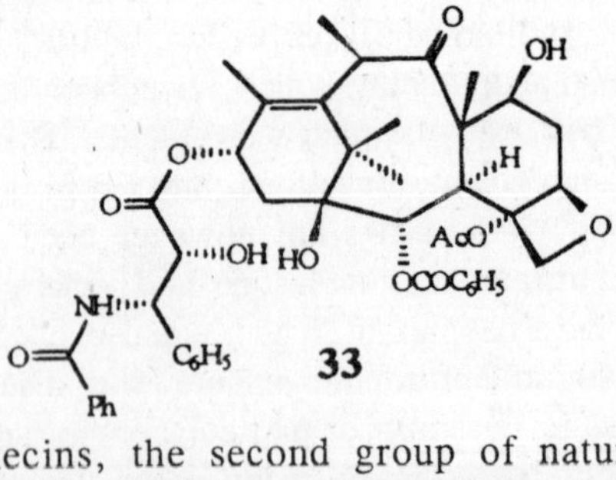

O
OH
O
H
O
AcO
OH HO
O
$OCOC_6H_5$
NH
O
C_6H_5
Ph

33

Camptothecins, the second group of natural antineoplastic compounds, are derivatives of the isoquinoline alkaloid camptothecin (34), first isolated from the Chinese tree *Camptotheca acuminata*. The alkaloid has been subjected to limited clinical trials but its effects

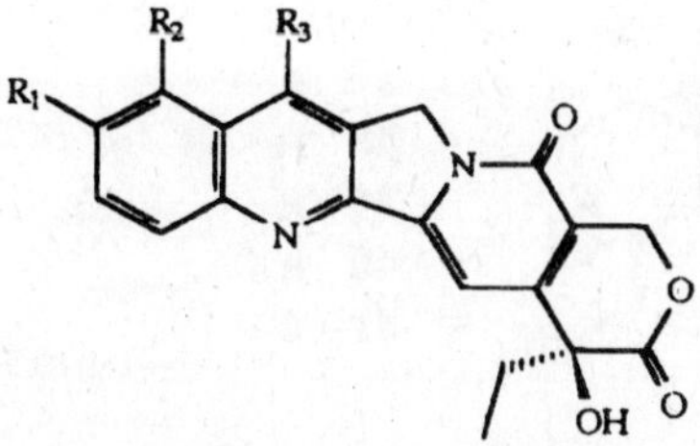

	R1	R2	R3
34	H	H	H
35	H	$CH_2NH(CH_3)_2$	OH
36	CH_2CH_3	H	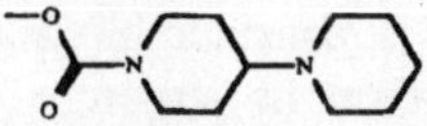

have not paralleled those seen in animal studies. The compound was found to have a serious side-effect, causing bleeding in the bladder and kidneys. Better results have however been observed in clinical trials of the relatively new camptothecian derivatives, topotecan (35) and irinotecan (36). Whereas several families of topoisomerase II inhibitors, such as anthracyclines, epipodophyllotoxins, acridines, and ellipticines, are known and widely used in clinical practice, the camptothecins are the unique representative of selective topoisomerase I inhibitors with clinical applications.

Artemisinin

Until the recent discovery of artemisinin (37) from the Chinese antimalarial plant, *Artemisia annua* (Qinghao), there had, for many years, been no further antiprotozoal drugs from higher plants. Also known as quinghaosu, this is an unusual endoperoxide sesquiterpenee lactone. Artemisinin has been found to be an effective antimalarial drug against both chloroquinine-resistant and chloroquinine-sensitive strains of *Plasmodium falciparum* as well as as against cerebral malaria. Artemisinin is currently in clinical use and in some parts of south-east Asia it seems to be the only effective drug against infections from multidrug resistant *P. falciparum*.

The significant biological activity, novel chemical structure and its low yield from natural sources have promoted efforts directed at its synthesis. In the past few years, a number of derivatives have been developed and found to be clinically active against malaria, including multi-drug resistant *P. falciparum*. For example, reduction of the lactone carbonyl of artemisinin yields dihydroartemisinin (38) from which the semi-synthetic products (39–41) have been prepared.

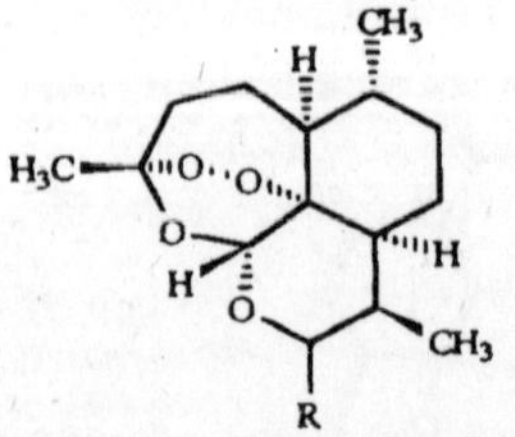

37 R = O
38 R = OH
39 R = —OMe
40 R = —OEt
41 R = —OCHOCH$_2$CH$_2$COONa

The World Health Organization and Rhone-Poulence Rorer have in fact collaborated in the development of artemeter (39). Registration of these products has been approved in six African countries and applications field in another eight countries. The current interest in artemisinin is considerable and it is possible that other antimalarial drugs based on its structure will be developed in the future, in a similar way to quinine being used as a template molecule for the development of chloroquine and mefloquine.

Conclusions

It is apparent that the plant kingdom is a rich source of biologically active natural products and no doubt it will continue to serve mankind in the future just as it has done since the dawn of history. This is likely in view of the fact that only a small proportion of plants, especially those of the tropical rain forests, have been thoroughly investigated for their medicinal potential. Plants are useful in their crude or advanced forms as drugs, and biologically active compounds from plants can serve as templates for the synthesis of modern drugs. Method of plant drug research have improved tremendously over the years, and much more has been learned about the basics of plant metabolism, plant analysis and even plant production. Looking ahead to the future, there are still many diseases such as AIDS, certain cancers, Parkinson's disease, muscular dystrophy, and cystic fibrosis which require improved and/or satisfactory cures. It is hoped that significant new plant drugs and new methods of producing them will continue to be discovered and developed.

6

FOREST PRODUCT WASTES

Over the last 25 years there has been considerable interest in the potential of producing fuel ethanol from biomass. The OPEC oil embargo of the 1970s resulted in a marked increase in the price of oil and influenced countries such as Brazil, Canada, Finland, Japan, Sweden and the USA to plan for better liquid fuel self-sufficiency. More recently research into fuels from renewable resources has been driven by environmental concerns, particularly the role of fossil fuel contribution to poor air quality and global warming. As a result there has been considerable research and discussion about the environmental advantages of using ethanol as a transportation fuel and as a gasoline supplement. The benefits of using ethanol and the ether form of ethanol, ethyl *tert*-butyl ether (ETBE), as an alternative to gasoline, have been discussed in detail.

Ethanol is a clean-burning, high-octane fuel that can be readily substituted for gasoline and its combustion results in significant reductions of toxic emissions such as formaldehyde, benzene and 1,3-butadiene. Blends of ethanol or ETBE with gasoline increase the octane of the mixture and can improve performance. Ethanol blends cause internal-combustion gasoline engines to run with leaner fuel mixtures and they reduce carbon monoxide emissions and it further lowers the Reid vapour pressure of gasoline, thereby decreasing the release of smog-forming compounds including ozone.

Ozone is recognized as being one of the most pervasive and persistent urban air-quality problems. Consequently, urban areas in the USA with heavy air pollution, such as areas of California and Colorado, have led the way towards implementation of ethanol (and other oxygenated fuel) vehicle regulations. When ethanol is produced from renewable sources such as biomass it can both decrease urban air pollution and reduce the accumulation of carbon dioxide, one of the greenhouse gases. Thus replacement of gasoline with ethanol, derived from renewable biomass feedstocks that sequester CO_2 during growth, is expected to reduce CO_2 emissions by 90-100 per cent. It has also been estimated that enough neat ethanol could be made from the cellulosic biomass residues that are currently available within the USA today to potentially replace twice the amount of gasoline consumed within the USA in 1994.

FEEDSTOCKS

Sugar and Starch

Ethanol, when used as a transportation fuel, can be generated from a number of feedstocks which are usually categorized into sugar, starch and lignocellulosic based materials. Sugar crops including sugar cane, sugar beets and sweet sorghum produce monomeric sugars (glucose, fructose and sucrose) that can be directly fermented to ethanol. Starch crops, including grains (corn, wheat, barley, grain sorghum) and tubers (potatoes, sweet potatoes) require an extra processing step, called hydrolysis, prior to fermen-tation. Hydrolysis converts the complex sugars or starches in the grains and tubers to monomeric sugars suitable for fermentation.

Fuel ethanol is currently produced from both sugar and starch based feedstocks with approximately 3 billion US gallons of ethanol produced from sugar cane in Brazil, 1 billion US gallons from corn in the USA, and 5.5 million US gallons from both corn and wheat in Canada. However, the use of these feedstocks for fuel production competes with other higher value usages such as food production. Current production of fuel ethanol is often based on excess agricultural production and it is generally recognized that this volume is too small in comparison with the anticipated levels of production required for total conversion of transportation fuel markets from gasoline to ethanol. It is also apparent that there is the potential for competition with food production for both the sugar and starch feedstocks and that prime agricultural lands normally required to produce the foodstuffs should not be diverted for fuel production.

Lignocellulosics

Lignocellulosic biomass is typically composed of a complex mixture of three polymers—cellulose, hemicellulose and lignin—and a small amount of other compounds that are loosely termed extractives. The fermentation of sugars derived from lignocellulosic feedstocks has proven to be more of a process design and operating challenge than traditional sugar or starch based processes. For example, there is a considerably wider variation in the type and nature of the processes and equipment needed to convert lignocellulosic feedstocks to ethanol. Although sugar, starch and lignocellulosic substrates can have compositional variability due to variations in the species of feedstock used, growing site, climate, age and the part of the plant used, lignocellulosic feedstocks have the following additional problems: proportional variability within the mixture of the three major components; differences in the types and amounts of extractives; and natural variability in the monomeric sugars that make up the hemicellulose component.

Acid vs. Enzymatic Hydrolysis of Lignocellulosics

Acid Hydrolysis of Lignocellulosics

Acid hydrolysis of biomass feedstocks has been studied and practised commercially for many years. Although several types of acid, including sulphurous, sulphuric, hydrochloric, hydrofluoric, phosphoric, nitric and formic have been used for hydrolysis, there are essentially two types of acid hydrolysis process, termed dilute and concentrated, with a number of genetic processes associated with each of these two options. Although the conversion of lignocellulosic to glucose via acid hydrolysis has been proven technically on a large commercial scale it is still considered that enzymatic hydrolysis has the potential to surpass greatly the efficiency of acid hydrolysis.

Major technical problems that have yet to be resolved using acid hydrolysis are: the corrosion of the reaction vessels; degradation of product sugars resulting in low yields; the need for neutralization before subsequent bioconversion; formation of numerous environmentally noxious by-products; high capital and operating cost; and solvent losses. Although a considerable amount of research is still directed towards these problem areas, the long-term outlook for acid based biomass to ethanol processes is still not overly optimistic as various economic projections indicate that several major technical problems have yet to be resolved before the economics of an acid based process are significantly more attractive.

Enzymatic Hydrolysis of Lignocellulosics

Enzymatic hydrolysis processes are relatively new and integrated processes have yet to be proven both technically and economically.

Enzyme based hydrolysis of lignocellulosics tends to show better promise than acid based hydrolysis, primarily because of the potential for higher sugar yields and the production of less toxic effluent streams. However, any proposed enzyme based bio-conversion process is generally more complex than an acid hydrolysis process as the enzymes tend to show more substrate specificity and require more carefully controlled reaction conditions. To date, a truly 'genetic' enzymatically-based biomass-to-ethanol process has been difficult to identify because of the heavy influence that the type of feedstock, type of by-products, number of unproven processes and equipment currently available will have on the design of such a process. However, it is generally acknowledged that a generic enzymatic-based process would include the following steps: pretreatment, fractionation, enzyme production, enzyme hydrolysis, fermentation, ethanol and other by-product recovery, and waste treatment.

The pioneering work that has been done at the pilot or demonstration scale has shown that the subprocess steps are all strongly interdependent. Thus it has been extremely difficult to identify the relative technical or economic merits of each of the subprocess variations and their subsequent influence on the final production cost of ethanol. Some of the process steps, such as fermentation and ethanol recovery, have been commercialized and often used as component steps in other industries such as brewery and distillery plants. These component process steps therefore have an established technoeconomic baseline and can be considered to be mature technologies.

The less mature process steps—pretreatment, fractionation, hydrolysis and pentose fermentation—have generally been compared on a relative technical or economic basis using laboratory, pilot-plant equipment or techno-economic modelling to simulate the entire, integrated process. There have been a number of pilot plants, two fully-integrated pilot plants and several smaller non-integrated pilot plants built and operated over the last 5 years. They have been primarily used to test the technical and economic feasibility of various aspects of the enzymatic conversion process. There have also been a number of attempts to model techno-economically the various process scenarios using laboratory/pilot-plant equipment.

Major Component Steps in an Enzyme Based Biomass-to-Ethanol Process

Pretreatment

Pretreatment is the process step required to make the relatively recalcitrant lignocellulosic material more easily digestible to the hydrolytic enzymes while preserving the yield of the original carbohydrates for fermentation. This can be accomplished by various mechanisms such as the removal of the lignin sheath, reduction of cellulose crystallinity, or by increasing the surface area that is accessible to the enzymes. However, inhibitory breakdown products can be formed if the pretreatment conditions used are too harsh.

The nature of the lignocellulosic substrate used has a major impact on this process step as a certain pretreatment, which may be effective with one lignocellulosic substrate, may prove to be ineffective on another. A number of reviews have covered pretreatment in detail and these have generally separated the different types of pretreatment into physical, chemical, biological and combinations of these methods. There appear to be four main pretreatment methods currently being researched and commercialized: organosolv, steam explosion, dilute-acid prehydrolysis. Of these various options, only the steam-explosion process has resulted in the substantial commercialization and sale of reactors by companies such as Stake Technology of Canada.

Fractionation

Fractionation is the subprocess step that separates the lignocellulosic slurry obtained after the pretreatment into the three main fractions of cellulose, hemicellulose and lignin. Subsequent fractionation after pretreatment is generally recognized as an efficient way of providing for separate processing of the individual components while recovering most of the material available in the original feedstock. There are generally two unit operations within the process which provide separation of both the hemicellulose and lignin components. The major product derived after these two fractionation steps is a cellulose rich residue which is subsequently hydrolyzed enzymatically. Although pretreatment and fractionation can be carried out simultaneously in processes such as organosolv, in processes such as steam explosion or acid hydrolysis it is usually carried out as two separate subprocess steps.

Due to the inter-related nature of the enzymatic based biomass-to-ethanol process, the type of feedstock and pretreatment method used will probably determine the fractionation procedure that is adopted. However, the greater the number of washing steps required, the higher the capital and operating costs will become, and the more likely that the net return on the investment will be negative. Hemicellulose, once it has been solubilized through pretreatment by SO_2^- steaming or dilute acid, can be processed in a number of different ways.

Currently, the xylose derived from agricultural or hardwood hemicelluloses cannot be readily fermented to ethanol. This will be discussed more fully in the subsequent fermentation section. Although there has been a considerable amount of work carried out on other hemicellulose derived products such as furfural, xylitol and single-cell protein this has not lead to any significant commercial products, partly because the few high-value products that were identified have too small a market volume. After pretreatment, lignin can generally be extracted from most lignocellulosic residues by a sodium hydroxide wash.

Lignin has a high heat content and has been used traditionally in the pulp and paper industry as a boiler fuel for process heat or cogeneration of steam and electricity. The potential for by-product utilization is immense because approximately 1 kg of lignin is produced per litre of ethanol. Although there have been a large number of high-value lignin-derived products identified, the operation of a few commercial-scale plants would probably saturate the world market for most of these applications.

Hydrolysis

The enzymatic hydrolysis of the cellulosic component of lignocellulosics requires the use of a complete cellulase enzyme complex containing various endoglucanases, exoglucanases and cellobiases. Various groups, due primarily to technical and economical reasons, have advocated the on-site production of cellulases rather than using the commercial cellulases sold by companies such as Novo-Nordisk, Genencor, Primalco and at least a further seven companies worldwide. These companies currently produce and market different types of cellulases for applications in areas such as textiles, detergents, animal feed and pulp and paper processing.

Cellulases are synthesized and excreted by various micro-organisms with certain fungi, primarily the *Trichoderma* species (notably *T. reesei*), among the most efficient producers. Generally, the amount of cellulase produced by wild-type strains of fungi or bacteria is too low to support an economical industrial process. For this reason strain improvement programmes were initiated in the mid-to-late 1970s and still continue to this day. Strains originally isolated using agar plating and isolation techniques have been improved by various methods, such as increasing the production of the whole cellulase complexes, increasing the resistance to glucose repression and enhancing pH and temperature tolerance.

Certain strains, such as *T. reesei* have remained remarkably stable, in a genetic sense, over the whole transition from laboratory-scale to precommercial production scale (30,000-litre fermenter). However, continued genetic improvement through both molecular biology and further use of traditional mutagenesis and screening protocols has not significantly improved the multifactorial characters such as specific activity, productivity or yields. Cellulase production is now possible at a cost well below expectations based on earlier economic studies. However, the cost of supplying enzymes for a biomass-to-ethanol process is still too high to allow the economic production of chemicals or fuels from lignocellulosic derived sugars.

Although on-site production of hemicellulose and glucose hydrolysates could provide a cheap source of substrates, the cost and effectiveness of on-site enzyme production has yet to be proven. Consequently, a significant amount of work on the production, mechanism and effectiveness of cellulase is continuing in this area. It can therefore be expected that, with increasing volumes of enzyme scales and the increased number of new applications in areas such as pulp and paper, the commercial cost of enzymes will continue to drop. As mentioned earlier, enzymatic hydrolysis is accomplished through the synergistic action of several cellulase components. Synergistic action means that the combined activity of the enzymes is greater than the sum of each of the components. The current mechanistic model primarily involves three main groups of enzymes that are required before cellulose can be hydrolyzed effectively to glucose.

The first component includes the endoglucanases, which attack the amorphous cellulose in a random action, producing more free which remove cellobiose units from both the reducing and non-reducing ends of cellulose chains. The third component includes the β-glucosidases which split the cellobiose units into monomeric glucose units. Each of the enzyme components is influenced by end-product inhibition and consequently the build-up of any of the products from any of the enzymatic reactions results in inhibition of the overall cellulose hydrolysis reaction. The cellulase enzyme complex has been isolated from a wide variety of organisms including anaerobic protozoa, aerobic fungi, and aerobic and anaerobic bacteria.

Enzymes from *trichoderma reesei*, which is an aerobic, mesophilic fungus, are the most extensively studied cellulases, essentially because all the necessary enzyme components for cellulose hydrolysis are produced extracellularly in high con-centrations and the organism can be grown in submerged aerobic culture. Furthermore, the cellulase complex produced is resistant to chemical inhibitors and remains stable for up to 48 hours at 50^{0}C. Although maximum cellulase activity for most fungal derived cellulases occurs at 50 ± 50^{0}C and pH of 4.0–5.0, cellulase complexes are known to differ substantially in their pH and temperature tolerance and in the ratio and amount of the different cellulase components. For example, *T. reesei* wild-type preparations are deficient in cellobiose, a β-glucosidase type enzyme, and result in an accumulation of cellobiose unless supplemented with the enzyme. However, there are induced mutant strains of *T. reesei* that display high β-glucosidase activity.

The high specificity of the cellulase enzymatic reaction should theoretically result in efficient hydrolysis of cellulose to glucose. In practice, the yields of glucose are influenced by many factors that can impact on both the rate and extent of hydrolysis. For example, it is known that the hydrolysis rate progressively declines with time due to a range of substrate and enzyme related factors. It has been shown that the surface area available for enzyme-substrate interaction is influenced by cellulose pore size and the shielding effects of hemicellulose and lignin.

The crystalline structure of cellulose excludes water molecules as well as any larger molecules, including the cellulase enzymes, and thus reduces the available surface area. Although it has been suggested that the crystalline regions of cellulose will be hydrolyzed at a much slower rate than the amorphous cellulose, due to the greater stability resulting from the interchain hydrogen bonding, this has not proven to be the case. Analysis of residual substrates has shown that the crystallinity remains unchanged as hydrolysis proceeds. As well as the surface area of the substrate limiting hydrolysis, both the rate and extent of the reaction are influenced by enzyme factors such as end-product inhibition, the irreversible and/or non-specific adsorption of cellulases onto the substrate, and the inactivation of key components of the cellulase complex.

There are various ways in which the effectiveness of the cellulases could be enhanced. For example, the low specific activity of commercial cellulase preparations has led to the requirement for high cellulase enzyme loadings. As a result, a considerable amount of research is now focused on learning more about the enzymatic and inhibitory mechanisms associated with the cellulase complex, screening for strains with enhanced enzymatic features (higher productivity, yield, resistance to end-product inhibition and higher specific activity) and the designing and testing of alternative operational and flow characteristics (e.g., fed-batch reactors, high enzyme concentrations, enzyme recycling) to enhance the activity and reuse of the cellulases.

Fermentation

Hexose Fermentation

The fermentation of glucose to ethanol was one of the first complex biological and chemical processes mastered by man. Alcohols became an important fuel and chemical feedstock in the mid-nineteenth century, predating the petrochemical industries of today. For example, most solvents and chemicals such as acetone, butanol and ethanol were originally produced from a number of carbohydrate feedstocks using a variety of conversion processes. However, with the rapid growth of the petroleum and petrochemical industry following World War I, fermentation research and development has been restricted primarily to the brewing and distilling industries and the last two decades of fermentation research have tried to extend the limits of traditional technologies rather than develop radically different processes. By optimizing the typical batch cycle, a batch fermentation which took 7 days in 1978 was reduced to 3 days by 1986. At the same time companies such as Melle-Boinot developed a system which operated in a mode between a batch and continuous fermentation and reduced the fermentation time to 16 hours. This was accomplished by recycling the yeast and residual fermentation substrate from earlier batches, thereby decreasing the volume of the fermenter and consequently increasing yields. Simultaneous ethanol distillation and advances in antibiotic research have also aided in the development of continuous fermentation processes. The ability to draw off the ethanol continuously as it is produced enables the system to keep a high level of productivity by removing the product which can slow down the metabolism of the yeast and eventually kill it. Advances in antibiotics were also required as continuous fermentation systems are vulnerable to outbreaks of infection and subsequent costly shutdowns.

The Biostil process incorporates many of these developments while other methods and technologies continue to be researched to increase the efficiency of ethanol production. Strategies include the development of flocculating yeasts, extractive fermentation, yeast immobilization, and continued research into modifying the various organisms through various classical and genetic engineering techniques.

Pentose Fermentation

The importance of being able to ferment the hemicellulose pentose derived sugars to the economics of the biomass-to-ethanol process has been emphasized by a number of authors. There are several reasons why the fermentation of pentoses to ethanol continues to be researched aggressively. These include the relative ease by which pentose can be recovered from most lignocellulosic substrates by methods such as dilute acid hydrolysis and acid catalyzed steam explosion; the rapidly expanding knowledge base on the biochemistry of ethanol production from xylose continues to offer potential ways of enhancing fermentation efficiency.

Finally, as mentioned above, a major driving force is the economic incentive that the extra ethanol from the xylose fraction of many biomass sources has on the overall ethanol process. The identification of a xylose-fermenting yeast, *Pachysolen tanno-philus*, in 1981 first indicated that ethanol could be derived from xylose and allowed projections to be made of the economic viability of converting both cellulose and hemicellulose derived sugars to ethanol. Other pentose fermenting organisms such as *Pichia stipitis* and *Candidae shihatae* have also been identified and characterized over the last 5 years.

The focus of most of this research has been to understand the limitations of the xylose fermentation and to use modern genetic engineering techniques to improve the ethanol yields and productivity of the yeasts. Some recent work has looked at the application of xylose-fermenting organisms in processing schemes using actual lignocellulosic sugar substrates. This has indicated that various problems such as inhibitory products and fermentation of mixed sugar streams have yet to be fully resolved. Several groups have been trying to manipulate certain bacteria and yeasts genetically so that they could incorporate the genes necessary for xylose fermentation to ethanol.

Metabolic engineering has been applied to *Erwina chrysanthemi*, *Escherichia coli*, *Klebsiella oxytoca*, *Klebsiella planticola* and *Zymomonas mobilis* and to *Saccharomyces cerevisiae*. So far the organisms which are most capable of fermenting both hexoses and pentoses have been *E. coli*, *K. oxytoca*, *Z. mobilis* and *S. cerevisiae*. Enteric bacteria such as *E. coli* do not grow well on xylose, even though they possess the necessary genes for xylose uptake and utilization. Normally, anaerobic fermentation of sugars with *E. coli* results in a range of products including lactate, acetate, succinate and formate with ethanol being only a minor product. Although engineered organisms can directly ferment xylose and other five-carbon sugars they tend to prefer a neutral pH. However, a neutral pH creates a greater demand for base and a higher potential for contamination by other organisms.

Ethanol Recovery

The beer resulting from a typical glucose fermentation usually contains about 8-12 per cent ethanol by volume. This dilute concentration is primarily a consequence of ethanol end-product inhibition. It is not possible to produce anhydrous ethanol by simple distillation as an azeotrope is formed at 95% ethanol; the azeotrope has a lower vapour pressure than either ethanol or water and is therefore preferentially distilled. A second step using a third component (e.g. benzene) to form another azeotrope with one or both of the original components has traditionally been employed. A considerable amount of work continues to be carried out to try to reduce the effects of end-product inhibition and the costs of conventional distillation (vapour recompression, cascade pressurization, super-critical fluid carbon dioxide) and dehydration (carbon dioxide extraction, solvent extraction, extractive fermen-tation, pervaporation, molecular sieves, adsorption).

Current and Future Status of Enzymatic Hydrolysis

As is apparent in this brief review, the bioconversion of ligno-cellulosics to ethanol is a complicated and strongly interdependent series of process steps. Currently there are no true examples of commercial or totally integrated demonstration-sized plants which can convert lignocellulosic materials to ethanol. Although some of the current and past pilot plants have been able to demonstrate the successful operation of entire sets of subprocess steps, these plants have not been able to operate continuously over a prolonged period of time. Hopefully, plants such as those at NREL in Colorado, USA, and others that will be potentially constructed in Sweden and Canada will provide the technical and operational experience that will allow the establishment of true commercial plants.

As a less expensive option, many researchers have attempted to assess the current techno-economic status and future potential of the various bioconversion processes by building techno economic models based on information obtained from both laboratory and pilot studies and from experience gained in the operation of similar processes in other industries, for example, ethanol from gain/corn. At this point in time, the comparison of these models appears to be the most direct way of providing a relative subprocess cost estimation. Although it is often difficult to compare model results directly as the basic tenets on which the models are based can differ substantially, there is general agreement that an enzyme based biomass-to-ethanol process could produce ethanol for about US$0.50 per litre based on the recovery of most of the cellulose and hemicellulose derived sugars and an energy credit for burned lignin.

More optimistic studies incorporating advances in genetic engineering, ethanol recovery and by-product credits have estimated that US$0.13-0.18 per litre of ethanol can be achieved. Although continued research will undoubtedly decrease the cost of producing biomass-to-ethanol it is probable that the eventual increase, both environmentally and economically, in the cost of petroleum derived fuels will provide the necessary incentive to establish biomass-to-ethanol processes.

7

DEFORESTATION

In the first half of the 1980s, an annual forest loss of 7200 square kilometers was recorded in the countries along the Gulf of Guinea, a figure which corresponded to 4-5% of the total remaining rainforest area. In 1985, 72 % of West Africa's rainforests had been transformed into fallow territory and an additional 9% had been opened up by timber exploitation. The future of West African rainforests as a living form of vegetation and a habitat for both man and animals is thus uncertain today. The biological diversity arid ecological equilibrium of the entire region is endangered. Some scientists fear that regional climate change has already begun due to large-scale deforestion and that what is left will be jeopardized by longer dry periods in the future. Foresters and the timber industry are discontent over forest destruction and an increasingly short supply of valuable hardwoods while the domestic timber needs of these countries are rising. Have we entered the last stage of a 500-year exploitation of the rainforest along the Gulf of Guinea?

Forest loss is often attributed to increasing human population and, indeed, the influx of farmers from the north worsens the situation drastically. In the Cote d'lvoire, for example, hundreds of thousands of farmers from Mali and Burkina Faso emigrated between 1966 and 1980 to the rapidly expanding areas of timber exploitation. The area of forest damaged by slash-and-burn agriculture almost doubled and affected 90% of the entire rainforest zone in 1980. In the southwestern Cote d'lvoire, where Tai National Park was established in 1972, the human population density had been recorded at an average of 1.3 persons per square kilometer. The inhabitants belonged to the tribes Krou,

Bakwe and Bete. Eight years later, the population density had risen to 7.7 persons per square kilometer. Timber exploitation had opened up the region and large-scale agricultural projects had attracted farmers from the north thereby making the original forest inhabitants a minority. The completion of the Buyo dam on the Sassandra River led additional settlers from the flooded regions to move into the area surrounding Tai National Park.

Overpopulation in the Sahel countries was not the only factor leading to the invasion of new settlers, however. The countries along the coast were themselves partly responsible. From 1969 to 1970, Ghana deported 300000 Nigerians and citizens of other West African countries. Fifteen years later, Nigeria revenged itself by employing the same tactic and deporting thousands of teachers and trained workers of Ghanaian nationality. Ghana's economic crisis of the early 19805 left many with no choke but to look to the forest for a new way of life.

Immigrant farmers clear the forest bit by bit using axes and bush knives, leaving the dried, remains of cut vegetation to be burned. The immigrants from Sahel countries are especially unfamiliar with the forest's sensitive soil. After only a few years harvest, it becomes depleted and infertile: Consequently, the farmer follows the path left by timber exploiters and moves deeper into the forest to clear his next plots of land. The exhaustive use of land for the temporary production of corn, plantains, cassava, yams and a few vegetables leads to an ever-increasing area of fallow land. A few tall trees and groups of smaller trees are all that is left protruding above high grass and thick, scrubby brush. A chaotic mosaic of farm plots fills out the picture. Badly scared wooded hills eroged slopes and the ruins of mud wall huts tell of the abandoned crop beds. Such land must lie fallow for some: years before it can be cleared again and replanted. Even then, it will yield but a few modest harvests. If the land is not too sloped and has not been entirely eroded of its soil, it will only regenerate after a period of many long years.

The native gatherers and planters who had practiced shifting agriculture for centuries in the forest did not do irreparable damage to the land. They never cleared sloped ground and they worked only small areas. Afterwards the plots were left to regenerate to full secondary forests. There are such areas of secondary forest throughout West Africa and they are scarcely distinguishable in structure from closed primary forest Some forest tribes in isolated areas have continued to practice shifting agriculture to this day and in over one hundred years, no lasting large scale damage has been done to the forests surrounding their villages.

The slash-and-burn agriculture practiced by the immigrant farmers does not increase the area of cultivated land in proportion to forest loss. That is the irony of the rainforest's destruction. Since the soil can only be worked for a short time and cannot support sustainable use in most areas, the actual area of land cultivated is merely displaced as the forest retreats and does not increase to a meaningful extent. That is why there is so much fallow land, unable to support either timber production or agriculture. Neither are there forest products to be gathered, nor much game to be hunted. Thus, it is not a choice between forest or agriculture, as many may wish to believe; rather, it is a choice between forest or a mosaic of farm plots with a great deal of fallow land inbetween.

Meanwhile, foresters and timber companies never cease to declare that they are responsible for removing comparatively few trees from the forest and that over 90% of the trees lost are sacrificied to slash-and-burn farming. Conservationists also sometimes divide the blame between the timber industry and the farmers according to who felled how many trees. Others mistakenly believe rainforest destruction to be connected with the problem of firewood. But the latter is a difficulty in dry tropical zones, where the lack of firewood leads to the destruction of open forests and other dry woody vegetation. Collecting firewood is generally not a problem in the rainforest, even seriously disturbed forest provides sufficient dead wood.

It is not that easy to claim certain people or a single factor solely responsible for forest loss: Actually, the destruction began much earlier this century when the original forest inhabitants were stripped of their autonomy and the forest administration was centralized in the interest of commercial timber exploitation, Forest loss is the result of complex interactions between cultural and commercial factors which eventually lead to uncontrolled destruction. But the tropical timber industry plays a key role in the process.

The Consequences of Selective Exploitation

An undisturbed area of rainforest in West Africa harbors about 180 larger tree species. Fewer than one quarter of those species are of economic value and only 10 to 15 are actually marketable timber. In spite of efforts to encourage the use of lesser known timber species, the market continues to concentrate on a fraction of the usable timber available.

In high-yield areas of exploitation in West Africa, there are usually more than 500 trees per hectare, which measure a diameter of over 10 centimeters. About one tenth of the trees are more than 30 centimeters thick and the largest specimens may have diameters of 200 - 300 centimeters above their buttresses. In spite of the fact that African rainforests have a higher growing stock than forests in other parts of the world, an average of only 12 - 13 cubic meters are harvested per hectare. That is three times less than in Southeast Asia and does not even equal the trunk volume of one large tree. In forest reserves – most of which are open to exploitation – minimal diameters are prescribed for felling, In Ghana that may be 68 or 120 centimeters depending on the species. But the low area harvest is not due to regulations. It has more to do with the timber companies themselves, who are only interested in the most valuable species: They "cream" the forest. Extremely selective methods of timber exploitation lead to only 7% of the timber available in West African forests being felled and marketed.

One might think that this kind of hyper-selective exploitation would be the best guarantee for a sustainable timber industry. After all, the purpose of the selective system is the repeated harvest of the same area after a felling cycle of some decades! Reality on the other hand, paints quite a different picture. Very selective exploitation is synonymous with very extensive exploitation and a low area yield quickens the pace at which further rainforest is opened up. Since the massive trunks can only be transported out of the forest over logging routes and feeder tracks, even selectively logged areas must be crisscrossed with a network of access roads. At least 10 kilometers of road must be allowed for every 10 square kilometers of rainforest. And they are the beginning of the end. Logging roads are the real reason why 90% of the slash-and-burn activities by immigrant farmers is concentrated in exploited areas. Poorly staffed and, under equipped forestry services are notable to supervise, let alone, control, the fast pace at which forests are opened up and exploited, nor the influx of farmers. The forest guard is of little interest to the timber companies, at best they may give him a pitiful smile and perhaps a small bribe. Many firms themselves no longer believe that their logging concession will survive an entire felling cycle.

The Forestry Crisis

At the beginning of the century, foresters assumed that moist tropical forests could be managed in a sustainable fashion similar to

European forests. On the basis of this assumption, African forest administration was centralized and a system of forest reserves was established against the will of local inhabitants. Today at the end of the century, foresters are more perplexed than ever as to how rainforests should be sustainably utilized, if at all. They have themselves begun to doubt the sustainability of sylvicultural systems. Too much forest has been lost as a consequence of opening up forest for timber exploitation. The combined selective exploitation system became discredited in Ghana since many valuable secondary species were destroyed and large quantities of poison were used in the course of improvement thinning. From 1958 to 1970, 2590 square kilometers of rainforest were managed under this system during which time, 188 tons of sodium arsenite were applied. Other methods of improving, timber yield were just as unsuccessful. After years of research and numerous tests, the Tropical Shelterwood System (TSS), which also required the use of sodium arsenite, proved to be a failure. Natural regeneration of valuable species under the TSS did not meet expectations. Enrichment Planting also proved unsuccessful. The seedlings of commercial species raised in tree nurseries at great expense and later planted in the forest were usually soon overgrown by ground herbs and vines. In both Nigeria and Ghana, the Tropical Shelterwood System and Enrichment Planting were abandoned in disappointment during the mid-1960s.

Tropical Foresters under Attack

Tropical foresters lead difficult lives today. They have been the object of international criticism and have been held responsible for rapid deforestation although they have always strived towards sustainable forest management. If foresters can be accused of anything, it would be the fact that they were too concerned with the primary product timber and neglected the forest's multiple other functions Although foresters are quick to point out the importance of secondary forest products, of game and gathered produce; those aspects were completely ignored in forest management practices Officially, all of Ghana's commercially exploited forests in forest reserves were considered "managed". A study by FAO, however, showed that forest management in the Kakum Forest Reserve "has been geared towards timber production with scant attention given to the potential of minor forest products to stimulate rural industry and the use of branch wood and rejected logs for fuelwood and charcoal. Employment in forest industry is minimal and the concept of forestry for rural development has been ignored". These findings are in crass contrast to Kakum's reputation for model forest management.

Especially serious is the fact that tropical foresters too long deceived the world by claiming that moist tropical forests could be sustainably logged of a few valuable timber species. In the meantime, they were applying inefficient methods and thoughtlessly poisoning "worthless" trees and secondary timber species at the danger of wildlife populations.

Endangered Forest Reserves

The apparent failure of the foresters in their strive to exploit valuable species in a sustainable way led them to forsake the complex management of natural forests in favour of intensive plantation forestry. As early as the 1960s, large-scale plantations of native timber such as limba, emeri, obeche and opepe were established in Nigeria as well as of the exotic species gmelina, teak and pinus. The experience gained during the pre-war years proved useful in helping to set up the new plantations. According to the FAO, industrial timber plantations, increased by approximately 71% in West Africa from 1981-85. Large-scale plantations were established especially in Nigeria and the Côte d'lvoire. Unfortunately, this did not mean the remaining natural forests were spared. The Nigerians did not hesitate to establish plantations within forest reserves. In Nigeria, the forestry service must prove the socio-economic value of trees if it wishes to protect forest reserves against conversion to other forms of land-use. The Subri Forest Reserve in Ghana was also transformed into a gmelina plantation, an act which was actually supported by the United Nations Development Programme (UNDP).

At the demand of local populations, which had never overcome the Ioss of their rights to land use in forest reserves, the Taungya System was also introduced. It entails the combined plantation of timber and agricultural crops on cleared land. During the first two to three years mixed crops are cultivated between the young trees. Afterwards, the farmer must forfeit his plot of land and leave it to the forester and his trees. The government retains, property and timber rights. Practically speaking, the Taungya System was little different from the traditional practice of shifting agriculture in which farmed plots are left after some years to allow for natural regeneration. With the introduction of the Taungya System, Ghana's entire forest plantation program attained only 60 % success It was difficult to supervise the system in the forest outside and the timber yield was accordingly

Table 7.1. Plantations of industrial timber in km². Firewood plantations, which were primarily established outside the rainforest zone, are not included.

	1980	*1985 (estimated)*
Benin	77.5	77.5
Ghana	262.5	319.5
Guinea	21.5	27.0
Guinea-Bissau	3.0	7.0
Cote d'lvoire	378.0	658.0
Liberia	63.0	163.0
Nigeria	1463.0	2703.0
Sierra Leone	53.0	63.0
Togo	75.5	92.5
West Africa	2397.0	4110.5

poor. Since the farmers have no share in the timber profits earned by the plantations, the Taungya System has also proved to be of limited success in Nigeria.

Aside from forest reserves, there will soon be no significant forested areas left in West Africa. Official forest policy in Ghana and Nigeria requires that areas not within forest reserves be opened up to other functions, notably agricultural use. Unfortunately, a combined use for both agricultural and timber purposes has scarcely been considered up to now, although it would be the best way of achieving a sustainable and ecologically balanced land-use. Although agroforesty has be come a popular term today, foresters – more than farmers – are skeptical of agroforestry methods. They would have to work with other timber species, use different Iogging practices and integrate the farmers into their work. Instead forestry service limits themselves to the use of less efficient but better-known methods of management in fares reserves.

Neither is there a guarantee that forest reserve will actually remain forest: It was necessary to declassify approximately one quarter of the original 33 000 squarc kilometers of fore' reserve in the Cote d'lvoire. The government agency for reforestation SODEFOR, assigned with the demarcation of the reserves, discovered numerous cleared areas. Entire forest reserves had vanished and today only 2400 square kilometers of permanent forest remain. In Nigeria, federalist attitudes prevent a uniform national forest policy. Forest reserves, which are practically the only forest left in the country today, fall under the

Table 7.2. Forest reserves (forests classees) in the rainforest zone of the most important West African timber export countries.

	Forest reserves (km²)	*Proportion of total closedforest area (1985)*
Liberia	16647	22.4%
Cote d'ivoire	24042	18.9%
Ghana	16788	20.5%
Nigeria	21221	15.8%

jurisdiction of the separate states. They are not always able to prevent farmers and loggers from over stepping the law. In Nigeria, deforestation continues at a rate of 350-400 square kilometers year and mainly affects forest reserves. Even well-stocked reserves are cleared to make way for plantations of oil palm, rubber, citrus fruits and cocoa although fallow land lies unused nearby.

THE RISE AND FALL OF TIMBER EXPORT

Tropical timber became a viable alternative to European wood after World War II, when trade with East European countries ceased and even more so when timber became noticeably scarce in western and southern Europe. With the upward economic trend in industrialized European countries, the demand for tropical hardwood was concentrated almost exclusively on West Africa. At the time, economic theory projected endless growth and particularly American economists were in favour of mobilizing the rainforest's timber supply and investing the profits in other more productive branches of economy. This attitude conflicted with the traditional principles of forest management, especially in the British colonies. But Europe's trade interests had long determined its relationship to West Africa and here again they proved to be stronger. Today, most of West Africa's natural forests are exploited. In the meantime, however, those countries domestic demand for timber has increased. This, combined with the fact that profits from round wood exports are skimmed off by trading companies and processing. In Europe, has led many governments to set export restrictions. But the European market has proved to be less stable than before the recession of 1975. Although Europe still imports tropical round wood almost exclusively from Africa, interest in sawn wood began to shift to Asia. The Africans were left in the cold.

Only four of West Africans nine countries produce significant quantities of tropical timber In order of increasing importance for today's export, they are: Nigeria, Liberia, Ghana and the Cote d'lvoire.

Although Nigeria looks back on a century of forest management, today it is scarcely able to cover its domestic need for timber. The country's population is more than double that of the other eight West African states combined, And the oil boom of the mid-1970s further strengthened the domestic demand for wood and wood products, Nigeria began to import more timber products (logs, sawn wood, veneers, pulp and paper) than it exported, The foreign trade balance continued to worsen until, in 1980, Nigeria showed a deficit of US$ 247 million spent for the import of wood products, The catastrophic situation had already led to a timber export ban in the 19705. At the same time, logging activities were intensified in the remaining forests. But a program of reforestation was also begun and appears to have been successful as far as the trade balance is concerned. FAO statistics for 1985 show the deficit reduced by U$$ 100 million. It is questionable, however, whether many intact rainforest areas will survive in Nigeria.

Liberia's timber industry is of lesser importance. Although practically the whole country was once covered with rainforest, its exports consisted mostly of rubber and of iron ore extracted from the Nimba Mountains. The first timber firm, the Maryland Logging Company, did not move into the southeastern corner of Liberia until 1965. Between 1971 and 1980, only 33 timber companies actively made use of their concessions although logging permits had been distributed over most of the country. In order to reduce logging activities and prevent the forests from quickly being creamed of their best specimens, the Liberian Forest Development Authority (FDA) limited annual exploitation within larger concessions to 4% of the total Area. Despite fears that Liberia may merely lie ten years behind the dramatic situation in the Cote d'lvoire, it has seldom reached more than one tenth its neighbour's annual round wood production.

Selling Out Ghana's Forests

Once Ghanaian tribal chiefs had been stripped of authority over the forests in their territory, the distribution of concessions was also centralized under the Ministry for Lands and Mineral Resources, Under Nkrumah, the government strived to promote small to middle-sized enterprises owned by Ghanaians and the distribution of timber concessions to foreign companies was thus reduced. One hundred concessions were granted to Ghanaians from 1961-71, only two to foreign companies. Until then, most timber rights had been in European hands; but now the large foreign concessions had been divided' and distributed among Ghanaian enterprises. The average size of a concession decreased from 686 square kilometers to a mere 41 square kilometers. By 1967, logging permits had been issued for 75% of 'the forest reserves and for all unreserved forests. The government's policy had drastic consequences. By 1970, the number of firms had risen from 121 to 361. More than half were subcontractors to the actual concession holder.

In spite of government loans to timber producers, many firms soon went bankrupt. A few lucky individuals, however, found their way from rags to riches. One example is Francis Osei Kyeremateng: "Franco" rented chain saws, one tractor and a truck in order to fell timber under contract to large concessionaires and sell it to a sawmill in Kumasi. He used the profits to purchase his own tractor and two used timber trucks. In 1967, he was able to exploit more than 500 hectares in the Subim Forest Reserve. Additional profits allowed him to add a bulldozer, a second tractor and another truck to his enterprise. After developing trade relations with a Dutch partner who was prepared to invest in his machinery, Franco gained the government's trust and was issued an import license for spare parts. Up to then, he had, only worked as a subcontractor to concession holders without timber rights of his own. Not until Acheampong came into office, whose government was considered corrupt throughout the country, did Franco Timbers receive its own concession - right in the middle of Bia National Park! In 1976, to thirds of the park had to be declassified to the status of game reserve in order to provide Franco Timbers and a number of other small concessionaries with logging permits. The pressure on the remaining natural forest reserves had drastically increased.

But Ghana's government program to promote native enterprises did not succeed. Many of the small firms fought costs much too high for what they profited. Few Ghanaians made their way to the top and could allow themselves the luxury of being chauffeured through the rainforest in a Mercedes like "Franco". Instead, more and more Lebanese moved into the timber industry, openly or by using small-scale Ghanaian enterprises as fronts.

Ghana's forest service, which had to deal with limited staff, funds and equipment in any case, stood before a particularly difficult task The government's policy of promoting small-scale enterprises led to relatively small concession areas with more intensive logging activities over a wider total area thus making supervision difficult. At the demand of timber concessionaires, all economic timber trees with diameters of at least 108 centimeters were allowed to be felled. The timber concessionaires had "convinced" the government that trees of greater diameter were "overmature" and would result in a deterioration of wood quality. For this reason, the felling cycle was also reduced from 25 to 15 years. The more liberal regulations were based on totally unfounded ideas - most rainforest trees reach much greater diameters without becoming "overmature" – and led to unnecessary destruction and damage. Ironically, large numbers of felled trunks rotted in the forest because there was no market for them.

The hoards of small-scale enterprises led to the downfall of many rainforest areas. Even in the forest reserves, loggers often did not follow the rules of selective exploitation and indiscriminately felled all economic species. Not much was left of the top canopy. Forest guards were bribed to label best quality trunks as second class in order to lower their export value. This reduced the country's hard currency income but the exporters had their European customers pay them the difference to a bank account abroad, an illegal practice still common in West Africa today.

Attempts at Rectifying Ghana's Timber Industry

Large timber companies, some of which had been active in Ghana since 1948, also suffered from the preference given to small-scale enterprises. Timber companies operating in the well-stocked moist semi-deciduous forests were especially hard hit by the government scheme: Gliksten West Africa, the Mim Timber Company and African Timber and Plywood (ATP). The Mim Timber Company had paid particular attention to, exploiting its concession carefully and protecting it from slash-and-burn clearing. In the 1970s, Mim was nationalized like many other foreign firms but instead of being rewarded for its considerate forest utilization, it was quite poorly treated. Not only were the older timber companies now struggling with the recession, their import licenses for spare parts were also restricted. Mim even lost some of its timber rights to small-scale enterprises favoured by Acheampong's government.

Today's government under Jerry Rawlings is trying to correct some of the mistakes made in the past; divided concessions have been returned to their original holders. In 1979, the decrease in timber production led to a log export ban for 14 species in order to promote the domestic timber processing industry, but also to encourage the exploitation of lesser known species such as pterygota, aningre, cardboard and the relatively common limba. Some of today's experts recommend returning to earlier methods of selective exploitation and 'a much longer felling cycle of 40 years. But today, Ghana's forests consist almost only of

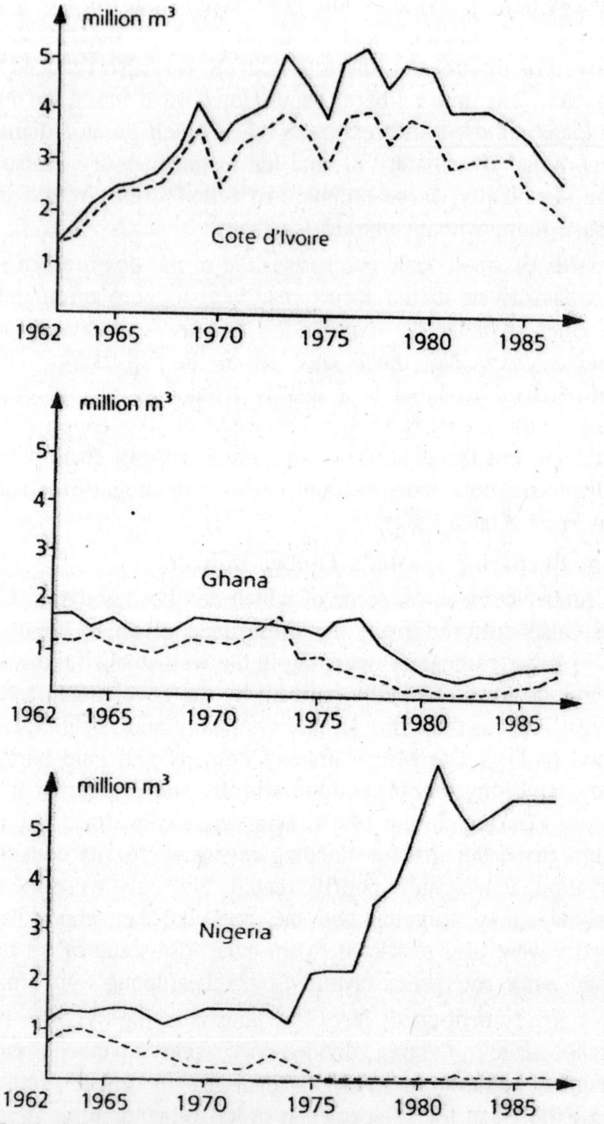

Fig. 7.1. Tropical timber production and export 1962-1987. The black lines indicate the total production of roundwood (logs). The broken lines indicate the export of roundwood, swanwood and woodbased panels.

forest reserves and even they have been too severely depleted of commercial species to attract further large foreign investors. Afrormosia, a tree species of limited distribution in West Africa, is listed today as rare and endangered. Half of Ghana's afrormosia stock once occurred within Mim concessions. New loans from the World Bank have tempted smaller British firms back to Ghana. They take over the management of timber companies like the Bibiani Logging Co. Ltd, improve their equipment and in return they can export timber to Great Britain. Since 1983, Ghana's timber production and export have begun to rise from an all time low. The question is, for how long.

Overexploitation in the Cote d'lvoiré

The Cote d'lvoire has been and continues to be by far Africa's, most important exporter of tropical timber Although this country with the liberal market economy on the Gulf of Guinea cannot yet compete with, Southeast Asia's timber giants in the "golden" timber years of, the. 1970s, the Cote d'lvoire did export one-fifth the volume of Indonesia's export. Indonesia, however, logs its, forests much more intensely because of the frequent occurrence of the dipterocarp species. In 1985, one quarter the value of Africa's total timber products export was covered by the Cote d'lvoire.

The Cote d'lvoire has a younger history of forest management than the former British colonies. Timber export remained insignificant until the. 1950s but after independence, it was boosted all the more to support the country's economic development. Nowhere else in Africa was the rainforest opened up so quickly and in such an uncoordinated manner as in the Cote d'lvoire. The production of industrial roundwood truly correspond to the market - 20 years ago (1969) the Cote d'lvoire exported nearly the entire quantity of timber felled. There were 2646 concessions distributed over 66000 square kilometers of forest, which is equal to the area of Sri Lanka. Contrary to most other West African timber producers who sought to develop their own forest industry, the Cote d'lvoire exported by far the majority of its timber in, round wood form. Only 30 years since the tropical timber boom really began, supplies are clearly showing signs of exhaustion. There is not much forest left to be opened up in the Cote d'lvoire. The export of the more valuable species - African mahogany, utile, sapele, gedu nohor and makore is steadily decreasing in favour of the faster growing obeche; a species often taken in a second felling, In any case, the Cote d'lvoire's, liberal economy seems to be leading towards Nigeria's situation of 15 years ago. A country whose forest area consists of only small, patches of secondary forest and whose timber exports threaten to collapse in the face of an increasing domestic demand for industrial timber:

Legacy of Colonial Power

Arthur Creech Jones, a former Secretary of State for the British colonies, described Britain's well meant colonial policy in West Africa early in the century: "To guide the colonial territories to responsible self-government within the Commonwealth in conditions that ensure to the people both a fair standard of living and freedom from oppression from any quarter". British colonies often refrained from establishing large plantations because it would have meant forcing the local inhabitants off their land. After their bad experiences with tribal chiefs in Ghana, the English sought to include the local population in the planning process and to allow the village chiefs to rule their territory. In accordance with this colonial philosophy, school systems were encouraged and developed in British West Africa. Today, the level of education in Ghana and Nigeria remains superior to that in French speaking West Africa.

France treated its colonies differently: French territory in West Africa was always considered part of the "Grande Nation". All property automatically belonged to the state unless an African had registered his land with the French authorities. The French administered their territories by their own colonial officers and did not delegate any power whatsoever to the native people. Throughout French West Africa and especially in the Cote d'lvoire, large tracts of land were given to foreign investors for the establishment of rubber, oil palm, pineapple and banana plantations Business and trade were very much oriented toward the French market and remain so today. Former French colonies have continued to be greatly dominated by foreign powers even after attaining independence. After the Cote d'lvoire became independent in 1960, it was not curious that the number of French citizens in the country had nearly doubled by 1972. In all English-speaking countries, on the other hand, the population of citizens belonging to the former colonial power had decreased. Today, English speaking West Africa tends to disdain its French speaking neighbours for their economic dependence on and factual control by the former colonial rulers Professor of Geography Reuben K. Udo from the University of Ibadan (Nigeria); for example, comments that former French colonies need more export' earnings to satisfy the, demands for goods on the part of the expatriate population and their African elite: "Some of whom tend to be more French than the French". In spite of relatively impressive growth rates in the national economy the Cote d'lvoire's rural areas have remained as backward and underdeveloped as ever. Udo considers it

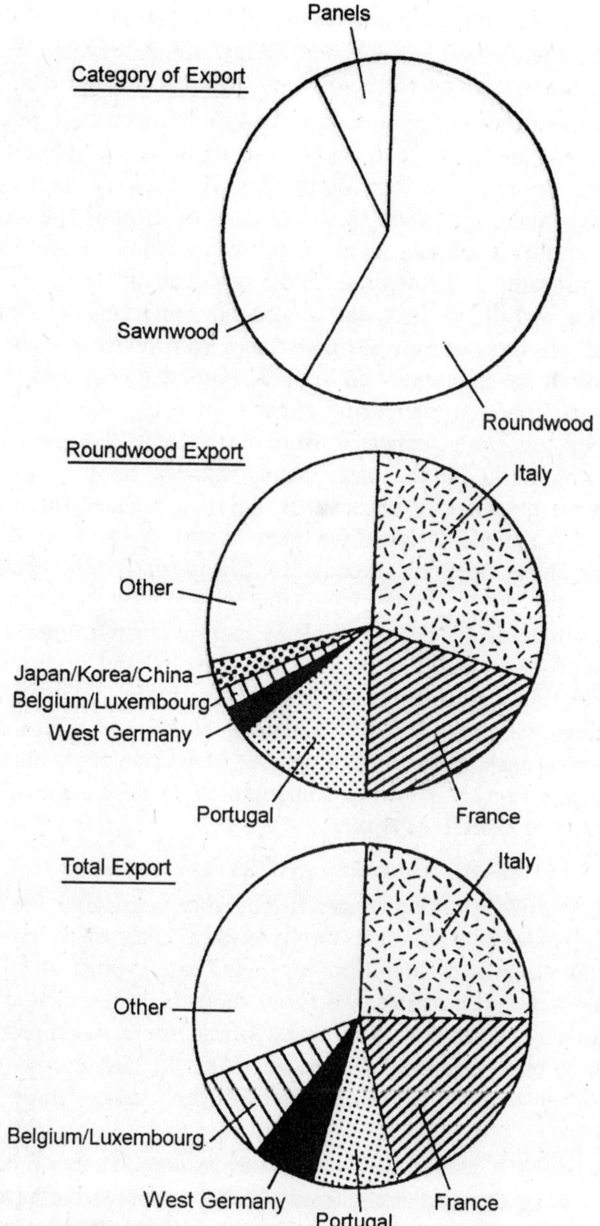

Fig. 7.2. Export and destinations of tropical timber from the Cote d'lvoire, 1985. Sawanwood and woodbased panels are expressed in roundwood equivalents.

an example of "growth without development". Whoever has seen crates of imported French, table wine and, Vichy mineral water standing beside clay huts all dusty roads will tend to share his opinion.

Old ties to France have also developed into timber trade relations. Although the Cote d'lvoire quickly rose to become Africa's most important timber exporter after World War II, not even the first step - sawing the trunks - was left to the country of origin. The majority of Ivorian timber continues to be exported as round wood logs to essentially the same destinations since the post-war timber crisis. Apart from France and Italy, Portugal is also an important consumer of Ivorian timber. Ivorian logs are used there to produce plywood and veneers, which are then exported to other European countries, rotably Britain! Since 1985, an increasing quantity of round wood (saw logs amid veneer logs) was exported from the Cote d'lvoire to Japan. European countries, oh the other hand, reduced their round wood imports, from the Cote d'lvoire in favour of a higher proportion of sandwood and panels. Originally timber export in the Cote d'lvoire had as elsewhere been the domain of European family firms, for example Victor Balet. Today, the enterprise consists of registered African companies based on African capital with timber rights, sawmills and other facilities in the Cote d'lvoire and in the central African Republic. Various large French firms are involved in the Ivorian timber business, BECOB, Lalanne, SCAF and SCOA among others. They in turn also control a number of Ivorian companies. And behind many a French industrial conglomerate stands, a French bank like the BNP or Credit Agricole.

The Same Mistakes in Central Africa?

While English-speaking countries tended to nationalize the timber industry, transform traditional family-owned enterprises into semi nationalized companies and limit or even ban export; the French merrily continued to dominate the forest industry in the Cote d'lvoire – but not to the best interest of the forest Ivorian round wood production wavered with export demand which shows that logging did not follow the rules of sustainable forest management but, rather, those of the free market.

But the party is over in the Cote d'lvoire as well. Timber production and export have dropped dramatically. Ivarian rainforests have been depleted and attention is slowly turning to Central Africa, where a great deal of rainforest still stands. Between 1981 and 1985, already two and a half times as much primary forest was opened up there as in West Africa. Interestingly enough, industrial conglomerates tend to keep to their language areas more than anything else. While the British timber industry concentrates its efforts increasingly in Southeast Asia. French firms do more business in Cameroon, Gabon and in the Central African Republic. But the large German Dangerous Group, active in tropical timber exploitation and processing worldwide, has also shifted its African business from the Cote d'lvoire to Cameroon and particularly to Za'lre. West Africa has served its purpose - in return, the countries along the Gulf of Guirlea will soon be able to puzzle over how to meet their own rising demands for industrial wood. So far, the timber plantation program has only produced significant yield as in Nigeria.

The danger is great that the mistakes made in West Africa over the past 30 years will be repeated in Central Africa Immigrant farmers have not as yet cleared as much land in the extensive forest areas of Central Africa as has been the case in West Africa, but the peculiarities of timber exploitation and the industry's methods have not changed. In 1978, Jack Westoby a prominent forest economist at FAG described the situation at the World Forestry Congress in Jakarta: "Forest industries have made little or no contribution to socio-economic development in the underdeveloped world certainly not the significant contribution that was envisaged for them a couple of decades ago Indeed, the probability is, that such forest industries (...) served but to deflect attention from real needs, diverted resources from what should have been the true priorities, and served to promote socio-economic under development". Hansjurg Steinlin, Professor for global forestry at the University of Freiburgi. Br., still comes to the same conclusion a decade later. Steinlin states, "The capital made available by timber harvests was not reinvested in agriculture and forest management, instead it was withdrawn for the most part from the rural regions and trickled in sometimes dubious ways to the cities where it was spent on consumer goods or invested in unproductive ways. The costs to the national economy caused by forest loss are well above the profits". These are not the words of fundamentalist conservationists but the opinions of experienced tropical foresters who have the courage to speak out. Their statements are especially true in West Africa. In view of the catastrophic consequences of timber exploitation in closed tropical forests for the ecology, local populations and national economies; African governments, foreign investors, importer countries and consumers should today ask themselves if it might not be better to completely refrain from this form of rainforest utilization.

8

CONSERVATION OF FOREST

Forest inhabitants present the first sip of every calabash brimming with palm wine to their ancestors, allowing it to trickle into the ground as symbol of gratitude for the land and hunting grounds left to their use. Neither will a son unthinkingly sell his mother's hut. These people know the value of their old drums and of the forest which has supported them and their family for generations.

Tribal chiefs and village elders may have appeared to only be defending their rights to ancestral land as they resisted the centralization of the forest administration at the beginning of the century. But even then it was a question of conservation. Although the forest, inhabitants were not familiar with the term, their cultural and existential dependency on the forest and its gifts was synonymous with conservation. Their life meant conservation. Of course, neither did the colonial governments, the newly established forest administrations nor even many timber companies intentionally plan to destroy the forest. On the contrary, the creation of forest reserves was meant to place as much forest as possible under permanent protection.

Paradoxically today, in spite of the fact that everyone strived towards, forest conservation back then, or perhaps just because of that, exactly the opposite was achieved. The Incompatibility between tradition and modern forest management has already been dealt with in the first chapter of this book. To put it concisely: The forest conservation planned on paper, without consideration of local interests or effective methods of supervision, and combined with increasing pressure from the timber industry and immigrant farmers, culminated in forest destruction or, in the words of forest economist Westoby:

"Though every underdeveloped country now has a forest service, these forest services are nearly all woefully understaffed, and miserably underpaid. Because they exist, exploitation is facilitated; because they are weak, exploitation is not controlled. Because exploitation has been uncontrolled, and management non-existent, marginal farmers, shifting cultivators, and landless poor have followed in the wake of the loggers, completing the forest destruction" If the same mistakes are not to be repeated, forest conservation measures must be conceived with respect for local interests.

From Hunting Bans to Agroforestry

Forest management introduced conservation measures more to preserve the timber supply than to conserve biological diversity as a whole. And 20 years ago, on the other hand, conservationists gave little thought to the fate of West African rainforests, as an ecosystem. They were mainly concerned with aspects of species conservation and tried to preserve animals from being hunted, irrespective of rising threats to the forest as a whole. Even in the 1960s, it was apparently hard to imagine that mere patches of forest were soon to remain of West Africa's rainforests.

Conservationists made their recommendations accordingly. They modelled hunting after European traditions, with open and closed seasons, bans an certain species or on females and young offspring, and sometimes went as far as to completely ban hunting The use of traps and snares, the trade and even transport of bushmeat were also examined and actually prohibited in some West African countries. Of course, hunting regulations can be useful if local needs are taken into account and if the regulations can be enforced. But how is a village hunter to determine between a male or a female duiker antelope in the rainforest, and judge its age, if he often cannot even distinguish between an antelope and a monkey in the light of his carbide lamp? And when people cover their protein needs almost exclusively with bushmeat, what are they supposed to eat if hunting is suddenly not allowed for months on end? It is not surprising that West African hunting regulations have remained nothing but worthless pieces of paper and are scarcely respected anywhere. First, the Europeans deprived the forest inhabitants of their authority over the forest in the belief of so being able to better protect nature, Then, they tried to preserve wildlife resources with European-style hunting regulations, It would hardly have been possible to attempt more unsuitable methods of forest conservation and they were consequently of little success.

International Efforts

Today, there is a global demand for land-use planning in tropical rainforest areas. Sustainable, non-destructive methods of utilization should be the basis of such planning. But how can that demand be met when we still do not know how rainforests can be managed sustainably and when foresters knowingly cling to old methods despite their unsuitability?

The Tropical Forestry Action Plan conceived for 1987-91 by the World Resources Institute in cooperation with the Food and Agriculture Organization (FAO), the United Nations Development Programme (UNDP) and the World Bank with an initial budget of US$ 5.3 billion was developed with high hopes. Saving the world's forests was assumed to be a costly undertaking. Through increased investments in forestry, it was believed that the destruction could be halted. The Action Plan has since been judged more objectively. Forestry review reports of missions to various tropical forest countries do not look particularly promising. Although firewood and industrial timber plantations were included, old methods of timber exploitation were not questioned and a mere 8% of the budget was reserved for conservation projects. Significantly, the large teams of forest experts who judged the situation in Ghana, the Cote d'lvoire and in Cameroon scarcely included critical foresters and only a few forest conservationists.

The International Tropical Timber Organization (ITTO) also has yet to prove that its activities actually result in forest conservation. A part of its efforts aims at financing forest conservation projects under article 1 (H) of the International Tropical Timber Agreement (ITTA) established in 1984. In the long term, however, the treaty could prove to be an effective instrument for international forest conservation. It is the only commercial treaty to even mention tropical forest conservation, let alone declare it an aim. A further advantage of the ITTO is the equal participation of producer and consumer countries which enables critical voices in the tropical timber debate to also directly influence timber exploitation.

Budowski's Principles of Forest Conservation

International efforts to conserve tropical forests should not be overestimated. Especially not when new investments in the forest sector are supposed to correct what previous investments have destroyed. In view of today's continuing forest loss, not only are new methods needed but an entire new philosophy is necessary based on the urgent needs of conservation as well as the social and economic needs of today's forest inhabitants. In many rainforests throughout the world - and very much so in West Africa - preserving remaining undisturbed forest has to be the leitmotif of every planning concept. Forestry, too, must adhere to this principle. In other words: Forest utilization planning needs to concentrate on areas already opened up - secondary forests and fallows. In 1984, one of the most progressive tropical foresters, Gerardo Budowski, based his principles of forest utilization on just this need:

(a) *Agroforestry*. Integration of timber, firewood and fruit trees in agricultural plots based on traditional and modern methods.

(b) *Plantation of trees*. Reforestation with native and exotic species for the production of timber, pulp and fuel wood but never at the cost of natural forests. There is enough fallow land to be used for such purposes.

(c) *Secondary forest management*. Production of valuable timber species in already existing secondary forests, using methods of sustained production such as liberation cuttings.

(d) *Social forestry*. Production of timber, fuel wood, fibers, medicinal plants and charcoal by village communities, on a sustained basis also as part of agroforestry systems.

(e) *Buffer zones*. Management of forest zones surrounding national parks and other protected areas. Such areas provide an opportunity for foresters, and conservationists to prove their cooperation.

Protected forest areas are especially suitable for focusing the development of integral forest utilization. Inversely, a careful, sustainable land-use in zones surrounding protected areas is of vital importance to the areas themselves if they are not to be sacrificed to an increased demand for land.

Rainforest National Parks in West Africa

Until 1968, there was not a single strictly protected rainforest area in all of West Africa, with the exception of the 180 square kilometer large nature reserve in the Nimba mountains and the tiny Banco National Park north west of Abidjan. Later, Mont Peko National Park and Marahoue National Park were established in the Cote d'lvoire. The latter comprises over 1000 square kilometers of transitional zone to Guinea savannah, In 1972, Tai National Park was established in the southwestern Cote d'lvoire at the recommendation of the International Union for Conservation of Nature (IU(N) and WWF. The Tai Park - with an area of 3300 square kilometers, a buffer zone and the neighbouring N 'Zo Wildlife Reserve - remains the most important protected rainforest area in West Africa today. Although it has not been overly careful of its forests, one must admit that Africa's "land of economic wonder" did set aside integraliy protected areas earlier and in a more consistent manner than any other country along the Gulf of Guinea. Until very recently, Sierra Leone, Guinea and Nigeria had not managed to establish even one national park in the rainforest zone. The mangrove forests in Guinea Bissau, so very important for the fishing industry, were virtually unprotected. In 1989, however, a coastal wetlands management project was begun there. Within the scope of this project, a series of reserves are to be established which will allow multiple use of Guinea Bissau's coastal wetland resources. Also in 1989, the Nigerian Council of Ministers upon the recommendation of WWF approved two important rainforest areas in southeast Nigeria being declared a national park. The Cross River National Park will incorporate the Oban Division, a large area between the Cross River and the Cameroon border, and the Boshi-Okwangwo Division, a geographically separate forest area further north Including these new additions to the West African system of protected areas, only about 10500 square kilometers have national park or strict nature reserve status in the rainforest zone. An additional 3660 square kilometers are, classified as wildlife reserves. These figures comprise only 27% of the total rainforest area. An additional area of about 10000 square kilometers has been suggested for protection. The future reserve areas planned in Sierra Leone and Liberia, however, have been on a waiting list for some time and it is doubtful whether they will ever receive protected status. But whatever the case, the total protected rainforest area by far does not correspond to the importance that should be attributed to preserving biological diversity and the ecological balance in West Africa Of course, the forest reserve system is also vital, but as was mentioned earlier, many of the forest reserves suffer from illegal slash-and-burn clearing. Others have been exhausted by hunting or have even been transformed into timber plantations. High priority must therefore be given to creating additional strictly protected forest areas in West Africa.

Threats to National Parks in the Cote d'lvoire and Ghana

Uncoordinated and uncontrolled land-use almost had fatal consequences for West Africa's largest protected rainforest area, the 3300 square kilometer large Tai National Park in the southwestern Cote d'lvoire. The immigration of farmers from the Sahel region as of 1980 led to ever-increasing slash-and-burn activities in the immediate surrounding areas of the park. At the same time, wildlife came under increased hunting pressure. And at times, several hundred gold washers were present inside the park's boundaries. Timber companies also overstepped their rights in the northern areas. Aerial photographs of Tai National Park's border areas made in 1988 showed that farmers and 'timber exploiters did not encroach upon the buffer zone where it was clearly marked by a peripheral road. Clear demarcation is a simple but often crucial method of forest protection. Many forest reserves in West Africa have been sacrificed for want of clearly marked boundaries or because these were overgrown. An agreement between the Ivorian government and WWF on the management of the Tai region was signed in 1988 and obliges both parties to financially support the maintenance of Tai National Park. But it will not be easy to compensate for the earlier lack of land-use planning, nor to stabilize the situation which has resulted from destructive land-use around one of the most valuable rainforest areas in West Africa.

One of the former Chief Game and Wildlife Officers in Ghana, Emmanuel O.A. Asibey, was the first to press for protected areas representing all of the country's vegetation zones. Ghana possesses an extensive system of forest reserves but they, mainly serve the timber industry Bia National Park was established in 1974 and only two years later, it was reduced to a minimal 77 square kilometers under the pressure of several small timber enterprises. The remaining 228 square kilometers were declassified to game reserves and partially opened up to timber exploitation, In the same year, 1976, this misfortune was compensated by establishing Nini Suhien National Park and Ankasa Game Reserve in the moist southwest corner of the country. Together, they comprise 513 square kilometers. These areas suffer less pressure from the timber industry ever since the failure of the firm George Grant due to a lack of marketable timber species. In 1989, a further rainforest area in southern Ghana, the Kakum Forest Reserve, was suggested to be established as a national park.

Planning Sapo National Park

Liberia established its first strictly protected rainforest area in 1983. Sapo National Park, which covers an area of 1307 square kilometers, is still the only area of this status in the country. In 1978, Jacques Verschuren was assigned by WWF and IUCN to make recommendations for wildlife conservation and national parks based on a survey of the possibilities throughout the country. But the true responsibility for the establishment of Sapo National Park lies with

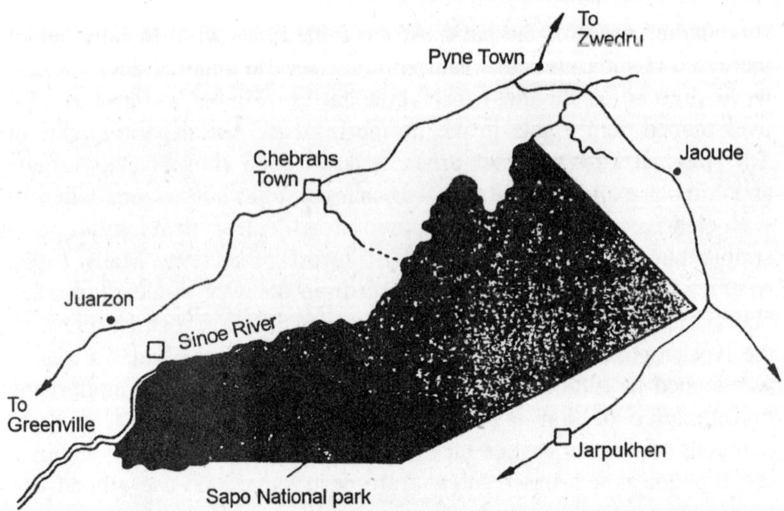

Fig. 8.1. Sapo National Park (Liberia) with centers of sustainable agricultural development.

Alexander Peal, Director of Liberian Wildlife and National Parks, Although timber concessions had already been distributed in the area and specific trees had already been marked for felling, he continued to strive patiently towards his aim, In order to secure the widest support possible for the protection and management of Sapo National Park, a seminar was held in 1985 in which representatives of the concerned ministries, the local population, WWF and IUCN participated. It was the beginning of the first integral management plan in West Africa. Besides the management of the park, the plan prescribed land-use and development in the surrounding areas. At first, local farmers suffered from fluctuating, and uncertain harvests and a lack of workers, The project now includes the development of sustainable agriculture.

Preserving the Balance in Korup

Today, the needs of the local population are taken into much greater consideration in planning new protected areas. In 1986, the establishment of Korup National Park placed the park's 1259 square kilometers within the framework of a comprehensive land-use concept. The korup area supposedly consists of the oldest rainforests in Africa. Situated at the edge of the center of endemism "West Central" in the wettest area of the continent, Korup harbors an accordingly high diversity of plant and animal species. Across the border in Nigeria,

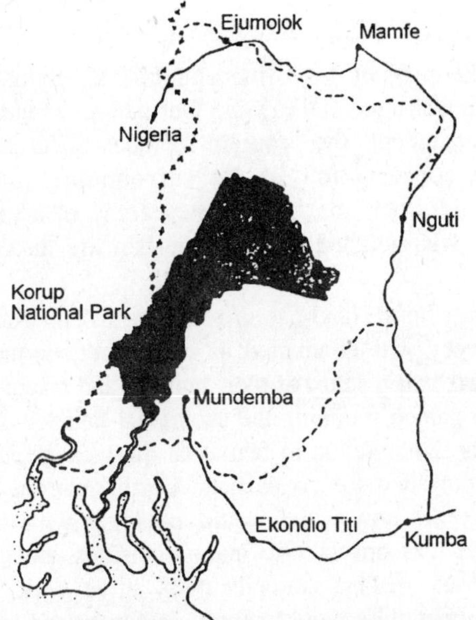

Fig. 8.2. Korup National Park with surrounding rural development zone.

the recently established Cross River National Park belongs to the same forest area. Thus, the entire southern border area between Nigeria and Cameroon has doubtlessly become a protected rainforest complex of global importance.

Hilly terrain and deep gorges have hindered the opening up of the Korup area. The population density has remained low despite patches of fertile basalt soil outside Korup National Park. Only the Pamol (Unilever) oil palm plantation had attracted people from other regions to settle in the humid southwest and eventually led to an increased demand for land. Forest villages in the Korup area can be reached only on foot along narrow paths through closed rainforest and are thus practically isolated from what we tend to call civilization They are often surrounded by small-scale farms where wonderfully mixed plots of plantains, cocoyams, cassava and vegetables are cultivated together with cocoa and coffee. There are often trees left standing within the plots. Tree species of the *Mimosaceae* family, *Albizia* spp. for example seem to be favourites with the farmers. Their feathery leaves cast partial shade on and probably fix nitrogen from the, they then pass on to the soil. Some of traditional farms in the Korup area are pefect examples of agroforestry and could serve as models for other regions. WWF has negotiated a complex and ambitious project with the government of Cameroon ensure the balance between nature conservation and land-use. The project is cofinanced by the British Overseas Development Administration (ODA) and German development Besides national park management, the program includes different aspects of natural resource conservation in the surrounding ranging from agroforestry and livestock to hunting. Research, education and the development of a well-adapted form of tourism are also included in the project.

In order to plan future land-use in rounding Korup National Park, a soil fertility survey was conducted as well as economic survey of the forest inhabitants and a study of their hunting and trapping methods. The knowledge so gained retaining the ecological balance of the Korup area and improving the situation in favour of the local population. And just this is of importance for roads near Korup National Park have been planned for years now which could endanger what has thus far been achieved. But it is not easy to make decisions, nor to put them into effect. The local village councils must agree with whatever is decided and sometimes they would simply prefer a road to finally put them in touch with the rest of the world.

Lessons for the Future

Land-use plans are only useful if they are feasible and supported by the local population. In this, context, the experience gained with the establishment of forest reserves earlier this century should be a lesson for the future. In the wake, of today's forest loss, many West African governments are considering careful land-use in regions surrounding the remaining forest areas. And at least farsighted politicians and, administrators are willing to work toward integral forest conservation. These officials have to be supported with moral and, even more importantly, material aid, in order for them to put their costly plans into action. Otherwise, industrialized countries will miss their last chance to save West African forests.

Development aid agencies are becoming increasingly interested in forest conservation projects which take the needs of forest inhabitants into account. But Africa is only beginning to see the truly sustainable use of rainforest today. Successful projects are urgently needed to serve as models for governments and investors. In addition, forest policy must refrain from the uncoordinated, large scale opening up of still more rainforest. The countries of Central Africa with their vast expanses of forest would by all means do, well to learn from the past decades of West African history.

9

FOREST PESTS

Since 1962, with the publication of *Silent Spring* by Rachel Carson highlighting the adverse effects of pesticides on birds, there has been renewed interest in biological pest control. Biological control is based on two ecological principles: that one organism can be used to control another organism; and that some of the organisms that can be used to control other organisms have a limited host range. Since this approach is close to nature's own way of controlling an organism, it has found widespread acceptance with the public.

Biological control is perceived, for good reasons, as being a highly selective and effective method that is long lasting. At the same time, some organisms have been used for practical or commercial purposes such as using yeast to make bread or beer since ancient times, and this use has been defined as 'biotechnology'. Beginning in the 1970s, biotechnology has taken a dramatically different turn. With the knowledge gained in recombinant DNA technology, it became possible to alter the genetic make-up of an organism by inserting foreign genes, deleting genes, or modifying the functions of genes.

The integration of traditional biological control with modern biotechnology has resulted in some exciting new developments, some of which will be outlined in this chapter. Modern biotechnology is an immensely powerful tool and has found applications in almost all walks of life, promising improved agricultural and forest products, health care, and crime detection, to mention a few. Unfortunately, research in biotechnology has become controversial, mainly because it is difficult for the general public to comprehend this field since it is mired in complex jargon. It has been cited as being a threat to environmental safety, violating natural laws, and religious zealots have even labelled it as trivializing the meaning of life! In this chapter we will examine some of the recent advances in pest control using biotechnology and attempt to allay some of the concerns of the public

Pests of Forests

Broadly speaking, there are three major groups of forest pests: pathogenic microorganisms competing vegetation, and insect pests. Historically many of these pests of economic importance have been managed by using chemical control agents such as chemical fungicides, herbicides and pesticides. While biological control methods have been attempted, there was no sustained interest until recently when some of the non-target effects of the chemical pesticides became apparent. After a cursory examination of the biological control of competing weeds and pathogenic organisms, much of the discussion will be focused on the control of insect pests.

Vegetation Management

Phytophagous biological control organisms have been tested as weed control agents for many decades; the organisms used have been either insects or microorganisms, including fungi, nematodes or mites. Testing for host specificity has been a major hurdle. In Australia, the common heliotrope *Heliotropium europaeum* was successfully controlled with the fungus *Uromyces heliotropii* and tests were conducted on 96 plants of the region for microscopic and macroscopic effects. Rather than continuing to depend on chemical herbicides, North American forestry is rapidly changing to 'ecosystem management', which is an effort to combine ecological principles, sustainable forests, and land stewardship ethics.

Since chemical herbicides are generally inexpensive and effective there has been a reluctance to invest in research on the use of alternative herbicides. Public belief that forested landscapes are among the only remaining unspoiled ecosystems has more recently lead to a search for other types of weed control agents including mycoherbicides. Some mycoherbicides have been successfully developed in recent years. *Chondrostereum purpureum* is common pathogen that invades the xylem vessels through fresh wounds and causes silverleaf disease in various hardwood shrubs and trees. Although *C. purpureum* is not host specific, it prefers broadleaf trees.

The fungus lives in living tissues or in trees that have been dead for less than 2 years. The airborne basidiospores infect tree wounds or stumps. Biotechnological approaches have been used to engineer herbicide resistance genes into the trees to protect them against herbicides that are sprayed to control competing vegetation. A sulphonyl urea herbicide, chlorosulfuron, was shown to inhibit cell division. Biochemical studies showed that it inhibits acetolactate synthase (ALS), which is required for the synthesis of isoleucine, leucine and valine.

Using the ALS gene as a probe, the ALS mutant gene from herbicide resistant plants was isolated. The resistance was conferred by selective amino acid substitution. When such a resistant ALS gene was cloned into the tobacco plant, the transgenic tobacco plant was found to be resistant gene that was transferred into the crop plant. In the case of phosphoinothricin, a gene that produce a detoxifying enzyme was found to be better than a resistant glutamine synthase gene. In the case of atrazine and bromoxynil, the herbicide binding protein or Q_β protein (32-kDa membrane protein in the chloroplast) was involved in the resistance mechanism. The resistant variety of the Q_β protein has some amino acid substitutions.

Plant Pathogens

Many species of bacteria, fungi and nematodes are pathogenic to plants in general. The molecular mode of action of phytopathogenic bacteria is being actively studied and the results of these investigations may pave the way for developing resistant varieties by recombinant DNA technology. *Erwinia*, *Pseudomonas* and *Xanthomonas* have genes that code for cellulase (endo-β-1,4-glucanase) but their role in pathogenicity has not been established. Proteases, production and export of extracellular enzymes, polysaccharides, plant growth substances, toxins and unknown products have all been implicated in pathogenicity and genes for many of them have been cloned. *Agrobacterium tumefaciens*, the soil bacterium that causes crown gall in dicotyledonous plants, has been by far the most studied and is extensively used for gene transfer. During the disease process, a segment of this bacterium's DNA (T-DNA) is transferred to the host plant and becomes integrated into the plant genome.

The T-DNA originates from a 200-kb plasmid and foreign genes can be inserted into this DNA for transfer into the host plant. The molecular biology of several fungal pathogens of plants has been well studied. A resistance gene may be cloned by a shot-gun method and thereby inserted into a host plant. The large genome size and, consequently, the size of the cloned DNA fragments however requires the screening of more than 10,000 transformed plants, which is an enormous task. Another method is the insertion of a transposable DNA sequence (transposable element) which in essence functions as a tag and can carry a resistance gene.

Nematodes

Resistance of phytopathogenic nematodes has been reported and has been traced to an H_1 resistance gene in certain cultivars of potato. While at this time this resistance gene has been shown for the potato cyst nematode, *Globodera rostochiensis*, similar studies can be extended to others that are pathogenic to trees such as the pinewood nematode. The excellent genetic information available for the free-living nematode *Caenorhabditis elegans* will serve as an elegant backdrop to characterizing the biochemical mechanism of resistance in parasitic forms such as the potato cyst nematode. Since the H_1 resistance gene has been shown to follow a Mendelian pattern, it lends itself to genetic manipulation.

Phytoalexins

Phytoalexins are low molecular weight, antimicrobial agents that are synthesized by plants in response to a pathogen or stress factor. Many compounds from the invading fungus or bacterium, such as oligoglucans, ethylene, chitosan oligomers, and polypeptides serve as elicitors for phytoalexin production in the host. The accumulation of phytoalexins at the infection site inhibits the growth of the fungus or bacterium and serves as a defence mechanism. The ability to produce phytoalexins confers a degree of resistance against the pathogen. Work that will lead to gene expression for phytoalexin accumulation and disease control is underway.

Viral Pathogens of Plants

Viral pathogens of plants are well known and transmission of many of them by sucking insects such as aphids and leafhoppers has been extensively studied. One of the novel ways of providing protection against the pathogenic viruses is similar to vaccination. The coat protein of the virus protects the host plant from viral infection. The exact mechanism for this protection has not yet been elucidated. For example, the cucumber mosaic virus (CMV) infects 775 species of plants from 85 different families and causes severe viral disease. The coat protein (CP) gene of this virus was inserted into tobacco leaf discs using *Agrobacterium tumefaciens*. Of the 22 transformant lines, 15 showed resistance to CMV. Such a technology may be extended to trees for protection against viral pathogens.

Insect Pests

Chemical and biological control of insect pest using parasites and predators dates back to the 1950s and has been extensively reviewed. Control of forest insect pests with the introduction of various egg parasites (*Trichogramma* sp.), external parasites (Tachinids), and internal parasites (Ichneumonids, Chalcids, etc.), has been attempted with various degrees of sources, but in general, the results have not been spectacular. However, success stories of classical examples such as the introduction of the Australian vedalia lady beetle in 1899 to control the cottony-cushion scale in Californian orange groves reinforces the need to continue this approach.

One of the areas that fact needs particular attention, especially in forestry, is the environmental impact of classical biological control agents. In the words of Howarth, 'Absence of evidence is not evidence of absence'. Microbial pathogens such as fungi, bacteria and viruses that cause diseases in insects have been tested extensively as biological control agents. Among the fungi, more than 50 genera contain species that are pathogenic to insects and are candidates for biological control. They have widely varied life cycles and host range and are transmitted primarily through either spores (sexual forms) or conidia (asexual forms). When a spore or a conidium lands on a susceptible host, it adheres to the cuticle, germinates and digests its entry into the insect by means of its germ tube.

The fungal mycelia soon overpower and mummify the insect. The conidia or spores are released and the life history starts all over again. *Beauveria bassiana* is an imperfect fungus that infects over 100 insect species from many orders; it has been used extensively in Russia and China for insect control. Identification of the various isolates (pathotypes) that are morphologically similar is being done with molecular techniques to resolve taxonomic problems. In addition, entomophthoraceous fungi have been reported from many insects, and many of them have been found to have a narrow host range.

Recently, recombinant DNA technology copies of a gene encoding a regulated cuticle-degrading protease from an entomopathogenic fungus, *Metarhizium anisopliae*, were inserted into the same fungus so that the enzyme was constitutively overproduced in *Manduca sexta* infected with the recombinant fungus. The insects ate less, died quickly and the cadavers were black due to melanization. The resulting cadavers were poor substrates for sporulation ensuring minimal persistence of the genetically altered fungus.

Phylum Protozoa is now considered a sub-Kingdom, and the class Microspora has now been elevated to a phylum and includes the entomopathogenic microsporidia; this is important from an insect control stand point. *Nosema locustae* has been registered for controlling grasshoppers. Microsporidia are obligate intracellular pathogens and the larvae are infected when they ingest the spores. The spore extrudes a hollow polar filament through which the sporoplasm is injected into the midgut cells where they multiply vegetatively. Many forest insect pests have microsporidia and some of them have been shown to be transovarially transmitted. They are quite infective but lack the virulence required to compete with other control measures. Their large genome has been an impediment to developing recombinant DNA techniques to increase their virulence by inserting foreign genes.

The bacterium *Bacillus thuringiensis* (Bt) is the most widely used pathogen for insect control in North America. Bt is a common organism that is found in the soil, insects, frass, grain dust and leaves. It was first isolated in 1902 as the causative agent for 'Sotto disease' in silkworm in Japan. It is a Gram-positive, aerobic, spore-forming bacterium, which produces a characteristic parasporal crystal that contains the insecticidal toxins.

The insecticidal parasporal proteins are activated by the midgut proteases and the activated toxin binds to a specific receptor on midgut cells of susceptible insects. The lysis and destruction of the midgut cells eventually leads to the death of the host. The genes that encode the insecticidal proteins are typically located on large transmissible plasmids that determine the host specificity of the isolate or serotype. Bt has more than 50 subspecies and produces a variety of crystal (Cry) proteins. These Cry proteins are classified according to their activity spectrum and molecular mass. Cry I and Cry II are active against lepidoptera and are 135 and 65 kDa, respectively, in size. The Cry III protein of 65 kDa size is active against coleoptera such as the Colorado potato beetle, *Leptinostarsa decemlineata*. Cry IV proteins range in size from 65 to 135 kDa and are effective against mosquitoes and blackflies. The presence of these toxin genes in the plasmids made it relatively easy to isolate and purify them, and in the 1980s most of them were cloned. These toxins have been engineered into insect pathogenic viruses, which is described later, as well as into plants and trees.

Viral Pathogens of Insects

Insect viruses causing epizootics have been recognized for nearly a century and one of the earliest such occurrences described in North

America was in 1913 by Glaser and Chapman on the wilt disease of the gypsy moth, *Lymantria dispar*, caused by a nuclear polyhedrosis virus (NPV). Perhaps one of the most dramatic controls ever reported was the control of the European pine sawfly, *Neodiprion sertifer*, in Ontario, Canada by an NPV isolated from dead larvae sent from Sweden. Various types of viruses are pathogenic to insects but one group, the Baculoviridae, is uniquely pathogenic only to insects. By far the largest group of insects affected by viruses is the Lepidoptera.

Baculoviruses and cytoplasmic polyhedrosis viruses form the two major groups of viruses that are infectious to insects. The host range of entomopathogenic viruses varies widely but generally it is quite narrow. Viruses such as the multicapsid nuclear polyhedrosis virus of the beet army worm, *Spodoptera exigua* (*Se*MNPV) are species specific whereas the virus of the alfalfa looper, *Autographa californica* (*Ac*MNPV) infects and replicates in at least 33 lepidopterous species from seven different families. However, most of the viruses have an intermediate hot range and are best described as genus specific, as is illustrated by *Hz*MNPV that infects several species of *Heliothis*, including *H. zea*. Many baculoviruses have been developed commercially or used in a practical manner for controlling specific pest.

The effective dosage is generally established in terms of the number of polyhedra or occlusion bodies (OB) required to affect 50 per cent of the treat insects (LD_{50}). Since the time taken to have an effect has an important bearing on the ability to protect the crop from damage, the LT_{50} or time taken to kill 50 per cent of the treated insects, usually in days, is also studied. Larvae typically become infected by NPV when they ingest the polyhedra on the foliage. The polyhedra dissolve in the midgut and the virions are released. These virions fuse with the microvilli of the midgut cell and go through the cytoplasm into the nucleus. The DNA unravels and the virions begin to replicate and give rise to an intranuclear region referred to as the virogenic stroma. Envelope formation and polyhedron synthesis results in the production of occlusion bodies. Some of the non-occluded virions (NOV) come of the cell as budded viruses that infect more cells.

Ultimately, when the cells break down and the entire insect liquefies, the occlusion bodies are released to start the cycle once again. The degree of susceptibility varies from species to species. Those insects showing low susceptibility will permit limited infection to only midgut cells, whereas others that are highly susceptible show infection to virtually all tissues. What confers host specificity has largely been unknown until recently when it was shown that specific

Table 9.1. Baculoviruses of commercial/practical use

Pest	*Virus*	*Status*
Cotton bollworm, Tobacco budworm, Corn earworm, Tomato fruitworm (*Heliothis* species): *Heliocoverpa* (=*Heliothis*) *zea*, *Heliothis virescens*, *H. armigera*, *H. paradoxa*, *H. peltigera*, *H. phloxiphaga*, *H. punctigera*	Single nucleocapsid NPV Registered as Viron H®, Bitrol-VH2, Eclar™	>1,000,000 ha treated in USA Dosage: 6×10^{11} occlusion bodies (OB) per hectare to 1.2×10^{12} OB/ha. Honeybees used to disseminate virus
Alfalfa looper, *Autographa californica*. Insects 43 species in 11 families. Used on Cabbage looper (*Trichoplusia ni*), Beet armyworm (*Spodoptera exigua*), Diamondback moth (*Plutella xylostella*), Douglas-fir tussock moth (*Orgyia pseudotsugata*)	Multiple nucleocapdis NPV. Commercial development as Guasano®, VPN 80	Being extensively tested. Dose: 2.5×10^{11} OH/ha to 2.5×10^{12} OB/ha
Velvetebean caterpillar, *Anticarsia gemmatalis*	At least five companies are producing commercial products of this MNPV	1 to 4×10^{6} ha annually. Dosage: 10^{4} OB/ha
Cassava caterpillar, *Erinnyis ello* in in Brazil. Cabbage looper, *Trichoplusia ni*	Granulosis virus (GV). Farmer level SNPV, MNPV, and GV. The MNPV is commercially produced as Bitrol VTN and Viron T	About 5×10^{3} ha annually
Celery looper, *Anagrapha falcifera*; also effective on *H. virescens*, *H. zea*, *T. ni*, European corn borer (*Ostrinia nubilalis*), *P. xylostella*	Patented by USDA and being commercializd by Sandoz	Kills host faster and at a lower doses than most other baculoviruses

Pest	*Virus*	*Status*
Grape leaf skeletonizer, *Harrisina brillians*	GV	Early stage of development but very promising. Dosage: 5.8 g/ha
Beet armyworm, *Spodoptera exigua*	SeNPV; Commercialized as Spod-X®	Effective on a large number of lepidoptera infesting vegetable crops. Dosage: 2.5×10^{11} OB/ha to 1.25×10^{12} OB/ha
Cotton leafworm, *Spodoptera littoralis*	NPV; Spodopterin®	Extensively tested in Egypt, 5×10^{12} OB/ha
Fall armyworm, *Spodoptera frugiperda*	NPV; produced by National Soybean Research Central in Brazil	>5000 ha in Brazil
Soybean semilooper, *Trichoplusia orichalcea*. Also controls *Chrysodeixis chalicites*	NPV in Zimbabwe, domestically produced	$>15 \times 10^6$ ha treated
Cabbage moth, *Mamestra brassicae* Effective on *H. zea*, *H. virescens*, *H. armigera*, *S. exigua*, and *Diperopsis watersi*	NPV; produced as Mamestrin®	Widely used in France
Coddling moth, *Cydia pomonella*	GV, produced as UCB 87; San 406; Decyde™, Carpovirusine®	Tested in Californian fruit orchards. Dosage: 2.5×10^{13} GV capsules/ha. Wide interest in commercialization of this GV
Indian meal moth, *Plodia interpunctella*	GV, patented by USDA	200 g of freeze dried product will treat 16 tons of dried fruit and nuts
Coconut rhinoceros beetle, *Oryctes rhinoceros* also controls	Non-occluded baculovirus discovered in Malaysia; infects adults as well	Palm industry in the countries of the of the South Pacific and Indian Ocean regions

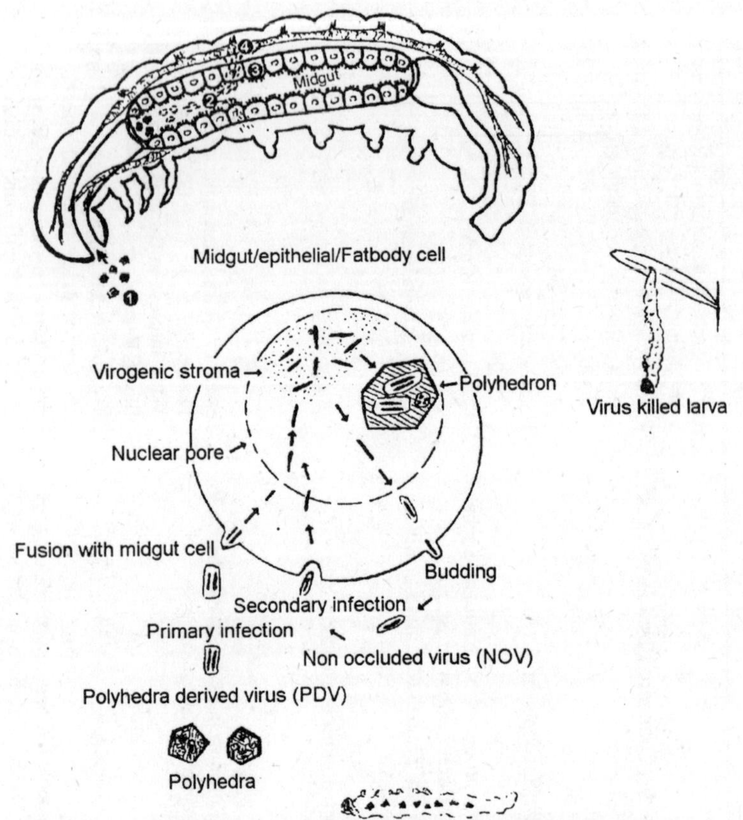

Fig. 9.1. Life cycle of a nuclear polyhedrosis virus.

regions of the DNA are necessary. Maeda et al. (1993) showed that a recombinant NPV containing portions of *Ac*MNPV and portions of *Bombyx mori* NPV (*Bm*MNPV) can infect *Bombyx mori* cells, but *Ac*MNPV is not infectious to these cells. Host shifts have been accomplished within closely related hosts and similar viruses. When cabbage looper larvae were fed large doses of the tussock moth NPV over 12 generations, it was possible to obtain a virus that would infect the cabbage looper. Virus control of insect pests is attractive because it is lasting, highly selective and effective. However, to compete against chemical control agents, they have to act fast, be more virulent and cheaper to produce.

The advent of recombinant DNA technology has made it possible to make the virus more virulent and fast acting. Since baculoviruses are propagated in eukaryotic cell lines (i.e., from insects), the expression of any foreign eukaryotic genes inserted into the baculovirus follows the eukaryotic pathway. All the post-translational processing such as phosphorylation, glycosylation, amidation, protein folding, etc., take place ensuring that the product is functional. It is for this reason that *Ac*MNPV has become the system of choice for expressing many eukaryotic genes that produce pharmaceutical products such as interferon.

Modified NPVs for Insect Control

Various types of genes from different sources have been inserted into the NPV to improve its virulence. The market potential for genetically modified NPVs as biocontrol agents is immense and only the surface has been scratched so far. It is now theoretically possible to develop transgenic viruses that are not only host specific but also as effective as conventional control agents.

Structure, Biology, and Ecology

Before embarking on genetic modification of the virus, it is essential that the biology of the virus is well understood. Fortunately, there is a fund of information in this area. The spruce budworm virus, *Choristoneura fumiferana*, multicapsid nuclear polyhedrosis virus (*Cf*MNPV) is one of the forestry-related viruses that has been well studied. The infectivity, host-range, LD_{50}, LT_{50} and ecology have to be studied to provide the base-line information for assaying the activities of the transformed viruses.

Biochemical Characterization

NPVs from different insects have been characterized to various degrees. The relatively small size of the circular dsDNA has made it possible to elucidate the structure. The genomes of *Ac*MNPV and *Bm*MNPV have been completely sequenced. The *Cf*MNPV has been mapped and some of the regions have been sequenced. Subsequently, using homologous probes, several genes such as polyhedrin, egt, and p10 have been identified and in many instances their functions have been described. The secret of success for genetic improvement of a virus depends *inter alia* on the availability of a cell line that grows well and permits rapid replication with no loss of fidelity but with retention of infectivity.

Development of Cell Lines

So far 26 continuous cell lines (1 embryonic, 4 midgut, 11 neonate larval and 10 ovarian) have been developed from the spruce budworm tissues. Most of the cell lines were found to be highly susceptible to

A

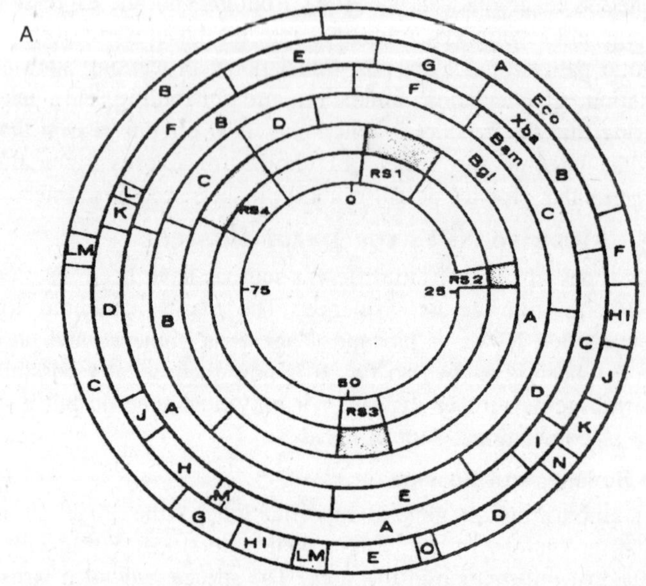

B

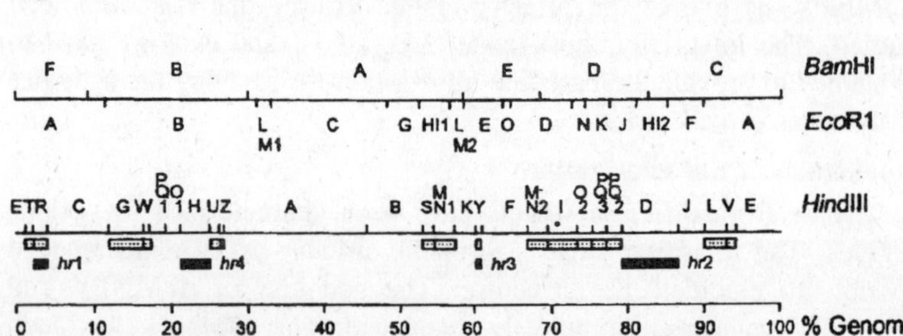

Fig. 9.2. Physical map of CfMNPV genome. A—Circular map with the zero position at the junction of BamH1 fragments B and F. B—Linearized version with the BamH1 fragment F to the left.

the virus and were used as experimental material for work on *Cf*MNPV. A plaque assay was developed using IPRI-CF-124T cells for purification of *Cf*MNPV. Initially, the cell lines were developed in Grace's insect tissue culture medium supplemented with 10-15 per cent fetal bovine serum (FBS). Since FBS is expensive, a search for a substitute especially for mass-culturing of cells for virus production resulted in identification of a cell line, CF-203, which grows well in Insect-Xpress medium supplemented with as low as 0.5 per cent serum and permits *Cf*MNPV replication.

Modification of Baculoviruses

The strategy is to introduce a foreign gene into the viral genome so that the resulting transgenic virus is more virulent and fast-acting than the wild type. Once a candidate foreign gene has been identified, it is inserted into a vector for transferring into the virus. This vector has to be constructed so that it efficiently transfers the foreign gene into the virus. The virus and the vector or recombinant plasmid are added together, or cotransfected, into permissive cells that allow homologous recombination resulting in the production of a few recombinant viruses. These recombinant viruses are then purified from the wild-type virus using a technique called plaque purification. The transgenic viruses can be propagated in the host insect larvae or permissive cell lines.

Promoter Selection

One of the primary requirements for producing a successfully modified virus for pest control is the incorporation of the proper promoter that will direct the expression of the foreign gene at the appropriate time and place. For instance, a fast-acting neurotoxin has to be secreted quickly into haemolymph close to the nervous system. Several late gene viral promoters such as polyhedrin and p10 have been used successfully. Large quantities of mRNA for genes expressed under these very late gene promoters will be produced, beginning 24 hours after infection. Polyhedrin promoter is the most commonly used promoter.

The advantage of using polyhedrin promoter in a virus where the polyhedrin gene has been removed is that the modified virus is produced without the polyhedrin in a non-occluded form and therefore does not survive in the environment beyond a generation of the host insect. This feature is attractive to both environ-mentalists because it does not persist in the environment, and to commercial producers because the virus has to be produced every year for repeated application. The disadvantage of using such a system is that there is no reliable quantitative bioassay to assess the effectiveness of non-occluded virions. Currently, the assay is performed by either injecting the modified virus, which can be time consuming, or by feeding the preoccluded virus which is difficult to quantify.

Many researchers have been persuaded to use the p10 promoter for the expression of foreign genes because of the difficulties encountered with non-occluded virus particles. The main disadvantage with the p10 promoter is that the modified virus will produce polyhedrin occlusion bodies that can persist and survive in the soil for a long time. Other promoters such as the combination of early and late promoters of baculoviruses and constitutive promoters such as the insect actin promoter that are active all the time have been tried, but none have enjoyed the success of the polyhedrin promoter.

Candidate Foreign Genes

The candidate genes that have been inserted into baculoviruses for improving their control potential; the most promising ones are those showing either the deletion of ecdysone glucosyl transferase (egt$^-$), or the expression of scorpion toxin, mite toxin or juvenile hormone esterase (JHE). The egt$^-$ virus has been one of the leading candidates for early registration because of its acceptance by the public. There is no foreign gene inserted into the egt$^-$ virus and by deleting this gene from the virus the moulting of the host larva is no longer prolonged, which results in less feeding damage. Other modified viruses such as the one expressing the scorpion toxin and the enzyme, JHE, are at various stages of evaluation. There are various developmental genes that have a regulatory function and may be tested in the future as candidates for insertion.

Future Considerations

Producing a genetically altered virus is at the early stages of development at present and there are several hurdles to be crossed before the modified virus can be successfully applied in the field. Some of the major problems that need to be solved are mass production, stability of the modified virus in the field, effect of modifications on the host range, effect of modified virus on non-target organisms, and formulation of the modified virus for field application. Mass producing a fast-acting transgenic virus in an insect host will be difficult because the virus will kill the insects before enough virus is produced. Strategies such as propagating the virus in cell cultures and using an inducible promoter than can be turned on at will by adding the inducers at the appropriate time will have to be employed. Mass production of recombinant viruses in SF-21 cells using large-scale fermenters appears promising. Most of the tests conducted on the modified viruses so far have indicated that the modifications have not affected the host range of the transformed virus and most of the non-target beneficial insects are not affected.

The occlusion bodies (OB) of baculoviruses are stable in the environment, especially in the soil, for several years. To circumvent this problem, Wood and his colleagues at the Boyce Thomson Research

Table 9.2. Modified baculoviruses for insect control

Gene inserted/deleted	*Effect*
Ecdysone glycosyl (transferase(egt)	Insects infected with egt-deletion consumed 50% less food than the ones infected with wild-type virus. Insects infected with egt-deletion mutant died sooner than those infected with wild-type virus
Diuretic hormone (DH)	Infection of *Bombyx mori* nuclear polyhedrosis virus expressing DH resulted in a decrease in haemolymph volume and the infected insects died one day earlier than controls
Juvenile hormone esterase	The recombinant *Ac*MNPV expressing JHE caused reduced feeding in neonate *T. ni* larvae. The feeding inhibition was not observed in later larval instars
Bacillus thuringiensis (Bt) delta toxin	No significant improvement in LD_{50} compared with wild-type virus
Androctonus australis insect specific neurotoxin (Aait)	*T. ni* larvae infected with recombinant virus expressing Aait, consumed 50% less diet and the LD_{50} was reduced slightly; there was a 25 decrease in survival time compared with controls.
Pyemotes tritici (mite) toxin (MT)	*Ac*MNPV expressing MT caused significant reduction in survival time, feeding and weight gain in *T. ni*

Institute have been working on a procedure of using a polyhedrin minus (null) preoccluded virus preparation for field application. They have shown that such a polyhedrin null virus disappears rapidly from the soil. A successful modified baculovirus is one that can outcompete a conventional chemical insecticide in its ability to kill faster and be produced at a competitive cost.

Some of the promising new strategies include using multiple genes for not only adversely interfering with feeding bout also derailing the normal development of the insect pest. The receptors and transcription factors that are involved in insect development will become one of the main target areas that will be used for adversely interfering with the normal developmental process. Integrating the rapidly developing field of biotechnology with insect molecular biology, endocrinology, physiology, ecology, cell culture and virology should make the dream of making an ideal recombinant virus a reality in the not too distant future.

Alternative Ways of Improving Baculoviruses

The traditional approach for improving baculoviruses is to modify the virus by either deleting an existing gene or adding a foreign gene into the viral genome. However, there are alternative ways of improving the baculoviruses as pest control agents. Selecting the more effective strains from the mixture of strains that occur in nature and optimizing the combinations of the more active strains is one method. Another approach is to alter the host range of an effective virus such as *Ac*MNPV so that it can infect other important pests such as the gypsy moth and the spruce budworm.

Strain Selection and Mixed Strains

The baculovirus isolates from nature contain a mixture of genetically heterogeneous populations. For example *Cf*MNPV field isolates contain at least two different viruses, and one of the two is more infectious to spruce budworm larvae. Two variants were isolated from field-collected *Pf*MNPV. A strain of codling moth granulosis virus that was 5.6 times more resistant to artificial ultraviolet light in the laboratory and survived twice as long as the wild type in the field was selected for development. Replication of *Ac*MNPV in the presence of 2-aminopurine resulted in a strain that had increased virulence.

Host Range Alteration

*Ac*MNPV is one of the most virulent and well-characterized baculoviruses. Unfortunately though, *Ac*MNPV does not infect some of the important forest pests such as the gypsy moth and the spruce budworm. When gypsy moth, *Lymantria dispar*, IPLB-LD652Y (Ld652Y) cells were infected with *Ac*MNPV alone the infection was aborted but, if they were coinfected with *Ld*MNPV, the *Ac*MNPV infection was enhanced. An *Ld*MNPV gene host range factor 1 (*hrf*-1) that enabled *Ac*MNPV to infect Ld652Y cells was isolated, cloned and inserted into *Ac*MNPV. Modified *Ac*MNPV expressing the *hrf*-1 gene can successfully infect *L. dispar* CF-203 cells inoculated with *Ac*MNPV showed a DNA ladder and morphological changes such as plasma membrane granulation, blebbing and nuclear fragmentation, which are characteristic of apoptosis.

The mRNA for the apoptosis suppressor gene p35 was detected 9 hours later in *Ac*MNPV-inoculated CF-203 cells than in SF-21 cells. Only a trace amount of mRNA for the *Ac*MNPV-inhibitor of apoptosis homologue (*Ac-iap*) gene and no mRNA for the late genes, *Ac*MNPV-polyhedrin (*Ac-polh*) and *Ac*MNPV-p10 (*Ac-p10*), were detected in *Ac*MNPV-inoculated CD-203 cells.

Inoculation of CF-203 cells with *Cf*MNPV at least 12 hours prior to inoculation with *Ac*MNPV prevented apoptosis-like cell death, and mRNAs for *Ac-iap*, *Ac-polh* and *Ac-p10* gene were expressed, resulting in successful virus replication and OB production. Work is currently in progress to identify the gene(s) in *Cf*MNPV that provide this protection and enhances *Ac*MNPV replication in CF-203 cells. Once this gene is identified, it should then be possible to engineer a recombinant *Ac*MNPV bearing this *Cf*MNPV gene similar to the recombinant *Ac*MNPV bearing the *Lymantria dispar* MNPV host range gene *hrf*-1. Such a recombinant *Ac*MNPV would most likely infect the spruce budworm and also will probably be more virulent than the wild-type *Cf*MNPV for this forest pest.

Other Applications of Biotechnology for Pest Control

The recombinant DNA technology used for altering the effectiveness of the virus can also be used on the insect. Incorporation of the genes into the host insect and its parasites and predators can be used in control strategies.

Transgenic Insects

Production of transgenic insects carrying an insecticidal gene under the control of an inducible promoter has been under investigation for several years. In this strategy the pest insect is transformed by incorporating a gene that is expressed under the control of an inducible promoter. The transformed insects are mass-produced and field-released to mate with natural populations. After a few generations when the population of the pest insect reaches damaging levels the inducers are sprayed.

The insecticidal gene is thereby induced resulting in the death of the pest species. This strategy is similar to the sterile male release technique and can be used in an integrated pest management strategy. Due to the lack of a good procedure for germ line transformation for pest insects this approach has not been very successful so far. With the recent cloning and characterization of transposons from several key pest insects it may be possible to produce transgenic insects in the near future.

Improvement of Parasites and Parasitoids

There have also been attempts to produce transgenic parasites and predators expressing genes that can enhance the survival of these organisms in the environment. Parasites and predators expressing insecticide resistance genes will work better in the integrated pest management strategies since they will survive insecticide treatments. This approach has had limited success due to the lack of availability of transformation protocols that can be used for producing transgenic parasites and predators. With the recent discovery of transposons in many insects this situation will soon change.

NATURAL ENEMIES OF FOREST

Greenhouse whitefly (*Trialeurodes vaporariorum*). 249 genera are known to be host plants of the greenhouse whitefly, *Trialeurodes vaporariorum*. Among the greenhouse host plants are cucumber, aubergine, paprika, tomato and many ornamentals. Among the latter are *Azalea*, *Calceolaria*, *Fuchsia*, *Pelargonium*, *poinsettia* and *Verbena*. The adult whitefly is attracted to yellow colours. Before alighting, the whitefly is unable to detect whether or not a plant is a suitable most. The females lay their eggs on the undersides of young apical leaves, often in circles on hairless hosts. The eggs hatch after 8 days (21-24°C) while further development consists of 1st. 2nd. 3rd and 4th instars and pupae whose development, at these temperatures, occupies, 6, 2, 3, 4 and 5 days respectively.

The newly hatched larvae ('crawlers' —1st instar) are initially mobile. They move for a few hours only and then settle. After inserting their mouthparts into leaf tissue, they lose their functional legs and remain static throughout the remainder of their development. After the third moult, there are three additional phases of development.

Table 9.3. Duration of Life Cycle in Trialeurodes vaporariorum and Encarsia formosa from egg to adult (in days) at different temperatures

Species	12°C	15°C	18°C	21°C	24°C	27°C	30°C	*Host Plant*
T. vaporariorum	103-123	65-72	37-42	25-30	22-25	—	18-21	Bean
E. formosa	—	—	29-39	25-35	16-24	13-17	—	Tomato

During the first (4th instar), the larve become flattened and in the second, this instar becomes thickened with lateral spines. The red eyes of the developing adult become visible although the shape of the pupa in third stage is same as in the second stage. Temperature governs the rate of growth so that the total developmental time varies from 18-123. Morality in the different developmental stages varies with type of host plant.

Table 9.4 The effect of the host plant on longevity in adult females of Trialeurodex vaporariorum, their egg production and mortality in the different developmental stages

	Aubergine	*Cucumber*	*Tomato*	*Sweeet pepper*
Longevity (days)	40.4	16.7	8.6	3.2
Total number of eggs	416	123	8.2	0.9
Mortality (%)	9.2	7.4	21.7	92.5

Through a slit in the dorsum of the pupa the adults emerge. The females commence oviposition after 1-2 days. Unmated females lay haploid eggs which produce males. Mated females produce both diploid female-producing eggs and haploid eggs. The longevity of the adult females depends on the host plant. Those host plants encouraging greatest longevity are also the most suitable for oviposition. With increasing density of whiteflies per leaf, egg production increases : it is also greater at high (26°C) rather than moderate temperatures (21°C) but the highest total egg production occurs at around 21°C. A humidity of 75-80% RH is optimal for both fecundity and longevity of the adults. The greenhouse whitefly has no stage specially adapted for hibernation. Survival is-dependent on suitable host plants throughout the year but, at low temperatures, the plant must have winter-hardy leaves. Eggs are the stage most tolerant to low tempetures and can survive up to 15 days at –3°C only 5 days at –6°C.

Parasitie Encarsia formosa

The larval stage, a pupa and the adult constitutes the developmental stages of this parasite. With the exception of the adult, development takes place within its host- the larvae and pupa of greenhouse whitefly. It volatile compound emanating from the whitefly honeydew attracts the adult parasite to its host can be detected over several metres. It usually lands to search for hosts only on whitefly-infested plants. and seldom on uninfested plants. The adult feeds both on whitefly honeydew and on the body fluids through a hole made in the whitefly larvae with the ovipositor. Males are rare and result from oviposition in parasitized scales (hyperparasitism) which may occur when the density of parasites is high. Cool temperatures also appear to increase production of males. Normally the sex ratio is 1 : 1 but twice as many as females may develop. The unparasitised and parasitized hosts can be distinguished by the wasp.

The parasitised is avoided for oviposition unless parasite density is high. Oviposition can take place in all four larval instars and the pupa but the parasites prefer the 3rd and 4th instars. The least mortality occurs in these stages and consequently these instars provide the best chances of successful parasitism. Oviposition in the 1st and 2nd whitefly instars results in high mortality of the parasite; consequently many of the young scales shrivel and die. Close examination will reveal multiple oviposition punctures. This mortality may, in some circum- stances, exceed that of parasitism. The females have a longevity of about 27, 21, 15, 8 and 3 days at temperatures of 18°, 21°, 24°, 27° and 30°C respectively under laboratory conditions. In a greenhouse experiment, the number of introduced parasites active on the plant was reduced to half in 4 days at 18°C and at 24-27°C a longevity of only 2-3 days was observed.

Low light intensity also reduces the longevity of adult parasites. When sugle plants are exposed in the laboratory the mean egg production is commonly reported to vary from 50-100 eggs per female, but as many as 350 eggs have been recorded from single females when single plants are exposed in the laboratory. Between 18 and 27°C there are only small differences in parasite fecundity. Most parasitization is recorded at humidities of 50-80% RH. Low light intensities seem to have a strong influence on fecundity. Very few eggs were laid below 4200 lux but at 7300 lux the parasites became fully reproductive in laboratory experiments at GCRI. Experience in UK greenhouses also shows that introduction of the parasite during the winter (before 1 March) achieves too low a parasitization for practical use. Parasitism is also influenced by the physical structure of the host plant. It is known that, on cucumber leaves, *E. Formosa* attacks fewer hosts than on tomato or aubergine. It is assumed that this effect is caused by the hairy leaves of cucumber, which reduce the walking speed of the wasp and contaminate it with honeydew from the glandular hairs.

The wasp, therefore, takes longer to clean its body on cucumber than on plants hosts with a different hair structure. Parasitization

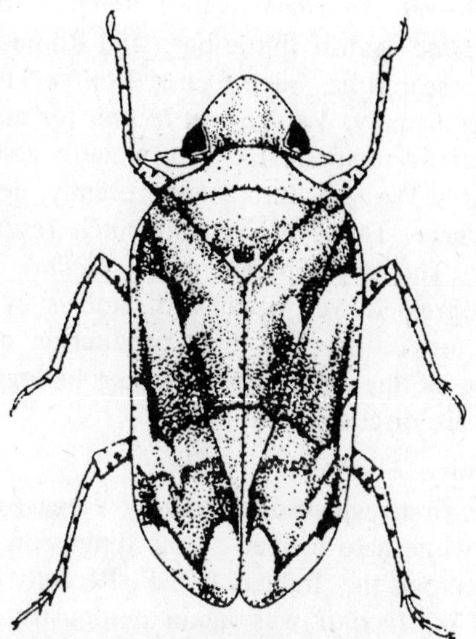

Fig. 9.3. Hilda patruelis.

declues as the quarterly of whitefly honeydew increases, independent of the nest plants. It follows, therefore, that dense whitefly populations hamper the parasite. A major factor affecting parasite efficiency is temperature in that flight is said to be inhibited below 17°C. However, *van Lenteren & Hulpas* (1983) have recently demonstrated flight at 12⁰C but there seems little doubt that direct radiation from sunlight plays an important role. Temperature plays a major role is deciding the duration of the parasite life cycle.

When half the development of the parasite is completed, the whitefly host turns black and the parasite finally emerges through a hole in the dorsum of the 'black scale'. The ecological information about greenhouse whitefly and its parasite suggests that the nature of the host plant is very important for the practical utilization of *E. formosa*. The effects of temperature and humidity are not fully understood but temperatures about 18°C and a humidity of between 50 and 80% RH seem to ensure effective parasitism and successful control of whitefly, providing the light intensity is sufficient and the whitefly population is low.

Biology of the Fungi Verticillium and Aschersonia

Several entomophathogenic fungi have been studied in connection with the biological control of insect pests and recently some success has been achieved. Examples are *Hirsutella thompsonii* against the citrus rust mite. *Nomuraea rileyi* against lepidopterous larvae and *Metarhizium anisopliae* against spittle bugs and Rhinoceros beetle. In glasshouse crops, research has been focussed on two fungi for use as microbial pesticides namely: *Verticillium lecanii* for control of aphids and whitefly, and *Aschersonia aleyrodis* for whitefly control. The latter has aroused interest in Western Europe only recently, despite successful experiments elsewhere. However, recent Dutch research has given promising results. The development of *V. lecanii* as a microbial insecticide has progressed well because of studies by researchers at GCRI. The two fungi differ in their production and application techniques because of the differences is their biology and ecology. These differences are discussed below.

Verticillium lecanii

V. lecanii was first resported in 1939 by Viegas, who referred to the characteristic white halo formed by the fungus on the scale insect *Coccus viridis* (Green) as the 'framers friend'. Recently the effectiveness on this insect of *V. lecanii* was again demonstrated in India by Easwaramoorthy & Jayaraj (1978). The fungus is a well-known cosmopolitan species described under several names, such as *Cephalosporium lecanii* and *Cephalosporium aphidicola*. Gams placed the toxonomy of the species in the genus *Verticillum*, mainly because of the arrangement of its coindiogenous cells in regular whorls. In his taxonomic study, *Gams* (1971) applied a rather broad species concept of *V. lecanii* and included in the tax on both small- and large-spored strains.

Recently *Evans* and *Samson* (1982), in their studies on entomogenous fungi from the Galapagos Islands, found that *V. lecanii* parasitizing coccids is associated with the ascomycete, *Torrubiella confragosa*. *V. lecanii* is not resticted to insect hosts. The species is commonly isolated from mouldy organic material, foodstuffs and soil. It is hyperparasitic on various fungi, such as rusts, agarics and even entomogenous fungi, and it is facultatively parasitic on various insects and arachnids, but has not been observed as a pathogen of mammals. On the insect, *V. lecanii* is found as cottony whitish colonies. On the aerial mycelium are condiophoes bearing awl-shaped phialides arranged in a characteristic verticillate manner. The cylindrical to ellipsoidal conidia are aggregated in a mucus.

In submerged cultures, blastospores are formed by a yeast-like budding process, while conida are readily produced by *V. lecanii* Hall (1980a) reported that virulence was not effected by successive transfers

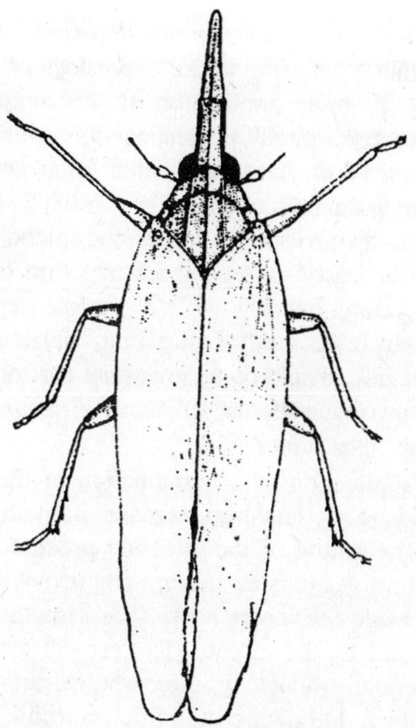

Fig. 9.4. Pyrilla perpusilla.

on artificial media nor by passage of conidia through the original host. Hall (1980b) isolated, from several sources, strains with different virulence towards the host, *Macrosiphoniella sanborni*. Currently, a strain with small spores for control of aphids and another with relatively large spores for control of whitefly larvae are used in commercial production. A product containing conidia of a different strain to be used against the cosmopolitan greenhouse pest, *Thrips tabaci*, is under development. Natural infections of insect populations by *V. lecanii* are common in the glasshouses in Western Europe. The inoculum which starts these epidemics probably originates from soil or mouldy organic material. By the use of Polyethylene Blackout sheets for manipulating flowering of chrysanthemums or the frequent use of overhead spray installations, the above mentioned infections can be induced & strongly enhanced by agricultural particles. The temperatures at which *V. lecani* grows and multiplies is between 15 and 15°C and humidities of 85-90% RH in the greenhouse.

High humidity must be present for at least 10-12 hours per day. Under these conditions, epidemics can occur within aphid or whitefly populations. The first infected insects are observed as white cottony particles ('fluffy-bodies') adhering to the undersides of the leaves 6-12 days after spraying. A sugle application of the fungus leads to the suppression of applied and whitefly populations for several months under favourable conditions. Most plant pathogenic fungi also grow best at the same temperature and humidity range, e.g. Botrytis sp. in tomatoes. Application of fungicides arrests the successful epizootic development of *V. lecanii*. In these cases, a second introduction of the fungus is necessary, after a safety interval of 1-2 weeks, depending on the fungicide used. Therefore, careful planning, particularly of aerial applications of fungicides, should be an important part of each integrated control programme involving the use of fungi. *V. lecanii* seems also to be sensitive to some insecticides.

However, the application of a combination of the fungus with a low dosage insecticide (e.g., fenthion) increases mortality in populations of *Coccus viridis*. The nature of the infection process by *V. lecanii* is not known. The fungus germinates and initially grows in an apparently saprobic manner outside the insect host. This growth might occur on the honeydew excreted by the insects. The growth also occurs, when applied as a commerical product, on the carbohydrate carrier material included in the product. Following the initial saprobic growth through natural orifices and between body segments. In contrast to A direct contact between a *V. lecanii* conidium and its future host is not necessary to accomplish infection, is contrast to other entamopathogenic fungi. It is not probable that conidia be dispersed in the greenhouse by air movement.

The conidia are sometimes dispersed by live insects and mites, as reported for *Metarhizium anisopliae* by Schabel (1982). In this respect, predatory mites and parasitic wasps might play a significant role. *V. lecanii* can occasionally be found infecting adult *Encarsia formosa* as well. However, the influence of such fungal infections on the wasp population is very limited.

Ascherossonia aleyrodis

The genus *Aschersonia* belongs to the family Coelomycetes of the class Fungi Imperfecti and contains over 30 species mostly found in the (sub-) tropics. All known species are highly host specific and all have been described from scale insects (*Coccidae*) and whiteflies (*Aleyrodidae*). In nature, some species are associated with species of the ascomycete, *Hypocrella*. *A. aleyrodis* was first described from citrus whitefly larvae in Florida. *A. placenta*, a common fungus on whiteflies in subtropical and tropical countries in Asia, differing mainly in the bright organe-red colour resembles *A. aleyrcdis*. After the turn of the century, *A. aleyrodis* was successfully introduced in Florida as a bio-insecticide in populations of *Dialeurodes citri* (Ashmead) by Fawcett (1908) and Berger (1907).

In some regions, whiteflies are still effectively controlled by epizootics following these original applications. Microscopical studies on the citrus whitefly (*Dialeurodes citri* (Ashmead) naturally infected with the fungus, *Aschersonia aleyrodis* Webber, show that the conidia are one-celled, fusiform, smooth-walled propagules produced in slime by phialides. These phialides are arranged in cavities, or pycnidia soon after the hyphae rupture the dorsal cutcle sporulation occurs early in the infection process and produce mat-like pustules of white mycelia on the host surface. Infection of whitefly larvae by *A. aleyrodis* is easily detected by the naked eye because of the bright orange, slimy spore masses formed under humid conditions on the bodies of the larvae. A yellowish discolouration of the larvae or a whitish mycellium protruding from the host can be observed, in drier conditions. In greenhouses, the-species has been found to be highly host-specific.

The species was never found infecting whitefly adults nor any other arthropod species, during several years of experimentation in the Netherlands. On various mycological media, the species can be successfully grown. For isolation and maintenance in the laboratory malt extract agar is the most favourable. Deterioration of the colonies has been observed on several media currently in use prior to or during sporulation. The colonies appear white and cottony after 1 week of growth. Light (350-420 nm) seems to induce sporulation and the characteristic yellow-orange pigmentation. After several transfers, the fungus grows and sporulates less vigorously; this contrasts with *V. lecanii*. This deterioration of a strain seems to be a common phenomenon in entomogenous hyphomycetes and has also been reported for the common *Metarhizium anisopliae* and *Beauveria bassiana*.

Therefore, in order to maintain viability and infectivity regular passage through the insect host followed by subsequent re-isolation, or suitable storage of the original isolate is recommended. Conidia of *A. aleyrodis* rapidly penetrate the cuticle of whitefly larvae. after the initial contact. The exact nature of the infection process is not yet known. Most infection occurs during the night following the introduction of conidia under greenhouse conditions. Once inside the host, the fungus is lethal, despite low humidity conditions in the green-house. Therefore, closing the ventilators of the greenhouse or the sides of plastic houses for 1 night following application of the fungus is sufficient to ensure infection. The first macroscopical symptoms of infection appear after 8 days. Melting of the two large fat bodies within whitefly larvae may be observed. Direct contact between a conidium and its future host is necessary in the absence of initial phase of saprobic growth. Therefore, emphasis has to be placed on adequate spray techniques when using preparations of this fungus. Clustering of the conidia in the spray solution can be avoided by the addition of detergents. Control of the greenhouse whitefly (*Trialeurodes vaporariorum*) by treating young larvae with conidia of A. aleyrodis has been studied in heated greenhouse in the Netherlands. Spontaneous reinfection was not observed but artificial infection succeeded both in rainy periods and during sunny weather. A dose of 2 X10^8 conidia of *A. aleyrodia*/plant, applied as an ultra low volume spray to a cucumber crop, caused 75% mortality. *A. aleyrodis* never occurred in the control plots.

The fungus did not affect the ratio between numbers of whitefly and its prasite, *Encarsia formosa*. Repeated applications are necessary to maintain the pathogen in the insect population, because of lack of dispersing agents (e.g., wind and rain) in the greenhouse. Kogan and Seryapin (1978) and Ramakers and Samson (1983) reported that, to accomplish almost complete kill, a dose of about 10^{13} conidia/ha was necessary in a cucumber crop. Kristova (1971) claimed permanent control by additional sprays of water following a single application of the fungus, but her findings could not be confirmed in our experiments. For humans and other vertebrates little is known about the safety of A. aleyodis. However, the fungus does not grow above 31°C and no cases. The different characteristics of *A. aleyrodis* and *V. lecanii* open a wide range of possible uses for these fungi within integrated control programmes. The environmental conditions and the efficacy of the other biological control agents in use are the factors on which the choice of fungus depends.

RED SPIDER MITE AND THE PREDATOR PHYTOSEIULUS PERSIMILIS

The major pest of both ornamental and vegetable plants throughout the world are Red Spider Mite (Terranychus Urticae [T. Telarius]) Red spider mite, also known as two spotted mite. *T. urticae* has five developmental stages; egg, larva, protonymph, deutonymph and adult, each nymphal stage having both a feeding and resting stage. Females lay spherical eggs (0.14 mm diameter) on the undersides of leaves.

The small, whitish larva has three pairs of legs while the protonymph and older stages have eight legs. Sexual characters become obvious at the deutonymph stage, those individuals with elongated bodies developing into males and those with rounded bodies into females. Males are attracted to female deutonymphal resting stages by pheromones, so that females mate immediately on maturing and begin laying eggs within 36 hours.

Unfertilized eggs produce males while fertilized ova produce both males and females. At 20°C and 36% RH a female will lay 7.3 eggs/day while at high humidites (95% RH) reproduction declines to about 4.9 eggs/day. The multiplication rate per generationis some 31x. The life cycle at 32, 21,18 and 15.5°C takes 3.5,14.5, 21 and 30 days respecitvely. The normal sex ratio is 3:1. Mites feed on cell chloroplasts, producing characteristic minute, yellowish, speckled feeding marks which may coalesce, causing leaves to shrivel an die. If the number of mites on a plant becomes excessive they migrate to the apical leaves where they produce silken webs. Individuals may then drop as much as a metre on a silken thread down which others climb creating a 'rope' with a ball of jostling individuals at the end. Such ropes are readily dispersed to other plants, either by wind or by physical transport by workers or equipment. Because of their small size and rapid rate of multiplication, numbers are best estimated by relating them to damage symptoms.

The economic threshold of damage on established cucumber plants, above which crop loss occurs, is 1.9, while an index of 2.5 will cause a 40% loss after 5 weeks (the time required for cucumber fruits to develop). On cucumbers, the maximum rate of increase in leaf damage is 1.0 in 12 days.

On tomatoes, a similar threshold (2.0), equivalent to about 30% of photosynthetic area, initiates crop loss, while the maximum rate of increase recorded is 2.7 in 16 days. It is interesting to note that the rate of damage increase is similar in both tomatoes and cucumbers although the mean growing temperatures are 16 and 21°C, respectively. Recently a new form of damge caused by a different red spider mite. *Tetranychus cinnabarinus*, which is plum red in colour, has appeared in several parts of the UK and the Netherlands. The typical speckling symptoms do not appear but, instead, infested leaflets become prematurely chlorotic with small transparent lesions.

The damage is caused by remarkably few mites and closely resembles magnesium deficiency.Bright yellow patches develop on the

Table 9.5. Definition of intensities of mite damage to cucumber leaves

Damage index	*Definition*	*Mite population* (adult plus nymphs) *per 6.45 cm²*
0	No damage	0
1	Incipient damge on or two 120 mm feeding patches	3
2	Feeding patches tending to coalesce, only 40% of leaf affected	12
3	60% of leaf with feeding marks as chlorotic patches	107
4	Dense feeding marks over entire leaf, but appearance still green	228
5	As 4 but leaft blanched and starting to shrivel	592

leaflets and necrotic patches from these gradually coalesce until the whole leaf withers and dies. Darker stripes may be seen leading from infested leaflets into the stipe, though the main stem is not affected. The characteristic feeding marks associated with red spider mites may or may not be present. If left unattended, the lower leaves wither and die rapidly and total deaths of plants has been observed. The damage seems to be caused by injected toxin which experiments at the GCRI confirmed were neither systemic nor viral. Under natural conditions, *T. urticae* overwinters as diapausing mated females, diapause being induced by shortening daylength, unfavourable food supply and low temperatures. Diapause is not normally terminated until the following spring when favourable conditions return. Both protonymphs and deutonymphs are sensitive, and respond, to shortening daylength.

The diapausing female spider mite is typically deep orange-red in colour—this colour being assumed within 3-5 days of maturation. Once this colour has developed, feeding ceases and the mites migrate from the plants to seek winter hibernation sites, usually within cracks and crevices in the greenhouse structure. Daylength is important in controlling the onset of diapause and, in Sothern England, the critical daylenght is about $13^1/_2$ hours, this period decreasing by 1 hour for each 3° fall in latitude. The intensity of illumination needed to induce a photoperiodic response in the developing nymphs, is about 3.5 lux. As with certain plants, breaks in the long dark cycle reduces the incidence of diapause, so long as the break is at least 2 hours and each portion of the broken dark period is less than 8 hours. This response enables growers to set up more economic lighting regimes by reducing the current load.

Low temperatures, as may be experienced in the greenhouse when the heating is turned off, will also favour the onset of diapause, as will the availability of only a poor food source on senescing leaves. This occurs commonly, in September on old main-crop cucumber plants, whereas younger second-crop plants growing at the same time carry few diapausing mites. Once diapause has been induced, the females become positively geotactic and negatively phototrophic. They thus show relatively little lateral dispersal so that, each year, new infestations tend to arrive in same part of the greenhouse. Diapause is normally terminated only by a fixed period of chilling—an adaptation to ensure that mites do not become prematurely active on warm winter days. In the greenhouse, emergence usually begins when the heat is turned on for a new season's crop, although this is not always the case.

Extensive research in the USSR has revealed that the pattern of emergence from diapause is goverend by the combination of factors which induced hibernation in the first place. Hence, in some years, emergence has been delayed until April or even May, despite the fact that the greenhouse has been heated for several weeks. The scale of an infestation in the spring is, therefore, governed by the number of mites which enter diapause in the late summer. Sex determination is arrhenotokous or haplodiploid (females develop from fertilized eggs and have a normal complement of chromosomes). The male on the other hand has only one set of chromosomes so that mutations will be immediately expressed. Thus, there is a rapid interaction between mutation and natural selection, enhancing the potential for rapid development of immunity to pesticides.

Red Spider Mite Predator (*Phytoseiulus persimilis*)

This predator was originally known as *P. riegeli* Dosse and *P. tardi* Lombardinin. It was accidentally brought from Chile to Germany on orchid roots and subsequently sent to many other parts of the world. Since the early 1960s, extensive research has been conducted both in Europe and North America, and its ability to control. *T. urticae* on a wide range of host plants has been clearly demonstrated. The adult female is an organe-red, pear-shaped mite rather longer than its prey.

The nymphs are oval and very pale pink in colour. Females lay eggs singly on the undersides of leaves among colonies of *T. urticae*. The eggs are large (2 x size of *T. urticae* eggs). When first laid they are translucent turning pink-orange. After about 3 days (at 20°C) a six-legged larva hatches and a day later it moults into an eight-legged protonymph which actively searches for food, eating 4-5 eggs before developing into a deutonymph. The deutonymph stages last about 2 days during which some 6 eggs or young mite stages may be eaten. Adults eat about 7 mites/day.

The sex ratio is approximately 4 : 1 and when egg-laying begins prey consumption doubles. Oviposition continues for about 3 weeks at a rate of 2-3 eggs/day (total about 54). Unmated females will not reproduce. Under experimental conditions, at 20°C, the predator population increases 44 x in a mean generation time of 17 days. This is equivalent to a weekly increase of 4.6 x compared with that of 2.7 x by its host. Given these statistics, it is not surprising that *P. persimilis*

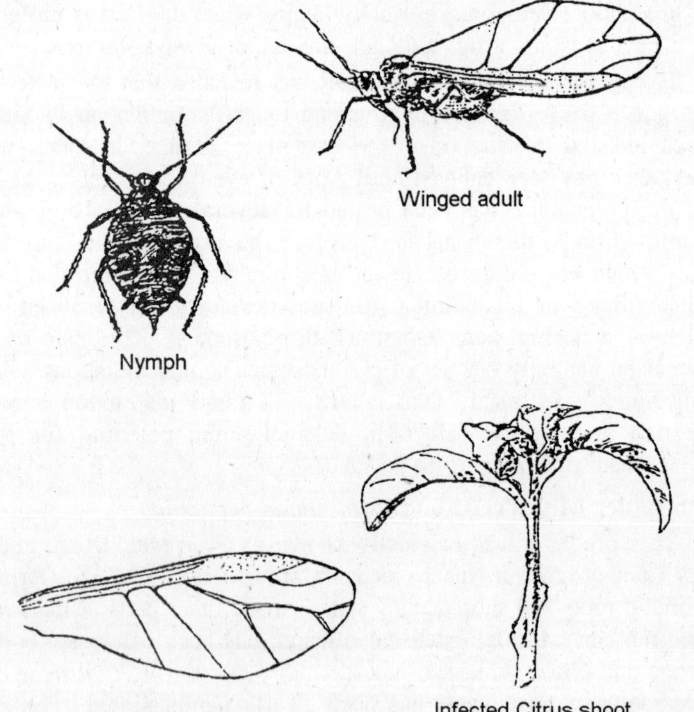

Fig. 9.5. Toxoptera citricida.

is a most effective predator and has been considered by some to be too effective as it often eradicates its prey from a greenhouse. At 20°C, a 300 x population increase occurs in 30 dyas while at 26°C this figure rises to about 200,000 x. Above 30°C, predators to not thrive thought *T. utricae* continues to develop rapidly. In greenhouses, temperature is perhaps the most important factor governing the time required to achieve control of mite populations. This becomes particularly important when cool outdoor conditions demand that heating the greenhouse temperature above ambient depends solely on pipe-heat.

Spatial variations within the greenhouse caused by the pipe lay-out create differences in the speed and efficiency of predator control. Various studies have shown that decreasing the relative humidity increases its searching, feeding and egg-laying capacity, although predator development ceases below 60% RH when oviposition and longevity also decline sharply. This explains the downward migration of predators form the apical foliage of cucumbers in hot shiny weather and may justify the selection of more tolerant strains which have been obtained following extensive experiments in Leningrad. Here, Voroshilov (1979) claims to have increased the heat tolerance of certain strains by 8-10 x. In practice, migration and extensive searching for prey occurs only when the latter becomes scarce within the immediate vicinity. Several species of phytoseiid mites have been the subject of genetic improvement projects and high levels of tolerance to parathion have been obtained with *P. persimilis*. Strains tolerant to carbaryl (x 10), diazinon and pyrazophos have been detected in Europe, while a project is underway in New Zealand to obtain pyrethroid resistance. Attempts to select for diazinon and pyrazophos resistance have been successful on a laboratory scale but less so in mass culture.

Thrips and their Natural Enemies

Thrips are small, slender, insects commonly called 'thunderflies' by country folk in the UK. Many are of tropical origin but have become widely established on ornaments in greenhouses. They may cause serious damge to cucumbers, carnations, roses and other flowering plants.

Biology

The life cycle comprises the egg, two larval, one prepupal and one pupal instar. The adults have two pairs of narrow wings fringed with long, fine hairs which, when at rest, are laid parallel along the back. It is convenient to consider the commonest species. *Thrips tabaci*, as typical of the several other pest species. *T. tabaci* is about 1 mm long and greyish yellow-brown in colour. The antennae are yellow-brown and seven-segmented. The legs are yellow, shaded with brown, the wings yellow brown.

The yonger stages are yellow-green. Males are very rare the females reproducing parthenogentically. Under summer conditions, the females each lay about 60 whitish, uniform eggs singly within a slit cut by ovipositor in leaf or flower tissues. One end protrudes from the slit to facilitate emergene of the newly hatched larva. The first stage is only 0.4 mm long and has bright red eyes on an abnormaly large head. Larval development is completed in 10-14 days when the larva drop to the ground to form prepupae which, in less than 2 days, turn into a pupa. The antennae of the prepupae are, unlike the pupae, not turned back over the head. The adults develop within the pupae in 4-7 days. Normally, the pupae are found on the soil surface or in natural cavities up to 15 mm below the surface. Thrips are gregarious and large numbers are found together on a single leaf or flower. They feed on sap after piercing tissues with their mouthparts. The tissues around the feeding punctures become desiccated, giving the leaves or petals a flecked appearance; indeed, on the rapidly expanding leaves of cucumbers, these flecks enlarge to become 'windows'. Thrips usually lie alongside prominent veins so that a concentration of damage occurs where the principal veins radiate from the petiole.

Thrips are very susceptible to pesticides so that they rarely become serious pests where fully chemcial pest and disease programmes are used. However, where biological control of major pests is practised, thrips create serious problems as they occupy niches on the plant (more than 50% of the population on the lower surfaces with a tendency of a greater numbers of occur on the young upper leaves) occupied by mites and whiteflies. It has, therefore, not proved possible to kill thrips on their host plants without affecting mite predators and whitefly parasites. Attention was therefore directed to the prepupae, which are found immediately below the plants, since larvae fall to the ground rather than walking down the main stem of the host. In recent years, in the face of escalating fuel costs, greenhouse cultural techniques have changed dramatically. Soil sterlization by steam of methyl bromide is no longer practised and the roots are now protected from disease by the use of rock-wool or peat-bolsters.

Thrips are, therefore, able to overwinter freely and now attack young plants in mid-winter whereas attacks fromerly occurred only in early summer when the pest immigrated into greenhouses from outdoors.

Control

When cucumbers were cultivated in manure beds and hose-watered, the soil and pathways were kept very wet—indeed, fequently waterlogged and it was possible to predict where thrip damage could be expected. If the paths were dry, symptoms were almost universally pesent but where they were wet no damage occurred. This effect was partially caused by drowning but was also due to encouragement of fungal epizootics which are discussed later in this section. Conversely, drip-watering associated with the new above-soil growing techniques led to dry floors on which thrips readily survived with a consequent high rate of population increase on the plants above. This development coincided with a trend to earlier planting so that the first pesticides (γ- HCH and diazinon), which had been used to successfully control pupating thrips, caused the death of parasites and predators of other pests when toxic vapours reached lethal concentrations in closed greenhouses. Pickford (1984) investigated a range of other non-volatile, persistent materials but only the novel 50/50 mixture of polybutene and water, to which the insecticide delta-methrin had been admixed, achieved control - reducing populations on the leaves from 40/cm^2 to less than 2/cm^2 within 4 weeks of treatment. Subsequent large-scale trials demonstrated that this control lasted 10 weeks. Where damge had occurred at the time of treatment, 'control' was apparently slow as damged leaves remained on the plant but, in reality, thrip populations dropped sharly within a few days.

The product concerned is now marketed as Thripstick and this selective control method could well be used on other crops when it would play to lay polythene sheeting along the plant rows to facilitate treatment. The considerable efforts were made to identify potentially useful biological control techniques for thrips before the development of the thripstick concept. The Commonwealth Institute of Biological Control was commissioned to seek natural enemies in onion crops in Central and Southern Europe. The most interesting agent found was the fungus, *Entomophthora parvispora*. Outdoor epizootics were first found from early July but by September attacks were widespread. Soon after the integument of the thrips is penetrated by the germ-tube of a conidial spore, the body becomes filled with rectangular hyphal bodies, which increase in number by fission and kill the host insect in 3-6 days. In nymphs, the entire body surface becomes covered with single, unbranched conidia, each bearing a single spore which is spherical but bears a knob-like projection. In the case of adults, this conidial growth is restricted to the intersegmental membranes, which are markedly stretched by the compact mass of hyphal bodies within.

As autumn approaches, the hyphal bodies change into brown resting spores. Attacked individuals containing these spores turn black and are washed or blown from the foliage by winter storms and release the spores on the soil surface. Only these resting spores survive the winter. Field studies suggested that, regardless of the suitability of the environment, epizootics are largely dependent on host density. This restriction is similar to that found in many *Entomophthora* sp. affecting aphids. There is, therefore, no prospect of using this species as a microbial insecticide but its presence in glasshouses is no doubt a contributory factor in depressing population increases in cucumber crops grown in damp soil. In Dutch cucumber-houses Samson et al. (1979) found another species, *E. thripidum*.

The fungus was not found before mid-August and epizootics did not occur before mid-October. This species differs from *E. parvispora* in that the spores are broadly ellipsoidal with a broad, truncate base and pointed apex. Long sporophores appear along the intersegmental membranes from which mature spores are forcibly ejected. Before the fungus sporulates, infected thrips move to an elevated part of the leaf to facilitate spore release. The fungus completes its life cylce in the insect host within 4 days. Where this fungus occurs, it can almost eliminate a thrip population within 2 weeks. Sporulation occurs continuously but is ceases in bright sunshine. This fungus has not been isolated in pure culture and so any development of microbial control will probably depend on *Verticillium lecanii*, which also attacks thrips. In glass-house experiments on cucumbers, *Verticillium*, killed more than 80% of the thrips within 6 days.

In view of the commercial development of this fungus for control of aphids and whiteflies, the potential for another specific product is evident. However, it is the development of predators of thrip control which has excited most interest. As the result of a planning decision within the Working Party, it was decided to concentrate biological control work on thrips at Naaldwijk while GCRI investigated the chemical approach. Studies by Ramakers (1980, 1983) have demonstrated the potential of the predatory mites, *Amblyseius mackenziei* and *A. cucumeris*, for thrip control, especially in situations where their reproductive rate is somewhat reduced by damp growing conditions.

These predators are pear-shaped, pale whitish brown and ative mites. They are noticeably smaller and flattened compared with *Phytoseiulus*. They lay smaller eggs which are white whereas the eggs of spider mite predators are tinted with brown. Another difference is that *Amblyseius* eggs are often attacked to plant hairs. In experiments where 28 predators were released on 2 out of 17 cucumber plants, *Amblyseius* spread to all the plants within 5 weeks and a sharp decline in the thrips population was observed after 8-10 weeks. A major advantage of this predator is that, unlike *Phytoseiulus*, it can survive the absence of its prey by taking other food, such as spider mite nymphs.

Hence, although the number of predators declines after control has been achieved, the proportion of leaves on which *Amblyseius* can be found remains high for some weeks. Although both *Amblyseius* spp. and *Phytoseiulus* prey upon each other to some extent, they are able to co-exist. Undoubtedly, the main interest in these predators lies in the case with which they can be mass-produced. Both species are reared on a flour mite. *Acarus farris*, whichi itself feeds on wheat bran within a stainless steel drum which is slowly rotated and within which the humidity can be accurately controlled. Up to 100,000 predators can be produced per litre of rearing volume on food costing less than £0.10p.

Biology of Glasshouse Leaf-Hopper and Its Parasite

Zygina pallidifrons

While several native leaf-hoppers may occasionally occur in greenhouses, the most important is the green-house leaf-hopper *Zygina palidifrons*. This species was first recorded as a greenhouse pest in the UK in 1918 and increased rapidly during the period 1920 to 1940. These leaf-hoppers are relatively easily controlled using modern pesticides but, with the increasing use of biological control methods for other pests, they are once more becoming important on many holdings. *Z. pallidifrons* is a small (3-4 mm long) pale-coloured jassid which is long-lived and extremely active, capable of developing serious infestations both under summer greenhouse conditions and within cages in controlled environment conditions. It has a wide host range including tomato, cucumber, geranium. *Nicotiana*, french bean, fuchsia, chrysanthemum, cotton and hop among the plants attacked. Several overlapping generations occur through the summer and the leaf-hoppers can overwinter on weeds such as chickweed. Leaf-hoppers feed only on the leaves; stems or buds are never touched.

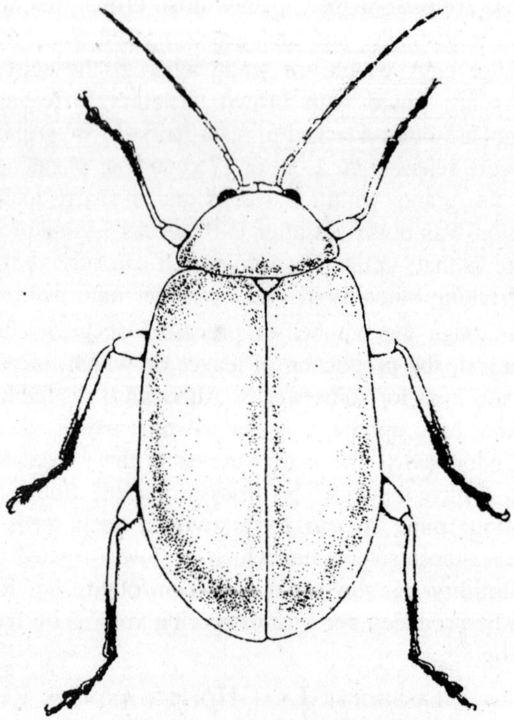

Fig. 9.6. Ootheca mutabilis.

The characteristic damage appears as a mottled area on the upper leaf surface caused by individual leaf-hoppers feeding from the underside. In extreme cases, the mottled areas becomes confluent, rendering the leaf white, bleached and shriveled. All the young developmental stages resemble the adult and cause a similar type of damage. Smith (1926) observed that the feeding punctures continued to enlarge even after the removal of the insect because damaged cells around the feeding puncture collapse and become full of air. Our observations showed that the area of damage varied depending on host plant. Whether this reflected host preferences or cell size within the leaf tissue was not determined. At 24°C, most feeding occurred on cucumber (17 mm²/24 hours) and at least on *Nicotiana* (4 mm²/24 hours). Temperature also affects the rate of feeding. The area of damage caused by feeding punctures on tomato at 26°C (14 mm²/24 hours) was approximately twice that of the area affected at the 18°C (5.14 mm²/24 hours). Very little feeding occurs at temperatures below 14 or above 30°C. Provided with water, but no food, leaf-hoppers kept at 24°C survived only 3 days.

The feeding punctures disfigure ornamental subjects and weaken or stunt seelings. In addition, the leaf-hoppers produce honeydew which supports the growth of sooty moults and hence may create a problem on food crops such as tomatoes. Development of the left-hopper has been reported as lasting from 25 days in summer to 85 days in winter. Our own studies have been made at four temperatures and show that, as with other insects, development is greatly influenced by temperature. There are five nymphal instars. The moulted skins characteristically remain attached to the plant by the stylets and, as they are white, have been referred to as 'ghost flies'. At 18°C, egg incubation takes approximately 17 days while the life cycle to adult emergence is complete in 42 days. At 30°C, egg incubation takes 8 days and adults emerge in 23 days. However, this temperature is very nearly at the upper lethal level for development so that few individuals mature successfully. Adults live for a long period. MacGill (1932) recording a life of up to 4 months. At temperatures near to 35°C, however, they die in a few hours. Adults readily jump and fly. When a severely infested plant is disturbed, they fly up and however temporarily in a similar manner to whitefly. The nymphal stages, however, are relatively slow moving and appear to spend most of their development on the leaf on which they are hatched.

The adults are able to locate and colonize other host plants with remarkable ease, dispersing readily around the green-house. Below 14°C, very little activity takes place and leaf-hoppers become sluggish. The sexes are easy to distinguish, the females having an obvious ovipositor on the ventral surface. Males and females occur in equal numbers,. although the females appear to be rather longer lived and hence dominate in severe infestations. Females are not sexually mature until a week or more old, although mating and courtship have not been observed in detail. In experiments to determine the age at which oviposition begins, newly emerged females were confined in clip cages on leaves with males. Eggs are nearly always laid singly, the leaf-hoppers preferring to oviposit in secondary rather than major leaf veins. In many cases, no eggs were laid, suggesting a reluctance to oviposit or perhaps mate under these conditions.

As with other Hemiptera, egg production appears to be inversely related to temperature. Individual adults maintained at low temperatures contained more eggs in the ovaries than those kept at high temperatures. More eggs were liad at 18°C than at 30°C. We found it particularly difficult to find eggs laid within the leaf veins of cucumber hosts and usually waited for the egg to hatch. In general, the lower fecundity, the long maturation period, an unwillingness to mate, oviposition site discrimination and the difficulty in detecting newly laid eggs make experimental procedures fairly challenging

The Parasite Anagrus Atomus Haliday

The principal parasite of greenhouse leaf-hopper is the mymarid wasp, *Anagrus atomus*. As with other mymarids, this wasp is a parasite of the egg stage of their leaf-hopper host. Mymarids are minute, short-lived wasps with a complement of fully mature eggs which are laid as quickly as possible. While the parasites seem readily able to find and attack leaf-hopper eggs, the percentage of parasitized hosts remains small. At 24°C, development take about 16 days. Towards the end of parasite incubation, parasitized eggs may be clearly seen as they develop a redddish hue. Parasites of such an early developmental stage are unbale to exercise effective control of the leaf-hopper. We believe that an attempt to achieve biological control using this mymarid alone is unlikely to be successful. While this wasp can be bred relatively easily in culture, there are several handling problems; eggs desiccate within detached leaves maintained for parasite emergence and the adult wasp is too short-lived for distribution to nurseries.

Leaf-Miners and Their Parasites (L.R. Wardlow)

The three most troublesome leaf-miner species (*Liriomyza bryoniae*). Tomato leaf-miner attacks both tomatoes and cucumber and will survive on some outdoor weed, e.g., sowthistle. The pest is important where greenhouse soil is not sterlized as leaf-miner pupae can then survive in the ground from one crop to the next. Crops grown by the *Nuteint-Film Method* (NFT) or in peat bags are particularly susceptible to this pest, especially where the floor is covered with plastic sheeting.

(*Chromatomyia syngenesiae*) Chrysanthemum Leaf-miner has a wide host range including many weeds : it is a severe pest of chrysanthemums with some cultivars being particularly prone to attack. This species pupates inside the leaf where it is difficult to control with insecticides.

(*Liriomyza trifolii*) American Serpentine Leaf-miner also has a wide host range and attacks most major protected crops. Like tomato leaf-miner, this species also pupates on the ground and is likely to thrive under similar conditions. The pest was imported into Europe from the USA comparatively recently via various African and Mediterranean nurseries, where it is now a serious problem due to its resistance to insecticides. In the UK, it is a notifiable pest under Statutory Plant Health Regulations and outbreaks have to be eradicated

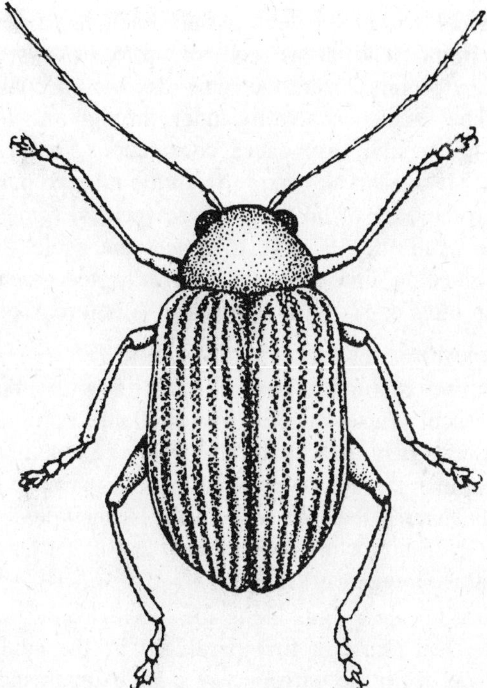

Fig. 9.7. Colaspis hypochlora.

as quickly as possible. Insecticides currently recommended to control this pest would seriously interfere with biological control programmes for other pests.

Leaf-Miner Biology

Tomato and American serpentine leaf-miner adults are difficult to distinguish with the unaided eye. Both are small black flies (2.5 mm long) with yellow spots on the thorax between their wings. It is most important for nurserymen to have a correct identification made of the species on their crops. Chrysanthemum leaf-miner is larger (3 mm long) and a dark grey colour. Adult leaf-miners feed on the leaf sap produced when the female fly inserts her ovipositor into the upper leaf surface to seek a suitable site for inserting an egg within the tissue. These oviposition marks soon show up as pale white spots on the upper surfaces of the leaves.

Only a proportion of the punctures are eventually chosen as egg-laying sites. Each females lays an average of 60 eggs during a 2-3 week life. After about 1 week the eggs hatch into small translucent larva which tunnel within the leaf tissue. Each larva forms a pale white tunnel or mine. The larvae feed for up to 10 days, moulting 3 times, and as they become larger the mine also becomes larger, longer and broader. The mines usually meander through the leaf but the American leaf-miner may also cause conspicuous sharply curled or blotched mines. Mature larvae emerge from the mine to pupate (falling to the ground in the case of both *Liriomyza* species) for about 9 days after which the adult flies emerge to repeat the cycle. Leaf-miners are capable of breeding throughout the year in heated greenhouses and are deceptive in their capacity to reproduce to outbreak proportions.

Leaf-Miner Parasites

There are two distinct types of parasite with many species attributable to each. Three species are available commercially but several other species may occur naturally where commercial biological control of leaf-miner larvae. After hatching, the parasite larvae feed at a rate which ensures that the leaf-miner is not killed until it has pupated. Only 1 parasite matures within each leaf-miner larva, although more than 1 parasite egg may be laid.

Ectoparasites lay their eggs alongside the leaf-miner larva within its mine but the leaf-miner is first paralysed by the adult so that it cannot move away from the parasite egg : the ectoparasite larva then feeds on the leaf-miner externally. Up to 6 parasites have been found developing within 1 mine, although the adults subsequently vary in size. Once a leaf-miner is attacked by an ectoparaite, the mine develops no further and, if it is a small young mine, it may not be detectable as the leaf grows.

Commercially Available Parasites

Dacnusa sibirica (Braconidae) is a small black endoparasite (2-3 mm long) with long flexible antennae (same length as its body). Parasites are supplied to nurserymen either as pupae in small cardboard release-boxes or as adults in plastic tubes. *Opius pallipes* and other species of *Dacnusa* may also be found amongst commercial supplies but they operate in a similar manner. The female parasite uses her antennae to locate a leaf-miner larva within a leaf, whereupon she inserts a transparent oval egg with her ovipositor. Each female lives for about 2 weeks, during which time she may lay up to 90 eggs. Eggs hatch within 4 days, the larvae taking about 16 days to mature within the leaf-miner pupae. With the aid of a transmitted light microscope, it is possible to dissect out leaf-miner larvae from the leaves before pupation to check parasitism.

Diglyphus isaea (Eulophidae) is an ectoparasite and is common on outdoor weeds from June onwards in the UK. The adult is small (1-2 mm long) and black with a metallic green sheen : its antennae are much shorter than those of *Dacnusa sibirica*. Little is known about the fecundity of *D. isaea* but a female probably lays about 60 eggs during her life span. When the parasite has paralyzed the leaf-miner, she inserts an egg through the leaf, placing it adjacent to the host. The parasite larva hatches within 2 days, passing through three stages during the next 6 days. Before turning into a pale turquoise pupa, the larva builds 6 to 8 columns with frass within the mine; these act like 'pit props' to prevent damage to the pupa. The pupa then turns dark brown before the adult emerges through a hole chewed in the leaf 6-9 days later. The frass columns remain in the mine and are a useful indication of the degree of parasitism. *Diglyphus* spp., are able to parasitize leaf-miners already parasitized by Dacnusa spp., and hence they becomes the dominant parasites when the hot conditions of mid-summer favour thier activity. Adult *Diglyphus* also feed on leaf-miner larvae to obtain protein—an essential ingredient of their diet to maintain egg production.

Biology of Aphids and Their Parasites in Greenhouses

Aphids rank with spider mites and whiteflies as the most serious pests of greenhouse crops. There are many more species than of the other pest groups but, until recently, they have proved more amenable to chemical control. However, resistant strains are appearing and, with increasing use of biological control against the other pests, it is becoming more necessary to find aphid control measures which are compatible with biological control.

Biology of Greenhouse Species Morphology

Aphids (Homoptera, Aphididae) are small (2 mm) soft-bodied insects which live on plants in dense colonies. The body is generally pear-shaped and lacks obvious segmentation or division into head, thorax and abdomen. The legs and antennae are slender and the hind end of the abdomen bears a pair of tubular wax glands, the cornicles. Two forms of adult occur : the apterae, which are wingless, and the alatae, which are winged. The latter appear particularly in crowded conditions.

Feeding

Aphids feed on plant sap by inserting the slender stylets of their mouthparts through the plant tissue and into the sieve tubes. Since the phloem sap is low in amino acids but rich in sugars, the aphids must take in large quantities of sap to meet their amino acid requirements, and pass out the remaining sugary liquid, or honeydew, droplets of which are ejected for considerable distances around the aphid. The honeydew not only clogs the stomata of the leaves, but encourages the growth of sooty moulds which prevent light from reaching the photosynthetic tissues. The aphids weaken the plant by draining its resources and may cause severe distortion of growth and, additionally, are a common means of transmitting plant viruses from infected to healthy plants.

Host Range

Aphids are highly adapted as plant parasites, showing their widest diversity and specialization in temperate regions. Most groups of plants have one or more aphids specific to them. On the other hand, some species infest a wide range of hosts. Many aphids alternate between summer host plants and a woody winter host on which they reproduce sexually and lay overwintering eggs. However, under glass, reproduction is continually asexual even throught the winter or, as with the rose aphid (*Macrosiphum rosae* L.) the rose is strictly its winter host. No aphid species is confined entirely to the greenhouse, although a strain of Myzus persicae Sulz, has become highly adapted to chrysanthemums and to many insecticides applied to them, and is probably confined to greenhouse culture. Aphids can thus be considered under two categories : the polyphagous species, attacking a wide range of hosts, and the oligophagous species, confined to a single host.

The most important polyphagous species are *M. persicae*, which infests mainly Solanaceae and chrysanthemums, *Aphis gossypii* Glover, on cucumberss and chrysanthemums and *Macrosiphum euphorbiae* Thom. and *Aulacorthum solani* Kalt., which are chiefly pests of Solanaceae but, like the previous two species, can affect many other plants. *Aulacorthum circumflexum* Bekt., attacks a wide range of ornamentals, particularly underglass. Oligophagous species include *Nasonovia ribisnigri* Mosl., *Hyperomyzus lactucae* L. and *Acyrthosiphon lactucae* Pass. on lettuce. *Dysaphis tulipae* B.d.F and *Myzus ascalonicus* Donc., on bulbs and *Macrosiphoniella sanborni* Gill and *Brachycaudus helichrysi* Kalt. on chrysanthemums.

Reproduction

The reproduction of aphids is highly adapted to exploit a new temporary habitat by rapid population increase; they what are known as 'r-strategists'. They achieve this end in several ways. On greenhouse crops, as on other summer hosts, all individuals are females and therefore all contribute to population growth. The young are bornfully formed and able to feed immediately. They grow rapidly, moulting four times before they mature, often within a week or less. Because fertilization is not required, ova can start developing within an aphid as soon as, or even before, it is born. By the time a female matures, several young are fully developed in her oviducts and ready to be born. Young are then produced at a rate of 3 or even 6 a day for several weeks. The body structure of aphids is considerably simplified to perform only the functions of feeding and reproduction, while retaining the ability to walk. Even wings and flight muscles are dispensed with, except when these are needed to escape to a new food source. Thus all nutrition is directed to the needs of reproduction.

Development of Aphid Populations Dispersion and Establishment

Because aphids increase so rapidly on short-lived hosts, they must have mechanisms to prevent overcrowding and to disperse to new hosts. They therefore react to their own population density by both walking and flying off and by restricting their own reproductive rate. The initial invasion of a greenhouse in the spring is therefore often by outdoor alate migrants entering the vents. These may be aphids leaving their winters hosts, or flying between summer hosts, but fight cannot occur until outdoor temperature are adequate. Thus, in 1982, the first *M. persicae* trapped, from the South to the North of France, at Pau by 11 April, Orleans by 9 May, Colmar by 6 June and at Arras by 4 July (data from ACTAPHID suction trap network).

Immigration may also be influenced by the size of vents and their time of opening. Aphids may also be distributed between and within nurseries on propagating materials. This is particularly the case with chrysanthemums and other crops where cuttings are supplied by a few specialist producers. Several crops such as lettuce, chrysanthemums, carnations and roses, are grown in greenhouses throughout the year. Aphids may readily move from one crop to the next. Continuity may also result if weeds or old crops are left through the winter.

Distribution within a Crop

The initial infestation of a crop is usually at isolated foci. Rapid reproduction at these points produces dense colonies which, if recognized in time, can be controlled by localized treatments. Aphids soon begin to wander to neighbouring plants, however, particularly in species such as *Myzus persicae* where the adults are not inclined to settle. As colonies become more dense, aatae are produced and disseminate the infestation throughtout the crop. The distribution of aphids on individual plants depends on the aphid species and its density and on the species, cultivar and age of the plants. Thus, on Solanaceae, *M. persicae* prefers the lower leaves and *M. euphorbiae* the upper leaves. On chrysanthemums, *M. persicae* prefers the upper leaves, but moves to the middle leaves of susceptible cultivars as the population density increases, and then migrates to the flowers when they appear. In contrast, *M. sanborni* feeds to the stems of chrysanthemums while Brachycaudus helichrysi feeds in the growing point.

Population Growth Rates

Within a greenhouse, environmental factors are constant and the natural enemies of aphids are usually absent. An aphid population is therefore able to grow exponentially for a considerable period, i.e., the numbers increase by a fixed proportion (q) each day. When the log of the number is plotted against time an approximately straight line results. The scopes of these lines (calculated between the arrows) are known as the r_m values (0.22, 0.29, 0.20 and 0.29) and the antilog gives the daily increase. q. (1.25. 1.34, 1.22 and 1.34). A more meaningful expression of increase rate is the weekly increase, q^7, which gives values of 5, 8, 4 and 8 times a week respectively. The rate of increase is determined by two factors of the aphid life history; the development time (d) from birth to first reproduction, and the number of female young (M) produced in an equivalent time. With aphids, all young are normally female. Thus increase rates can be calculated either from the slope of population graphs, as above, or from d and M, since the weekly increase rate

$$q^7 = M\frac{5.2}{d}$$

For example if an aphid first reproduces at 7 days old and then produces 20 young in the next 7 days, the weekly increase rate will be $20^{5.2/7}$ or 2.48 times.

The rate of increase is greatly influenced by factors such as temperature and host plant. For example, A. gossypii increases at only 4 x a week on aubergines, yet it will increase at 12 x on cucumber under glass and as much as 23 x under ideal laboratory conditions. The intrinsic increase rate (r_m) is proportional to temperature between two limits : a lower developmental threshold, usually near 0°C, and an upper lethal limit at about 25°C. This temperature is often excceded under glass in southern countries, but aphids are able to survive if night temperatures are low enough.

Biology of Parasites

All aphid parasites are Hymenoptera, or wasps in the broad sense, and belong to two families; the Aphidiidae, which are most important and are all aphid parasites, and the Aphelinidae which also parasitize other insects, such as scales and white flies.

The Aphididae include many important genera : *Aphidius*, *Praon*, *Ephedrus*, *Lysiphlebus*, *Monoctonus* and *Trioxys*. The adults are small (2 mm) slender wasps with black, brown, orange or yellow colouration. They live for only 1 or 2 weeks at 15-20°C when fed with honeydew or nectar. Their populations comprise rather more (60%) females than males. After mating, the female inserts her ovipositor into an aphid, usually by bending her abdomen forwards between her legs, and lay a minute (0.1 mm long) egg in its body cavity. Certain aphid instars are preferred by any one parasite species, although any instar is usually acceptable. Once within the aphid, the eggs expands to several times its original size. After a few days, the larva hatches and begins feeding osmotically. The larva grows, passing through three instars, without interfering markedly with the development or behaviour of the aphid. By the 4th instar, the aphid has usually become adult and the parasite has consumed all the internal tissues of the aphid, completely filling its cuticle. The larva then cuts a slit in the underside of the aphid, attaches the cuticle to the leaf by silk and then spins a cocoon within the aphid, where it pupates. This is the 'mummy' stage and resembles a swollen, papery aphid, yellow, brown or sometimes black (*Ephedrus*) in colour. Parasites of the genus Praon spin a cocoon beneath the empty skin of the aphid. When mature, the adult parasite cuts a circular lid in the top of the mummy, leaving behind only a few pellets of meconium. At 21°C, the mummy of *Ephedrus cerasicola* Stary appears after 12 days and the adult 9.5 days later. For *Aphidius matricariae* Hal., the equivalent times are 8.5 and 5 days. An adult females parasite may make several hundred oviposition attempts during its life, but only a small proportion of the eggs laid will develop successfully to adulthood. Under laboratory condition up to about 100 adults will eventually be produced, of which perhaps 60 will be female. Since development takes about 2 weeks the maximum population increase rate can be calculated as about 4.5 x a week, using the formula described for aphids. In practice, within a greenhouse, the increase rate may be considerably lower.

The Aphelinidae include one genus of importance : *Aphelinus*. The adults are small (1 mm) and thickset, the wings are short with a reduced venation, and the antennae are elbowed. The females inserts its ovipositor by backing up to the aphid. An egg may then be laid or the female may turn and feed from the puncture. Either process can lead to the death of the aphid. The mummy is black, retaining the original size and shape of the aphid, and the exit hole is ragged. Otherwise these parasites resemble the Aphidiidae in biological details such as development time and fecundity. The adults livesomewhat longer.

Biology of the Midge Aphidoletes and its Potential for Biological Control

Little is known of those gall-midge species which are predatory on leaf-aphids. However, research on their biology has increased recently and it has become evident that the role of midges in regulating the abundance of aphids in nature is greater than has been previously assumed. Three species are known to be predators of aphids : *Aphidoletes aphidimyza* (Rond.), *A. urticariae* (Kieffer) and *Monobremia subterranea* (Kieffer). Only *A. aphidimyza* has been investigated with respect to its suitability for the control of pest aphids in greenhouses. A. aphidimyza is a holarctic species. It is known in the USA, Canada, Japan and in most European countries. For instance, in Finland, this species is very common and abundant, occurring far to the north, up to latitude 68°C.

Biology of Aphidoletes Aphidimyza

The adult midge is about 2 mm long. slender with long legs. The sexes can easily be separated on the basis of the structure of the antennae. The male antennae are long, grey with long setae and bent backwards. The female antennae are shorter, thicker and darker in colour. Monogenic reproduction is characteristic of the aphid midge, i.e. all progeny from a single female are either males or females. In one series of experiments, the ratio of males to females was 1:1.7. The adults to not live long. Uygun (1971) observed that their life span averaged 1 week, the male living for as lightly shorter time. In the experimental glasshouses of the Agricultural Research Centre in Finland, they have survived for up to 2 weeks, but in the wild state lives are much shorter, probably only a few days. The adult midges feed on the honeydew secreted by aphids. They are active only at night and during dusk. In the daytime, they remain immobile in shaded parts of the plants. The females oviposit, usually under the leaves, only on plants infested by aphids. Egg-laying is particular prolific in aphid colonies where it is brought about by olfactory, chemical or tactile stimulation by the aphids, or their secretions, either alone or in conjunction with other properties of the plants.

The prey species has not been observed to have any effect on the egg-laying activity of the female, but the species of plant and even the variety has a clear effect. According to Miesner (1975), the differences between plant species as regards oviposition are due to leaf structure, hairiness etc. He also found that midges deposited more eggs near adult aphids than larvae. The females deposit about 100 eggs. In Uygun's (1971) experiments, the average number of eggs was only about 70, most of which were deposited during the first 2-4 days following emergence. According to El Titi (1972), the number of eggs is almost directly proportional to the aphid density. The eggs are 0.3 mm long and 0.1 mm broad, orange in colour, smooth and shiny. At room temperature, the egg stage lasts for 2-3 days. The larvae emerge from the anterior end of the egg. Bouchard et al. (1981) studied the development of eggs in the laboratory at a constant temperature of 23°C when the incubation period lasted 2 days.

The newly hatched larvae are only 0.3 mm long. When fully grown, they are 2-3 mm long, elongated, narrowing at both ends. The colour of the larvae varies from light orange to red, depending on the food source. There are four larval instar. The larvae develop only if they are able to feed on aphids. They cannot survive by feeding on scale insects and mites, but they are polyphagous as regards aphids. Observations so far show that the larvae feed on over 60 different species of aphids, but the range of prey is apparently much wider. The prey includes all the common aphid pests encountered in greenhouse, e.g. *Myzus persicae* (Sulz.), *Aphid gossypii* Glov., *Macrosiphum rosae* L. and *M. euphorbiae* Thomas. In nature, the larvae take 7-14 days to develop, depending on the temperature and food supply. Uygun (1971) found that development took 7 days at 15°C, 3.8 days at 21°C, and 3.0 days at 27°C. According to the laboratory studies of Bouchard et al. (1981), the development took 5.5 days at a constant temperature of 23°C. Immediately after hatching, the larvae start searching for aphids on which to feed.

Accordingly to Wilbert (1972), the larvae must find their first prey within a few hours. He observed that newly hatched larvae are capable of moving 63 mm without food and estimated that larvae are able to detect aphids within an area of 2.7 mm^2. In contrast to most other predators of aphids, A. aphidimyza larvae are able to locate their prey from quite a distance—1st instar larvae from about 3 mm.

According to Wilbert (1974), larvae mainly locate their prey by olfactory means, but vision may play some part in the mechanism because larvae also react to the presence of sand grains of the same size as aphids. Aphids make only limited attempts to escape when a larva approaches, 1st instar larvae do not produce any escape reactions in young aphids, but some of the adult aphids move away when a larva approaches. Larvae usually attack aphids by biting their leg joints. The larvae then excrete a toxin which paralyzes and kills the aphid. The dead aphids are initially green but gradually turn black and desiccate.

Many aphids remain attached to the leaves and hang downwards, suspended by their proboscis. Mayr (1975) showed that the salivary toxin paralyzes the prey within a couple of minutes. As the aphid ceases to struggle, the larva usually bites into its thorax. The contents of the aphid are dissolved by the toxin within 10 minutes and the midge larva than sucks its prey dry. The composition of the toxin is not known. According to Mayr (1975), a homogenate prepared from the salivary glands did not con- tain any proteases. It contained a phenoloxidase, which was inhibited by phenolthiourea. Investigations in Finland have shown that the saliva contains the enzyme hyaluronidase, which occurs commonly in the toxins of many animals. The salivary gland also contains glutaminic acid in clearly higher concentrations than other tissues. It is possible that the glutaminic acid is partly responsible for the paralyzing effect of saliva. According to Uygun (1971), the larvae require only 7 small-sized *Myzus persicae* to develop into pupae, but Nijweldt referred to other observations in which midge larvae were able to complete development if they ate 5 full-grown or 15 small-sized *M. persicae*. If there are plenty of aphids present, the midge larvae kill and eat many more than are needed for their development. Uygun (1971) found that the more and the larger the aphids available, the larger the number killed and left uneaten. At lower temperature, larval development takes longer and the larvae eat more aphids.

Similarly, the drier the air, the greater is the number of aphids eaten. After the larva has grown to its full size, it crawls down the stem of the plant or falls to the ground. It then burrows down to a depth of about 3 cm and builds a cocoon. This cocoon is formed from a large number of light-coloured sticky threads and is covered by small stones, aphid skins, larval excreta etc. It is oblong, about 1.8 mm long and 0.7 mm broad. The cocoons are very difficult to find in the soil. Pupation takes place 2-4 days after the cocoon has been formed. The pupa is 1.4 mm long and 0.5 mm broad. Initially it is orange-coloured but later turns brown. At room temperature, the pupal stage lasts for 10-14 days. In natural conditions, *A. aphidimyza* overwinters in the cocoon. The larvae diapause in the cocoons from September onwards. They pupate in spring and the adults emerge in the middle of May. In the high greenhouse temperatures, diapause starts later in autumn and finishes earlier in spring.

Under laboratory conditions, aphid midges can be reared throughout the year, without diapause, if they are kept in a 16.8 hours light : dark cycle at room temperature. Short illumination periods and low temperature induce diapause. According to Havelka (1980), the critical daylength at 20^{0}C for midges collected from Leningrad is 17 hours and for those from Kishinev 15.5 hours. Diapause is induced in the last larval instar 1 day before the cocoon is made and in the cocoon. Before emergence, the pupae come out of their cocoons and move up to the soil surface. Adults emerge head forwards from a split formed behind the middle point of the pupal body. Emergence takes 2-3 minutes. Adults fly within 10 mimutes of emergence.

Suitability of the Aphid Midge as a Control Agent

One of the most important tasks in assessing the suitability of biological control agents is to determine the most suitable developmental stage for transferring them to the plants. Both midge eggs and larvae can easily be transferred to the greenhouse on the leaves on which they have been reared. However, despatch to the customer in these stages is not profitable because they are easily killed during transport, primarily as a result of dessication and lack of food. It is possible to introduce either adult midges or cocoons in to the glasshouse. Adults have been spread either by transferring them straight to the glasshouse or by maintaining permanent mass production there. EI Titi (1974) and Markkula et al. (1979), however, did not obtain good results when adult midges were spread to greenhouse cultures. El Titi (1974) obtained slightly more promising result by maintaining an `open' midge culture in the greenhouse.

Mass Production of Cocoons

In practice, great numbers of cocoons are needed for satisfactory control. The following five-stage, mass production method has been developed at the Agricultural Research Centre:

1. The peat layer containing cocoons is sent to greenhouse growers a couple of days before the adult midges emerge.

2. Capsicums are sown at 2-week intervals and cultivated in a greenhouse as food for *Myzus persicae*.
3. When the number of aphids has increased to about 2000 per plant, 70 female and 30 male midges are placed in each cage. After 2 days, the midges will have deposited about 3000 eggs. The plants are removed and the adult midges are killed.
4. When the larvae have reached the final instar, leaves containing larvae are detached from the plants and placed on sand within small plastic containers. The containers are filled with moist sand to a height of 4 cm. On top of this is placed a sheet of nylon gauze and a thin layer of peat. 3 or 4 leaves are usually put into each container so as to give about 200 larvae per container. The larvae pupate in the peat layer.
5. When the plants are 20-30 cm high they are placed in cages, 3 plants in each cage, and about 50 aphids are placed on each plant.

The method of Bondarenko and Asyakin (1975) is basically the same and involves the same work stages. On essntial difference is that cocoons are sieved out from the sand, their number estimated, and they are then transferred to the greenhouse without sand.

Commercial Use

On the basis of the studies made in the Department of Pest Investigation of the Agricultural Research Centre, a Finnish firm decided to commence mass production and marketing of the aphid midges in 1978. The following instructions were drawn up for growers on the basis of research and practical experience:

'Peat, containing aphid midge pupae, is spread around the plants immediately after the appearance of the first aphids. One pupa per three aphids or, depending on the number of aphids present 2-5 cocoons per m^2 should be applied. Treatment should be repeated after 2-4 weeks to ensure good results.' A short description to the life cycle and behaviour of aphid midge was also added to the directions.

The control results in commercial greenhouses have been consistently good and no serious failures have occurred. Where the control has not been successful, the reason has almost invariably been because the control agents were introduced too late, when they were unable to prevent the increase of the aphid. The main reasons for the success of the aphid midge as a biological control agent are:

1. Adult midges are able to fly to aphid-infested plants even in large glasshouses.

2. Mass production is easy and hence economical.
3. The aphid midge forms a permanent population in the glasshouse. It can even survive the winter if the growth substrate of the plants is not changed and no harmful disinfectants used.
4. The midge larvae are motile and thus are able of find new prey. Aphids do not readily escape.
5. Cocoons readily withstand transport and distribution.
6. The larger the aphid population, the more aphids the midge larvae destroy.
7. The midge larvae kill and eat all the pest aphids in a greenhouse.

The aphids midge has given control in greenhouses superior to that afforded by other predators or parasites.

Biology of Glasshouse Mealybugs and Their Predators and Parasitoids

General Biology of Mealybugs

Mealybugs are small soft-bodies insects with sucking mouthparts belonging to the same order as aphid, whitefly and scale insects. They are named after the white waxy material which covers the bodies of all but the youngest nymphal instars. Most species feed on the aerial parts of plants, but some are root-feeders and others gall-producers. Mealybug feeding reduces plant vigour, causes a yellowing of the foliage, sometimes distortion and frequently defoliation of the host lant. Mealybugs produce copious quantities of honeydew. Secondary damge is caused by the growth of sooty moulds on these honeydews. The moulds cover leaves, reduce photosynthetic ability and, along with the white waxy secretions produced by the mealybugs, make the plants unsightly. There are some 15 species recorded from glasshouses. The most common and probably the most damaging under galss, is the common or citrus mealybug. *Planococcus citri* (Risso). This species is tolerant of a broad range of environmental conditions and host plants and is found on over 25 plant families. There are two other common species.

The longtailed mealybug, *Pseudococcus adonidum* (L.), has a more restricted host range and frequently conceals itself in leaf whorls. The vine mealybug (*Pseudococcus obscurus* Essig) is a cold tolerant speices more common in the USA. The species are distinguished by the shape, form and length of the wax filaments, e.g., *P. longispinus* has tail filaments, which are almost as long as the body itself. *P. citri* produces both sexes in appropriately equal numbers and is the only species which has been shown to mate. Other species can reproduce by parthenogenesis. The adult male is a delicate winged insect with a very short active life. Female mealybugs are wingless, ovoid insects up to 5 mm long when full grown.

All species lay eggs (except *P. longispinus* which is viviparous). Eggs are small, about 0.3 mm long, and are laid within a protective mass of waxy threads. Egg-laying takes 5-10 days and the female shrinks and finally dies when the egg mass is complete. The numbers of eggs laid varies with temperature; *P. citri* produces les than 100 eggs above 30° C, but in excess of 400 at 18° C. The eggs hatch into a dispersive crawler stage, which searches for new feeding sites on which to settles. Following settlement, the male spins an elongate white, waxy cocoon and undergoes matamorphosis. The female nymphs have three moults and are mobile throughout their lives. Development can be completed over a wide range of temperature : *p. citri* requires about 30 days at 30°C to around 90 days at 18°C.

Chemical Control of Mealybugs

Mealybugs are predominantly tropical and subtropical in origin and introduction of the pest is usually via infeceted plant material. Thus plants should be inspected thoroughly and, if possible, quarantined before being brought into the glasshouse, ornamental collection or amenity area. The insecticides most commonly used against mealybugs include diazinon, dimethoate, formothion, malathion and nicotine. Aldicarb applied to the soil may be safely used with some biological control agents and Thripstick, (polybutenes mixed with detamethrin) painted on to stems has also been used with some success in amenity areas. While sprays may be effective in controlling early nymphal stages of mealybugs, general chemical control is difficult for several reasons. Mealybugs tend to congregate in inaccessible places, e.g., leaf whorls, nodes, fruit calices, buds and flowers. They are protected from sprays by their waxy coat and they are often pests on ornamental plants which are sensitive to pesticides.

Biological Control of Mealybugs Predators

There are many parasitic hymenopterans, predators and fungal diseases which attack mealybugs. Probably the most widely used and successful to date is the predatory coccinellid, *Cryptolaemus montrouzieri* Mulsant. Insectaries in the USA produced 30 million beetles per annum primarily for release on *Citrus* (Fisher, 1963). The adult is a brown beetle about 4 mm long with an orange head, prothorax, wing tips and abdomen. Females mate soon after emergence and begin to lay eggs some 5 days later. They lay their eggs singly into mealybug egg masses, up to a maximum of 500 eggs, at a rate of about 10 eggs per day. The total number of eggs produced is strongly influenced by adult diet and starvation halts egg production. All stages are predatory on mealybugs. Adults and young larvae prefer host eggs and young nymphs, whilst larger larvae will consume mealybugs of any size. *C. montrouzieri* is polyphagous and will eat other homopterans, such as scales, if food is in short supply. Larvae are cannabalistic and should not be confined together without food. The larvae growth to 13 mm in length and, in the later instars, have a covering of waxy filaments, so resembling their host. At 21° C, larvae may consume over 250. 2nd and 3rd instar mealybugs in completing their development. Temperature has a marked effect on the life cycle; development is complete in about 25 days at 30° C, but requires 72 days at 18° C. The adult beetles are most active in sunny conditions. Their searching behaviour in unproductive above 33°C and they become torpid below 16°C. The larvae show a similar activity pattern over this temperature range with peak useful activity at around 28°C.

C. montrouzieri has been widely used in glasshouses. Whitcomb (1940) obtained good resuls under favourable conditions on *Gardenia* in Massacusetts. Panis and Brun (1971) reported satisfactory control of *P. citri* on various ornamentals, provided that temperatures were above 20°C. Below this temperature, the predator's efficacy drops markedly. Because it is a predator, it is effective when hosts are plentiful, but will rarely eliminate them. Doutt (1951) found *C. montrouzieri* inadequate alone, but by supplementing with parasitic hymenopterans obtained satisfactory control. Another predatory beelte, *Nephus reunioni* Chazeau, has been used in the glasshouse in France with some success.

Parasitoids

A wide range of parasitoids are found attacking mealybugs. They are generally host specific and attack a relatively narrow age range of the pest species. The most widely used parasitoid for control for *P. citri* is probably the encyrtid, *Leptomastix dactylopii* Howard. Techniques for mass rearing of this parasitoid are already in practice. It is a moderate-sized chalcid, about 3 mm long and yellow brown in colour. It attacks large nymphs and adult females of *P. citri* and can lay 20 or more eggs a day at 30° C. The adults are long-lived, given food and high humidity. The life cycle is completed in 12 days at 35° C and 45 days at 18°C. It has been succesfully used in many cases as a supplement to predatory beetles. In France, a combination of

Leptomastix dactylopii and *Crytolaemus montrouzieri* gave complete control of *Planococcus citri* on *Clivia* and crotons and reasonble control on *Pelargonium*, *Saintpaulia*, *Cattleya* and *Pilae*. *L. dactylopii* and *Nephus reunioni* gave excellent results on bromeliads. Similarly good control has been achieved in the Uk on a on a wide range of heated ornamentals. Mealybus populations tend to consist of many overlapping generations and a parasitoid attacking only a limited age range may take a long time to gain control.

Parasitoids with different host age ranges released simultaneously are being evaluated for their control potential for *P. citri*, *Anagyrus pseudococci* is slightly smaller than *L. dactylopii* and attacks half-to-full-grown nymphs. The female is brown with distinctive white antenna and male is generally small and black in colour. Its longevity and egg production are similar to those of *L. dactylopii* but the life cycle is always a day or two shorter. It seems to be more active under bright light conditions. *Leptomastidea abnormis* is a pale yellow brown, 2 mm long parasitoid with distintive banded wings held aloft. It atacks young 2nd instar mealybugs. While the adult is shorter-lived, its egg production is lightly higher than those of the other two species. The life cycle is longer, taking 19 and 46 days at 30° and 18° respectively. It is more sensitive to high temperature, probably due to the susceptibility of its smaller hosts. All these parasitoids reproduce by laying an egg into an appropriately sized mealybug.

The larva develops as an endoparasitoid eating out the mealybug before pupating within the skin of the mummified host. *Crytolaemus montrouzieri* will eat newly parasitized mealybugs but appears to find them unpalatable once mummified. All three of the above parasitoids have been shown to co-exist with the predator under glasshouse conditions. During the summer months, this combination of parasitoids and predator has produced excellent control. The ladybird effectively clears areas of heavy infestation, particularly egg masses, whilst the parasitoids maintain less serious infestations at low level with percentage parasitism up to 90% on some plants.

During the winter in glasshouses maintained at about 20°C, *C. montrouzieri* all but disappears and, whilst the parasitoids manage to maintain a small population, they seem unable to prevent pest populations from building up. Overall adequate control is achieved, but further work on regular inoculative releases is going on in an attempt to improve control during the winter. In France, a number of parasitoids have been used for the control of other mealybug species. Complete control of *Pseudococcus obscurus* was obtained using either the parasitoid

Pseydaphycus maculipennis alone on bromeliads and *Kentia* or with *C. montrouzierion* cacti or with *N. reunioni* on ferns. Satisfactory control was obtained using *P. maculipennis* on cyclamen and with *C. montrouzieri* on *Clivia*. Another parasitoid, *Tetracnemoidea peregrina*, has been used successfully against *P. longispinus* on ferns and *C. montrouzieri* on *Dracaena*. This combination also gave control of *Pseudococcus obscurus* on cacti.

Culture and Release of Natural Enemies

The citrus mealybug may be readily reared on potato sprouts through the year. At Wye, they prefer to use tubers with short sprouts raised dry rather than planted in soil at 26°C and approx 60% RH. Great care must be taken to choose sound tubers and maintain cleaniness in order to avoid infestations of mites which can rapidly destroy the culture, particulaly at high relative humidities. Reasonable numbers of predators and parasitoids can be reared in plastic boxes provided with tubers infested with large numbers of mealybugs. Care must be taken to avoid contamination of the mealybug cultures with predators and parasitoids. On parasitoid, *Pauridia peregrina* Timberlake, has proved particularly troublesome. In particular, ants should be destroyed as these will protect the mealybugs for their honeydew and hamper control. Temperatures should be adjusted to favour the parasitoids and predator, i.e. 22° to 27°C for at least several hours per day. To avoid excessive heating costs, nigh-time temperatures could be dropped a few degrees with probably little harm to most plants.

As a rough guide, predators or parasitoids should be released at a rate of 5/m^2 of infested planted area. Vents and doors should be screened to prevent escape and, during winter, some secondary glazing used to reduce heat loss and avoid trapping parasitoids in cold mositure films on the glass. Releases should be made on infested plants preferably in the early morning or evening when low light levels and temperature will prevent excessive dispersal. Plants should be monitored at least once a week by checking new growth to detect mummified mealybugs or predatory larvae. If possible, repeat releases weekly for 1 month to ensure that all stages are parasitized.

Biology of Glasshouse Scale Insects and Their Parasitoids

General Biology

Glasshouse scale insects can be divided into two broad categories. The first comprise the many species of armoured scale, or Diaspidae, which, while common, are usually restricted to a limited range of hosts. The second are the soft scales, or Lecanidae, of which there are several very common and troublesome members which are highly polyphagous. These include *Coccus hesperidum* L., *Saisettia coffeae* and *Saisettia oleae*. Studies in Britain have concentrated on *S. coffeae* which, in our experience, has the widest host range in heated glasshouses. We have found *C. hesperidum* more common on interior plantings. These scale insects are essentially pests of the tropics and subtropics. Soft scales are round dome-shaped insects which, when full grown, are up to 5 mm in length. Young scales are usually light brown in colour becoming brown or almost black at maturity. The female scale insect produces a mass of eggs over many days and then dies. In *C. hesperidum*, these hatch within her body and number from 80 to 250. In *S. coffeae*, from 500 to 2000 or more eggs are produced beneath the female's body while *S. oleae* has rather fewer eggs. The eggs hatches into a dispersive crawler stage which settles onto a suitable part of the plant. Mortality at this stage may be as high as 80% and is influenced by both humidity and plant host. Soft scales feed from the phloem and may be found on the stem or on leaves where they associated with the veins. While the plant may show the little signs of damage from individual feeding, a large population will cause yellowing or defoliation.

The main damaging effects are caused by the growth of sooty moulds on the copious amounts of honeydew which the scales produce. *C. hesperidum* produces considerably more honeydew than the other species. While scale insects are relatively slow-growing, they compensate for this by their large numbers of offspring. A few individuals left unchecked can therefore build into a very large population by the end of the season. We have recorded over 37 plant families attacked, ranging from ferns to orchids, and including representatives of most flowering and decorative leaf ornamentals. The family Acanthaceae seems to be the most susceptible to *S. coffeae* and also the most tolerant of high populations. The duration of the life cycle of *S. coffeae* ranges from 95 days at 18°C to 51 days at 28°C. They are unable to develop at temperatures of 30°C or above. The scales therefore appear most troublesome in the autumn and spring or indoors at temperatures around 20°C.

10

Chemical Destruction of Pests

Human beings have learned to line and compete with the insect world, even though insects appeared long before humans did. According to recent discoveries humanoids have exited on earth more than 3 million years, while insects are known to have existed for 250 million years. We can guess that the first materials used by our primitive ancestors that could be classed an insecticides (repellents) in the crudest definition of the word were mud and dust spread over their skin to repel biting and tickling insects, a practice that resembles the habits of water buffalo, pigs and elephants. History doesn't tell us very much about chemicals used against insects.

The earliest records of insecticides pertain to the burning of "brimstone" (sulfur) as a fumigant. Pliny the Elder (AD 23-79) recorded most of the earlier insecticide uses in his Natural History. Gall from a green lizard to protect apples from worms and rot were also included in it a variety of materials have been used with doubtful results: extracts of pepper and tobacco, hot water, soapy water, whitewash, vinegar, turpentine, fish oil, brine, lye and many others.

Even as recently as 1940, our insecticide supply was limited to several arsenicals, petroleum oils, nicotine, pyrethrum, rotenone, sulfur, hydrogen cyanide gas, and cryolite. World War II opened the Chemical Era with the introduction of a totally new concept of insect control chemical–synthetic organic insecticides, the first of which was DDT.

ORGANOCHLORINES

As the names indicates the *organochlorines* are insecticides that contain carbon chlorine and hydrogen. They are also referred to by other names : *chlorinated hydrocarbons*, *chlorinated organics*, *chlorinated insecticides*, *chlorinated synthetics*.

DDT and Related Insecticides

DDT affect human health agriculture and the environment. It can be considered the pesticide of greater of historical important Since EPA canceled all uses of DDT effective from January 1, The story of its rise of stardom, carrying with it the Nobel Prize, and decline to infamy is rather sensational and should be briefly narrated for the uninitiated. DDT which is more than 100 years old is probably the best known and most notorious chemical of this century. It is the most fascinating, and remains to be acknowledged as the most useful insecticide developed. It was first synthesized in 1873, by a German graduate student who had no idea of its tremendous insecticidal value, and after synthesis it was put on the shelf and forgotten. In 1939 a Swiss entomologist, Dr. Paul Miller, rediscovered DDT while searching for a long-lasting insecticide against the clothes moth. DDT proved to be extremely effective against flies and mosquitoes, ultimately bringing to Dr. Mller the Nobel Prize in medicine in 1948 for his lifesaving discovery. We should bear in mind that its most beneficial use was in public health, for malaria control, and in many nations it still is so used.

More that 1.8 billion kg of DDT have been used throughout the world for insect control since 1940, and 80 percent of that amount was used in agriculture. Production reached its maximum in the United States in 1961, when 73 million kg were manufactured. The greatest agricultural benefits from DDT have been in the control of the Colorado potato beetle and several other potato insect, the codling moth on apples, corn earworm, cotton bollworm, tobacco budworm, pink bollworm or cotton, and the worm complex on vegetables. It has been most useful against the gypsy moth and the spruce budworm in forest. From the point of view of human medicine, DDT has been most successful against mosquitoes that transmit malaria and yellow fever, against body lice that can be carry typhus, and against fleas that are vectors of plague.

One of the most surprising features of DDT was its low cost. Most of that sold to the World Health Organization went for less than

22 cents pound. Without question, it was the most economical insecticide ever sold. A federal ban on the use of DDT, declared by the EPA on January 1, 1973, named DDT an environmental hazard due to its long residual life and to its accumulation, along with the metabolite DDE, in food chains, where it proved to be detrimental to certain forms of wildlife. It is no longer available to the grower or home-owner.

DDT belongs to the chemical class of diphenyl aliphatics, and as the name indicates it consist of an aliphatic, or straight carbon chain, with two (di-) phenyl rings attached, as in the illustrations. DDT was first known chemically as *dichloro diphenyl trichloroethane*, hence DDT. Five members of DDT are of importance because they all had an early role in pest control : TDE (or DDD), methoxychlor, ethylan, dicofol, and chloro-benzilate. The latter two are not really insecticides, but rather are acarocodes (miticides).

How does DDT Kill? The mode of action is not very clear. In some complex manner it destroys the delicate balance of sodium and potassium within the neuron, thereby preventing it from conducting impulses normally. In order to understand some of the well-documented evils attributed to it let us consider a few important pents concerning DDT. The first point is DDT's chemical stability, DDT and TDE are *persistent*, that is, their chemical stability gives the products long lives in soil and aquatic environments and in animal and plant tissues. They are not readily broken down by microorganisms, enzymes, heat, or ultraviolet light. The remaining DDT relatives are considered nonpersistent. Second, DDT has been reported in chemical literature is the most insoluble compound ever made sure that DDT'S solubility in water is only about six parts per billion part (ppb) of water. However, it is quite soluble in fatty tissue, and, as a consequence of its resistance to metabolism, it is readily stored in fatty tissue of any animal ingesting DDT along or DDT dissolved in the food it eats, even when it is part of another animal.

DDT gets accumulated in every animal that preys on the other animals because of the fait eat it is not readily metabolized and thus not exerted. It also accumulates in animals thateat plant tissue bearing even traces of DDT. For example, the dairy cow excretes (or secretes) a large share of the ingested DDT in its milk fat. Humans drink milk and eat the fatted calf, and thereby ingest DDT. The same story is repeated in food chains ending in the osprey, falcon, golden eagle, seagull, pelican, and so on. The principle of those food chain oddities is this : Just as DDT, any chemical that possesses the characteristics of stability and fat solubility will follow the same biological magnification (*biomagnification*). The polychlorinated biphenyls (PCBs), a group of chemicals that have no insecticidal properties, are stable and fat soluble and have climbed the food chain just as DDT has. Other insecticides incriminated to some extent in biomanginification, belonging to the organochlorine group, are TDE, DDE (a major metabolite of DDT), dieldrin, aldrin, several isomers of HCH, endrin, heptachlor and mirex.

The rise and fall of DDT contains a lesson, and this is perhaps as good a place as any to moralize. Because of DDT's great success in World War II against body lice in Neples, during the typhus outbreak, and in the Pacific, against mosquitoes known to carry malaria, after the war it was rapidly adopted for agricultural use with inadequate basic knowledge. And, because of its effectiveness against a host of agricultural insect pests and its ridiculously low cost, it was overused, and abused, land then—when it caused problems-was banned in rather a panic. DDT moved to be highly effective against body lice in Neples, during world war II in typhus our break, and in the pacific against mesquitves which carried malaria.

Due to the above mentioned reasons DDT was readily adopted for agricultural use without knowing much about its disadvantages. Only when it started to cause problems, it was banned, rather in a panic. A lesson that should be learnt is that no matter how effective it is against a host of agricultural insect pests, a how cheap it is, there is on absolute need for an informect caution and according to available knowledge correct way of employing a specific chemical for pest control. We need basic research performed in autonomous institutions not subjected to competition in the economic marketplace. And because this research it basic, as opposed to applied, it will of necessity be slow, expensive, long-term, and not immediately applicable. But our social policy must support such research, to enable us to cope with—if not to avoid-those chemicals that prove to pose dangers to our environment as well as our health.

Hexachlorocyclohexane (HCH)

Hexachlorocyclohexane (HCH)–previously erroneously called benzenhaxachloride (BHC)–was first discovered in 1825. But, like DDT, it was not known to have insecticidal properties until 1940, when French and British entomologists found in the material to be active against all insects tested. It is made by chlorinating berizence, which results in a product made up of several isomers, that is molecules containing the same kinds and numbers of atoms but differing in the internal arrangement of those atoms.

HCH, for instance, has five isomers, named, after the Greek letters, *alpha*, *beta*, *gamma*, *delta* and *epsilon*. After much laboratory work in isolating and identifying these isomers, the chemists found to their great surprise that only the gamma isomer had insecticidal properties. In a normal mixture of HCH, the gamma isomer makes up only about 12 per cent of the total, leaving the other four isomer as inert material or insecticidally inactive ingredients. Since the gamma isomer is the only active ingredient, methods were developed to manufacture lindane, a product containing 99 per cent gamma isomer, which is effective against most insect, because of its cest being high it is impractical for crop use. Technical grade HCH has one highly undesirable characteristic, a prominent musty order and flavour.

The order is form the inert isomers, which are more persistent than the orderless gamma isomer in animal and plant tissues as well as in soil. As a result, root and tuber crops planted in soils previously treated with HCH retain its order and are usually unsalable. The same problem is reported with leafy vegtables, poultry, eggs, and milk that directly or indirectly come in contact with HCH residues. The effects of HCH on insects and mammals superficially resemble those of DDT. Lindane is a neurotoxicant whose effects are normally seen within hours and result in increased activity, tremors, and convulsions leading to prostration. Lindane is orderless and has a high degree of volatility. It quickly became popular as a household fumigant sold as pellets to be attached to light bulbs or to small, decorative electric wall vaporizers. These were later found to be hazardous to humans and house pets and were removed from the market.

Cyclodienes

The cyclodienes, also known as the *diene-organochlorine insecticides*, are of more recent origin than DDT (1939) and HCH (1940) which were developed after World War II and are therefore of more recent origin than DDT (1939) and HCH (1940). The eight compounds listed here were first described in the scientific literature or patented in the year indicated : chlordane, 1945; aldrin and dieldrin, 1948; heptachlor, 1949; endrin, 1951; endosulfan, 1956; and chlordecone (Kepone) 1958. Other cyclodienes developed in the United States and Germany are of minor importance in a general survey. These include isodrin, adodan, bromodan and telodrin. Cyclodienes, which are stable in soil & relatively stable to ultraviolet action of sunlight are persistent insecticides. Consequently, they have been used in greatest quantity as soil insecticides (especially chlordane, heptachlor, aldrin, and dieldrin), for the control of termites and soil-borne insects whose immature stages (larvae) feed on the roots of plant. Because of their persistence, the use of cyclodienes on crops was restricted; undesirable residues remained beyond the time for harvest.

To understand the effectiveness of cylodienes as termite control agents, consider in the year of their development are still protected from damage more than thirty years later. These insecticides are the most effective long-lasting, economical, and safest termite control agents known. However, several other soil insects became resistant to these materials in agriculture, resulting in a rapid decline in their use. In 1975 EPA banned most of the agricultural uses of cyclodienes. The most valuable, and produced in the greatest quantity, were chlordane and dieldrin. Structures of the common cyclodienes are presented to illustrate their similarity and complexity. The nomenclature and chemistry of the cyclodienes are quite complicated.

The cyclodienes have three-dimensional structures and thus possess stereoisomers; that is, forms that have the same kinds and numbers of atoms, but their atoms differ in their spatial arrangement. For instance endrin is a stereoisomer of deildrin. The toxic effects of not very clear. Cyclodienes on insects mammals and birds are of equal intensity but more on fishes perhaps because when the compound is introduced into water the fish continually respire and ingest any toxic compound contained in their aquatic environment. The modes of action of the cyclodienes are not clearly under-stood. It is known that they are neurotoxicants, that have effects similar to those of DDT and HCH. They appear to affect all animals in generally the same way, first with nervous activity followed by termors, convulsions, and prostration. The cyclodienes undoubtedly disturb the delicate balance of sodium and potassium within the neuron but in a way differing from that of DDT and HCH.

Polychlorotepene Insecticides

Toxapliene (1947) and strobane (1951) are the only two polychloroterpene material. Neither have ever been considered urban insecticides. Toxaphene is manufactured by the chlorination of camphene, a pine tree derivative. Toxaphene had by far the greatest use of any single insecticide in agriculture. It was used on cotton, first in combination with DDT, for alone it has a low order of toxicity to insects. In 1965, after a number of cotton insects became resistant of DDT, toxaphene was formulated in combination with methyl parathion, an organophosphate insecticide discussed later in this chapter. As late as 1976 some 11.8 million kg of toxaphene was used on cotton, or 41 per cent of all insecticides on cotton that year.

Toxaphene is an extraordinary mixture of more than 177 polychlorinated derivatives, which are 10-carbon compounds including CI_6, CI_7, CI_8, CI_9 and CI_{10} constituents. Most are probably isomeric CI_7., CI_8, and CI_9. bornanes. No single component makes up more than a small percentage of the technical mixture. The toxaphene components of greater concern are those most toxic to mammals and fish. One of these is toxicant A, shown in its three-dimensional form. Toxicant A makes up only 3 per cent of technical toxaphene, but it is 18 times more toxic to mice, 6 times more toxic to houseflies, and 36 times more toxic to goldfish than technical toxaphene. These materials are persistent in the soil, though not as persistant as the cyclodienes, and narish in three to four weeks from the surfaces of mosts plant tissues. This disappearance is attributed more to volatility than to actual metabolism or photolysis (disintegration from the effects of ultraviolet light in sunlight). They are fairly easily metabolized by mammals and birds, are not stored in body fat to any great extent, as are DDT, HCH, or the cyclodienes. Despite low toxicity to insects, mammals, and brids fish the highly susceptible to toxaphene poisoning, in the same order of magnitude as to the cyclodienes.

The modes of action for toxaphene and strobane are similar to the cyclodiene insecticides, acting on the neurons and causing an imbalance in sodium and potassium ions.

Organophosphates

The organophosphate compounds have been replaced by the chemically unstable organophosphate (OP) insecticides, especially with regard to use around the home and garden. *Organophosphate* is usually used as a generic term to include all the insecticides containing phosphorous. The OPs have several other commonly used names, some of which are organic phosphates, phosphorus insecticides, nerve gas relatives, phosphates, phosphate insecticides, and phosphours esters or phosphoric acid esters. They are all derived from phosphoric acid and are generally the most toxic of all pesticides to vertebrate animals. Because of their chemical structures and mode of action, they are related to the "nerve gases." Their insecticidal action was observed in Germany during World War II in the study of materials closely related to the nerve gases sarin, soman and tabun.

Initially the discovery was made is search of substitutes for nicotine, which was in critically low supply is Germany. The OPs have two distinctive features. First, they are generally much more toxic to vertebrates than are the organichlorine insecticides, and, second, they are chemically unstable or nonpersistent. It is this latter quality that brings them into agricultural use as substitutes for the persistent organochlorines, particularly DDT. The OPs exert their toxic action by inhibiting certain important enzymes of the nervous system, cholinesterases (ChE). This leads to the accumulation of acetycholine (ACh), which interferes with the neuromuscular junction producing rapid twitching of voluntary muscles and finally paralysis.

OPs that have attached to their phosphorous atoms combinations of different alcohols and different phosphours acids are termed esters. Esters of phospherous have varying combinations of oxygen, sulfur & nitrogen. The nuclie of the six subclasses of OPs are shown to help explain some of the seemingly odd chemical names gives to these insecticides. The Ops are divided into three groups—the aliphatic, phenyl and heterocyclic derivatives.

Aliphatic Derivatives

The term *aliphatic* literally means "carbon chain," and the linear arrangement of carbon atoms differentiates them from ring or cyclic structures. All the aliphatic OPs are simple phosphoric acid derivatives bearing short carbon chains. TEPP was the first OP introduced into agriculture is the only useful pyrophosphate and is probably the most toxic. It was never available for home use. Because TEPP is very unstable in water, it hydrolyzes (breaks down) quickly after spraying on crops and disappears with 12 to 24 hours.

The oldest and most heavily used aliphatic OP is Malathion introduced it was quickly adopted by agriculture for use on most vegetables, fruits, and forage crops for control of an extensive range of insect pests. Malathion is so safe that it is suitable for home use aho since it is safe to use around pets, fast acting and can controlled practically every kind insect including garden and household aphids and cockroaches. It is so safe that it is perscribed by physicians for use on humans for the control of head, body, and crab lice. It commonly appears in flea powders for dogs, cats, and other domestic animals, and is used in dips for the control of mange mites.

In 1981, and again in 1982, malathion became the insecticide of choice in the control of the Mediterranean fruit fly, which had invaded the rich fruit-growing areas of California. Malathion was mixed with a protein bait made of molasses and yeast and sprayed from ground equipment and by helicopter over the infested and surrounding areas. Both male and female and female fruit flies are attracted to the bait and die a few hors after feeding on the tasty morsels. The bait formulation applied by helicopter is the most selective and inoffensive of all forms and methods of malathion use. With this technique malathion is appled at the astonishingly low rate of 171 g/ha mixed with 684 g of the bait. When applied by ground equipment it is used at the rate of 2 kg of active ingredient in 378 L of spray per hectare as a foliar or vegetation spray. This malathion-bait mixture was used successfully in the eradication of the Medfly from Florida in 1956-1957, and again in 1962-1963, from Texas in 1966, and from Los Angeles in 1975-1976. It was again placed in service in the brief 1981 Florida outbreak of the Medfly, because of its exceptionally low acute toxicity to human and other warm-blooded animals.

Trichlorfon is a chlorinated OP, which has been useful for crop pest control and fly control around barns and others farm buildings. Monocroptophos is an aliphatic OP containing nitrogen. It is a plant-systemic insecaticide, but it has had limited use in agriculture because of its high mammalian toxicity. It is not available to the home gardener. Systemic insecticides are those that are taken into the roots of plants and translocated to the above-ground parts, where they are toxic to any sucking insects feeding on the plant juices. Normally caterpillars and other plan tissue-feeding insects are not controlled, because they do not ingest enough of the systemic-containing juices to be affected.

Contained among the alophatic derivatives are several plant systemics, dimethoate, dicrotophos, oxydemetonmethyl, and disulfoton, and of which can be used safely by the homeowner. Dichlorvos is an aliphatic OP with a very high vapour pressure, giving it strong fumigant qualities. It has been incorporated into polychlorovinly resin pet collars and pest strips, from which it is released slowly. It lasts several months and is useful for insect control in the home and other closed areas.

Mevinphos is a highly toxic OP. Because of its short insecticidal life, Mevinphos can be used in commerical vegetable production. It can be applied up to one day before harvest for insect control, yet it leaves no residues on the crop to be eaten by the consumer. Two of the recent arrivals in the aliphatic organophosphate structures are methamidophos and acephate. Both have proved highly useful in agriculture, especially for vegetable insect control. In summary, the aliphatic organophosphate insecticides are the simplest in structure of the organophosphate molecules. They have wide range of toxicites, and several possess a relatively high water solubility, giving them plant-systemic qualities several of which are important around the home.

Phenyl Derivatives

When the Benzene ring is attached to other groups it is referred to as *phenyl*. The phenyl OPs contain a benzene ring with one of the ring hydrogens replaced by attachment of the phosphorus moiety and others frequently replaced by Cl, NO_2, CH_3, CN, or S. The phenyl OPs are generally more stable than the aliphatic OPs; consequently their residues are longer latsting. Parathion is the most known of the phenyl OPs, being 1947, the second phosphate insecticide introduced into agriculture. The first, TEPP, was introduced in 1946. As a result of it's age and utility, parathion's total usage is greater than that of many of the less useful materials combined. Ethyl parathion was the first phenyl derivative used commerically and, because of its harmful effects has not been available for home use.

Methyl parathion became available in 1949 and proved to be more useful than (ethyl) parathion because of its lower toxicity to humans and domestic animals and borader range of insect control. Its shorter residual life also makes it more desirable in certain instances. This material is also not used by the layperson. Systemic insecticides are also found in the phenyl OPs. They are, however, usually animals systemics used for the control of the cattle grub; ronnel and crufomate are examples. Stirofos is a home-safe OP much like malathion in its overall usefulness against home and livestock pests. Profenophos and Sulprofos are two of the more recently registered phenyl derivatives that have a wide of insecticidal activity and are used only on field crops today. Isofenphos is used as a soil insecticide in field crops and vegetables, against corn rootworm and onion maggot, and also for white grubs, chinch, bugs, and sod webworms in turf.

Heterocyclic Derivatives

The term *heterocyclic* means that the ring structures are composed of different or unlike atoms. In heterocyclic compound, for example, one or more of the carbon atoms is replaced by oxygen, nitrogen or sulfur, and the ring may have three, five or six atoms. The first insecticide made available in this group was probably diazinon, in 1952. Note that the six-membered ring contains two nitrogen atoms, very likely the source of its proprietary name, since one of the constituents used its manufacture is pyrimidine, a diazine. Diazinon is a comparatively relatively safe OP that has an surpirsingly good track record around the home. It has been effective for practically every conceivable use : insects in the home, lawn, garden, ornamentals, around pets, and for fly control in stables and pet quarters. The second oldest of this group is Azinphosmethly (1954) and is used in U.S. agriculture. It serves both as an insecticide and acaricide in cotton production and is not available to the layperson.

Chlorphyrifos has become the most frequently used insecticided by pest control operators in homes and restaurants for controlling cockroaches and other household insects. Methidathion is not particularly new, but it has in the last few years acquired registrations for forage and field crops, true fruits, and crops for an extraordinary wide variety of insect and mite pests. Phosmet has a set of registration credentials similar to methidathion, including the infamous boll weevil and the plum curculio, two closely related weevil pests. Dialifor was first introduced in the mid-1960s as were methidathion and phosmet. It uses are somewhat more limited, however, to apples, grapes, pecans and citrus.

The heterocyclic organophosphates have generally longer lasting residnes than many of the aliphatic not simple molecules. Also, because of the complexity of their molecular structure, their breakdown products (metabolites) are frequently many, making their residues sometimes difficult to measure in the laboratory. Consequently, their use by growers on food crops is somewhat less than either of the other two groups of phosphorus- containing insecticides.

Organosulfurs

The organosulfurs, as the name suggests, have sulfur as their central atom. They resemble the DDT structure in that most have two phenyl rings. In hot weather dusting sulfer alone is a good Acaricide (miticide).

The organosulfurs, however, are far superior, requiring much less material to achieve control because sulfur in combination with phenyl rings is particularly toxic to mites. Of greater interest, however, is that the organosulfurs have very low toxicity to insects. As a result, they are used for selective mite control. This group has one other valuable property.

They are usually ovicidal as well as being toxic to the young and adult mites. Tetradifon is one of the acaricides and typically bears the sulfur and twin phenyl rings, as do most of the organosulfurs. No doubt the oldest of this group is Aramite, introduced in 1951. Notice that Aramite has only one phenyl ring and is, therefore, an exception to the general rule that organosulfurs have two phenyl rings.

Carbamates

Since the organphsphate insectides are derivatives of phosphoric acid, the carbamates must be derivatives of carbamic acid HO—C—NH_2, And like the organophosphates, the mode of action of the carbamates is that of inhibiting the vital enzyme, chloinesterase (ChE). In 1951 the carbamate insecticides were introduced by the eigy Chemical Company in Switzerland. They fell by the wayside because the first ones were not very effective, while being quite costly. The early carbamates are shown in the margin at the right.

At the time it was not known that the N,N-dimethyl carbamates, as shown in these structures, were generally less toxic to insects than the N-methyl carbamates, which were developed later and which make up the bulk on the currently used materials. In 1956, Carbasyl which was the first successful carbanate, was introduced. More of it has been worldwide than all the remaining carbamates combined. Two distinct qualities have made it the most popular material : very low mammalian oral and dermal toxicity and a rather broad spectrum of insect control. This has led to its wide use as a lawn and garden insecticide. Notice that carbarly is an *N-methyl carbamate*. Most of the carbamates are plant systemics, indicating that they have a high water solubility, which allows them to be taken into the roots or leaves. They are also not readily metabolized by the plants.

Methomyl, oxamly, aldicarb, and carbofuran have distinct systemic characteristics, making them useful also as nematicidies. Of these, only aldicarb and carbofuram are used as soil insecticides and nematicides. Under rare circumstances, adlicarb has been detected in shallow groundwater following certain uses. Methomyl has proved especially effective for worm control on vegetables. Bufencarb is used in agriculture exclusively as a soil insecticide, becoming a repalcement for the long- residual organo-chlorine insecticides, aldrin, dieldrin and heptachlor.

Methiocarb, aminocarb, and promecarb and effective againt foliage- and fruit-eating insects. Methiocarb and aminocarb are both excellent molluscicides, used for slug and snail control in flower gardens and orgnamentals. Methiocarb is also registered as a bird repellent for cherries and blueberries and as a seed dressing. For cockroaches and other household insects that develop resistance to the organochlorines & organophosphates, propoxure is highly effective.

It is used by most structural pest control operators for cockroaches and other household insects in restaurants, kitchens and homes. For home use it is formulated in bottled sprays. Similarly, bendiocarb has found its greatest use in the United States as residual household insecticide. In summary, the carbamates are inhibitors of cholinesterase, are plant systemics in several instance, and are, for the most part, wide ranged in effectiveness, being used as insecticides, miticides, and molluscidides.

Formamidines

The formamidines consist a new, small, promising group of insecticides. Three examples are chloridimeform, formetanate, and amitraz. They are effective against the eggs and very young caterpillars of several moths of agricultural importance, and are also effective against most stages, of mites and ticks. Thus, they are classed as ovicides, insecticides and acaricides. Late in 1976, chlordimeform was removed from the market by its manufactures, Ciba-Geigy Corporation, land Nor-Am Agricultural Products, Inc., because it proved to be carcinogenic to a cancer-prone strain of laboratory mice during high-level, lifetime feeding studies.

In 1978 it was returned for use on cotton, but under very strict application restrictions. Their present value lies in the control of organophosphate and carbamates-resistant pests. Poisoning symptoms are distinctly deferent from other materials. It has been proposed that one possible machanism of action is the inhibition of the enzyme monoamine oxidase. This results in the accumulation of compounds termed *biogenic amines*. Thus formamidines introduce a new mode of action for the insecticides and acaricides. This fact alone makes them extremely useful, for we are slowly losing ground in the battle or insect resistance to the modes of action of the older insecticide groups.

Thiocyanates

Thicyanates have easily recognized structural formulas. Remembering the *theion* of the Greek word for "sulfur" and that the cyanides or cyanates end in –CN we have molecules that bear- SCN, or thiocynate endings. These insecticides have very distinct, creoste like odours, comparatively safe to use around humans and animals, and the astonishingly quick knockdown of flying insects. Their mode of action is somewhat complex and can be simply to interfere with cellular respiration and metabolism. These materials may be found in aerosols to be used around horses and other farm animals. However, with the appearance of the synthetic pyrethroids, the thiocyanates have deceased demand and will probably sood disappear.

DINITROPHENOLS

They act by uncoupling oxidative phosphorylaction or basically by preventing the utilization of nutritional energy. In the 1930s, certain dinitrophenols were give by ininformed physicians to their overweight patients ot induce rapid weight loss. They were extremely effective, but quite toxic, and their use resulted in several widely publicized deaths. The older of this group is DNOC (3,5-dinitro-o-cresol), introduced as an insecticixe in 1982. DNOC has also used as an ovicide, herbicide, fungicide, and blossom-thinning agent. Its use has declined today to herbicidal applications in which all plants are to be killed. Dinoseb is used as a dormant fruit spray for control of many insects and mites. Another a caricide which was introduced in 1960 in Binapacryl Dinocap in 1949) is still another as well as fungicide and is one of the rare materials made up of several related molecular structures, only one of which is shown. Dinocap is particularly effective against powdery mildew fungi. Owing to its safety to green plants, it has often replaced the phytotoxic sulfur that is so effective against powdery mildews. In summary, the dinitrophenols have been used as pesticide in practically all classification: ovicides, insecticides, acaricides, herbicides, fungicides, and blossom-thinning agents.

Organotins

The organotins are a relatively new group of acaricides, which double as fungicides. Of particular interest here in cyhenxatin, one of the most selective acaricides presently known introduced in 1967. Proved to be most effective against mites on deciduous fruits, citrus, greenhouse crops and ornamentals is fenbutatinoxide which was introduced somewhat later. The mode of action of this group is not completely known but is believed to be the inhibition of oxidative phosphorylation at the site of dinitrophenol uncoupling (the production of energy in the form of adenosine triphosphate, ATP). These trial tins also inhibit photophosphorylation in chlorplasts (the chlorophyll-bearing subcellular units) and can thus serve as algicides.

Botanicals

Botanical insecticides are of great interest to many, because they are "natural" insecticides, toxicants derived from plants. Historically, the plant materials have been in use longer than any other group, with the possible exception of sulfur. Tobacco, pyrethrum, derris, hellebore, quassia, and turpentine were some of the more important plant products is use before the organized search for insecticides began. Some of the widely used insecticides come from plants. The flowers leaves, and roots are tinely ground and used in this form, or the toxic ingredients are extracted and used alone or in mixtures with other toxicants.

There are five natural or botanically derived insecticides that are of interest to gardeners in general, but especially to the organic gardener : pyrethrum, rotenone, sabadilla, ryania and nicotine. All except nicotine are exempt from the requirement of a tolerance when applied to growing fruit and vegetables. This is, they can be eaten anytime after application, but these batanical insecticides must be used according to label directions. Batanical insecticide use reached its maximum in the United States in 1966 and has declined steadily since.

Pyrethrum is now the only botanical of significance in use, typically in rapid knowdown sprays in combination with synergists and one or more synthetic organic insecticides formulated for use in the home and garden. Botanical insecticides are naturally occuring chemicals, synthesized by plants. They are really no safer than most of the currently available synthetic insecticides, at least as compared to those available to the layman. These chemicals would be unaffordable as insecticides if they were synthesized in the laboratory, which is also possible, as Botanicals are expensive to extract from plant tissues.

Nicotine

Smoking tobacco was introduced to England in 1585 by Sir Walter Releigh. As early as 1690, water extracts of tobacco were reported as being used to kill sucking insects on garden plants. As early as about 1890, the active principle in tobacco extracts was known to be nicotine, and, from that time on, extracts were sold as commercial insecticides, for home, farm and orchard. Today organic gardeners may soak a cigar or two in water overnight and spray insect-infested plants with the extract, achieving some success. "Black Leaf 40," which has long been a favourite garden spray, is a concentrate containing 40 per cent nicotine sulfate. Today steam distillation or solvent extraction are the two processes for the commercial extraction of Nicotine from Tobacco.

Nicotine which is a physiological compounds is an alkaids & contains nitrogen. It shows prominent physiological properties. Other well-known alkaids, which are not insecticides, are caffeine (found in tea and coffee), quinine (from cinchona bark), morphine (from the opiumpoppy), concaine (from coca leaves), ricinine (a poison in castor oil beans), *Strychnos nux vomica*), confine (from spotted hemlock, the posion that killed Socrates), and, finally, LSD (a haflucinogenic derived from the ergot fungus attacking grain). As its mode action, nicotine mimics acetylocholine (ACh) at the neuromuscular (nerve-muscle) junction in mammals, the results in twitching, convulsions, and death, all in rapid order. In insects, the same action is observed, but only in the gangila of their central nervous systems.

Nicotine sulfur, as it is commonly marketed, is highly toxic to all warm-blooded animals, as well as insects; for example, the LD_{50} (dose that proves lethal for 50 per cent to the test population) for rats is 50-60 mig/kg. This makes it the most hazardous of the botanical insecticides of home gardeners. It has been used with great success since before the turn of the century. Dusts are very much toxic to humans hence are not available for garden use.

Nicotine sulfate us used primarily for piercing-sucking insects such as leafhoppers, aphids, scales, trips and whiteflies, but it can kill all insects and spider mites on which it is sprayed directly. Many caterpillar pests, however, are very resistant to nicotine. It is more effective during warm weather, but degrades quickly. It is registered for use on flowering plants, and ornamental shrubs and trees to control aphids, merlybugs, scales and thrips, lace bugs, leafminers, leafhoppers, rose slugs, and spider mites. Its use for most greenhouse pests is also acceptable. Nicotine sulfate is registered for use on a variety of vegetables and fruit trees, but it cannot be used in most cases within seven days of harvest, as required by EPA. There are several ornamental plants that are sensitive to nicotine, such as roses. The label should identify those sensitive plants. Nicotine is also registered for out-of-door use as a dog and can repellent as well as for furniture in the home. Additionally, tobacco dust in acceptable as a dog and rabbit repellent out-of-doors.

Rotenone

Rotenoids, the retenone-related materials, have been used as crop insecticides since 1848, when they were applied to plants to control leaf-eating caterpillars. However, they have been used for centuries (at least since 1649) in South America to paralyze fish, causing them to surface. Roteniods are produced in the roots of two genera of the legume (bean) family : *Derris*, grown in Malaya and the East Indies, and *Lonchcarpus* (also called cubed or cube), grown in south America. Rotenone has an oral LD_{50} of approximately 350 mg/kg (in rats) and has been used for generations as the ideal general garden insecticides. It is harmless to plant, highly toxic to fish kind many insects, especially caterpillars, moderately toxic to warm-blooded animals, and leaves no harmful residues on vegetables. There is no waiting interval between application and harvest of a food corp.

Rotenone is marketed as spray concentrates and ready to use dust, it is both a contact & a stomach poison to insects. It kills insects slowly, but causes them to stop their feeding almost immediately. Like all the other botanical insecticides its life in the sun is short, one to three days. It is useful against caterpillars, aphids, beetles, true bugs, leafhoppers, thrips, spider mites, ants, rose slugs, whiteflies, sawflies, bagworms, armyworms, cutworms, leafrolles, midges and a host of other pets. Next to pyrethrum, rotenone is probably second in the number of approved use, exceeding 1000. Rotenone is the most useful piscicide available for reclaiming lakes for game fishing. It eliminates all fish, closing the lake of reintroduction of rough species. After treatment, the lake can be restrocked with the desired species. Rotenone is a selective piscicide in that it kills all fish at dosages that are relatively nontoxic to fish foiod organisms. It also breaks down quickly leaving no residues harmful to the fish used for restocking. The recommended rate is 0.5 part of rotenone to one million of water (PPM), or 5.1 kg per hectarameter of water (1.36 pounds per acre-foot).

Sabadilla

Sabadilla is extracted from the seeds of a member of the lily lfamily. Its oral $LD_{50}$is approximately 5000 mg/kg, making it the least toxic to warm blooded animals of the five botanical insecticides discussed. It acts as both contact stomach poison for insect. Cevatridine ($C_{32}H_{49}NO_9$) and veratridine ($C_{36}H_{51}NO_{11}$) are the two known active alkaloids that are included in Sabadilla. Neither chemical structure has been established. It is irritating to human eyes and causes violent sneezing in some sensitive individuals. It deteriorates rapidly in sunlight and can be used safely on food crops with no waiting interval required by the EPA.

Sabadilla is probably the most difficult of the five botanical insecticides to purchase, simply because there was hardly any demand for it for about 15 years. Sabadilla is registered for most commonly grown vegetables and will control caterpillars, grasshoppers, beetles, leafhoppers, thrips chinch bugs, stink bugs, larlequin and squash bugs, other true bugs, and patato psyllids. It is not very useful against and will not control spider mites.

Ryania

Ryania is a safe insecticide, quite safe for humans & domestic animals so safe that no waiting is required between the time of application to food crops and harvest, as there is for most other insecticides. Ryania is made from the ground roots of the ryania shrub grown in Trinidad and, like nicotine, belongs to the chemical class of alkaloids. It has an oral LD_{50} of approximately 750 mg/kg. It is a slow-acting insecticides, requiring as long as 24 hours to kill. Insects exposed to ryania usually stop their feeding almost immediately, making it particularly useful for caterpillars.

Ryanodine ($C_{25}H_{35}No_9$), is the active principle of ryania, and its chemical structure is still not determined. Ryanodine affects insect muscles directly by preventing contraction, resembling the effects of strychnine in mammals. The preferred uses for ryania are against fruit-and foliage-eating caterpillars on fruit trees, especially the codling moth on apple trees. However, it is useful against almost all plant-feeding insects, making it an ideal material for small orchards of deciduous fruits. It is not effective against spider mites. Ryania is exempt from a waiting period between application and harvest and is registered by the EPA for the control of a host of insect pests on a wide variety of plants, shrubs and trees.

Vegetable garden pests include aphids, cabbage loopers, Colorado patato beetles, corn borers, cucumber beetles, diamond back moths, flea beeles, leafhoppers, Mexican bean beetle, spittle bugs, and tomato hornworms. Ryania is registered for deciduous fruit trees of control aphids (except the woodly aphids), codling moth, Japanese beetles, and cherry fruit fly. It has long been used to control citrus thrips on all citrus. Though not very effective, ryania can be used in the home to control ants, silverfish, cockroaches, spiders and crickets. On ornamentals it is registered for aphids and lace bugs. It can used on roses against aphids, Japanese beetles, thrips, and whiteflies; on brambles, for aphids, raspberry fruitworms, and sawflies; and on grapes for aphids (except the woolly aphid) kand the Japanese beetles. Ryania is difficult to obtain since its importation into the United States has been stopped by its major distributor.

Pyrethrum

Pyrethrum is extracted from the flowers of a chrysanthemum grown in Kenya, Africa and Ecuador, South America. It has an oral LD_{50} of approximately 1500 mg/kg and is one of the oldest household insecticides available. In the early 19th century during the Napoleonic wars, ground dried flower heads were used to control body lice. Pyrethrum acts on insects with phenomenal speed causing immediate paralysis, thus its popularity in fast knockdown household aerosol spray. However, unless it is formulated with one of the synergists, most of the paralyzed insects recover to once again become pests. Pyrethrum is formulated as household sprays and aerosols and is available as spray concentrates and dusts for use on vegetables, fruit trees, ornamental shrubs, and flowering plants at any stage of growth. Vegetables and fruit sprayed of dusted with pyrethrum may be harvested or eaten immediately; there is no waiting interval required between application and harvest of the food crop. Pyrethrum has been approved by EPA, and has more uses than any other insecticides, numbering in thousand because of its general sagety to humans & domestic animals & its effectiveness against practically every known crawling and flying insect pest.

It is a mixture of four compounds: pyrethrins I and II and cinerin I and II. Their structures can be assembled by attaching the R1 and R2 in their proper positions on the large ester structure to the left.

Synthetic Pyrethroids

The natural insecticide is quite unstable in sunlight and aho it is very costly, therefore, it is seldom used for the agricultural purposes. Recently however, several synthetic pyrthrin-like materials have become available and are referred to as synthetic pyrethroids These meterials are very stable in sunlight and are generally effective against most agricultural kpests when used at the low rate of 0.11 to 0.32 kig/ha. Examples are permethrin (Ambuhs® or Pounce®) and fenvalerate (Pydrin®). The synthetic pyrethroids, or more correctly *pyrethroids*, have a rather long and successful history.

For ease of classification, they are placed in four categories, or generations. The first generation contains but one pyrethroids, allethrin (Pynamin). Allethrin was commercially available in 1949. It consists of 22 chemical reactions to produce the final insecticide, in this sense it marked the beginning of an era of complex syntheses. Allethrin in merely a synthetic duplicate of cinerin I (a component of pyrethrum), with a slightly more stable side chain, and it is more persistent than pyrethrum. Equally effective against houseflies and mosquitoes, but less so against cockroaches and other insects it was readily synergized by the common pyrethrum synergists.

The second generation includes tetramethrin (Neo-Pynamin), which appeared in 1965. It gives stronger knockdown of flying insects than allethrin and is readily synergized. Resemthrin (NRDC-104, SBP-1382), and FMC-17370) appeared in 1967, is approximatley 20 times more effective than pyrthrum is housefly knockdown, and is not synergized to any appreciable extent with pyrethrum synergists. Bioresmethrin (NRDC-107, FMC-18739, and RU-11484), also described in 1967, is

50 times more effective than pyrethrum against normal (suceptible to insecticides) houseflies, and also not synergized with pyrthrum synergists. Both resmethrin and bioresme-thrin and more stable than pyrethrum, and decompose fairly rapidly on exposure to air and sunlight, which explains why they were never developed for agricultural use. (Resemthrim has become·the most used of the second generation pyrethroids for sprays and aerosols to control flying and crawling insects indoors.) In 1969 Bioallethrin (d-trans-allethrin) was introduced & it is more potent than allethrin and readily synergized, but it is not as effective as resmelthrin. The last of this period was phenothrin (Sumithrin®), introduced in 1973. It, too, is intermediate in quality and slightly enhanced by synergists. The third generation includes fenvalerate (Pydrin®) and permethrin (Ambush, Pounce, and Pramex), which appeared in 1972 and 1973 respectively. These became the first agricultural pyrethroids because of their exceptional insecticidal activity (0.11 kgAI/ha) and their *photostability*. Photostability means they are unaffected even by ultraviolet in sunlight, lasting four to seven days on crop foliage as effective residues.

The contemporary forth generation, still being developed and regsitered, is truly exciting, for their rates of application are again reduced to one-tenth of the previous generation, or to the order of 0.11 to 0.06 kg AI/ha required of the phenomenal compared to the rate of 1.1 to 2.3 kg) AI/ha. This is truly phenomenal compared to the rate of 1.1 to 2.3 kg) AI/ha required of the organophosphate, carbamate, and organochlorine insecticides. Emerging in this truly revolutionary form of chemical insect control are the pyrthroids; cypermethrin (Ammo® Cymbush®, and Ripcord®), fenpropathrin, flucythrinate (Pay-Off®), fluvalinate (marvil®), and decamethrin (Decis®). All these insecticides are photostable, providing long residual effectiveness in the field, and are not significantly improved with the addition of pyrethrin synergists.

Synergists or Activators

Activators or Synergists as the name indicates are not in themselves considered toxic or insecticidal, but are materials used with insecticides to synergize or enhance the activity of the insecticides. Synergists are added to certain insecticides in the ratio of 8 : 1 or 10 : 1. The first synergist was introduced in 1940 to increase the effectiveness of pyrethrum. Since then many materials have been introduced, but only a few are still marketed beccause of cost and ineffectiveness. Synergists are found in practically all the "bug-bomb" aerosols to enchance the action of the fast knockdown insecticides pyrethrum, allethrin, and sometimes resemthrin against flying insects. Although initially developed for use with pyrethrum, they have since been observed to synergize some, but not all, organophosphates, organochlorines, carbamates, as well as a few of the botanical, or plant- derived, insecticides.

The mode of action of the synergists is to inhibit mixed-function oxidases, enzymes that metabolize foreign com- pounds, which in this instance would be the preythrum. The most popular synergists belong to the only two molecular groups, or moieties. The first is the methylendioxyphenyl moeity. The R_1 and R_2 are simple or oxygenated dcarbon chains or other groups of varying combinations. The second synergistic moiety does have a single name but is characterized by either of the following structures. Notice that all three moieties involve a five-membered ring associated with two oxygens. Because their mode of action k is the inhibition of insecticide-metabolizing enzymes, it is likely that this steric three-dimensional structure is generally the most effective in enzyme binding.

The synergists are usually used in sprays prepared for the home and garden, stored grain, and on livestock, particularly in dairy kbarns. Synergists are quite expensive, thus seldom if ever used on crops. Sesamin was the name given to a material containing the methyl endioxpenhyl groups, first is sesame oil. As mentioned earlier, many compounds having this moeity are synergistic, but the structures of piperonyl butoxide, mostly in livestock and animal shelter sprays. In summary, the synergists are used in many of the insecticide mixtures for home, garden and barn. Their mode of action of their binding to oxidative enzymes the would otherwise degrade the insecticide.

Inorganics

These insecticides which do not contain carbon are called Inorganic insecticides. Usually they are white and crystalline, resembling the salts. They are stable chemicals, do not evaporate, and are frequently soluble in water. They are mentioned here for their historical siignificance. Sulfur, 1, is very likely the oldest known *effective insecticide*. Sulfur and sulfur candles were burned by our great-grandparents for every conceivable purpose, from bedbug fumigation to the cleansing of a house just removed from medical quarntine of smallpox.

Sulfur is a highly useful; pesticide in integrated pest management programmes where target pest specificity is important. Sulfur dusts are especially toxic to mites of every variety, such chiggers and spider mites, thrips, newly-hatched scale insects, and as a stomach poison for some caterpillars. Sulfur dusts and sprays are also fungicidal particularly against powdery mildews. Several other inorganic materials have been used insecticides. These include compounds of mercury, boron, thallium, arsenic, antimony, selenium and fluoride. The only of these used extensively today is arsenic, which is used in two forms, the arsenites (salts of arsenious acid) and the arsenates(salts of arsenic acid).

The first commonly used arsenical was Paris green (green because of its copper content). It's a water soluble assenite. Next was lead arsenate. Finally, the third and last of these arsenicals was calcium arsenate, which was used for a time on vegetables in the 1930s and on cotton in the 1930s and 1940s. *Arsenicals* are truly stomach poisons, exerting their toxic action following ingestion by the insects. Their action is attributed to the arsenate or arsenate ion. The arsenicals have a rather complex mechanism of action. First, they uncouple oxidative phosphorylation (bysubstitution of the arsenite ion for phosphourus), a major enter-producing step of the cell. Second, the arsenate ion inhibits certain enzymes that contain enzymes that contain sulfhydryl (-SH) groups. And, finally both the arrsenite and arsenate ions coagulate protein by causing the shape or configuration of proteins to change.

Arsenical insecticides were very useful agricultural tools form 1930 until 1956, as we were making the transition form the simple to the complex synthetic molecules. They were, in fact, responsible for the initiation of large-scale insecticide applications eventually leading to the intensive use of fungicides and herbicides in modern agriculture.

Fluorine insecticides also included organic fluorine compounds, but these were of little importance and seldom used. The inorganic fluorides were sodium fluoride, used for cockroach and ant control around the home, and barium fluosilicate, sodium silicofluoride, and cryolite (NaF, $BaSiF_6$, and Na_3ALF_6, respectively). The last three were used for a time in plant protection. The fluoride ion inhibits many enzymes that contain iron, calcium and magnesium. Several of these enzymes are involved in energy production in cells, as in the case of phosphatases and phosphorylases.

Boric acid (H_3BO_4), used as an insecticide against cockroaches and other crawling household pests in the 1930s and 1940s, has returned in the 1980s. Although manufacturers claim it is "safe, does not evaporate, and continued to kill for years," in fact, it is only moderately effective, acting as both a stomach poison and adsorber of insect cuticle wax. The last group of inorganics are the silica gels or silica aergels. These are light, white fluffy silicates, used for household insect control. The silica aerogels kill insects by adsorbing waxes from the insect cuticle, permitting the continuous loss of water from the insect body. The insects then gradually become desiccated and die from dehydration. These include Dir-Die®, Drianone®, and Drione®. The latter two are fortified with pyrethrum and synergists, which enchance their effectiveness.

Fumigants

The fumigants are small, volatile, organic molecules that become gases at temperatures above 5°C. They are usually heavier than air and commonly contain one or more of the halogens (CL, Br, or F). Most are highly penetrating, reaching through large masses of materials. They are used to kill insects eggs, and certain microorganims in buildings, warehouses, grain elevators, soils, and green-houses and in packaged products such as dried fruits, lbeans, grain, land breakfast cereals. Fumigants, as a group, are narcotics.

The mechanism of action of the fumigants are more physical than chemical. The fumigants are liposoluble (fat soluble); they have common symptomogoly; their effects are reversi- ble; and their activity is altered very little by structural changes in their molecules. Narcotics induce narosis, sleep, or unconsciouness, which is effect in their action on insects Liposolubility appears to be an important factor in the action of fumigants, since these narcotics lodge in lipid-containing tissues, which are found in the nervous system.

Microbials

Certain microbes or micro-organisms are and used for controlling the insects, hence are called microbial insecticides like mammals insects are susceptible to diseases caused by fungi, bacteria, and viruses. In several instaces, these have been isolated, cultured, and mass-produced for use as pesticiedes. The insect disease-causing microorganisms do not harm other animals or plants. The reverse of this is also true. This method of insect control is ideal in that the diseases are usually rather specific. Undoubtedly the future holds many such materials in the arsenal of insecticides, since several new insect pathogens are identified each year. However, at the persent only a few are produced commercially and approved by the EPA for us on food and feed crops. There is still some concern regarding the every remote chance of human susceptibility to these diseases of invertebrate animals, hence the slow advances into this relatively new field exceptional precautionary testing. The microorganism *Bacillus thuringiensis* is a disease-causing bacterium whose spore are necessary induction. These spores produce compounds that injure the gut of the insect larve in such a way that invasion of the body cavity follows. This organism produces four substances toxic to insect.

The first, and most important, is a crytalline protein whose ingestion by caterpillars results in paralysis of their gut. The second is a toxin, a water, a water-soluble nucleotide derivative, that passes unchanged in the manure. The commerical preparation of Bacillus caused the loss of remaining two substance which are enymes. Only one insect virus has been registered for agricultural use by the EPA. Two of the most destructive pest caterpillars is agriculture, known as the *Heliothis* nuclear polyhedrosis virus, it is specific for *Heliothis zea* (corn earworm, cotton bollworm) and *Heliothis virescens* (tobacco budworm).

Recently registration has been extended not only for cotton but also for all crops attacked by *Heliothis* species including beams, corn, lettuce, okra, peppers, sorghum, soyabeans, tobacco and tomatoes. Proprietary names for this knaturally occuring viral pathogen are Elcar® and Biotrol VHZ® . Several other insect viruses are in the development stage, all of which are aimed at caterpillars and are only experimentally available. Viruses are highly specific and have modes of action that may not be identical throughout. Generally, the viruses result in crystalline proteins that are eaten by the larva and begin their activity in the gut. The virus units then pass through the gut wall and into the blood. There are units multiply rapidly and take over complete genetic control of the cells, causing thier death. A recent and innovative development in the agricultural use of microbial insecticides is the addition of feeding or gustatory stimulants.

The feeding stimulants apparently attract the caterpillars to treated foliage, which increases their consumption of the microbial. Two successfully marketed products are Coax® and Gustol® , both of which are wettable powders and used at 1.1 to 2.3 kg/ha. Abbott Lboratories developed a mycoacaricide, mycar miticide which is a new biological control. The microorganism is *Hirsutella thompsonii*, a parasitic fungus that infects and kills the citrus rust mite. Under optimum conditions *H. thompsonni* can infect spider mites and other nontarget mites.

It is, however, consistenty effective only against the citrus rust mite; this it is selective miticide. When sprayed on plants the spores grow into colonies that attach to the mite. In the presence of ample free moisture the spores germinates and infects the mite. The mite dies in about three days, and the fungus spread, continuing to propagate itself. In this manner it offers potentially long residual effectiveness. Because the active agent is a fungus, all commercial fungicides, copper chemicals, and certain other metal salts such as zinc, lead, and manganese are detrimental to *H.thompsonii*. Because of its specificity *H. thompsonii* should be highly compatible with other suppression techniques used in the integrated past managemnt of citrus crops. For the control in grasshoppers, Sandoz Inc. developed a new biological control, *Nosema Locustae*. Marketed under the name NOLOC® and Trojan 10®, the microorganism is a protozoan. Depending on the method of application, climatic conditions, and grasshopper density, the protozoa kill up 50 per cent of the insects and sterilize up to 30 per cent of the survivors. Maximum effect occurs over a two to four-week period. Through subsequent generation by transmission through the eggs upto three or four years the residual effect of a single treatment continues to control grasshoppers.

Insect Growth Regulators

The first generation insecticides were the stomach poisons, such as the arsenicals, heavy metals, and fluorine compounds. The second generation includes the familiar contact insecticides roganochlorines, organophosphates, carbamates and formamidines. The third generation of insecticides are the *biorationals*. These chemicals are environmetally sound, closely resembling or identical to chemicals produce by insects and plants. Among these are the insect growth regulators (IGRs), a relatively new group of chemical compounds that alter growth and developments in insects. Their effects have been observed on embryonic and larval and nymphal development on metamorphosis, on reproduction in both males and females, on behaviour, and on several forms of diapause. They include ecdysone (the molting hormone), juvenile sghormone (JH), JH mimic, JH analog (JHA), and their broader synonyms, juvenoids and juvegens.

More recently another growth effect, chitin inhibition, has been identified and is discussed later, with the EPA-registered IGRs. The IGRs are effective when applied in very minute quantities and apparently have no undersirable effects on humans and wildlife. They are, however, nonspecific, since they affect not only the target species, but most other arthropods as well. IGRs may play an important role in future insect control, consequently, when used with precision. Several hormone producing glands in insects perform the principal functions of which are the control of reproductive processes, motting land metamorphosis. Here we are interested only in the hormone ecdysone, which is responsible for molting, and JH, which inhibits or prevents metamorphosis. When insects are treated with ecdysones, they usually die in all stages of growth, making ecdysones similar to second-generation insecticides. One attractive feature of ecdysones are potential tools is their widespread distribution in plants,, and these may play as yet unrecognized roles in insect-plant relationships. Keen interest has been directed toward JHs. These are not in the usual sense, toxic to insects. Instead of killing directly, they interfere in the normal mechanisms of development and cause the insects to die before reaching the adult stage.

One JH is the classical juvabione, found in the wood of balsam fir. Its effect was discovered quite by accident when paper towels made from this source were used to line insect-rearing containers, and the insects' development was suppressed. Some of these plant-derived substances actually serve to inhibit the development of insects feeding thereon, thus protecting the host plant. These are referred to broadly as antijuvenile hormones, or more accurately, *antiallatotropins*. Recently, antillatotropins, called *precocenes*, have been discovered. These are considered a potential fourth generation of insect control agents.

Incidentally, the name precocene results from the precocious metamorphosis stimulated by compounds having the chromene nucleus. It is known that precocenes depress the level of juvenile hormone below that normally found in immature insects, although the mode of action is still unclear. Dramatic results with JHs have been obtained in the laboratory, the most promising effects being on mosquito larvae, caterpillars, and hemipterans (bugs), although effects have been observed on practically all insect orders. Most insect species respond to treatment with JHs by producing extra larval, nymphal, or pupal forms that vary from giant, almost perfect, forms, to intermediates of all sorts between the immatures and the adults. For the most part, the periods of greatest sentivity for metamorphic inhibition are the last larval or nymphal stages and the pupa, in those having complete metamorphosis. One recognizable problem is the precision of timing applications to achieve meximum damaging effect on the uncoming life stage of a particular insect.

For practical purposes. IGRs could be used on crops to suppress damaging insect numbers. They would be applied with the purpose lof preventing pupal development or adult emergence, thus keeping the insects in the immature stages, resulting eventually in their deaths. To date, only three IGRs are registred by the EPA. The first, methoprena (Altosid®), manufactured by the Zoecon Corporation, was registered early in 1975 as a mosquito growth regulator, for use against second-through fourth-larval-stage floodwater mosquitoes at 0.11 to 0.14 kg/ha to prevent adult emergence. Larvae exposed to methoprene continue their development to the pupal stage, when they die. When applied to pupae or adult mosquitoes. Additionally methoprene has been formulated as Precor for indoor control of dogs and cats fleas. It acts by interrupting the flea's life cycle at the larval stage, preventing emergence of adult fleas for lup to 75 days. Its use in combination with a conventional insecticides is usually necessary to control adult fleas not affected by the growth regulator.

Methoprene is also registered for use on tobacco to control cigarette beetles (KabatØ), on cattle feed to control horn flies, and on mushrom-growing media to control hungus gnats (ApexØ). In order to control mosquitoes in drinking water it has been approved by the World Health Organization for its use. The second IGR is diflubenzuron (Dimilin®), manufactured by Thompson-Hayward Chemical Company. Currently registered for gypsy moth caterpillars in forest and for the boll weevil in cotton, it is awaiting registration for a wide variety of pests.

Experimentally, it has controlled insect pests in forest, woody ornamentals, fruit, vegetables, cotton, soyabeans, citrus, larvae of flies, midge, gnats, and mosquitoes : on mosquitoes, a dose as small as 1.5g/ha is effective. Diflubenzuron is not truly a growth regulator of the juvenoid class but rather another insecticide with a different mode of action. However, it is tentatively classed with the IGRs. It acts on the larval stages of most insects by inhibiting or blocking the synthesis of chitin, a vital and almost indestructible part of the hard outer covering of insects, the exoskeleton. The third, and most recent, IGR is kinoporene (EnstarØ),also developed the Zoecon Corporation. It is effective against aphids, whiteflies, mealybugs, and scales (both soft and armored) on ornamental plants and vegetable seed crops grown in greenhouses and shadehouses. It is specific for insects in the order Homoptera, and results in a gradual reduction rathar than an immediate kill, by inhibiting development, reduction egg-laying, killing eggs already laid, and sterilizing mature whiteflies and aphids.

It is virtually nontoxic to humans and other warm blodded animals because it is specific for insects like all other IGRs. Cans IGRs become successful pest control agents? Certainly they can in time. They will, however, have to meet general criteria for other pests control agents;

thus they must be effective in reducing insect populations below economic damage levels, be competitive with second-generation insecticides in cost, and have no undersirable side effects. In summary, IGRs hold intriguing possibilities for future use in practical insect control. It should be kept in mind that IGRs are insect-controlling chemicals and thus fall within the same legal confines as other insecticides. Being Toxic to populations of insects rather than to individuals they are however distinguished from other. Likewise the ability to control the fecundity (reproductive capacity) of the pest to the cause of the ultimate success of any pest control agent.

Insect Repellents

Historically, repellents have included smokes, plants huge in dwellings or rubbed on the skin as the fresh plant or brews, oils, pitches, tars, and various earths applied to the body. Camel urine sprinkled on the clothing has been of value, although questionable, in certain locales. Camphor crystals sprinkled among woolens have been used for decades to repel clothes moths. Before humans developed a more edified approach to insect olfaction and behaviour, it was assumed that if a substance was repugnant to humans it would likewise be repellent to annoying insects. Prior to World War II, there were only four principal repellents: (1) oil of citronella, discovered in 1901, used also as a hair- dressing fragrance by certain Eastern cultures, probably to control lice and other head ectoparasites; (2) dimethyl, phthalate, discovered in 1929, (3) Indalone® introduced in 1937, and (4) Rutgers 612, which became available in 1939. It became essential to find new repellents that would survive both time and dilution by perspiration, with the onslaught of World War II and the introduction of American military personnel into new environments, particularly the tropics.

The ideal repellent would be nontoxic and nonirritating to humans, nonplasticizing, and longlasting (12 hours) against mosquitoes, biting flies, ticks, fleas and chiggers. Unfortunately, the ideal repellent has still not been found. Some repellents have unpleasant odours, require massive dosages, are oily or effective only for a short time, irritate the skin, or soften paint and plastics. Insect repellents come in every conceivable formulation - undiluted, diluted in cosmetic solvent with added fragrance, aerosols, creams, lotions, treated cloths to be rubbed on the skin, grease sticks, powders, suntan oils, and clothes-impregnating laundry emulsions.

Regardless of the formulation, the periods of protection they offer vary with the chemical, individual, the general environment, insect species, and avidity of the insect. What happens to repellents once applied ? Why aren't they effective longer than one or two hours? No single answer is satisfactory–but generally it is because they evaporate, are absorbed by the skin, are lost by abrasion of clothing or other surfaces, and are diluted by perspiration. The following chemical structures are those of the most commonly found in today's repellents. Of these, diethyl toluamide (Delphene®) is by far superior to all others against biting and mosquitoes.

Insecticide Selectivity

We must supplement insecticides with other forms of insect control as there are no main tool or insect control at least or the foreseeable future. Selective insecticides must be used and insecticides must be used in selective way, lest the effect of beneficial insects and natural enemies be minimizeds in any programme requiring multiple insecticide applications. Insecticides affect various insects differently. An insecticide that is lethal against one group may have little, if any, effect on another. Generally, however, most insecticides kill many kinds of insects; broad-spectrum insecticides are those that kill more kinds than others. A selective pesticide is one that is toxic to some pests, but has little or no effect on other similar species. For example, a selective herbicide is one that kills certain undersirable species of weeds while harming the crop plants little or not at all. Certain fungicides are selective to the point that they control only powdery mildews and no other fungi.

A selective insecticide kills selected insects, but sprares many or most of the other insects, including beneficial species, either through different toxic action or the manner in which the insecticide us used. Though desirable the development of such a product would be uneconomical for the manufactures since not enough of the spectes specific insecticide could be sold to recoup research development and marketing costs. Thus, the chemical industry seek rather to develop a general purpose, broad-spectrum chemical that will control not only elm leaf beetles, but boll weevils on cotton, caterpillars on vegetables, the gypsy moth in deciduous forest, green bugs in small grains, alfalfa weevis, the codling moth in apples, and scales on citrus.

General-purpose insecticides offer the best possible incentives in the economic market : satisfied growers and contented stock-holders. A selective insecticide, in the narrowest use of term, simply means that the active ingredient is inherently more toxic to one group of insects than to others; in other words most groups of insects are physiologically more tolerant to the chemical than are the few readily killed by it. More commonly, selective is used to designate an insecticide that does not harm a beneficial species of insect while killing pest species. This physiological selectivity results from differences between target and nontarget species in (1) penetration rate of the toxicant, (2) tissue binding and loss of the toxicant, (3) the speed of toxicant and metabolite excretion, (4) metabolic alteration or detoxification, (5) target sites of action or biochemical lesion, or (6) polyfactorial selectivity where more than one of the above processes is involved. (For a clear, detailed discussion of physiological selectivity, see Hollingworth, 1976.)

Physiologically nonselective insecticides may achieve use selectivity if they are applied in such a way that certain insect groups are more adversely affected than others. Use selectivity may result from the timing of the application, the formulation used, the dosage level, or numerous there techniques. From a practical standpoint this approach offers the most immediate hope of being included in precision integrated pest management programmes. The selective use of an insecticide to kill a particular pest while permitting other insects to escape, particularly beneficials, achieves the same selective effect as the use of physiologically selective insecticides. The existence of both the pest and the desirable species, and utilize some difference in their habits, distribution, or biology to devise a discriminatory method of application, all these must be taken into a count by the planner if they use selectivity.

Although some insecticides are intrinsically more toxic physiologically to certain insects, and some are equally toxic to different species, they can be used selectively to affect pests more than beneficial insects. Insecticide selectivity thus can be achieved not only by restricted toxicity but also by precision in timing, the calculation of effective rates of application, the use of materials with short residual lives, methods of application such as seed treatment, spot treatments restricted to areas in which pests vastly outnumber beneficials, or use of those formulations that tend to enhance the survival of beneficials.

In general, selectivity is obtained by one of the following paractices : (1) use of physiologically selective insecticides that are more toxic to pest species than to others; (2) timing of applications such that detrimental effects on the pest's natural enemies are minimized; and (3) reduction of dosages to levels that adequately control the target pest while sparing relatively large numbers of natural enemies of the target pest and other potential pests. The selective use of insecticides is not simple.

In most instances it requires an intimate knowledge of not only the target pest but also the secondary pests beneficial species. Researchers are directing their efforts towards integrating the use of insecticides and beneficial insects. Effective insect control will require both toxicological research in the development of physiologically selective insecticides and applied ecological research in the use of available insecticides to achieve selective action. The selective use of insecticides requires an intimate knowledge of not only the target pest but also the secondary pests beneficial species.

Application of Insecticides

Insecticides are the chemical substances used in controlling the pests. The usefulness of any insecticide depends in a very large measure upon its proper application, and this is determined by the properties of the insecticide, the nature of the pest or pest complex to be controlled, and the site to which the application is to be made. The three general methods of applying insecticides are as sprays, in which water or oil is used as the carrier for the toxicant, as dusts, in which a fine dry powder is the carrier, and as fumigants, in which the insecticide in applied as a gas. The equipment for the application of insecticides ranges from such simple devices as the puff duster and "flit gun" to complex machines such as the mist blower and spraying helicopter, and this development is entirely a product of the last 100 years. Before that time, liquid insecticides were applied by a bundle of twigs, a feather, or a brush broom, and dusts by a bellows or blowing tube.

The progress which has been made is a product of detailed knowledge of physics and engineering coupled with a vast amount of trial and error. Much remains to be learned, and relatively simple devices may yet be produced which will effect vertiable revolutions, as for example, the development of the aerosol "bomb," which from its humble begining in 1942 has become a standard household article, of which 65,900,000 units were sold in 1959 for insect control.

Cautions in Insecticide Applications

Usually insecticides are applied when populations of a pest species reach the economic threshold. In this way economic damage is prevented and needless treatments are avoided. Other factor must often be con- sidered as well, such as the timing of applications so as to coincide with the stage of development of the insect pest which is most easily killed or with the stage in the seasonal development of the plant when it well best withstand the treatment. Timing to observe the safe interval before harvest which is required to attenuate insecticide residues to legal levels and to avoid periods of bloom for protection of bees and other pollinating insects is also extremely important. Since proper timing varies widely with different crops, different insecticides, and in various areas of the country, the grower should follow only approved spray programmes of state and federal agencies, observe all label precautions and directions, and whenever in doubt should secure the advice of a trained entomologist who knows local conditions regarding spray programmes for different crops and insects. In general, the earlier the insecticide is applied after the insects appear, the easier it is to destroy them, but in most cases applications should be made only when populations reach economic thresholds.

Most of insecticides are violent poisons to human beings and livestock, as well as to insects. Therefore, they should be plainly labeled and, together with mixing vessels, kept out of reach of children. Animals must be kept away from liquid sprays and not allowed to pasture in treated areas. All discarded insecticide containers should be burned or buried. The spray applicator should familiarize himself with the hazards of various insecticides before use and determine the proper protective measures necessary for safe application, as furnished by the manufacturer.

In general, these will include the use of protective clothing, rubber gloves, and goggles when handling spray concentrates and a protective mask if there is any possibility of inhaling toxic dust, mist, or vapour. Prolonged wetting by sprays or other contamination should be avoided, and clothes changed at least twice daily, followed by the liberal application of soap and water to remove any skin contamination. In rainy weather the spraying and dusting should be avoided although many sprays will adhere satisfactorily to plants if the spray has time to dry before rain falls. Winter sprays should not be applied when the temperature is below freezing or when the trees are wet with snow or rain. When possible, spraying should also be avoided in very hot weather, above 90°F, because of increase susceptibility of plants to insecticide damage and because of the increased hazard to the operator from skin and inhalation absorption of poisons.

Sprays and Spraying

Historically, dusts have been the simplest formulations of pesticides to manufacture and the easiest to apply. In recent years, because of the increased effectiveness of the new organic insecticides, concentrate sprays have largely replaced dusts on many field and vegetable crops. Sprays are made up of solutions, emulsions, or suspensions of the toxicant. The liquid phase is usually water, but light oils are also employed. Insecticidal sprays are con- veniently described as space sprays or aerosols, directed against flying insects, and residual sprays, applied to surfaces of plants, animals, or structures frequented by insects.

Importance of Droplet Size

The size property of spray droplet is very significant and conveniently measured in microns (μ a or 0.001 millimeter). In every spray cloud there is a considerable spectrum of droplet sizes and the cloud is most conveniently characterized by a mean value which expresses the normal frequency distrubution of the droplets. The most commonly used characteristic is the mass median diameter MMD or D_m, which is that throretical droplet diameter which divides the volume of the spray into equal parts. The surface median diameter SMD or D_o is the theoretical droplet diameter which has the same surface to volume ratio as that of the total spray. D_m is a useful measure of the effectiveness of the spray in terms of the amount of active material deposited per unit area, while D_o defines the amount of exposed liquid surface and thus the coverage which may be obtained. D_m range from 1.1 to 1.6 times D_o, depending upon the nature of the atomizing device. However, with the common fan, swirl, and twin-fluid atomizers used in the application of insecticides. The average ration D_m/D_o is relatively constant with a value of 1.28, as studied by Fraser.

Droplet-size Requirements

The droplet-size of the sprays as per requirements for various insecticidal spraying operations cover a 300-fold range of droplet diameters and a 27,000,000 range of droplet volumes and extend from the 1-to30- micron size of true aerosols to the 100- to 500-micron size of hydraulic sprays. With contact sprays, the zone of efficiency for air-blast sprays is about 30 to 80 microns and for hydraulically driven sprays, between 100 and 300 microns. Special problems are encountered in aircraft spraying, and in general the most efficient range is from 100 to 300 microns.

Space sprays or aerosols

The principle of space spraying is to suspend a cloud of droplets in the space through which the insect pests are flying and thus to force the insect to accumulate a lethal deposit by colliding with the droplets. The successful application of this method is dependent upon physical laws governing the behaviour of aerosols, which are defined as colloidal suspensions of matter in air and invole an understanding of the insect flight behaviour. It is clear that the insecticide will be effective only as long as the droplets remain suspended in the free-air space.

Spraying Equipment

There are Narious types of spraying equipments. The size and type of sprayer to be used will depend upon the amount and kind of work to be done. However, spraying is at best a disagreeable task, and every effort should be made to have equipment of sufficient capacity so that the work will be done thoroughly and efficiently. The best spraying equipment can easily be ruined by failure to give it proper care. Clean water should always be pumped through the sprayer after use, the flush out all corrosive spray materials, and the metal parts should be oiled to prevent rust.

It is not advisable to apply insecticides with spraying equipment which has previously been used for the application of herbicides of the plant-growth-regulator type such as 2,4-dichloro-phenoxyacetic acid (2,4-D), because very small traces of such materials may seriously injure certain plants. There are many types of sprayers, but the most common sprays are hydraulic sprayers, which employ only pressure nozzles for the formation and distribution of the spray, and air-blast sprayers, which utilize an air stream for distribution and/or breakup of the spray.

Hydraulic Sprayers

The various types of hydraulic sprayers include (a) the compression sprayer, which is actually a special type in which compressed air is used to force the liquid through a pressure atomizing nozzle. The most familiar type is a 4-gallon cylindrical tank with a hand piston pump which is operated at 40 to 80 pounds per square inch and is very popular with the home gardener. The bucket or stirrup pump sprayer (b) has a single-or double-action plunger pump clamped into a 2-gallon bucket and operates at up to 150 pounds per square inch; (c) the napsack sprayer is a 2- to 5-gallon tank carried as a napsack and containing a diaphragm pump and agitator operations at 50 to 80 pounds per square inch by a lever carried under the operator's shoulder. These are especially suitable for small garden operations or treatments in inaccessible spots, as in mosquito larviciding or residual house spraying. The barrel pump (d) is a larger plunger-type spray pump which operates at a pressure of 200 to 300 pounds per square inch and uses a 15- to 45-gallon container as a reservior. The wheelbarrow sprayer (e) is essentially a portable barrel pump which is suitable for spraying small fields, orchards, or farm buildings. Most modern wheelbarrow sprayers have rubber tires and contain a two-cycle gasoline-engine-driven pump of 1.5 to 3.0 gallons per minute to 200 to 250 pounds per square inch and have a capacity of 15 to 50 gallons. Hydraulic power sprayers (f) range from the power whellbarrow sprayer through trailer-type field and row-crop sprayers to truck-mounted orchard sprayers. These power sprayers have 50- to 500-gallon capacities, operate up to 400 to 800 pounds per square inch, and have discharge capacities ranging from 5 to 80 gallons per minute. Discharge may be carried through one or more spray hoses or through a horizontal or vertical spray boon equipped with multiple swirl spray nozzles.

Parts of a sprayer

The important components of a spray outfit are similar for the various types, some of which are as follows: The cylinder is the portion of the pump in which the pressure is developed. It must be of noncorrosife material, and in large power sprayers, which have two to four cylinders, the lining is generally of acid-resistant porcelain. The plunger or piston forces the spray liquid through the cylinder and is made to fit tightly inside the cylinder by means of packing. Plungers may be fitted with molded rubber and fabric plunger cups which act as inside packing, expanding against the cylinder wall on the pressure stroke, or outside packing may be used which is compressed against stainless-steel plungers. Valves, usually of the ball type, and valves seats made of hardened stainless steel, direct the flow of spray liquid.

They must be readily accessible for cleaning in case of clogging by particles of dirt or spray materials. An air chamber is used to equalize the pressure and remove excessive strain on the pump. The discharge opening leading to the nozzle is located at the bottom of the air chamber. The tank, in which the spray ingredients are mixed and held, is usually constructed of metal with an enamel lining or of stainless steel. Since many spray ingredients, such as wettable powders, are not soluble in water, an agitator in necessary to keep the finely divided particles in suspension or the emulsion evenly distributed. In power sprayers this is commonly effected by two or more flat paddles or propellers on a rotating shaft near the bottom of the tank. A pressure gage indicates the pressure being maintained, and the pressure regulator maintains uniform pressure on the spray nozzles and allows the pump to operate at a greatly reduced load when spray is not being discharged. This is accomplished by a spring-and-ball valve, which can be set to lift at the desired pressure and permit the excess liquid to bypass to the tank. Strainers, over the intake to the tank and over the suction or intake pipe leading to the cylinders, keep the spray liquid free of troublesome foreign matter. The discharge pipe should be free from abrupt angles that cut down the pressure between pump and nozzles. The hose for orchard spraying shoed be at least 25 feet long, of ½ - to ¾ -inch inside diameter and four-to seven-ply strength.

The friction of the spray liquid against the inside surfaces of the spray hose results in a considerable loss of pressure at the nozzle. For example, with a 50-foot hose ½ -inch in diameter and a flow rate of 10 gallons per minute, the friction loos in 70 pounds per square inch. The pump of most power sprayers is of the direct-displacement-plunger type. The recent development of high-capacity, high-pressure boom sprayers for orchard spraying has been possible through the utilization of centrifugal pumps with capacities of up to 125 gallons per minute at pressures of 800 to 1,000 pounds per square inch. Such pumps, however, are subject to severe wear by abrasie wettable powders. Spray booms. The boom is a light hollow tube or pipe which is used to carry the spray liquid under pressure from the pump to one or more nozzles. The simplest type is the spray rod of lance, which is a tube from 3 to 8 or even 12 feet in length, with a cut off valve at one end and a simple swirl spray or flat fan nozzle at the other. With power sprayers, a broom or fog-drive gun in sometimes used for spraying fruit trees. This consists of a spray rod from 3 to 5 feet long, with a cutoff at the base and a group of three to eight nozzles at the tip.

Residual spraying indoors

The spraying of houses and barns with a heavy deposit of a long-lasting residual insecticide is widely practiced for the control of flies, mosquitoes, bed bugs, cookroaches, silverfish, and ectoparasites of animals and is one of the principal weapons for the eradication of malaria. This type of application is most efficiently performed with a small-capacity, portable spray pump such as the napsack, compression, or bucket sprayer or the wheelbarrow power sprayer. The World Health Organization has specified that residual-spraying operations be conducted with a spray pump having a regulator to produce a constant pressure of 40 pounds per square inch and that a flash fan nozzle discharging at 0.2 gallon perminute with a spray angle of 60 to 65 degrees be used.

During the spraying operation, the nozzle should be held approximately 18 inches away from the surface being streated, and about 150 to 250 square feet of wall surface should be covered per minute. Adherence to the suggested conditions will avoid wasteful and unsightly discharge and produce a spray of maximum impingement and deposition.

Air-Blast Sprayers

In the air-blast sprayers a relatively large volume of high-velocity air is used to break up the spray droplets and to carry them to the target, as in the twin-fluid atomizers. For convenience, however, we shall also discuss air-blast equipment in which the spray may be produced by other means but dispersed by means of an air blast. The common hand atomizer or "flit gun" is perhaps the simplest familiar device of this type. Here a piston-type air pump furnishes the air blast, which also forces the spray liquid from a reservior up a small-diameter delivery tube, and atomization results from the apposition of the air and liquid streams, according to equation. The compressd air-paint spray gun is a larger example of the type. In the use of air-blast equipment for the treatment of field or orchard crops the 30- to 80-micron droplet range seems most suitable because of the questions of coverage and dynamic catch, and thus the matter of air volume and velocity is of great importance. This is particularly true in orchard spraying, where it is necessary to have sufficient air-moving capacity to agitate the air in all parts of the tree and to displace most of it.

It has already been stated that volumes of air required with various-sized delivery tubes to produce adequate velocities at various distances from the blower. It is evidence that to secure adequate dynamic catch of 30-micron droplets at distances of 25 to 50 feet from the bolwer, very large volumes of air, ranging, from 7,500 to 28,000 cubic feet per minute are required. It has been shown that to spray a moderate-sized orchard tree 20 by 20 by 20 feet (8,000 cubic feet) with a mist blower travelling at 0.5 mile per hour, 17,600 cubic feet per minute of spray are required, and of course this requirement is directly proportional to the volume of the tree and the speed of travel of the sprayer.

Table 10.1. Air Velocities at Various Distances

Diameter of Round outlet, in.	*Volume of air, cu. ft./min.*	*Velocity at indicated distance from blower, m.p.h.*				
		Outlet	*10 ft.*	*25ft.*	*50ft.*	*100ft.*
4	1,300	170	40	8	2	0
8	3,800	125	40	10	3	0
12	7,500	125	60	30	7	2.5
24	28,000	120	75	40	17	7
54	27,000	50	35	30	8	3

Two types of air-blast sprayers have been constructed the spray blower and the mist blower. In the spray blower, the liquid is broken up by hydraulic nozzles and carried to the target by the air blast, while in the mist blower the spray liquid is finely dispersed by means of air-atomizing nozzles or spinning disks and then carried by the air blast. Both types of equipment employ axial-flow turbines or centrifugal fans to generate from 4,000 to 60,000 cubic feet of air per minute at velocities ranging from 60 to 250 miles per hour.

The successful application of air-blast sprayers to field and row crops is difficult because of problems in equalizing spray distribution at varying distances from the point of discharge. Various devices, including manifolds with a number of outlets, fishtails, elongated slots, and rotating or oscillating outlets to sweep the area, have improved the evenness of coverage. Air blasts of 3,500 to 4,000 cubic feet per minute at 60 miles per hour have given effective results over swaths of 15 to 35 feet. The commercial units available, however, are generally modifications of orchard sprayers and use air blasts of 20,000 to 40,000 cubic feet per minute at moderate velocities of 70 to 90 miles per hour to avoid crop damage, damage, directed at right angles to the path of travel from either one or both sides. The rows over which the machine passes are simultaneously sprayed with a low-volume boom. Such equipment will treat a swath 40 to 60 feet wide suing 5o to 100 gallons per acre. A number of large spray blowers are in extensive commercial use for orchard spraying, and the Speed Sprayer is perhaps the best known. This equipment will apply from 50 to 500 or more gallons per acre and delivers up to 45,000 cubic feet per minute of air, with nozzle pressures of 50 to 70 pounds per square inch and pump capacities of 55 to 140 gallons per minute. The spray is delivered into the air blast from as many as 58 to 264 swirl spray nozzles.

The spray duster employs 40,000 cubic feet per minute of air passing through two vertical fishtail outlets to distribute high-pressure spray at 100 to 1,000 gallons per acre from vertical banks of nozzles. The air flow is periodically changed in direction by the oscillation of a hinged section of the outlet to aid the spray penetration by moving leaves and twigs. The most difficult problem with air-blast sprayers in orchard spraying is equalizing the coverage between the top and bottom of the tree.

Aerosol Generators

In the aerosol culture, we have raised being bombs, hair sprays, under arm deodorants, adhesives, car wax, fabnc, finishers etc. Aerosols for insecticidal use have been produced by a number of methods: (a) by burning the insecticide; (b) by spraying a solution of insecticide onto a heated surface; (c) by forcing the insecticide, dissloved in a liquefied, low-boiling gas through a capillary tube; (d) by spraying at high pressure through a swirl spray nozzle of low capacity; (e) by forcing a solution of insecticide between two closely apposed and rapidly spinning disks; and (f) by the use of a high-velocity stream of gas, air, or steam acting upon a stream of liquid in some type of twinfluid atomizer. The exhaust aerosol generator uses the hot exhaust gases from an internal-combusion engine to produce atomization.

The droplet size is directly proportional to the ratio of flow of the liquid to the flow of air and can be predicated. The use of the hot exhaust gases favours the production of droplets of aerosol dimensions because of the very high velocitics, 600 to 1,400 feet per second, obtainable with the hot gases and aerosols are not, however, produced at pressures below 25 pounds per square inch gage. These low-or moderate-pressure aerosols require a more critical nozzle design than the simple capillary tube of the high-pressure aerosoal. In order to introduce turbulence and the formation of small bubbles of gas which serve as nuclei for boiling, a mixing chamber is provided into which the liquefied gas flows through a 0.015-inch-diameter constriction and from which the mixture issues through a 0.020-inch orifice. The dispenser value consists of a ball of metal or nylon held by a spring against a valves seat of synthetic rubber. The use of low-pressure aerosols requires higher boiling propellants or mixtures such as 54 per cent dichlorodifluoromethane and 46 per cent trichlorofiuoro-methane, which develops 37 pounds per square inch gage to 70°F.

Other useful combinations include the addition of up to 25 per cent by volume of isobutane of n-pentane to the above mixture, II and III, I and IV, and I and V from Table. Mextures such as these form bubbles in the nozzle more readily than single- component propellants and produce better aerosol dispersion at low pressures. The insecticids most commonly dispersed by the liquefied-gas method are DDT, methoxychlor synergized pyrethrins or allethrin, lindane, chlordane and dieldrin. High purification is necessary to prevent clogging of the capillary nozzle and decomposition of the insecticide and consequent corrosion of the container, although this can be inhibited by including 0.1 per cent propylene oxide. Auxiliary solvents such as petroleum distiallates, polymethylnaphthalenes, or cyclohexanone have been used to solubilize the insecticides in the propellant gas. A small percentage of nonvolatile material such as 10-W lubrication oil has been found effective in preventing too rapid volatilization of the aeroso droplets. The ultimate droplet size is determined by the concentration of nonvolatile materials, and the optimum for flying insects of 5 to 20 microns (D_m 10 to 5 microns) is obtained with about 20 per cent nonvolatile material in a high pressure formulation and about 15 per cent in a low-pressure formulation. Typical formulations of both types are:

High-pressure Aerosal	Per Cent
DDT	3
Pyrethrins, 20% extract	1
Alkylated naphthalenes	16
Dichlorodifluoromethane	80

Low-pressure Aerosol	Per Cent
Methoxychlor	2.0
Pyrethrins	0.25
Piperonyl butoxide	1.0
Alkylated naphthalenes	11.75
Dichlorodifluoromethane	30.0
Trichloromonofluoromethane	55.0

Such aerosols should be used at the rate of 2 to 4 grams per 1,000 cubic feet of space and the ischarge rate is approximately 1 gram per second. The most popular containers are the 1-pound size are available for larger enclosures and for greenhouse work. For the latter purpose a formulation of 5 to 10 per cent parathion or TEPP in methyl chloride, 90 to 95 per cent, is widely used in 10-pound bomb with a 2-foot rod and nozzle. This should be used only when wearing a protective mask. The liquefied-gas method has been used also to produce bombs delivering residual- type sprays for the control of cockroaches, ants and clothes moths and carpet beetles, at a low pressure of 20 pounds per square inch gage. For this purpose, the amount of propellant is reduced to 30 to 35 per cent of the total, and this produces a relatively coarse discharge of about 30 to 35 microns, which settles rapidly and has good wetting properties. Typical formulations are:

Roach and Ant Spray	Per Cent
Dieldrin	0.5
Pyrethrins	0.04
Piperonyl butoxide	0.1
Petroleum distillate	69.36
Propellant	30.0

Mothproofing Spray	Per Cent
DDT	3.0
Perthane	3.0
Petroleum distillate	59.0
Propellant	35.0

Dusts and Dusting

Dusting is thc oldest and the simplest method of poisoning plants for insect control it has been much more extensively practices during the past 50 years. This is largely due to the following undesirable features of dusting: (a) decreased efficiency due to less efficient deposition on the plant, (b) increased drift problems with poisonous materials, (c) increased cost of dust diluents compared with water, (d) tendency of carrier and toxicant to separate in the air unless the diluent particles are coated with the toxicant, (e) difficulties in incorporating several insecticides or other agricultural chemicals into a single dust, and (f) incrased hazard to operator from inhalation of toxic dusts. Despite the disadvantages, dusting is in many cases much easier, lighter, and several times faster than thorough coverage spraying. The equipment is considerably simpler and lighter than the spray rig and can be better used in hilly territory and under muddy conditions.

Dusting is obviously the favoured means of insect control in regions with a limited water supply and is a useful means of achieving insect control just prior to harvest without exceeding insecticide-residue tolerances. Most insecticidal dusts are very finely divided, and typical surface mean diameters are talc 1.8 microns, pyrophyllite 2.2 microns, lead arsenate 6 to 10 microns, calcium arsenate 1 to microns, and ground rotenone roots 6 microns. Such dusts pass nearly completely through a 325-mesh screen of 44 micron aperture. Thus when failling free in air these dust particles should behave similarly to aerosol droplets.

However, dust particles not only very greatly in size and shape but also tend to agglomerate during the dusting operation, so that many particles adhere tightly together, and it is very difficult to predict their settling and drifting pattern. Since the settling velocity of these small particles is directly proportional to particle density, dusts of such materials as lead and calcium arsenates settle considerable faster than dusts of botanicals such as pyrethrum or rotenone. The density of thedust diluent and the presence of dush conditioners such as stabilizers and fluffing agents also affect the dusting behaviour. The electrostatic charge on dust particles has often been suggested as a means of importance in causing the dust to adhere to plant surfaces which are negatively charged. A number of devices have been designed to increase the charge on the insecticidal dusts, either by friction or by passing the dust particles through a flow of positive ions from a highpotential electrical discharge. Inorganic dusts such as arsenicals, fluorides, copper, lead, and sulfur assume positive charges, while botanicals assume negative charges. Diluents such as pyrophyllite and gypsum are also positively charged, and diatomite, clays, and tacls are negatively charged. The use of electrostatically charged dusts has been claimed to prevent agglomeration, to increase adherence and even distribution on both sides of leaves, and to increase the dust deposition as much as 4 to 10 times.

Insecticidal dusts are commonly applied to crop plants at rates of 10 to 50 pounds per acre. However, organic insecticides such as DDT give somewhat similar insect control as long as the amount of active ingredient and plant coverage are constant, regardless of whether applied as 3 to 10 pre cent dust. The use of dusts impregnated with oily materials such as mineral oil or polymethyl naphtalenes has sometimes been of advantage in increasing deposits and decreasing drift. For some insecticidal applications, such as in the control of the European corn borer in the whorls of the corn plant, ants and other soil-inhabiting insects, and mosquito larvae in water under dense vegetation, the use of relatively coars granular dusts of 30- to 60-mesh (250 to 590 microns) serves to prevent the insecticide from adhering to plant foliage and enables it to reach the soil or water surface. The use of these granular materials also greatly decreases drift problems.

Dusting Equipment

A good duster, like a good sprayer, is one that will spread the insecticide—in this case in dry form—in such a manner as to give the most uniform coating possible to the plants being treated. The simplest dusters are the small hand dusters adapted to the home garden in which a plunger discharges an air blast through a chamber containing from 0.5 to 2.0 pounds of dust and the dust cloud is emitted through a small flared nozzle or tip. Next in size are the blower dusters, which consist of an enclosed fan rotated by a hand crank which sends a continuous blast of air through a small chamber into which the dust is fed by an adjustable gate. An agitator stirs the dusts in the hopper and provides for an even feed of the dust into the discharge chamber. The dust cloud is forced out through a delivery tube extending nearly to the ground, which may end in Y or fishtailed nozzle. Such a duster will contain 5 to 10 pounds of dust and can be used to protect 1 to 2 acres of truck crops. The most recent innovation in blower dusters is a back pack unit containing a small gasoline engine which drives a fan providing a steady stream of dust.

The bellous or knapsack duster of similar capacity uses the extension and compression of a bellows attached to the back of the duster to force air through the discharge chamber. This gives a discharge of the dust in puffs instead of the continuous stream as in the blower type. This design is best adapted to somewhat isolated plants such as small trees and shrubbery.

Traction dusters have been widely used for vegetable-and field-crop dusting, especially for small acreages of cotton. In this type the fan is driven by the wheel or wheels on which the duster runs. Such machines, containing 50 to 100 pounds of dust, may develop enough power to turn a 12- to 16-inch fan at 2,500 to 3,000 revolutions per minute and may operate with a boom containing up to eight nozzles for a four-row operation. Because the speed of the machines will vary with the rate at which they are drawn through the field and the wheels may slip in soft ground, it is always difficult to maintain an even discharge from traction-type dusters.

Power dusters operated by small gasoline engines are the most practical for orchard and field-crop work. The fan is operated at about 3,000 revolutions per minute. For field and row crops, booms up to 30 feet in length with from 8 to 18 delivery nozzles are used. These may be individually connected by flexible tubing to a peripheral manifold surrounding the fan, or they may be attached to a tapering hollow-boom manifold to equalize the discharge rates at each nozzle.

The *orchard dusters* commonly have a single discharge outlet or a double fishtail arrangement for discharging dust from both sides and a centrifugal or squirrel-cage fan to discharge large volumes of air, up to 20,000 to 40,000 cubic feet pet minute. This equipment will project dusts for considerable distances even to the tops of forest trees. In these machines the dust is mechanically fed by an agitator or metered by a worm or helix arrangement directly into the fan or blower, assuring a fairly even rate of discharge. However, in practice, the uniformity of discharge of power dusters may vary over a severalfold range because of the changes in the head of dust above the hopper opening and the tendency of dusts to cake and is greatly inferior in the respect to comparable spray equipment.

The most recent developments to remedy this deficiency include equipping the hopper with an elevator which lifts the dust to the top, where it is force-fed into the fan, or the use of a rotating hopper which scoops up the same measure of dust at each revolution and feeds it into the fan, and the employment of a conveyer-belt system at the bottom of the hopper which transports an even layer of dust through a variable shutter into the fan. Such desings have reduced the variability of discharge to a few per cent.

The *spray duster* was developed to apply dusts simultaneously with a mist spray from nozzles along the edge of the fishtail orifice, which served to wet the foliage and increase the initial deposit of dust.

Certain types of mist blowers are also equipped for simile- taneous spray-dusting, and results have been secured by the simultaneous emission of 1 gallon of aqueous oil emulsion to each pound of dust, which were equal to or better than results of high- pressure spraying. However, this type of application has been superseded by the use of concentrate sprays. Many other innovations have been developed for dust applications.

For use with volatile materials such as nicotine an hopper with a mixing attachment in which the dust is mixed immediately before application has been used. The performance of nicotine dusts has also been improved by partially confining them under a gasp of canvas trailer 10 to 30 feet wide dragged behind the duster for a distance of 10 to as much as 100 feet. The trailler serves to confine the vapour of the insecticide given off by the dus and to thus expose the insects to it for a longer period.

Spraying of Insecticides by Aircraft

Practically the fust use of the airplane for insect control was in the application of lead arsenate dusts to control the catalpa sphinx, Ceratomia catalpae, in Ohio in 1921. The advantages of aircraft applications in rapidity, cheapness, and ease of treatment were readily apparent, and the uses in creased rapidly. Calcium arsenate dust was applied by air in 1923 to control the cotton boll weevil, Anthonomus grandis, and the cotton leafworm, Alabama argillacea, and paris green dust was applied by air to control anopheline mosquito larvae in the same year. By 1925, forest insects were being dusted by air in Germany, the United States and Canade.

During the nest 20 years, most aircraft operations employed dusts because of the difficulties in formulating suitable sprays with the water-insoluble arsenicals. During the Second World War, malaria control became an essential adjunct to military operations in many areas of the globe and DDT was found to be exceptionally effective for mosquito control. However, its poor dusting qualities resulted in the development of aircraft spraying and literally hundreds of devices were employed using a range of aircraft such as the Piper Cub L-4 and Stearman PT-17 equipped with booms and nozzles, fighter planes with wing tanks, and heavy multiengined ships such as the B-25 bomber and C-47 transport with large tanks emptying through vertical discharge pipes. Both larviciding and adulticiding operations were proved practicable on the very largest scale and have since been extended to pest mosquito control in Alaska and Canada and to the control of the tsetse flies,

Glossina spp., in Central Africa and to black flies, Simulium spp., in the Adirondack mountains. Aircraft have been employed extensively for the control of locusts and grasshoppers by a veriety of means. Oil solutions of dinitro-o-cresol and BHC have been sprayed on swarms of *Locusta migratoria migratoriodes* both in flight and at rest on the ground. Aldrin, chlordane, and toxaphene have also been used both as sprays and baits for various species of Melanoplus, while arsenical-molasses baits have been applied on a very wide scale. Aircraft applications have been used very successfully for the control of forest insects where other means of application are completely impractical.

Notable campaigns have involved the use of calcium arsenate dust and, more recently. of DDT dusts and sprays for the control of the gypsy moth, Porthetria dispar, and of DDT sprays of the spruce budworm, Choristoneura fumiferana. It has been estimated that in the gypsy moth operations, the payload of a single C-47 airplane treats an area as large as that which could be covered by a truck-mounted spray rig in 4 years. Today, in the United States, the airplane plays a major role in the appication of pesticides or example, in 1955, 45,316,000 acres were treated by air for insect control and 265,808,000 pounds of dust and 51,274,000 gallons of spray were applied. On California farms in the same year, of a total of 5,756,941 acres treated by commercial pest-control operators, 4,853,462 were treated by air craft. The aircraft has brought an astonishing increase in efficiency to many insect-control operations. An ordinary dusting plane flying at 100 miles per hour can treat an area at the rate of about 10 to 40 acres per minute, depending upon the effective swath width, varying from 50 to 200 feet; allowing for an operating period of only about 3 hours per day and the time required for loading, from 500 to 2,000 acres are commonly treated. Even greater retes of treatment are obtained in specific operations with larger aircraft. Thus in mosquito-larviciding operations, several square miles may be treated in an hour, and in grasshopper-bait spreading operations with a C-47, 10,000 acres have been treated per day. In tussock moth, Hemerocampa leucosigma, control, 450,000 acres of forest were sprayed within a few weeks.

The aircraft operations have also made insecticidal applications possible in many areas which were previously inaccessible. These included swamps and marshes where mosquitoes and other biting insects breed, jungles and forests, vast plains areas where grasshoppers and locusts are found, and certain cultivated crops such as rice, sugarcane, mature corn, and cotton, where ground treatment is impractical or destructive. In assessing the place of aircraft in any insect-control operation, it is well to keep in mind that the advantages of aircraft are (a) speed and timeliness of application, (b) freedom from crop injury and soil compaction, (c) no need for farmer preparation of area to be treated, and (d) accessibility of all types of areas. Against these must be balanced the disadvantages: (a) dependency upon optimum weather conditions, (b) lack of uniform coverage, especially under leaves, (c) difficulty in confining application to treatment area which results in severe drift problems, (d) very hazardous operation, with equipment and sometimes human lives lost through accidents, (e) expense of operation and inefficency on small acreages, and (f) inflexibility after application has begun due to difficulty in communication with pilot. The use of the airplane or helicopter for the application of insecticides introduces and additional dimension of complexity into the operation, that of the turbulences imparted to the air by the rotation of the propeller and the down draft resulting from the flight of the aircraft. The influence of these factors on sprays and dusts has been given a great deal of study, and the principles involved are well understood although they are often ignored in practice. A thorough appreciation of these factors is very important in designing and operating aircraft application equipment which will have the maximum effectiveness on the insects to be controlled are reduce hazardous or objectionable drift to a minimum.

Airflow

The lift of an aircraft in flight is obtained by imparting a downward motion to the air. This downwash or downdraft may amount to about 600 feet per minute for the ordinary biplane flying at 80 to 100 miles per hour and as much as 1,100 feet per minute for the helicopter. The downdrafts helps to carry the insecticidal discharge toward the ground and also moves foliage, which aids in penetration and distribution of the insecticide. The lift in secured by the airfoil of the wing and results in a decreased air pressure above the wing and an increased pressure below it. As a result, the high-pressure air under the wing flows out and around the wing tips to the low-pressure area above the wing, producing a rotary movement at each wing tip, the trailing wing-tip vortex, which may persist for several seconds after the passage of the aircraft. Superimposed on these forces in the rotary slipstresm of the propeller, which displaces the airflow in a counterclockwise direction. The velocities of the downdraft and the wing-tip vortices increase as the speed of the aircraft decreases, since the downward displacement of the air must equal the lift required to support the aircraft. With the helicopter, the forces are very similar. Pronounced vortices with outward and upward components occur at the ends of the rotor, while the downdraft is most pronounced under the central section of the rotor. The strength of these forces is greatest when the helicopter is hovering, and they are materially decreased under conditions of normal forward flight.

Fungicides

Strictly speaking chemicals used to kill or halt the development of fungi. However, for our purposes we shall consider them as chemicals used to control bacterial as well as fungal plant pathogens, the causal agents of most plant diseases. Other organsim like viruses, rickettisias, algae, nematodes, mycoplasma like organism and parasitic seed plants causes plant diseases. In this chapter we discuss only those chemicals used for control of fungi and bacteria. Of plant diseases here are hundreds of examples which include storage rots, seedling diseases, root rots, gall diseases, vascular wilts, leaf blights, rusts, smuts, mildews, and viral diseases. These can, in many instances, be controlled by the early and continued application of selected fungicides that either kill the pathogens or inhibit their development. With today's fungicides most plant diseases can be controlled to some extent.

Phytophthora and phizoctonia rots Fusarium, verticillium and bacterial wilts and the viruses, are among those that are only beginning to be controlled with chemicals. The difficulties with these diseases are that they either occur below ground, and thus beyond the reach of fungicides, or they are systemic within the plant. Fungus is a plant living in close quarers with its host so fungal diseases are basically more difficult to control with chemicals than are insects. This explains the difficulty of finding selective chemicals that kill the fungus without harming the plant. Also, fungi that can be controlled by fungicides may undergo secondary cycles rapidly and produce from 12 to 25 "generations" during a 3-month growing season. Consequently, repeated applications of protective fungicides may be necessary, due to plant growth dilution and removal by rain and other weathering. Before there is any evidence of disease Fungicides must be applied to plants during stages when they are vulnerable to inoculation by pathogens, before there is any evidence of disease. Those fungicides referred to as chemotherapeutants can help to control certain disease after the symptoms appear. Also, protective fungicides are commonly used, even after symptoms of diseaese have appeared.

Eradicant fungicides are usually applied directly to the pathogen during its overwintering stage, long before disease has begun and symptoms have appeared. However, the fungicide must be applied as protect spray, in advance of the pathogens, to prevent the disease are in the case of crops, whose sale depends on appearance, such as lettuce and celery. In our present arsenal there are about 225 fungicidal materials, most of which are recently discovered. Most of these act as protectants, preventing spore germination and subsequent fungal penetration of plant tissues. Protectants are applied repeatedly to cover new plant growth and to replenish the fungicide that has deteriorated or has been washed off by rain.

The application principle for fungicides differs from that of herbicides and insecticides. Only that portion of the plant that has a coating of dust or spray film of fungicide is protected from disease. Thus a good uniform coverage is essential. Fungicides, with several new exceptions, are not systemic in their action. They are applied as sprays or dusts, but sprays are preferable, since the films stick more readily, remain longer, can be applied during any time of the day, and result in less off-target drift. Thanks to modern chemistry, many of the serious diseases of grain crops are controlled by treating the seeds with selective materials. Other are controlled with resistant varieties. Diseases of fruit and vegetable are often controlled by sprays or dusts of fungicides. Historically, fungicides have relied on sulfur, copper, and mercury compounds, and even today most of our plant diseases could controlled by these groups.

The development of organic fungicides vests in the reason, that sulfur and copper compounds can retard growth in sensitive plants. These sometimes have greater fungicidal activity and usually have less phytotoxicity. In organic forms of copper, sulfur, land mercury, until recently and metallic complexes of cadmium, chromium and zinc along with a variety of organic compounds are inclusions of the general purpose fungicides for agriculture whereas the general purpose lawn and garden fungicides are few in number and are usually organic compounds. The general-purpose lawn and garden fungicides are few in number and are usually organic compounds.

Inorganic Fungicides

Sulfur

Sulfur in many forms is probably the oldest effective fungicide known and is still a very useful garden fungicide. There are three physical forms of formulations of sulfur used as fungicides. The first is finely grounds sulfur dust that contains 1 to 5 per cent clay or talc to assist in dusting qualities. The sulfur in this form may be used as a carrier for another fungicides or an insecticide. The second is flotation or colloidal sulfur, which is so very find that it must be formulated as a wet paste in order to be mixed with water. It would be impossible to mix this with water when it is in its original dry, microparticle size, as it would merely flow but would merely float. Wettable sulfur is the third form; it is finely ground with a wetting agent so that it will mix readily with water for spraying. The easiest to use, of course, is dusting sulfure, applied when plants are slightly moist with the morning dew. The particle size of wettable sulfur should be no longer than 77 μm for controlling the most effective disease. A good grade of dusting sulfur should pass through a 32.5-mesh or finer screen.

Copper

The majority of inorganic copper compounds are practically insoluble in water and are pretty blue, green, red, or yellow powders sold as fungicides. The various forms include Bordeaux mixture, name after the Bordeaux region in France, where it originated. Bordeaux is a chemically undefined mixture of copper sulfate and hydrated lime, which was accidentally discovered when sprayed on grapes in Bordeaux to scare off "freeloaders." It was soon observed that downy mildew, a disease of grapes, disappeared from the treated plants. From this unique origin began the commercialization of fungicides. The fungicidal as well as phytotoxic and properties are provided by the copper, ion, which becomes available from both the highly soluble and relatively insoluble copper salts. A few of the many inorganic copper compounds used over the years are presented.

The EPA has determined that no tolerance level need be set for a large number of copper compounds : Bordeaux mixture, copper acetate, copper carbonate-basic, copper-lime mixtures, copper oxychloride, copper silicate, copper sulfate, copper sulfate-basic copper-zinc-chromate, cuprous oxide, cupric oxide, and copper hydroxide.

A comment on solubility is appropriate at this point. In general, protective fungicides have low ionization constant, but in water some toxicant does go into solution. That small quantity absorbed by the fungal spore is then replaced in solution from the residue. The spore continues to accumulate the toxic ion in sublethal doses, whose cumulative effect is lethal. Except for powdery mildews,, water in the penetration court—the place on plant tissue softened by fungal mycelium, which permits it to penetrate the plant cutlicle—thus permits

Table 10.2. A sampling of the vast number of inorganic copper compounds used as fungicides.

Name	*Chemical formula*	*Uses*
Cupric sulfate	$CuSO_45H_2O$	Seed treatment and preparation of Bordeaux mixture
Cupric hydroxide (Kocide®)	$Cu(OH)_2$	Seed treatment, foliage spray, many fungal diseases
Copper oxychloride	$3Cu(OH)_2$ $CuCl_2$	Powdery mildrews
Copper oxychloride sulfate	$3Cu(OH)_2$ $CuCl_2$ $3Cu(OH)_2$ $CuSO_4$	Many fungal diseases
Copper ammonium carbonate (Copper-Count-N®)	Chemical complex (formular not known)	Many citrus, deciduous fruit, and vegetable diseases
Cuprous oxide	Cu_2O	Powdery mildews
Basic copper sulfate	$CuSO_4$ $Cu(OH)_2$ H_2O	Seed treatment and preparation of Bordeaux mixture
Curpric carbonate (malachite®)	$Cu(OH)_2$ $CuCO_2$	Many fungal diseases
Copper resinate (Citcop®)	Salts of fatty and rosin acids	Bacterial and fungal diseases of grapes, citrus, vegetables

spore germination and makes soluble the toxic portion of the fungicidal residue. To discourage killing all or portions as the host plant, the copper ion which being toxic to all plant cells must be used in dicrete dosages or in relatively insoluble forms. This is the basis for the use of relatively insoluble or "fixed" copper fungicides, which release only very low levels of copper, adequate for fungicidal activity, but not enough to affect the host plant. Copper compounds are not easily washed from leaves by rain, since they are relatively insoluble in water, and thus give longer protection against disease than do most of the organic meterials.

During spraying no special precaution is required as they are relatively safe to use. Although copper is an essential element for plants, there is some danger in an accumulation of copper in agricultural soils resulting from frequent and prolonged use. After using fixed copper for disease control a serious problem, in fact, of copper toxicity is being experienced by certain, citrus growers in Florida. The currently accepted theory for the mode of action of copper's fungistatic action is its nonspecific denaturation of protein. The Cu^{++} ion reacts with enzymes having reactive sulfhydryl group which would explain its toxicity to all forms of plant life.

Mercury

The inorganic mercurial fungicides are probably the most toxic of the fungicides. Mercury's fungicidal properties and toxicity to animals are due in part to the degree of association of divalent mercury ions, which are toxic to all forms of life. As a result, no mercury residues, are permitted in foods or feed. Over the past 30 years, many organic mercury compounds were developed, but they have been replaced by other organic fungicides.

Phenyl-mercury acetate (PMA) was useful for turf diseases, as a seed treatment, and as a dormant spray for fruit trees whereas ceresan is typical of those used as seed treatment. The mode of action for the mercurials is the nonselective or nonspecific inhibition of enzymes, especially those containing iron and sulfhydryl sites. With one or two exceptions, both organic and inorganic mercurial Fungicides have been banned from home and agricultural use by the EPA. This decision hinged on their toxicity to warm-blooded animals and accumulation of mercury in the environment.

Organic Fungicides

To replace the more harsh, less selective in organic materials many synthetic sulfur and other organic fungicides have been developed over the past 35 years. Most of them had no measurable build up effect on the environment after many years of use. Thiram, the first of the organic sulfur fungicides, was discovered in 1931; it was followed by many others. On 1943 and 1949 respectively, other new classes, the dithiocarbamates and dicarboxmides (Zineb and captan) was introduced. Now more than 200 fungicides of all classes are in use or in various stages of development. Several outstanding qualities are passessed by newer organic fungicides, that is being extremely efficient, smaller quantities are required than of those used in the past, usually lasts longer and are safe for crops, animals and the environment. Most of the newer fungicides also have very low phytotoxicity, many being at least ten times safer than the copper meterials. And most of them are readily degraded by soil microrganisms, thus preventing their accumulation in soils.

Dithiocarbamates

Among the dithiocarbamates we find the "old reliables" —thiram, meneb, ferbam, ziram, Vapam (SMDC), and zineb all developed in the early 1930s and 1940s. Such fungicides probably have greater popularity and use than all other fungicides combined. Except for systemic action, they are employed collectively in every use known for fungicides. The dithiocarbamates probably act by being matabolized to the isothiocyanate radical (- N = C = S), which inactivates the —SH groups in amino acids contained within the individual pathogen cells.

Thiazoles

The thiazoles, a class of compounds that offers a surprising chemical disposition, contains among others, ehtazol. The five-membered ring of the thiazoles is claved rather quickly under soil conditions to form either the fungicidal —N = C = S or a dithiocarbamate, depending on the structure of the parent molecule. Ethazol is used only as a soil fungicide and, as such, is exposed to the ring cleavage just mentioned. The probable mode of action is similar to that of the dithiocarbamates.

Triazines

The triazines structure, seen frequently in herbicides, is found in only one fungicide. A wide use for control of potato and tomato leaf spots and turf-grass diseases has been received by Anilazine which was introduced in 1955.

Substitued Aromatics

The substituted aromatics belong in a somewhat arbitrary classification assigned to the simple benzene derivatives that possess long-recognized fungicidal porperties. For seed treatment and as soil treatment to contract stinking smut of wheat, Hexachloro-benzene, was introduced in 1945. Pentachlorophenol (PCP) has been used since 1936 as a wood preservative as a seed treatment, and as a herbicide. Pentachloro-nitrobenzene (PCNB) was introduced in the 1930s as a fungicide for seed treatment and selected foliage applications. It is also availed as a soil treatment to restrain the pathogens of certain damping-off diseases of seedlings.

Chlorothalonil is a very useful, broad-spectrum foliage-protectant fungicide made available in 1964. And chloroneb, developed in 1965, is heavily used for cotton seedling and turf diseases. Dicloran (DCNA) is a highly useful fungicide against *Botrytis*, *Monilinia*, *Rhizopus*, *Sclerotinia*, and *Sclerotium* species, on a wide range of fruits and vegetables. Substituted aromatics are diverse in their modes of action.

Being generally fungistatic, they reduce growth rates and sporulation of fungi, probably by combining with $—NH_2$ or —SH groups of essential metabolic compounds.

Dicarboximides (Sulfenimides)

Dicarboximides are three extremely useful foliage protectant fungicides. Captan appeared in 1949 and is undoubtedly the most heavily used fungicide around the home of all classes; folpet appeared in 1962; and captafol (Difolatan®) appeared in 1961. They are used primarily as foliage dusts and sprays on fruits, vegetables, and ornamentals. Recommended for lawn and garden use, as seed treatment and as protectants formildews, late blight, and other diseases, the Dicarboximides are some of the safest of all pesticides available. Remember the garden adage, "When in doubt, use captan."

Many compounds containing the—SCC13 moiety are fungitoxic, a fact that indicates that group as a toxophore (molecular unit that account for the molecule's toxicity). Fungitoxicity of the dicarboximides is aparently nonspecific and is not a result of a single mode of action. The dicarboximides' lethal effect on disease organisms is probably due to the inhibition of the synthesis of amino compounds and enzymes containing the radical.

Systemic Fungicides

Only in recent years have successful systemic fungicides been marketed, and very few are available. Systemics are absorbed by the plant and carried by translocation through the cuticle and across leaves to the growing points. Most systemic fungicides have eradicant properties that stop the progress of existing infections. They are therapeutic in that they can be used to cure plant diseases. To give prolonged disease control a few of the systemics can be applied as soil treatment and are slowly absorbed assimilated through the roots. These systemics offer much better control of diseases than is possible with a protectant fungicide that require uniform application and remain essentially where it is sprayed onto the plant surfaces.

There is, however, some redistribution of protective fungicidal residues on the surfaces of sprayed or dusted plants, giving them longer residual activity than would be expected. Systemic constitute of perfect method of disease control by attacking the pathogen at its site of entry or activity, and they reduce the risk of contaminating the environment by frequent broadcast fungicidal treatments. Undoubtedly, as newer and more selective systemic molecules are synthesized, they will gradually replace the protectants that compose the bulk or our fungicidal arsenal. Those systemics currently in commercial ùse are mentioned in order of their appearence. None are available for home use.

Oxathiins

The first of the systemics to suceed in practice, introduced in 1966, were the Oxathiins, represented by carboxin and oxycarboxin. They are used as seed treatments for the cereal crop, particulary those affected by embryo-infecting smut fungi, and they have potential for other used. They are selectively toxic to the smuts, rusts, and to Rhizoctonis (Thanatephorus), organisms belonging to the Basidiomycetes. The apparent mode of action of the oxathiins beings with their selective concentration in the fungal cells, followed by the inhibition of succinic dehydrogenase, an important enzyme to respiration in the mitochondrial systems.

Benzimidazoles

The benzimidazoles, represented by benomyl and thiabendazole (TBZ), were introduced in 1968 and have received wide acceptance as systemic fungicides against a broad spectrum of diseases. Benomy has the widest spectrum of fungitoxic activity of all the newer systemics, including the Sclerotinia, Botrytis, and Rhizoctonia species, and the powdery mildews and apple scab. Thiabendazole has a similar spectrum of activity to that of benomyl. Introduced in 1969, thiophanate, although not a benzimidazole in its original structure, is converted to that group by the host plant land the fungus through their metabolism. Thiophanate has a fungitoxicity similar to that of benomyl. All three compounds have been used in foliar application, seed treatment, dipping of fruit or roots, and soil application. Their mode of action appears to be the induction of abnormalities in spore germination, cellular multiplication, and growth, as a result of their interference in the synthesis of that vital nucleic material, DNA.

A later addition to the benzimidazoles is carbendazium, introduced in 1973. The interesting quality of this systemic is its proved usefulness in the control of the formidable Dutch elm disease, in the formulation of Lignasan, hydrochloride salt, it is injected into the trunks of diseased trees, and results in a slow curative action.

Pyrimidines

The pyrimidine systemic fungicides appeared in the late 1960s, and include dimethirimol, ethirimol and bupirimate. They are very active against specific types of powdery mildews : for instance, dimethirimol work well on cucurbits. Ethirimol is for cereals and other field crops, and bupirimate controls powdery mildews on apples and greenhouse roses.

Organophosphates

Among the newer systemic fungicides are two organo-phosphorous meterials, IBP and Conen. Developed in Japan and introduced in 1965, both are effective against rice blast, stem rot, and rice sheath blight.

Acylalanines

Acylalanines are another new group of systemic fungicides which includes metalaxyl and funalacyl. They are effective against soil-borne diseases caused by *Pythium* and *Phytophthora* and foliar diseases caused by the phycomycetes (downy mildews). They show promise as foliar, soil, and seed treatments for agricultural crops. They offer systemic and corrective activity as well as residual-protectant activity. However, against the Ascomycetes, Basidio-mycetes and Fungi Imperfecti they have little or no activity.

Triazoles

The sole systemic fungicide of the triazole group is the Triadimefon which carries both protective and curative actions and is effective against mildews and rusts on vegetables, cereals, coffee, deciduous fruit, grapes and ornamentals.

Piperazines

The piperazine systemic fungicides include only one member at this time, triforine, which is amazingly effective against powdery mildew on any host. Additionally it is active against scab and other diseases of fruit and berries, rust and black spot on ornamentals, powdery mildew and other leaf diseases on cereals, rust on cereals, several diseases of vegetables, land storage diseases of fruit.

Imides

A second group of dicarboximides, the imides, are structurally significantly different from the originals. These systemic chemicals appeared during the 1970s. The group now includes procymidone, iprodione and vinclozolin. They are particularly effective against *Botrytis*, *Monilinia* and *Sclerotinia*. Iprodione is also active against Alternaris, Heminthosporium, Rhizoctonia, Corticium Typhula and Fusarium species.

Dinitrophenols

We have mentioned the dinitorphenols are insecticides and as herbicides. Their mode of action as fungicides is the same : the uncoupling of oxidative phosphorylation in cells with an attendant upset of the energy systems within the cells. Dinocap (karathane) has been since the late 1930s, both as an acaricide and for powdery mildew on a number of fruit and vegetable crops. Dinocap undoubtedly acts in the vapour phase, since it is quite effective against powdery mildews whose spores germinate in the absence of water. This is popular home fungicide.

Quinones

The quinones are a facinating chemical group that offers countless numbers of molecules that are potential fungicides. Chloranil is the first of these to appear (1937). Until the decorboxi-mides it was used heavily as a seed treatment and Foliar application. The most popular of this group, however, is dichlone. It is used on a number of fruit and vegetable crops and for treatment of ponds, to control blue-green algae. Dichlone affects cellular respiration in many fungi and acts by attaching to the —SH groups in enzymes, thus inhibiting their action and indirectly uncoupling oxidative phosphorylation.

Aliphatic Nitrogen Compounds

A fungicide that has proved effective in controlling certain diseases such as apple and pear and cherry leaf spot was introduced in the mid 1950s and is known as Dodine having disease specificity and right systemic qualities. It has disease speificity and slight systemic qualities. Its mode of action is not clear, but it is taken up rapidly by fungal cells, causing leakage in these cells, possible by alteration in membrane permeability. The guanidine nucleus of dodine is also known to inhibit the synthesis of RNA.

Fumigants

As with the insecticides, there are distinct hightly volatile, small-molecule fungicides that have fumigant action. They are unrelated chemically but are handled alike and are deal with as a single class in this book. Chlorophicrin was mentioned in as a waring agent, in grain fumigants, but it is also an ideal fumigant itself : It controls fungi, insects nematodes, and weed seeds in the soil. Equally effective against fungi, nematodes and weeds. Methyl-bromide, is also listed as a fumigant insecticide. Methylisothiocyanate (MIT) is closely related to the dithiocabamates and has a similar mode of action against fungi, nematodes and weeds. SMDC was listed, but not illustrated, in the dithiocarbamate fungicide, where it belongs chemically. SMDC decomposes in the soil to yield methylisothiocyanate. None of these is available for home use.

Antibiotics

Such antibiotics are penicillin, tetracycline, and chloramphenicol are used medically against human bacterial diseases. These are not involved in our present study. But we note in passing that the oxytetracylines are therapeutic against some of those mysterious mycoplasmalike diseases. As in the case of the medically important antibiotics the antibiotic fungicides are substance produced by microorganisms, which in very dilute concentrates inhibit growth and even destroy other microorganisms. To date, several hundred antibiotics have been reported to have fungicidal activity, and the chemical structures of about half of these are already known. The largest sources of antifungal anitbiotics is the actinomycetes, a group of lower plants. Two antibiotics streptomycin and cyclonezimide is obtained from one amuzion species, *streptomyces griseus*, which is found within the action mycetes.

Streptomycin is used as dust, spray, and seed treatment for the prevention of mostly of bacterial diseases such as blight on apples and pears, soft rot on leafy vegetable, and some seedling diseases. It is also effective against a few fungal diseases. Streptomycin, the mode of action of which is not clearly understood, probably interferes into synthesis of proteins. Despite the evidence of antibiotic-resistant strains, streptomycin has a place in the control of some bacterial diseases, and the tetracyclines may well play an important part in controlling some mycoplasmalike diseases of plant. Because streptomycin appears to have a single and specific site of action, resistance to it by both bacteria and mycoplasmas in inveitable.

Cycloheximide is a smaller, less complicated antibiotic, about which more is understood. First, cycloheximide is toxic to a wide range of organisms, including yeasts, filament-forming fungi, algae, protozoa higher plant and especially mammals. Surprisingly, it is inactive against bacteria, perhaps because the bacteria fail to absorb it. Cyclohximide cause growth inhibition in yeasts and filament forming fungi by inhibiting protein and RNA synthesis. Thus, with a fair amount of confidence, we can say that both streptomycin and cycloheximide act by inhibiting the synthesis of nucleic acids. In the control of powdery mildew, rusts, turf diseases and certain blights of Fungicide known as *Cycloheximide* was intorduced in 1948 which at present has become very popular. It is best known commercially under the name Acti-Dione. Because of its high acute toxicity, it cannot be purchased for home garden use. Blasticidin-S, discovered in 1955, is produced by the ferment-ation of Streptomyces griseochromogenses. Kasugamycin, introduced in 1963, is formed by Streptomyces kasugaenis, and Polyoxins are extracted from Streptomyces cacaoi. All three are Japanese contributions to the systemic antibiotics. The first two are effective against rice, blast, and the latter against rice sheath blight.

Actions of Fungicides

All agro chemical show their effects on different organic of the insect pests in different ways. Fungicidal action is usually expressed in one of two physically visible ways: The inhibition of spore germination or the inhibition of fungus growth. Most fungicides prevent spore germination or kill the spore immediately following germination. Some of these chemical inhibitors or toxicants also retard or halt fungus growth when applied after the infectious stage has developed. The newer systemics fungicides have eradicant properties and stop the progress of existing infections. What happens at the cellular level to cause these readily visible results? As currently viewed, all fungicides are metabolic inhibitors; that is, they block some vital metabolic process. For the sake of organization and simplicity, we can classify the modes of action into three broad groups: inhibitors of the electron transport chain, inhibitors of enzymes, and inhibitors of nucleic acid metabolism and protein synthesis.

Inhibitors of the Electron Transport Chain

Sulfur

Whenever certain pathogenic organisms and most mites come contact with sulfur and in also by its fumigant action at temperatures above 22°C they are killed. The fumigant effect is, however, somewhat secondary at marginal temperatures and under windy conditions. It is quite effective in controlling powdery mildews of plants that are not unduly sensitive to sulfur. Unlike those of any other fungus, spores of powdery mildews will germinate in the absence of a film of water in the penetration court (a spot on the tissue that is "softened" prior to penetration by spore). Sulfur is absorbed by fungi in the vapour state, land its fumigant effect—acting at a distance—is undoubtedly important in killing spores of powdery mildews. Sulfur interferes in electron transport along the cytochromes and is then reduced to hydrogen sulfide (H_2S), a toxic entity to most cellular proteins. The way fungi respond to sulfur suggests that sulfur can stimulate enzyme activity. The reduction of sulfur to hydrogen sulfide (H_2S) by fungi is a metabolic process that diverts protons (H^+) from steps of normal hydrogenation reactions. This reduction is aerobic (requires oxygen) and involves a cytochrome system, possibly cytochrome, a respiratory enzyme involved in the oxidation of nutritional components and foreign compounds. Sulfur presumably serves as an acceptor of hydrogen atoms from dehydrogenases, and then activates to full capacity the enzymic steps preceding sulfur reduction.

Oxathiins

Carboxin and oxycarboxin are the only two oxthiins currently in use. Carboxin inhibits glucose and acetate oxidation by intact fungi, and noncompetitively inhibits succinate, but not $NADH_2$, oxidation by mitochondria. This effect occurs in the electron transport chain of respiration. Succinate accumulates in carboxin-treated cells of fungi, suggesting that inhibition of succinate oxidation is the primary site of action. Oxycarboxin, though less toxic, has the same mode of action.

Enzyme Inhibitors

Copper

There are several inorganic copper compounds like protectants meterials applied before the pathogen appears, to protect plants from inoculation. They prevent the spread of an infection but cannot eradicate an existing one. Thus, the site of copper fungicidal action must be the fungal spore. Copper ions are concentrated by fungal spores from the surrounding medium, some up to 100-fold over that in the immediate environment. This high concentration of copper inside the spore supports the generally held view that the fungitoxic activity of copper ions is due to nonspecific attraction for various groups in the cell, such as imidazole, carboxyl, phosphate, or thiol, resulting in nonspecific denaturation of protein and enzymes. The currently accepted theory for the mode of action of copper's fungistatic action is its nonspecific denaturation of protein. The cupric ion (Cu^{++}) reacts with enzyme having reactive sulfhydryl (–SH) groups, which explains copper's toxicity to all forms of plant life, and especially its toxicity to the vulnerable copper-concentrating spores and cells.

Mercury

The fungicides of mercury compounds fungicides are purely historical and classical toxicologic interest, for they are no longer registered except for occassional use. Considerable concern over the widespread use of mercury pesticides focused on the toxic nature of mercury itself and the discovery in 1970 that methyl mercury (CH_3Hg^+)—which is more toxic to life than aryl (aromatic-ring derivatives) mercurials or inorganic salts of mercury—is synthesized in the biosphere. As a result, most registrations for mercury fungicides were canceled.

The biochemical basis for mercury's toxicity is generally though to consist to interactions with the thiol groups of proteins, where mercury ions (HG^{++}) form compounds attaching to one or two sulfurs. Since there are so many functional -SH groups in a living system, it is virtually impossible to select one reaction of mercury is being the most important to its toxic effect. Organic mercury is different only in that its chemical form is R-Hg^{+} rather than Hg^{++}. The organic mercurials are more soluble in lipid than the inorganic Hg^{++}, enabling them to penetrate more readily into cells and tissues. In general, inorganic mercury is a more effective enzyme inhibitor than organic mercury, though the organic forms remains as potent toxicants.

Dithiocarbamates

This category includes in the dithiocarbamates, the oldest group of the organic fungicides, are maneb, ferbam, zineb, manzate, dithana, polyram and ziram. The dithiocarbamates may act by being metabolized to the isothio-cyanate radical (-N = C = S), which inactivates the -SH groups in amino acids, proteins, and enzymes contained within the individual pathogen. It is difficult to establish exactly how they act since they are unstable, and the chemical nature of the fungitoxic agent(s) is not known for certain.

A more recent theory tends to discount the isothiocyanates as toxic products, suggesting instead that ethylene thiuram disulfide. An important function in both the lower and higher plants that may help explain the mode of action for not only the dithiocarbamate fungicides but also others, including those derived from the heavy metals, is *chelation*. A chelate is an organic ring structure composed of a metal atom linked to a ring by nitrogen, oxygen, or sulfur. Particularly as they involve enzymes, chelates are powerful and essential entities in the metabolic procesed of plant. Some of the metals required by the higher plants and fungi in trace amount assist enzymes in conducting their routine duties of metabolism. The metal may be active in this role as a chelate with the biological component.

One of the generally accepted theories to explain the fungicidal activity of copper, mercury, cadmium, and other heavy metals is the formation of chelates within the fungal cells. The chelates, in turn, disrupt protein synthesis and metabolism. And since the most critical protein of cells are enzymes the metals required in trace amounts appearing in abundance or excessive quantities are equivalent to the introduction of potent poisons in the cells. If the chelation correct, it would account for the mode of action for the organic and inorganic heavy metal fungicides, for the formation of isothiocyanates from the dithiocarbamate molecules, and for the potency of the heavy-metal dithiocarbamates.

Certain fungicides are in themselves chelating agents. They attain to the scarce metal components, such as Fe, Mg, and Zn, within the cells, literally robbing cells of essential materials. In summary, chelation of heavy metals plays an important role in both the life and the death of cells.

Thiazoles

Ethazol, tricyclazole, and Busan-72 belong to the thiazole group. The unstable five-member ring of the thiazoles is broken rapidly under soil conditions to form either the fungicidal –N = C = S or a dithiocarbamate, depending on the structure of the parent chemical. The isothiocyanates inactivates –SH or –SR groups in amino acids, proteins, and enzymes contained within the individual pathogen. Thus the site of action is nonspecific.

Substituted Aromatics

The substituted aromatics are diverse in their modes of action. Being generally fungistatic, they reduce growth rates and sporulation of fungi, probably by combining with amino (–NH_2), –SH, or SR groups in essential amino acids, proteins, or enzymes. Hexachlorobenzene possesses some fumigant qualities, especially with wheat bunt, but is mode of action is unknown. Chlorthalonil is believed to work by inactivation of thiol groups in the fungal cell. Chloroneb may act by inhibiting DNA synthesis. PCNB is effective against many species of fungi having chitin in their cell walls, but is virtually inactive against fungi in which chitin is either absent or present in small quantities, for example, *Pythium* and Phytophthora. Thus, there is indirect evidence that PCNB may act by interferring with chitin synthesis. Pentachlorophenol (PCP) block the formation of ATP by uncoupling oxidative phosphorylation.

Dicarboximides (Sulfenimides)

Captan, folpet, and captafol are the early members of the dicarboximide class of fungicides. They probably act nonspecifically, because the nature of the reactions between the fungicides and components of the fungal cells are not definitely established. It is generally believed that -SH or -SR groups are likely reaction sites. However, folpet inhibits isolated chymotrypsin, which does not contain thiol groups, so that reactions not involving thiol groups could be involved in fungicidal action.

Quinones

Belonging to the quinones are dichlone and chloranil. Fungal spores take up a large amount of dichlone before expiring, which suggests that dichlone exerts its toxicity by a simultaneous action on a variety of loci in major metabolic pathways. It is not clear what chemical reactions quinones undergo in the fungus. They do react readily with thiols, and they probably enter into a variety of other reactions in the cell, including combination with amino groups. The primary toxic effect of quinones therefore be due to reaction with -SH or -SR and $-NH_2$ groups of vital enzymes.

Inhibitors of Nucleic Acid Metabolism and Protein Synthesis

Benzimidazoles

The benzimidazoles include benomyl, thiabendazole and thiophanate. They are not toxic to fungi in their original state, but must be converted to their ester metabolites, which are known to be the toxic entitles. These metabolites cause morphological distortion of germinating spores and probably act by inhibiting DNA synthesis, or by interfering with some closely related aspect of cell or nuclear division.

Antibiotics

Cycloheximide is a protein synthesis inhibitor—it inhibit the incorporation of amino acids into protein. As a consequence of its interference with protein synthesis, it may also inhibit DNA synthesis. Cycloheximide is toxic not only to fungi but also to plants, and it has an oral LD_{50} in the rate of 2.5 mg/kg, by far the most toxic of the fungicides.

Streptomycin probably inhibits protein synthesis by binding to the ribosome, one molecule of streptomycin per ribosome. It also cause misreading of the genetic code, though this is not likely the primary effect.

Aliphatic Nitrogen Compounds

Dodine has a nonspecific mode of action, but it is generally agreed that it acts interfering with membrane structure. There is indirect evidence that its primary side of action is the mitochondrial membrane. The quanidine nucleus of dodine is also known to inhibit the synthesis of RNA.

Triazines

Anilazine is the only fungicide belonging to the triazine class of fungicides. The ultimate site and mechanism of action are unknown. However, the fungicide does react with $-NH_2$ groups and less readily with –SH or –SR. Consequently, it appears likely that anilazine cause inhibition of a variety of cell processes by nonspecific combination with vital cell components.

11

Insect Pest Management

There is a number of potential management tactics available; selection should be based on economic conditions, agronomic requirements of the crop, pest situation, meterological conditions, and many other factors. Once a crop is planted, for example, it is too late to choose another variety. The frequent use of two tactics, planting of pest-resistant crop varieties and application of insecticides, reflects the desire of most agriculturalists to avoid frequent monitoring of pest populations and to eliminate the need for advance planning. Planning a resistant variety may free the farmer from a particular insect problem. If the farmer fails to utilize a resistant variety or one is not available, it is often most convenient to resort to insecticides to prevent pest outbreaks. The use of one tactic certainly does not preclude the use of others. For example, insecticides may be used if plant resistance is not completely satisfactory or if biological control agents do not provide satisfactory suppression. The integration of several tactis into an effective program requires knowledge of pest life history, crop requirements, and available suppression tactics.

Regulations

To prevent entry and establishment of foreign pests. Government agencies sometimes establish regulations designed. Also, once pests become established, regulations may be directed at containment, suppression, or eradication of pests. This process is sometimes referred to as *regulatory control*. Quarantines limit movement of pests, usually by preventing transport of products that could harbor pests, by requiring inspection or by requiring fumigation to kill hidden pests. The international movement of many important pests has been limited by quarantines, and inspection is required at most international borders as well as to some state boundaries. Quarantine programmes are not always effective. For example, two pests that have recently arrived in North America in spite of quarantine programmes are the face fly, a pest of livestock, and the cereal leaf beetle, a pest of small grains. When quarantines are not effective and potentially damaging insects are successfully established, regulatory agencies sometimes resort to pest control activities.

The principal concern regarding selection of tactics usually is effectiveness, not economy, and chemical insecticides are usually employed. *Eradication* is an effort to eliminate pests from a geographic area. If the infested georgraphic area is relative small, and effective suppressive tactics are available, eradication is possible. For example, the Mediterranean fruit fly has been introduced accidentally to the United States on several occasions and has been eradicated successfully; effective population-monitoring techniques and suppressive tactics were available and were applied to relatively small geographic areas.

Proposed eradication programmes aimed at well-established pests such as boll weevil and fire ant probably are not feasible because of the extensive area infested and the disruptive effects associated with insecticide treatment of large areas. When eradication programmes are not successful or not feasible, regulatory agencies sometimes intiate containment or suppression programmes. *Containment* programmes attempt to limit the spread of pests through their potential habitable environment, and therefore limit economic loss.

Suppression programmes attempt to reduce pest population levels and associated damage, usually because the pest inhabits too large an area for containment. *Suppression* programmes supported by regulatory agencies generally are limited to pest species that cause severe loss over large geographic areas; the pest are too abundant or too widespread to be managed by individual landowners. Grasshopper control on rangeland is an example of a regularly conducted suppression programme. Federal agencies coordinate grasshopper suppression efforts, and the cost of the programme is shared by rachers and state and federal governments.

Host Resistance

Selection of a host by an insect involves four major steps : (1) finding the habitat, (2) settling, (3) settling, (3) sampling or tasting, and (4) ingestion. Host selection is a complex process, and different stimuli are involved in long-distance and in short-distance orientation.

Any host-related factors that disrupt the host selection process provide the basis for host resistance, or unsuitability of the host for an insect. Mechanisms of host resistance have been classified in several ways.

Physical resistance refers to morphological characteristics of a host that lead to its unsuitability. Host size, shape, colour, toughness, succulence, and presence of trichomes (leaf hairs) contribute to physical resistance.

Chemical resistance refers to toxins or to nutritional and metabolic factors of a host that lead to its unsuitability. It has been seen that plants frequently have physical or chemical attributes that serve important functions as protective agents. Plants also vary in their nutritional adequacy. Some species characteristically have low levels of essential nutrients, such as protein; other possess digestibility-reducing herbivores to use the nutrients.

An alternative approach is to attribute resistance to nonpreference, antibiosis, or tolerance. *Nonpreference* refers to insect responses to host characteristics that lead away from the use of the host for food, oviposition, or shelter. It has been observed that the striped borer moth. *Chilo suppressalis*, shows a strong preference for oviposition on rice varieties that are taller and have wider and smoother leaf blades. Even when borer populations are low, susceptible varieties receive large numbers of eggs while resistant varieties receives few or none. Antibiosis refers to delecterious effects on insect survival or life history resulting from feeding on a resistant host. Very young corn plants are resistant from feeding on a resistant host. Very young corn plants are resistant to survival of European corn borer because of complex toxic substance called by the acronym DIMBOA.

Certain inbred varieties maintain high levels of DIMBOA in their whorls at later stages of development and are relatively resistant to corn borer. Tolerance refers to the ability of a host to grow and reproduce normally while supporting a pest population that would be damaging to a susceptible host. It has been found that certain resistant varieties of corn any support as many earworms (Heliothis zea) as susceptible varieties do, but most remain with the silk channel (after pollination) and do not penetrate the ear. Frequently for insect pest population suppression resistance crop varieties are used. If a resistant variety proves to have a smaller yield than susceptible varieties, this must be more than compensated for by reduced costs of control. Plant breeders usually try to combine insect and pathogen resistance into the same cultivar, so the value of such varieties is even greater.

Hessian flies and greenbug aphids are important insect pests of wheat and sorghum, respectively, and resistant cultivars are the principal tactics employed to alleviate insect damage in these crops.

As is the case with any plant characteristics, however, host plant resistance may be modified by environmental conditions. Resistance of wheat varieties to Hessian fly, for example, may be reduced by high temperatures. Similarly, fertilizer application can make plants more or less susceptible to attack by insects, depending on the type of fertilizer and insect species. Also, through natural selection insects sometimes develop races that overcome the source of resistance.

Biological Control

As stated already that insect populations are naturally affected by a wide variety of environmental factors, both biotic and abiotic. The action of these factors is often termed *natural control*. One aspect of natural control is *biological control*, which involves populations regulation by the use of biotic agents. Biological control agents traditionally have been considered to be predators, parasitoids, and microbial pathogens, although other biotic factors such as host plant characteristics could be considered in this category.

The principal distinguishing feature regarding predators, parasitoids, and pathogens is their potential to respond in a density-dependent manner. Both predators and parasitoids have long been acknowledged to be important components in natural control. In addition, there have been several outstandingly successful manipulations of predators and parasitoids to achieve better biological control. Sometimes a species may be both a parasitoids and a predator. For example, adults of the chalcidoid wasp *Tetrastichus asparagi* deposit their eggs within the eggs of asparagus beetles. The wasp larvae develop within the beetle larvae, killing the beetles just prior to pupation. Thus *T. asparagi* is termed an egg-larval parasitoid. Adult *T. asparagi* also feed on the eggs of asparagus beetles. This is the predaceus nature of the species. Insect predators and parasitoids play a very important role in biological control programmes through introduction, conservation, and augmentation.

Introduction of exotic predators and parasitoids entails the search for natural enemies in foreign countries and their introduction into areas where pest insects are causing damage. This is generally done where pests were accidentally introduced into new areas without their normal complement of natural enemies. Most of the spectacular successes achieved with biological control have involved introduction.

(a)

(b)

Fig. 11.1. (a) Plants of susceptible variety of corn damaged by European corn borer. (b) A resistant variety that shows little damage. Each was experimentally infested with 100 corn borer eggs per plant.

Perhaps the best-known example of biological control involving a predator concerns the cottonycushion scale and vedalia beetle.

Conservation of predators and parasitoids emphasizes the importance of preserving naturally occurring beneficial species. Conservation may involve either careful use of insecticides to avoid accidental mortality among beneficial groups of manipulation of the environment to make it more suitable for them, as by planting flowering plants to provide a source of nectar for adult parasitoids. An example of parasitoid conservation occurs in vineyards where wild black-berries are allowed to grow. The grape leafhopper, which is a serious pest of grape, is attacked by an egg parasitoid. The chalcicidoid egg parasitoids, *Anagrus epos*, overwinters successfully only when an alternative host, a leafhopper that inhabit blackberry, is present. Thus, the presence of blackberries and associated nonpest leafhoppers enables maintenance of the agents that attack the pestiferous grape leafhopper.

Augmentation of predators and parasitoids involves, the culture and repeated release of natural enemies to suppress pest populations. The beneficial insects may occur naturally, but at low densities, or they may be exotic species that do not persist in their new environment. An example of parasitoid augmentation is the Mexican bean beetle suppression programme developed by Allen Steinhaur and his associated at the University of Maryland. The Mexican bean beetle is a pest of several varieties of beans. Although it has been a serious pest of soybeans, as the acreage devoted to soybean increases, Mexican bean

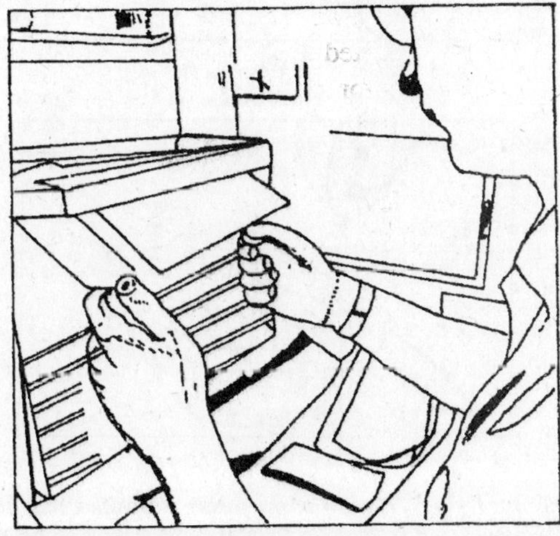

Fig. 11.2. Laboratory augmentation of small chalcidoid wasps of the genus Trichogramma.

beetle damage also increases. There is a distinct possibility that soybean growers could become "locked" into a chemical control program if insecticides are applied to soybean regularly. Experience with other crops has demonstrated that if insecticides are applied routinely, insectiside-resistant populations often develop. Also, insects that are not pests sometimes attain pest status when beneficial insects are inadvertently killed by excessive insecticide use. To forestall these potential problems, the chalcidoid parasitoid *Pediobius foveolatus* is released annual to suppress Mexican bean beetle. Pediobius was imported from India and cannot survive Maryland winters; thus beetles and parasitoids are cultured, and parasitoids released, such spring.

Since Mexican bean beetles prefer snap beans over soybeans, soybean growers are encouragd to plant a few rows of snap beans to attract emerging. Mexican bean beetles away from the soybean crop. Pediobius then is released into the snap beans, where the Mexican bean beetles are congregated. Although the bean beetles eventually

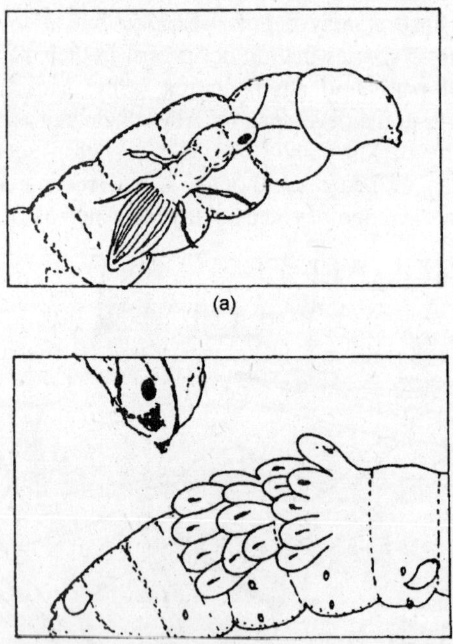

Fig. 11.3. Goniozous legneri, a wasp of the family Bethylidae that has been improved from Uruguay and released in California for control of the naval orangeworm: (a) adult wasp on the host caterpillar; (b) larvae of the parasitoid developing on the caterpillar.

move to thc soybean crop, the parasitoids become sufficiently abundant, and are sufficiently mobile, to prevent excessive damage by bean beetles. In addition to suppression of pests attacking orchard and field crops, augmentation programmes show particular promise for control of dung-breeding pests. Parasitoids frequently are released into poultry and cattle production facilities to alleviate dungbreeding fly problems because many of the fly pests are insecticide resistant. Also, it is important not to contaminate livestock with insecticides soon before they are marketed. These are to the use of predators and parasitoids for insect pest suppression?

There are three principal advantages : permanence, safety, and economy (although all may not apply to any one situation). Many predators and parasitoids, unlike Pediobius, are self-perpetuating. The vedalia beetle, for example, required little assistance once established. Although the initial cost of locating, culturing, and releasing predators and parasites may be quite high, experience has demonstrated that this is very economical method of pest suppression if an appropriate predator or parasitoid can be located. Also, there is less danger of selection for resistant pest populations. Predators and parasitoids can coevolve with their hosts). However, the development of complete immunity of parasitoids has rarely been reported.

Lastly, release of predators and parasitoids has had no significant adverse environmental effects. The pest environment influences the probability that naturally occurring biological control will be successful. Also, the nature of the environment should be considered carefully when attempting to manage a pest situation through manipulation of predators and parasitoids. There are many types of pest situations, but the extremes are probably best represented by the forest environment and agroecosystem.

Biological Control in a Forest Environment

In most forest environments, the long-term average insect population densities are below the economic injury level. Occasionally a pest population suddenly increases to damaging level and then usually declines precipitously. The problem in this type of environment is to *stabilize* pest population fluctuations. It is important, therefore, to introduce density-dependent mortality factors that will exert greater impact on pest populations as they become more abundant. Density-independent factors are important because they help to maintain pest populations below injurious levels, but is probably the absence or presence of density-dependent factors that determines population trends.

The introduction of exotic predators and parasitoids may be the most appropriate tactic in the forest environment. Another pest of eastern forests, the gypsy moth, has proved more intractable. Over 40 species of predators and parasitoids have been introduced and at least 12 of these are well-established. The severity of periodic defoliation of tree in urban areas and in parklands has, however, led to demands for aerial applications of insecticides, and these have not favoured the success of biological control programme. The severe outbreaks of 1981 have reinforced efforts to develop an integrated programme for the gypsy moth, which will include biological control as an important element.

Biological Control in an Agro-ecosystem

In many agroecosystems population fluctuations are not the problem; rather, the average population density exceeds the economic injury level. This can result from a number of factors : (1) the crop may have a very low EIL, such that few pests can be tolerated; (2) the crop may be a very suitable food source, promoting good pest survival and reproduction; (3) the pests may be well-adapted to exploit disturbed monocultures (r- strategists); and (4) the pests may be releatively free from natural enemies. In such an environment, our objective is to reduce average pest densities rather than to reduce the severity of outbreaks. We need to introduce mortality factors that on the average destroy a portion of the pest generation that is equal to, or exceeds, the reproductive ability of the pest. Density-independent factors, in addition to density-dependent factors, are of value here. Insecticides might be more effective than predators and parasitoids in this environment, or we can utilize predators, parasitoids, or perhaps pathogens in an augmentative approach where they applied regularly, as are insecticides. Many agroecosystems also display characteristics of a forest environment. Deciduous fruit trees and rangelands, for example, may be somewhat intermediate between the typical forest environment and agroecosystem as described above. Selection of pest suppression tactics will be influenced by the unique environment characterisitics associated with each. The potential value of predators and parasitoids in a crop environment also is influenced by the pest-crop relationship. For many natural enemies, there must be a minimum level of hosts (pests) present in the crop for these potential control agents to be supported at effective levels.

Fruit and flower crops, among others, which cannot tolerate large numbers of direct pests, may not be amenable to predator and parasitoids utilization as compared to forage crops, which often can support considerable damage. Biological control is a tactic of wide appeal in an age of environmental awareness. Practitioners can point to important successes, but it is only fair to say that there have been many instances in which control was disappointing. Other problems arise from the difficulties of identification of these often minute organisms. When parasitoid wasps of the genus *Aphytis* were introduced for control of California red scale, results were inconsistent. Still many thousands of species of parasitoid Hymenoptera and Diptera are left that have yet to be discovered and studies.

Pathogenic Biological Control

The microbial control agents or pathogens also are important in naturally occurring biological control. The potential for pathogens in applied biological control probably exceeds that of many other pest management tactics, including predators and parasitoids. However, development of pathogen-based systems of pest management has proceeded slowly. The difficulties associated with identification, culture, and registration and microbial agents account for much of the delay in intergration of pathogens into pest management programmes. In many ways, pathogens are very similar to parasitoids. They are most effective against the immature stages of insects, and adults tend to be less susceptible or immune. As is often the case with parasitoids, they develop internally, and a single host can produce many pathogens.

Pathogens often has a rather specific host relationship (narrow host range), much like parasitoids. However, active host "selection" is rarely involved; the pathogenic organisms are ingested inadvertently or spread by air, water, or oviposition by parasitoids. Acute, lethal infections are common, but chronic, debilitating infections also occur, whereas the attack of parasitoids is almost always fatal. There is a variety of pathogens including viruses, bacteria, fungi, protozoa, and nematodes. Not all are beneficial from our point of view, for some attack useful insects such as the honey bee. The most widespread diseases of adult honey bees is nosema, caused by the protozoan *Nosema apis*. American foulbrood and European foulbrood are important diseases of honey bee larvae and are caused by two species in the baceterial genus *Bacillus*. However, microbial agents that attack noxious insects are being taken.

Viruses

Viruses are the acellular organisms and as usually particles of many insect viruses are enclosed in protein crystals called *inclusion*

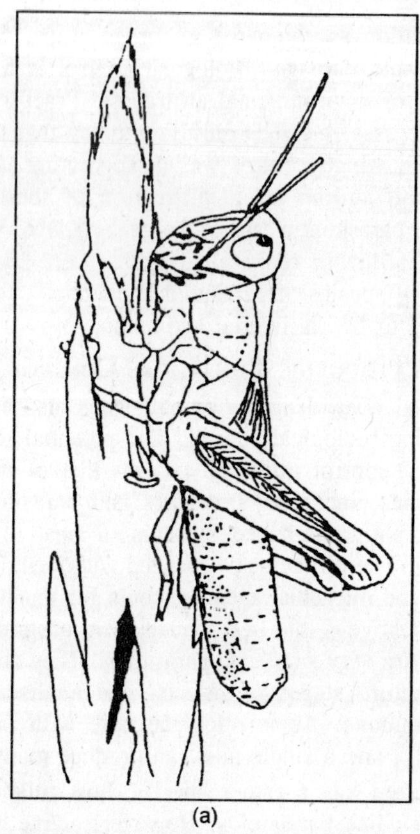

(a)

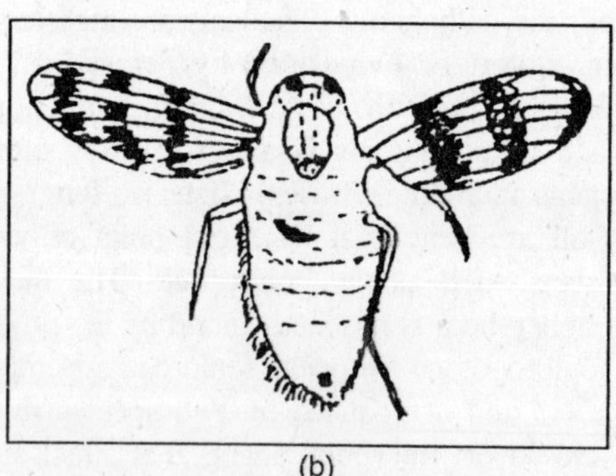

(b)

Fig. 11.4. Insects that have succumbed to fungi of the genus Entomophthora. (a) An immature grasshopper that is infected with E. grylli. Infected grasshopper typically climb to the tops of plants and die with their legs wrapped tightly around the plant. (b) A fly that has succumed to E. muscae.

bodies. The principal types of inclusion viruses are Nuclear Polyhedrosis Virus (NPV), Granulosis Virus (GV), Cytoplasmic Polyhedrosis Virus (CPV), and entomopox virus. *Non-inclusion viruses* occur in insects but are difficult to detect without an electron microscope and are not well-known. NPVs multiply in the cell nucleus. Tissues most commonly infected are the epidermis, fat body, blood cells, and tracheae in Lepidotpera. In phytophagous Hymenoptera, midgut cells are infected. Infected larvae rarely exhibit symptoms of infection until just before death, when the epidermis darkens and becomes shiny. Virus infection sometimes induces a change in larval behaviour whereby the insect climbs to the highest point available prior to death. After death the integument ruptures, releasing millions of polyhedral inclusion bodies that contaminate the food plant. This enhances the probability that other insects will accientally ingest inclusion bodies and become infected. This change in behaviour is sometimes induced by other pathogens as well. As usual the GVs multiply in both the nucleus and the cytoplasm of host cells.

The fat body is the principal site of infection, but the epidermis ad tracheae are sometimes infected. Symptoms of infection are similar to NPV infection. Lepidoptera are common hosts. CPVs develop in the cytoplasm of the host cells. The midgut is infected, and Lepidoptera larvae are the usual hosts. The disease tends to be debilitating; diseased larvae exhibit loss of appetite, are smaller, and develop slowly. Insects that are infected but not killed may have a reduced reproductive capacity. CPVs are not as host specific as are the other two virus groups mentioned previously. Entomopox viruses multiply in the cell cytoplasm of fat body and blood cells. They are found in Coleoptera, Lepidoptera, Diptera and Orthoptera. Symptoms of infection are variable. Viruses seen to play a significant role in the pest management. They are usually quite specific, which allows entomologists to suppress pest populations without undue disruption of beneficial insects.

Insect viruses can be applied with conventional insecticide application equipment. They are not harmful to mammals, and they are tolerant of many adverse environmental conditions. The main limitations to the use of viruses include our inability to produce them economically their susceptibility to ultraviolet radiation and certain other adverse environmental conditions, and the reluctance to apply disease-causing agents to food crops. Commerical production of insect viruses still is quite limited. "Elcar" is an example of a nuclear polyhedrosis virus that is commercially available. It is active against several species of lepidopteran pests in the genus *Heliothis*, but thus far its use is restricted to cotton.

Bacteria

Bacteria are the prokaryotic organism most and important bacterial pathogens of insects form resistant spores and thus can survive unfavourable conditions quite well. Non-spore-forming bacteria are common in the digestive tracts of insects, but they are only pathogenic when they invade the hemocoel; this occurs under unusual conditions such as stress or injury. There has been little effort to utilize non-spore-forming bacteria as microbial agents; some are pathogenic to mammals. The best-know insect pathogens among the spore-forming bacteria include *Bacillus thuringiensis* and *B. popilliae*. *B. thuringiensis* was first isolated from silkworm larvae by Japanese workers about 1900.

There has since been extensive research on this organism, and several strains infecting a wide variety of insects are recognized; however, it is most frequently applied against lepidopterous larvae. It has been pointed out that the organism was easy to produce in large quantities and to disseminate as a "microbial insecticide." Infected caterpillars become sluggish and eventually discoloured and flaccid; after death they produce odors of putrifaction. Hundreds of tons of *B. thuringiensis* spores are now being produced commercially each year, under such names as "Thuricide," Dipel," and "Biotrol." The bacterial cells contain a toxic protein crystal as well as spore. When dissolved in the insect, the crystal causes paralysis of the gut. However, both spore and crystal are usually required for effective action. *B. popilliae* is effective against the larvae of Japanese beetles and produces "*milky disease*," the name resulting from the milky-white appearance of infected grubs. *B. popilliae* persists in the soil for some time, where *B. thuringiensis* is less persistent and must be reapplied regularly.

Fungi

There is a wide variety of fungi and most of them contain some insect pathogens. Entomopathogenic fungi often are not very specific. Fungal pathogens are usually transmitted from host to host by spores; unlike viruses and bacteria, fungi are capable of penetrating the insect directly through the integument. Fungi, more than any other insect pathogen, require favourable environmental conditions for development of *epizootics*, or outbreak of disease. This seems to be due to the need for high humidity that usually is required for germination of fungal spores. Fungi can often be cultured on artificial media, but infectivity is reduced. Fungi are important naturally occurring biological control agents. Some species have been used successfully to reduce pest populations, *Verticillium lecanii* is used for biocontrol of aphids and scales affecting greenhouse crops *Beauveria bassiana* is applied against a variety of pests and *Metarhizium anisopliae*—is used for controlling spittlebugs on sugarcane. Similarly for suppression of citrus rust mites Hirsutella thompsoni is used.

Protozoa

These are the microscopic a cellular organisms faming a heterogenous assemblage of organisms. Many groups, including the flagellates, gregarines, and amoebae, may be pathogenic to insects. The order Microsporida, especially pathogens of genus *Nosema*, has received considerable attention by entomologists. Microsporidans can be transmitted orally or via the egg. They are not very specific and often cause a chronic disease that results in lowered fecundity or sterlity. Nosema locustae affects a large number of grasshopper will normally produce enough spores to treat 3 to 4 acres of rangeland. Nosema spores usually are mixed with bran to make a bait that grasshopper ingest readily. Nosema also can be applied in conjunction with a reduced amount of insecticides to provide rapid, but residual, suppression of grasshopper populations.

Nematodes

Nematodes are the helminthic organisms and traditionally have been treated as microbial pathogens, but it would perhaps be more logical to consider than as microparasites and place them in a separate category. Several nematodes are parasitic on insects. The infective stage of the nematode penetrates the insect directly or is ingested, and reproduces inside the host. The insect is killed by the exit of the nematodes or by release of a bacterium carried by the worms. Reesimermis nielseni nematodes appear promising for suppression of mosquito populations.

Nematodes are cultured in mosquito larvae at a cost of about 10 cents per million infective jugenile nemas and are applied at a rate of about 100 nemas per square meter of water surface. Steinernema feltiae has a broad host range and has been used experimentally for control of many insects. The nematode penetrates the insect hemocoel and releases bacteria. The bacteria kill the host, and the nematodes feed on the bacteria and host tissue. Large numbers of infective nematodes can be produced from a single host. *S. feltiae* also can be cultured on artificial media with production costs as low as 2 cents per million nematodes.

Biological Control of Weeds

Weed constitute quite another class of pests, and the possibility of controlling them with *phytophagous insects* 'has long intrigued entomologists. Programmes of this nature cannot be undertaken without careful preparation, however, as there as several problems to be considered:

1. The insects must be introduced without natural enemies from their native home and must survive the attacks of predators and parasitoids in their new home. When scale insects (Coccoidae) were introduced to South Africa to control prickly-pear cacti, for example, they were ineffective because of predation by lady beetles. In this instance insecticides were used to destroy these "beneficial" beetles, permitting the scale insects to destroy the cacti.
2. The insects may be monophagous or so narrowly oligophagous that they are unable to survive on desirable plants. For example, biological control of thistles is hampered by the presence of related, cultivated plants such as safflower and many garden flowers, which may be attacked.
3. The weeds must have sufficient negative economic effect to justify the effort. Some seeds have desirable attributes, either as sources of nectar for bees or parasitoid wasps or as cover for game birds.

The best-known example of successful use of insects to control weeds concerns pricklypear cacti (Opuntia species) in Australia. Cacti are not native to Australia, but the introduction of pricklypears for ornamental purposes resulted in many parts of eastern Australia being overrun by stands of cacti so dense as to be virtually impenetrable for humans and livestock. In 1925, eggs of a small moth, appropriately called Cactoblastis cactorum were brought from Argentina. The larvae were reared on cacti, and over time some 3 billion eggs were released in the field. The result was a dramatic decline in the abundance of pricklypear cacti. Today, the cacti survive in small pataches here and there, but the moths usually find and destroy them. Not every effort at weed control by insects has met with success, however. Attempts to control lantana in various parts of the tropics, for example, have had limited success. There are at present a number of ongoing projects, such as those for leafy spurge, alligator weed, and water hyacinth, the results of which are not yet clear.

GENETICAL INSECT CONTROL

Reproduction in pest insects can be disrupted by releasing sterile or genetically insects into natural populations. This approach of using insects of self-destruction is known as *autocidal control*. Utilization of these techniques is dependent on our ability to produce economically large numbers of insects for release. Also, the insects released must be successful competitors with members of the natural population for mates. Several genetic mechanisms exist that can, at least theoretically, be manipulated to reduce the reproductive capacity of pests. The use of *lethal mutations* involves introduction of genes that are lethal under certain conditions. When the specific conditions occur, a breakdown in normal physiological function occurs. For example, the inability to diapause could be introduced into a population, which would lead to mortality in winter.

The use of *translocations* involves release of insects bearing chromosomes with translocations (gene exchange between nonhomologous chromosomes). Crosses between normal and translocation strains could result in death of the developing embryo because genetic information would be missing. These tech- niques appear promising but as yet have not been well tested under field conditions. Autocidal control using *sterile insect release* has, however, been demonstrated to be practical and is current in use. The genetic constitution of the natural population is not altered, but reproduction is disrupted. Any treatment that provides sterile but functional adult insects may be satisfactory; gamma irradiation is commonly used. Sterile males, females, or both may be released to achieve suppression, but usually only sterile males are used.

After release sterile insects mate with normal, nonsterile adults in the population, thus reducing their reproductive potential. This approach may be useful against other insect pests, but there are some limitations to the tactic. The principal limiting factors for such programmes are that (1) we must be able to sterilize insects, but without reducing their ability to compete effectively with nonsterile insects for mates; (2) we must be able to rear insects in large numbers, economically; and (3) the native population must reach low levels of abundance at sometime in their seasonal life history (naturally or through suppression), so that we can release an advantageous ration of sterile insects to nonsterile ones. The second of these factors might be circumvented if it were possible to develop a safe and effective chemosterilant that could be applied in the way that insecticides are applied. However, this remains for the future.

Cultural Techniques

Management of insect populations through *cultural techniques* involves modification of the environment to make it less attractive or suitable for pests through standard agronomic (cultural) practices. Cultural techniques do not require special machinery or equipment, but for cultural techniques to be successful a thorough knowledge of insect life history is essential. Cultural techniques depend on disrupting a favourable biological or physical condition; obviously we must know what is favourable for the insect pest before we can be disruptive. Common cultural technique include tillage, sanitation, crop rotation, timing of harvest and planting, water management, and use of trap crops. Tillage, or soil preparation, will influence thermal and moisture conditions as well as the physical structure of the soil. Also, insects may be killed directly or may be brought to the surface where they susceptible to predation and desiccation. An example of an insect that is affected by tillage is the pale western cutworm, a pest of small grains. Females of this moth prefer bare soil for oviposition, and if tillage is delayed until after the oviposition period, cropland may escape attack. Also, caked soil is unsuitable for cutworm larvae, which burrow beneath the soil surface, so postponing tillage reduces survival of this stage. Lastly, high soil moisture, which can be induced by irrigation or by packing the soil, will drive cutworm larvae to the soil surface, where they are readily attacked by parasitoids.

Sanitation, a clean culture involves removal of weeds or crop residues that might harbor insect pests. In general, crop pests are not monophagous, and weeds may serve as regular, alternate hosts. The European corn borer, for example, attacks over 200 different plants, many of which are weeds. Weeds may harbor pests that infect crop plants as they become suitable hosts, or weeds may attract pests that than spread to crop plants as the weeds are consumed. Beet web-worms, for example, that are known to be much more destructive to sugar beet fields harboring lambsquarter and Russian thistle; apparently the adults prefer to oviposit on these plants. European corn borers survive the winder as full-grown larvae in crop residue. Where corn borer populations are high, crop residue should be shredded and used for animals fodder. Destruction, or deep lowing of crop residue, will alleviate many insect problems. The trend toward reduced tillage and no tillage in American agriculture seems likely to be exaccrabate certain pest problems because crop residues remain to harbor insects. Where parasitoids have potential to exert significant suppressive effect on pest populations, a thorough consideration of their biology should be made before recommending indiscriminate weed control. Many adult parasitoids are much more effective when they feed on nectar from flowering plants, including weeds.

Thus certain weeds, especially those that do not harbor pests directly, may be valuable in that they supply nourishment of beneficial insects. Crop rotation is the alternating the type of crop grown at a given, location. It often provides effective management of pest populations. Crop rotation is particularly effective where insect pests are not very mobile. Management of western corn rootworms, for example, is feasible through rotation of corn with a nonhost, such as soybeans. Rootworms overwinters as eggs in soil, and larvae that develop in spring and early summer have limited mobility. Thus eggs deposited in corn fields produce larvae that perish for lack of suitable food when soybean or another unsuitable host follows corn in a rotation sequence. Insects pests may be abundant for a releatively brief period of the growing season or may be able to damage the crop only during a specific stage in growth. Thus, it may be possible to *time planting* or *harvest* such that the crop is not available, or not in a susceptible stage, when the pests are active. Lack of susceptibility because of differences in timing also is called *phenological asynchrony*. A well-known example of phinological asynchrony invovles the Hessian fly, a pest of wheat.

It is practical to delay planting wheat in the autumn until after the brief period of adult activity, allowing the wheat crop to escape infestation. The availability of free water or soil moisture influences the abundance of many insect pests. *Water management*, when combined with knowledge of insect response to water, can be used to regulate insect pest abundance. For example, many species of mosquitoes breed only in temporary pools of waster. Modification of land contours to prevent pooling removes potential breeding sites. Alternatively, water can be permanent impounded in areas where temporary pooling occurs. Permanent impoundments are less likely to breed mosquitoes because fish and other predators that inhabit permanent water feed on the mosquito larvae, and also because some species will not oviposit in such habitats.

Sometimes insects can be lured away from the principal crop when a small area is planted to a more attractive plant, or if a small part of the crop is planted early. The attractant crop, or portion of the crop, is called a *trap crop*. When a trap crop is infested with insects, it is destroyed or treated in some manner to destroy the insects.

The advantage of trap crop use is that it eliminates the need to control insects on the main crop, which reduces expense and insecticides contamination. For spruce beetle control it is possible to lure the beetles to recently felled or girdled tree, which is highly attractive to beetles and serves as a trap. The trap crop (tree) may be injected with cacodylic acid, a poison containing arsenic, prior to felling or girdling. Thus, the beetles are killed they burrow into the treated tree, and healthy nearby tress are spared attack.

Physical and Mechanical Techniques

The physical and mechanical techniques of insect pest suppression is the oldes, and in some cases most primitive. The suppression of insect pests by physical and mechanical techniques are measures taken to destroy insect pests, to disrupt normal physiological function (other than with insecticides or similar chemicals), or to modify the environment to make it unsuitable for insect pests. Physical and mechanical suppression methods may be distinguished from cultural methods by the use of special equipment or operations in addition to the normal agronomic (cultural) procedures. Physical and mechanical methods often provide immediate and tangible results; hence, they are popular. On the other hand, they may be costly or labour intensive and therefore not feasible for commerical agriculture.

Physical techniques utilize physical properties of the environment in such a manner as to destroy pests. As is the case with many other suppression methods, thorough knowledge of insect life history is useful for effective pest suppression using these techniques. For example, we may need to know the physiological response of a particular insect to certain temperature or humidity conditions, or the behavioural response to certain visual stimuli. Temperature is also proved very effective certain pests. Cold storage of fruit, especially when accompanied by modification of gaseous atmosphere, will kill some internal pests. Burning (flaming) crop stubble and field margins is useful for destroying both insect and weeds pests. Reflection by aluminium mulch will repel certain flying pests, especially aphids; this is especially valuable when attempting to protect a crop from insect-borne plant disease. Light plays a very important role in the management. It traps are usually used for pest monitoring, but when employed in sufficient number they can effect significant reduction in pest abundance. Other attractants such as pheromone or visual sticky traps can remove pests similarly. Hand-picking is useful for home gardeners or in societies where labour is not expensive.

Chemical Basis of Behaviour

The manner in which many insect species locate mates, recognize food, and determine suitable oviposition sites may be regulated, at least in part, by chemical stimuli. When chemical stimuli have been identified and synthesized, it is sometimes possible to modify insect pest behaviour to alleviate damage by using these chemicals. The chemicals that have received most attention, and that currently are most practical for insect management, are sex pheromones. Other chemicals that probably will prove useful in the future are other types of pheromones, kairomones, repellents, and feeding deterrents. Organic gardening techniques such as companionate planting purportedly have a chemical basis.

Sex pheromones are as usual are the products of the glands pound directly into the air. They are often used to monitor insect activity. A pheromone dispenser usually is placed in a sticky trap, and the number of insects captured is used to ascertain the need for, and timing of suppression programmes. Sex pheromones are available for many insect pests, especially Lepidoptera. Examples include "Disparlure" for attracting gypsy moth, and "Grandlure" for boll weevil. Sex pheromones also can be used to disrupt mating by saturating the atmosphere with the proper chemical stimulus. In a saturated atmosphere insects cannot orient properly and locate mates. Thus reproduction is inhibited and damage reduced. "Nomate PBW" is a commerical available sex pheromone formulation that disrupts reproduction in pink bollworm when the product is applied to cotton.

Aggregation pheromones are basically secreted to attract the entire population. Thus, they are produced by some insect species to facilitate group attack of a host. Aggregation pheromones are best known from bark beetles, where attack by a large number of beetles allows the invaders to overwhelm the host's defenses. Bark beetles also produce antiaggregation pheromones. Either type of pheromone could be useful for pest management. Aggregation pheromones could be used to attract bark beetles to a trap, while antiaggregation pheromones could protect particular trees from attack.

In cockroaches there are stink glands in the abdomen to produce an aggregation pheromone that can be used to attract them to a particular location or trap. Also, aggregation pheromone can be used to offset the repellency sometimes associated with insecticides and thereby increase insecticide efficacy. There are certain insects mark their oviposition site with a pheromone; this is best known in certain parasitoid wasps and phytophagous flies. *Oviposition-deterring pheromones* keep insects from depositing too many eggs in a single host, which could result in over-crowding and insufficient food for developing larvae. Apple maggot and cherry fruitflies, for example, produce oviposition-deterring pheromones. When synthetic pheromone becomes available, it may be possible to apply it to fruit and thus protect the crop from injury. Some insects release *alarm pheromones* when they are attacked or otherwise disturbe to warn other members of the species that danger is nearby.

Alarm pheromones are known from bees, termites, aphids, and other insects. Aphid alarm pheromone also alerts attending ants to disturbance, and the ants rush to the defense of the aphids, which are valued by the ants as a source of sugary honeydew. Social insects such as ants and termites, and some pre- social insects such as tent caterpillars, also produce *trail pheromones*. Alarm and trail pheromones conceivably could be used to disrupt pest behaviours, but application thus far has been lacking. There are certain chemical substances called *kairomones* which are interspecific messengers that benefit the receiver of the chemical stimulus but are deleterious to the producer. Predatory and parasitic insects apparently use kairomones as an aid in locating host insects.

The chemical tricosane, for example, which is associated with corn earworm, attracts *Trichogramma* wasps to the pest insect. When tricosane is applied to a field containing corn earworm eggs, the wasps are stimulated to higher levels of activity, and a higher degree of parasitism results. Plants also produce kairomones, which are used by herbivorous insects in locating a host plant or in allowing the insect to recognize the host. In breeding for resistant crop plants, breeders should attempt to delete these chemical stimuli from the varietal phenotype. It would not be necessary to kill insects if we could deter them from attacking us and the things that we value. Repellents and feeding deterrents, therefore, reduce the need for insect control. *Repellents* are chemical that cause insects to make oriented movements away from the source of the chemical. The best-known repellent is deet, the active ingredient in mosquito repellent. *Feeding deterrents* inhibit feeding but do not necessarily repel insects. Currently there is considerable interest in azadirachtin, a chemical extracted from seeds of the neem tree, because it deters feeding by a large number of insect pests.

Certain "organic" gardening practices such as companionate planting reportedly result in insect repellence or deterrence.

Companionate planting is intercropping of "repellent" or "confusing" plants with the crop plants. The best-known example of a companionate plant is marigold, which supposedly repels pest insects from crop plants or masks the attractant odors from plants, thereby preventing pests from locating their hosts. There is no scientific evidence to support the concept of companionate planting although increasing plant diversity through intercropping may be a successful practice. Some of the plant species reportedly useful as companionate plants, such as garlic and onions, do contain natural insecticides. Organic gardeners might achieve better levels of plants protection by applying aqueous extracts of these plants to kill pests as they appear.

Chemical Disruption of Physiology

The most frequently, the pest management tactic used in technologically advanced societies is application of chemical insecticides to disrupt the physiology of the pest insect. Some pests can be effectively managed without insecticides, and some crops require insecticide application for protection only occasionally. However, insecticides have been widely employed since about 1900, and although their use is likely to diminish in the future, it is not likely to be completely eliminated. When insect populations or damage approach the economic threshold rapidly, insecticides often are the only practical suppression tactic.

In other words, it may take too long to augment the beneficial insect population, or it may be too late to initiate cultural or other suppression tactics. Insecticides, or pathogens that can be used like insecticides (microbial insecticides), can suppress pest populations quickely. Insecticides also offer a wide range of properties that make them useful for many different pests situations. For example, insecticide formulations are available for foliar, livestock, aquatic, soil, and stored-product pests. Relatively long-lasting or short-lived materials can be purchased. Finally, the cost of insecticides often is low relative to expected return on investment. For example, under some conditions each dollar invested in potato insect suppression results in a $29.00 increase in yield. A farmer may view insecticides as a good investment and insurance against unforeseen disaster. Variation in insecticide properties often is related to the chemical origin of the product.

Natural and synthetic inorganic insecticides are still available, but only to a limited extent; they were commonly used before the development of synthetic organics. Today, synthetic organic insecticides dominate the insecticide market, although natural organics are popular among some home gardeners. Biological insecticides, or microbial pathogens, have been discussed previously.

Natural inorganic insecticides are naturally occurring minerals. *Cryolite* is an example of an infrequently used natural inorganic that acts as a stomach poison for chewing insects. Sulfur is useful for suppressing mites, but it is more widely used as a fungicide. The toxicity of these two mammals is very low. Similarly *synthetic inorganic insecticides* are chemical modifications of naturally occurring minerals. Examples include the arsenicals paris green, lead arsenate, and calcium arsenate. Paris green was first used against Colorado potato beetles about 1865. Lead arsenate became popular for gypsy moth control around 1890. Calcium arsenate was targeted principally against boll weevil. Arsenicals are very toxic to mammals.

Sorptive dusts are inorganics that are used for structural pest control and grain protection. The dusts usually are silicon dioxide powders that abrade and disrupt the wax layer of the insect cuticle, leading to desiccation. Sorptive dusts are not very toxic to mammals.

Natural organic insecticides are principally botanical in origin. Pyrethrum has been used as an insecticide for at least 2000 years in the form of finely ground *chrysanthemum* flowers. The insecticidal properties are due to pyrethrins, which can be extracted from the flowers. It is less expensive to produce synthetic analogs of the active ingredients, called pyrethroids, than to extract them from plants. Pyrethroids are available commercially and have a low toxicity to mammals. Water extracts of tobacco plants were used by American colonists for insect control prior to 1700. The alkaloid nicotine is principally responsible for the insecticidal properties. Nicotine is used in the form of nicotine sulfate and is an effective aphicide; however, it is quite toxic to mammals. Ryania and rotenone are additional examples of infreqeuntly used plant-derived insecticides. Their mammalian toxicity is low to moderate. Petroleum derivatives are useful insecticides and acaricides that are releatively non-toxic to mammals. Dormant oils are heavy oil applied when plants are dormant, because oil is toxic to foliage. Summer oils are lighweight oils that are safer for use on plant foliage.

Synthetic organic insecticides are widely used in commercial agriculture. The principal groups are the chlorinated hydrocarbons, organophosphates, and carbamates. Other groups, such as the insect growth regulators, probably will assume greater importance as environmental standards change, as the frequency of insecticide resistance increases, and as the need for selective insecticides becomes more acute.

Chlorinated hydrocarbons, also known as organochlorines, are some of the oldest and best-known insecticides. As the name implies, they contain chlorine, hydrogen and carbon. Most notorious of the chlorinated hydrocarbons is DDT, one of the most useful, effective, low-cost insecticides every produced. DDT also is quite persistant; poor biodegradability combined with overuse led to severe restrictions on its use in the United States starting in 1973. Its adverse effects were demonstrated particularly among predatory birds and mammals, which were especially susceptible to ingesting large quantities of insecticide by way of its increasing concentration in higher levels of food chains. Other chlorinated hydrocarbons formerly used to a great extent include aldrin, dieldrin, chlordane, heptachlor, lindane and mirex. Like DDT, most chlorinated hydrocarbons are quite residual and therefore useful where long-term control is desired. These materials were widely used as soil insecticides and as seed treatments, and some are still employed in structural pest control.

In general, their use is restricted or prohibited in the United States, although they are employed in some other countries. Some chloriated hydrocarbons such as methoxychlor and kelthane are not very persistent and are still in use. The chemically unstable *organophosphates* are derived from phosphoric acid and have replaced many of the chlorinated hydrocarbons. They are related to military "nerve gas," and some are very toxic to mammals. Because they are chemically unstable, they are not very persistent. Common organophosphates include ronnel, disulfoton, dichloreos, methyl parathion, diazinon, chlorpyrifos and malathion. Their properties differ significantly. Malathion is a very safe insecticide and acaricide, while parathion is quite toxic to mammals. Dichlorvos is a fumigant that is frequently incorporated into pet collars. Ronnel is used on livestock. Chlorpyrifos is used almost exclusively for household pest control. Many of the organophosphates are systemics. *Systemic insecticides* are absorbed and translocated through the animal or plants; ronnel and acephate are examples.

The *carbamates* are derived from carbamic acid. The first successful carbamate was carbaryl. It is widely used because it kills a broad spectrum of pests and its mammalian toxicity is fairly low. Other common carbamates include propoxur for cockroach control, aldicarb for field crop and ornamental pests, pirimicarb for aphids, and carbofuran for a variety of insects. Many carbamates also are effective nematicides. Some carbamates are quite selective and kill only certain insects. Their mammalian toxicity is extremely variable. The use of carbamates is increasing as selective suppression of pests is emphasized in pest management programmes, and resistance to organo- phosphates becomes more common among pest species.

Insect growth regulators probably will assume an important role in pest management as they become more readily available. Insect growth regulators may act as hormones of antihormones and may have diverse effects, such as disruption of molting. Diflubenzuron, methoprene, and kinoprene are examples of commercially available insect growth regulators. Diflubenzuron interferes with cuticle formation, while methoprene and kinoprene act similarly to juvenile hormone. Various insecticide affect different body agains to paralise the pest.

Organophosphates and carbamates are acetycholinesterase inhibitors; thus they inhibit transmission of nerve impluses. Chlorinated hydrocarbons appears to disrupt nervous transmission also, but by causing a sodium-potassium imbalance in the neurones. Rotenone inactivates the enzyme glutamic acid oxidase. Nicotine affects acetylcholine receptors in some unknown manner. The pyrethroid mode of action is not understood, but nervous transmission is interrupted. Sorptive dusts cause desiccation by disrupting the cuticular wax layer. Petroleum oils have a different effect—a thin layer of oil impedes gas exchange, so insects suffocate. Thus, insecticides provide a variety of ways to disrupt physiological processes in insects, ultimately leading to death.

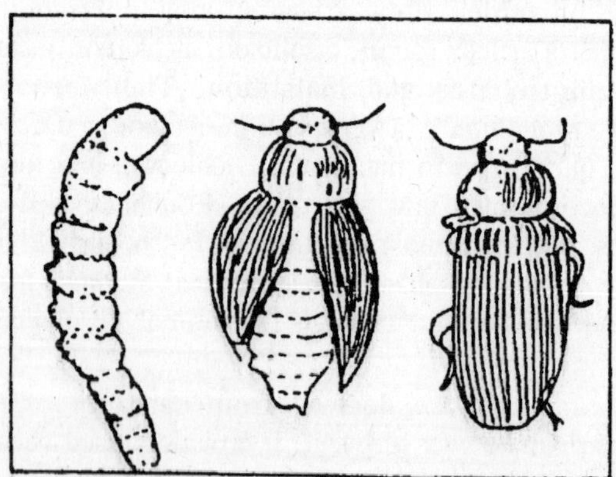

Fig. 11.5. The pupa of the yellow mealworm (left), when treated with juvenile hormone analog, produces an abnormal adult that is unable to reproduce (center). A normal adult mealworm is shown at the right.

Formulation and Application of Insecticides

Discovery of a chemical that will disrupt the physiology of insects is only part of the process that will lead to plant and animal protection. An insecticide must be prepared in such a way that it is available for practical use; this process is called *formulation*. There is a variety of equipment for delivering insecticide formulations to the target organisms is as diverse as the formulations available. Safety and convenience are important considerations for insecticide application in urban and suburban environments.

Aerosol applicators utilize compressed gas as a propellent and are popular because no preparation is required. However, they are very expensive to use. *Resin strips* release a vapor that usually is useful in enclosed areas only. *Compressed air sprayers* are inexpensive and easy to use but are useful for small applications only. *Hose end sprayers* are equally convenient and inexpensive and are useful for larger areas and small trees, but calibration is difficult. Agricultural insecticide application is more concerned with efficacy and economics. Although the initial expenditure for application equipment may be quite high, large areas may be treated effficiently.

Hydraulic sprays are commonly used for many filed crops. *Low-pressure hydraulic sprayers* are releatively inexpensive and versatile; they commonly are attached to tractors, trailers, and aircraft. *High-pressure hydraulic sprayers* are more expensive but provide better penetration of foliage. However, high pressure results in small droplet size, which can lead to dangerous insecticide drift. Drift also is a problem with *dusters*. Dusts provide good penetration of foliage but poor coverage. *Granule applicators* overcome the problem of drift because the insecticide is formulated in particles too large to be blown by the wing. However, granule applicators are expensive, and granules do not stick to foliage.

Air blast sprayers inject liquid formulation into a stream of air. Large air blast sprayers are called mist blowers and are used to treat orchards, shade trees, and livestock. Small backpack, or knapsack, air blast sprayers utilize the same principle but cannot be used for large trees. Specialized applicators are produced for other uses, such as suppression of medically important insects and greenhouse pests. *Ultra-low-volume applicators* apply very small droplets of undiluted insecticide.

Ultra-low-volume applications sometimes are used for suppression of mosquitoes, cockroaches, and grasshoppers. Application equipment is expensive, but little insecticide is required. Thermogenerators, or

Table 11.1. Components and types of insecticide formulations

I. Components of commercial insecticide formulations

1. *Active ingredient* : The toxicant or poisonous substance responsible for insecticidal properties; usually given in % or 1b/gal
2. *Inert ingredient* : The nonpoisonous diluting material; sometimes called carrier or solvent
3. *Surfactant* : Surface active agent enhancing useful properties of the formulation; examples are wetting agents or stickers, which assist the spread of the liquid formulation over the target organism and promote retention, respectively; emulsifiers are surfactants that cause an even dispersion of one liquid throughout a second liquid, in which it is not soluble
4. *Synergist* : A nontoxic material than when added to a toxicant, produces a more toxic product by competing for, or inhibiting, detoxifying enzymes.

II. Types of commercial insecticide formulation

1. *Solution* (S) : A solid, liquid, or gas dissolved in a liquid to make a homogeneous mixture
2. *Emulsifiable concentrate* (EC) : A liquid containing an emulsified active ingredient; when added to water, EC formulations normally turn milky white; usually contains a high concentration of toxicant
3. *Wettable power* (WP) : A dry formulation that is suspended in water; requires constant agitation to prevent the toxicant from precipitating; usually contains a high concentration of toxicant
4. *Soluble powder* (SP) : A dry active ingredient that dissolves in water to form a solution; usually contains a high concentration of toxicant
5. *Flowable* (F) : A solid or semisolid suspended in liquid with surfactants to provide the characteristics of a solution rather than a suspension
6. *Dust* (D) : A dry formulation diluted with another dry material; usually contains a low concentration of toxicant
7. *Granules* (G) : Dry formulation similar to dust but consisting of larger particles; usually contains a low concentration of toxicant
8. *Aerosol and fog* : Very fine droplets of carrier containing toxicant; produced by propellant, air blast, or heated gas; usually contains a low concentration of toxicant; provides little residual deposit
9. Smoke : Very fine solid particles containing toxicant; produced by burning; little residual deposit
10. Vapor : Vapors released from resin strips, or liquids that act as fumigants
11. Encapsulation : Active ingredient is encapsulated (enclosed) to slow inactivation and prolong activity
12. Bait : An attractant, usually some type of food, that contains a toxicant

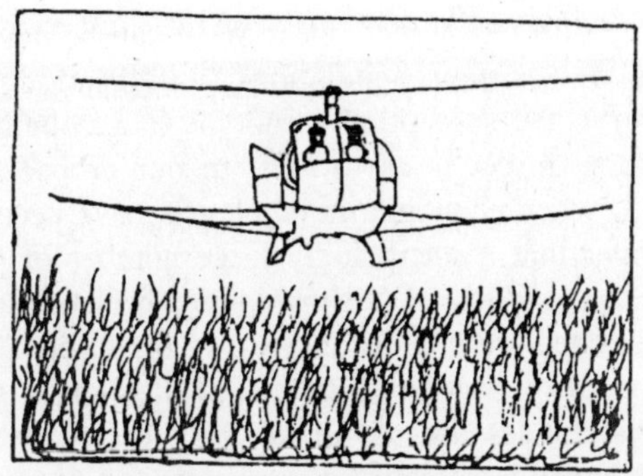

Fig. 11.6. Spraying vineyards with a suitably equipped helicopter. Downdraft is produced by the rotor blader.

foggers, disperse aerosol droplets in a cloud of fog that is produced by vaporization from a heat source. Thermogenerators commonly are used to kill adult mosquitoes outdoors and greenhouse pests indoors. In recent years aerial application of insecticides has become widespread, especially where there are broad acreages of single crops. Planes have also been used extensively in forested areas, for example, in control of spruce budworm. Helicopters are especially useful in irregular terrain or where landing strips are not available. Aerial spraying by an experienced pilot under suitable wather conditions may result in rapid coverage of wide expanses of crops with little drift to nontarget areas.

Disadvantages of Insecticides

Insecticides provide us with useful, practical tools for insect pest suppression, but they do have disadvantages. These include selection for insecticide-resistant strains, outbreaks of secondary pests, and adverse effects on nontarget organisms. Resistance to insecticides may be the major factor to restrict insecticide use in the future. Normal insect populations apparently contain some members that are resistant to insecticide. Insecticide use, especially when inducing high levels of mortality, selects for survival of an insecticide-resistant genotype. Under continued selection pressure the resistant strain becomes dominant and the population no longer is susceptible to insecticidal control. New insecticides with differeing modes of action may be substituted, but the selection process may be repeated, sometimes with alarming speed. The magnitude of the insecticide resistance problem first became apparent with house fly populations in 1946-1947.

Susceptibility to DDT was lost after only two years of selection. Since then, numerous species have exhibited partial or complete resistance to many different insecticides. What can be done to prevent the development of resistant populations ? Relaxation of selection pressure to preserve the susceptible genotype is an obvious solution. Can we allow some insect pests to exist in our crops? As we have already discussed, when economic injury levels have been established we usually discover that a surprisingly large number of pests can be present with no economic loss. We should avoid broad-scale application of insecticide; untreated areas allow survival of the susceptible genotype and enhance survival of beneficial insects. Utilization of tactics other than chemical insecticides are useful to delay to prevent resistance. Alternating insecticides is sometimes recommended but may result in selection for resistance to several insecticides simultaneously.

Secondary pests are pests that do not attain pest status in the absence of insecticide treatments but become damaging when insecticides are used. Some insects normally are checked by biological control agents. When insecticides are used, predators and parasites may be killed more effectively than secondary pest species; the pests than attain high, damaging population levels unimpeded by natural biological control agents. Red-banded leaf-roller in an example of an induced, or secondary, pest that now has attained key pest status in apple orchards. Mites commonly are induced pests, not only because their natural enemies have been destroyed, but because insecticides may induce physiological change in the host plant and stimulate mite reproduction. Pest species are not the only organisms that are affected adversely by insecticide application. We have already mentioned that beneficial predators and parasitoids may be killed by applications aimed at pest insects.

Pollinators, such as honey bees, frequently are destroyed by insecticides. Wildlife, especially birds and fish, are sometimes killed by direct contact with insecticides or by eating insecticide-contaminated insects. Residues of persistent insecticides, such as DDT, have been shown to assumulate in predators. Tertiary consumers, such as raptors and humans, may ingest large quantities of insecticide. It is probably fair to assume that humans are healthier when not ingesting insecticide residues. Even plants that are presumably benefiting from insecticide application do not always escape injury. Even applied at recommended dosages, inhibition of pollen germination and fruit drop may result.

Problems and Prospects

Agriculturalists are continually faced with the rather difficult task of producing food and fiber of sufficient quantity and satisfy the world's consumers. At least in capitalist countries, this must be done at a profit. Entomologists contribute to agricultural production through plant and animal protection, and they contribute to human health indirectly through management of disease vectors. Entomologists have successful at their task but cannot relax their efforts. The demand for food, fiber, and protection from disease will grow as the world's population increases. Our successes thus far have been achieved in fossil fuel-rich economies. However, agriculture, including pest management, now is faced with a new order of economic realities as fossil fuel becomes more expensive or unavailable.

Economics will not allow frequent and expensive insecticide application, and environmental concerns will prohibit un-necessary residual insecticides. Thus, a re-examination of pest management practices is under way. Contemporary pest management programs are meeting the challenge of change in agricultural production. Insect pest management programs, based on the strategy and the tactics have been initiated in a number of crop agroecosystems—for example, cotton, alfalfa and apples. The IPM programme for cotton has been especially wide ranging. Cotton is attacked by several major pests, such as the boll weevil, pink bollworm, tobacco budworm, and cotton fleahopper. Heavy use of insecticides in the past resulted in the development of resistant strains of several of these pests resulted in the development of resistant strains of several of these pests as well as outbreaks of secondary pests such as aphids and spider mites.

The current programme in the United States relies on the cultivation of varieties of cotton that are both disease resistant and cold tolerant. These "short-season" varieties can be planted early and harvested early, before the major build-up of pest populations. Crop residues are destroyed or treated with insecticides to kill diapausing weevils. A variety of predators and parasitoids are being encouraged, including *Trichogramma. Nuclear Polyhedrosis Virus* (NPV) and *Bacillus Thuringiensis* (BT) have been widely tested, and the latter is in use. Pheromones of several pest species are available for trapping and for mating disruption, and sterilization techniques have met with some limited success with the boll weevil. Insecticide use has been reduced, and more selective chemicals are being employed. Cotton is a major crop in many parts of the world and is grown under a variety of conditions. The combination of tactics will inevitably vary, depending on climate, type of cotton grown, the complex of pests present, and the general economic situation. But IPM has brought about a fresh and hopeful approach to cotton problems.

Ecological Basis for Insect Pest Management

Insects are the great majority of known animals and many of them are enormously abundant as individuals. Entomologists must have an understanding of the factors that regulate insect populations and must also be able to measure or estimate population size and its potential impact on humans. It is important to known when numbers are great enough to justify artificial controls, to be able to evaluate the effectiveness of controls, and to have some basis for anticipating outbreaks. Population size is a reflection of *fecundity*, which is subject to several sources of variation, and of *mortality*, which may occur at any stage of the life cycle and result from many different environmental or other influences. The effects of immigration and emigration must also be considered. Students of population dynamics concern themselves greatly with causes of mortality and the search for *key factors* in reducing the numbers of individuals available for reproduction. Survival, whether in a natural environment or an *agroecosystem*, is often relatively poor. As we sample insect populations, it is important to remember that not only the current pest population but also the future population will affect agriculatural production. Large numbers of young insects can often be tolerated in a crop because natural mortality agents cause significant decreases in pest abundance before the insects become large enough to inflict serious injury.

Human often provide insects with a veritable plethora of food in the form of well-watered and fertilized crop monocultures. *Monocultures* are uniform stands of the same plant. *Polycultures* incorporate two or more types of crop plants into the same area and more closely resemble natural system. Insect pest survival may be enhanced by the abundance of suitable food provided by agricultural monocultures. Worse yet, the natural enemies of insects may be isolated from the crop and pest insects, or the beneficial insects may be killed by insecticides. We must understand the nature of mortality factors that affect insect populations so that we can predict the eventual size of the pest population and the resultant damage.

Population Dynamics

The term *population dynamics* is given to the forces that control population size, and their effects. The search for key factors in determining numbers available for reproduction is abetted by preparation of a *life table*, in which the influence of each mortality factor is quantified for each life stage. For example, studies conducted in Ontario, Canada, by D.G. Harcourt and his colleagues indicated that alfalfa weevil populations in that area are principally regulated by th fungus *Zoophthora phytonomi*. Although the parasitoid *Bathyplectes curculionis* had proved effective in other areas neither it nor the parasitoids *Patasoon luna* or *Tetrastichus incertus*. As the host density increases the effectiveness of the *Zophthora* fungus increases its effect is said to be *density dependent*. Such factors are of major importance in *population regulation*, that is, the maintenance of reasonably constant numbers in nature. *Density independent* factors tend to be unpredictable, catastrophic events such as unseasonal rainfall (or lack of rain), severe winter temperatures, and the like. Such factors can be important for suppression of insect populations, but they are not usually regulatory factors.

Insecticides often are density-independent mortality factors, especially when used on a scheduled rather than a need basis. Thus, they are effective in reducing pest population levels but are not *more* effective when density is high. When populations are monitored and insecticides are applied judiciously, insecticide use is somewhat more regulatory. The population *stability*, which is the ability of a system to absorb disturbance and return to an equilibrium state is maintained by the density-dependent mortality factors. For example, a system may be more stable in the presence of phytophagous insects when density-dependent mortality agents such as predators and parasitoids are present. Such agents prevents the herbivores from destroying their host plant, which would result in local-extinction of both herbivore.

Resilience is the capacity to adapt to change or to persist in a changing environment. When agriculturalists convert natural ecosystems to monocultural systems, they provide certain herbivores with vast amounts of food. Resilient herbivore species quickly adapt to this changed environment and increase in abundance. Predators and parasitoids may also respond numerically to the increased abundance of host insects, and the plants-herbivore-predator system could stabilize at a new, higher equilibrium state. Such a shift to a new equilibrium state may equally well be brought about by other factors, such as unusual weather conditions, shifts in resistance of host plants, or the indiscriminiate use of insecticides. It is important to understand the factors responsible for such shifts so that when possible we can prevent the shift to a higher, more damaging equilibrium state or so that we can induce the shift to a lower, less damaging state. This is especially true when the new equilibrium state is above the level of damage that is economically tolerable.

Characteristics of Pest Species

Certain species of insects have life history characteristics that make them more likely than are others to become agricultural pests. It has been suggested that such species normally frequent habitats of low stability. Also, the insects in these species tend to be small and mobile and to reproduce rapidly. Insects species with this set of attributes are known as *r-strategists*. In contrast, *K*-strategists which are less likely to be pests, occur in more stable habitats, *K*-strategists tend to have lower reproductie rates, are less dispersive, and are frequently larger (relative to *r*-strategists). These terms have been adapted from ecologists, who employ *r* for the intrinsic rate of increase of a population; *K*, for the carrying capacity of the environment. The assumption is that *r*-strategists make use of available resources to maximizer *r*, while *K*-strategists tend to maintain more stable populations that do not closely approach carrying capacity.

In general, r-strategists quickly utilize resources available to them, often achieving pest status and sometimes destroying their hosts before dispersing. Their resilience is seen in the rapidity with which they adapt to new resources. Natural enemics are often unable to keep up with, and to regulate populations of r-strategists. Rather they are frequently suppressed by shortage of food or by unfavourable weather.

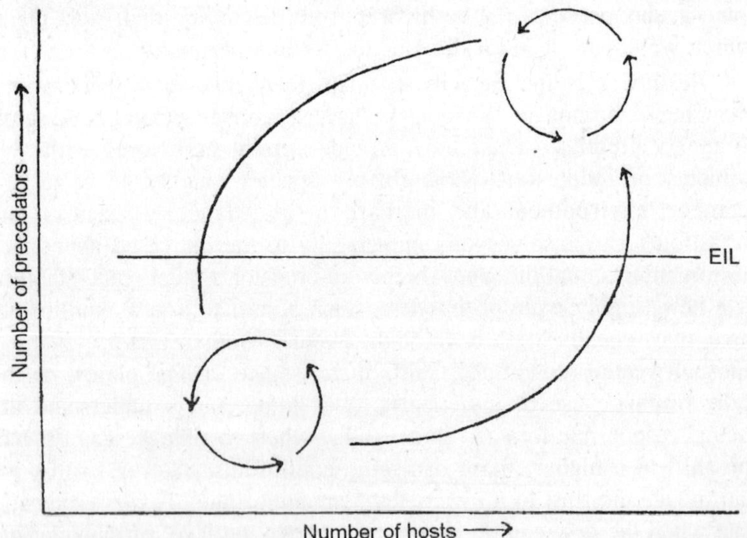

Fig. 11.7. Theoretical predator and host system with multiple equilibrium positions. EIL—economic injury level.

Examples of r-strategists include aphids, house flies, and some locusts. On the other hand, K-strategists rarely become so abundant as to destroy their food supply. Populations of K-strategists do not undergo violent fluctuations and usually are regulated by density-dependent mortality factors.

Table 11.2. Some characteristics of r-selected and K-selected species

	r-selected	*K-selected*
Type of habitat	Often unstable, impermanent	Usually more stable
Reproduction	Rapid under favourable conditions	Generally slower
Development	Many eggs laid	Fewer offspring produced
	Relatively rapid	Often slower
	Often multivoltine	Often univoltine, or extending over more than 1 year
Mortality	Often catastrophic, density independent	More constant, density dependent
Population size	Very variable in time	Fairly constant in time
Capacity to disperse	Very high	Often lower
Brood care	Absent	Sometimes present
Body size	Often very small	Often larger
Inter- and intra-specific competition	Variable, often reduced	Usually keen
Ultimate result	High productivity	Efficient use of resources

In short, they tend to be stable species occurring in stable environments. Examples include the tsetse fly and the codling moth, both of which are considered to be serious pests not because they threaten to destroy their hosts, but because human values are such that we do not wish to tolerate sleeping sickness or blemished apples. Many insects that are K-strategists are never numerous enough to become pests. Now, it is very clear that most insects are neither extreme r-strategists or K-strategists. Rather, they may be said to occupy some point on an r-K continuum, although many of them tend toward one or the other extreme. K-strategists can often be managed through modification of their environment or disruption of reproduction, since they do not adapt quickly to change. In contrast r-strategists are often controlled with insecticides, although the use of resistant hosts is likely to prove more effective in the long run because of the resilience that these pests exhibit. In all instances of pests management, it is important not to disrupt the natural enemy population, as this can lead to biotic release of the pest and attainment of higher population levels.

Even species that are normally quite stable can become rather resilient, and damaging, if stable elements of the insects' habitat are removed. Strategies of population regulation that are inherent within the population are said to be *intrinsic*; they may also be described as "self-regulating" in that they involve mechanisms that alter fecundity or rate of dispersal, depending on population density or food availability. Intrinsic factors are thus always density dependent. In contrast, *extrinsic* factors (arising outside the population) may be either density dependent (such as predators) or density independent (such as weather changes). We shall consider these three categories separately, though in some individual cases all may be operative.

Intrinsic, Density-dependent Factors

Many species have mechanisms that lead to dispersal or to reduced population growth well before their food supply has become completely exhausted. Studies of the bean aphid by M.J. Way, of Imperial College, London, showed that wingless parthenogenetic females multiply faster in initial populations of 8 than in populations of 2, 4, 16, or 32. However, the multiplication rate decreases as populations increase. He concluded that the optimal reproductive rate is realized only when the number of insects per plant is relatively low. Under crowded conditions, progeny tend to be smaller than average, to have reduced fecundity, and to include an increased number of winged individuals capable of moving to other plants or other fields. Similar results have been found in several other aphid species. Mechanisms for such "self-imposed" regulation appear to reside in the genes and to be triggered by changes in the quality and flow of nutrients in the plants.

Bark beetles of the genus Dendroctonus are major pests of conifers, especially in the southern and western United States. Colonization of a tree involves the production of attractant pheromones and the inoculation of the tree with fungi, resulting in a mass attack on a susceptible tree. Having reached a suitable host tree, females make galleries beneath the bark in which to lay their eggs; the larvae hatching from these eggs tunnel beneath the bark, often eventually causing the death of the tree. In some species of Dendroctonus, at least, females

Table 11.3. Multiplication rates of bean Aphid populations developing from different numbers of initial wingless, parthenogenetic females in field cages.

Initial no. of	*Multiplication rate*		
Adult females	between *days 9-17*	between *days 17-23*	between *days 23-44*
2	x 29	x 20	x 17
4	x 41	x 22	x 6
8	x 46	x 15	x 3
16	x 36	x 11	x 2
16	x 36	x 11	x 2
32	x 27	x 7	x 2

produce "territorial chirps" by means of stridulatory ridges on the posterior ends of their bodies. These signals are evidently perceived by other females, causing them either to move to another part of the tree or to dig shorter galleries in which fewer eggs are laid. Experiments by J. A. Rudinsky and R.R. Michael, or Oregon State University, showed that 81% of female western pine beetles (Dendroctonus brevicomis) did not approach confined, chirping females closer than 5 cm. The galleries of this species are usually spaced about 9 cm apart, suggesting that chirping plays a role in maintaining such spacing. Females also chirp more rapidly in the close presence of other females. A female along chirped 38 times in 5 minutes, while one surrounded by other females 1.3 cm away chirped 285 times in 5 minutes (these are averages based on several replications). It has been shown that at high population densities *Dendroctonus* females also attack tree both higher and lower in the trunks than they normally do.

In certain other genera of bark beetles no territorial mechanisms occur, and the large number of resulting crowded larvae scramble for the available space and food, and only some survive to maturity (scramble competition discussed further below). The increased intensity of *intraspecific competition* results in a decrease in oviposition rate, a slowing of rate of development, or an increased tendency to emigrate. In the absence of genetic mechanisms, crowding and shortage of food may result in cannibalism or other forms of interactions that result in extensive mortality. *Cannibalism* among entomorphagous species is common : larvae of solitary parasitoids, for example, often kill or suppress the development of other individuals occurring in the same

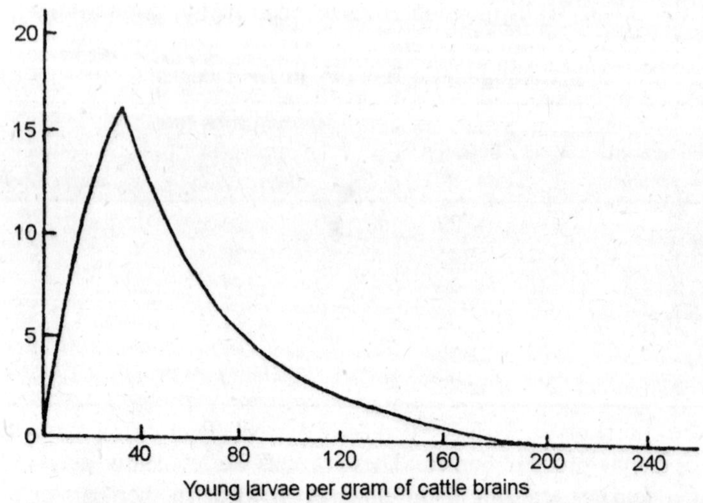

Fig. 11.8. Effect of competition for food among larvae of the sheep blow fly (Lucilia cuprina, Calliphoridae) on the number of adults produced. The food is homogenized cattle brains.

host. Cannibalism has also been reported among phytophagous insects under crowded conditions—for example, in flour bettles and in codling moth larvae. *Interference competition* occurs when crowd ing results in incomplete or unsuccessful copulations or ovipositions or in reduced access to feed. Or a few larger or more active individuals may unsurp to resources, as occurs in instances of male territoriality with respect to access to females. This is often called *contest competition*. Insects occurring in limited, widely spaced habitats (such as maggots in a carcass) often exhibit *scramble competition*. Of the sheep blow fly are reared on homogenized cattle brains, varying the number of larvae per gram of food. Up to about 30 per gram, most larvae produced adults.

At higher densities there was not enough food for all larvae to complete development, and in the resulting "scramble" only a small number reached adulthood—when over 180 per gram, most or all perishe. Although these studies were conducted in the laboratory, field studies have confirmed many sheep carcasses receive many more blow fly eggs than they can support, resulting in much mortality.

Extrinsic, Density-dependent Factors: Natural Enemies

Evidence that natural enemies play an important role in maintaining population numbers well below their maxima is wide-spread. Virtually all life-history studies of insect species have revealed the presence of one or (much more commonly) several predators, parasitoids, or

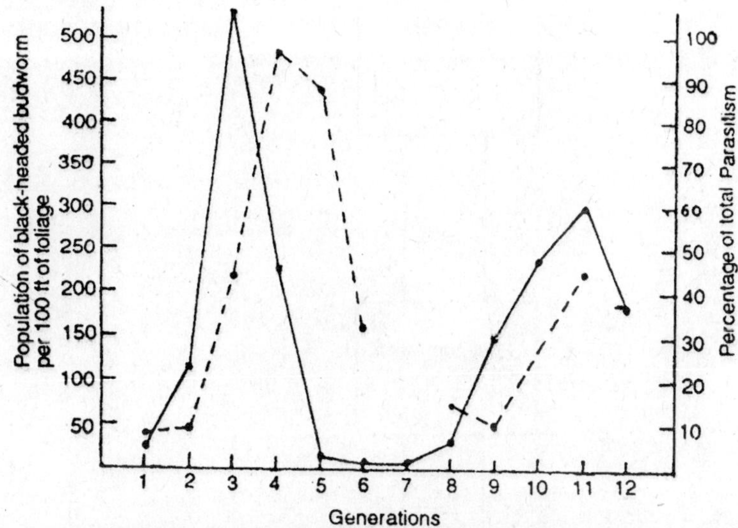

Fig. 11.9. Population size of the black-headed budworm (Acleris variana, Noctuidae) (solid line scale on left) in relation to that of its parasitoids (dashed line, scale on right)

diseases that are consistently present in nature. A small chalcid wasp was found to maintain 70% to 95% parasitization of the eggs of the red-headed pine in Illinois. A complex of ichneumon wasps and tachina flies was found to produce from 7% to 97% parasitism of the black-headed budworm resulting in population osciallations often characteristic of density-dependent factors. The importance of natural enemies in regulating numbers is dramatically demonstrated in instances of *biotic release*, that is, cases in which population is suddenly released from its natural enemies. This may occur when a predator or parasitoid is decimated by insecticides or when a species gains access to a new area where its normal enemies are absent. The Japanese beetle provides a good example of the latter. This insect reached very high populations and was incredibly destructive to lawns and to foliage following its accidental introduction in 1916 into the eastern United States, where its natural enemies do not occur. The U.S.D.A. sent a team of researchers, to Japan, beginning in 1920. Here the beetle is not a major pest, its numbers being keep low by several tachina flies and predatory wasps as well as by a bacterial disease of the grubs.

On tachina fly species alone was found to parasitize from 20% to 90% to the beetles. Import-ation of several of the parasitoids —and particularly the mass production and dissemination of spores of a

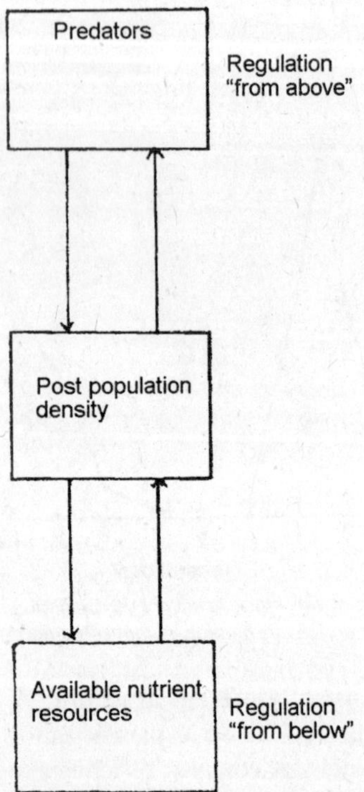

Fig. 11.10. The buildup of important cabbageworm.

bacterium causing "milky disease"—gradually reduced the bettle to the status of a minor pest in most parts of the eastern United States. Wide-spread use of DDT in 1950s and 1960s in some instances resulted in the destruction of major predators and the release of certain plant-feeders from these predators. For example, DDT was found to provide excellent control of imported cabbageworms. But as the plants grow, they send out new leaves on which the butterflies lay their eggs. In the absence of further spraying, the caterpillars consume the new foliage and eat into the center of the plant, while residues in the soil continue to control ground-living predators such as carabid beetles, which frequently kill 50% to 70% of the caterpillars in unsprayed plots. The red-banded leafroller was considered a pest of minor importance in fruit orchards in the eastern and midwestern United States prior to the introduction of DDT, being kept under control by a variety of arthropod enemies. The sudden appearance of this native insect as a major pest in the 1950s is believed to have resulted from destruction of many of its natural enemies by DDT and related insecticides.

During this same period, spider mites became major pests in the orchards in many parts of the world, again apparently the result of inhibition of their natural control agents, such as lady beetles, mirid bugs, the predatory mites. Some evidence was obtained that these insecticides may also increase the nutritive value of foliage and thus increase the fecundity of spider mites. In general, however, it appeared that the influence of insecticides on predator populations was primarily responsible for spider mite outbreaks. It has been demonstrated that one mirid bug eats up to 72 mites a day and can stabilize a population of about 2000 fruit tree red spider mites. But the bugs have only one generation a year, while the mites have several. Thus even a slight suppression of populations of the predator may set the stage for an outbreak of its prey. A species that does not normally attain pest status except when insecticides are employed in sometimes spoken of as a secondary pest.

Population Regulation by Extrinsic, Density-dependent Factors : Relative Shortage of Food

The effect of natural enemies may be thought of as "regulation from above." It has been proposed by white thought of as "regulation from above." It has been proposed by white that populations may alternatively be "limited from below," that is, limited by the amount of food available for normal growth and development. Young insects and other animals require food that is rich in nitrogen, since nitrogen is required for incorporation into body protein. Herbivorous animals may appear to have plenty of food available, yet there may be a relative shortage of food for the young that is rich in available nitrogen. This is reflected in the high mortality among early instars of many insects. White conceives of most environments as being harsh in the sense that food adequate for the development of the young is in short supply. Zoophagous animals utilize food that is rich in available nitrogen, but they are also "limited from below" by the abundance of their hosts. This may result in outbreaks of phytophagous. Since the weather patterns producing water stress are independent of population density, this provides an excellent demonstration of the interplay of density-independent and density-dependent factors in nature.

Population Changes Caused by Extrinsic, Density-independent Factors

Physical factors in the environment may have diverse effects on populations irrespective of their density. At extremes of temperature, moisture, or other factors, death occurs. Sudden onset of cold may be lethal, when gradual cooling to the same temperature may be much

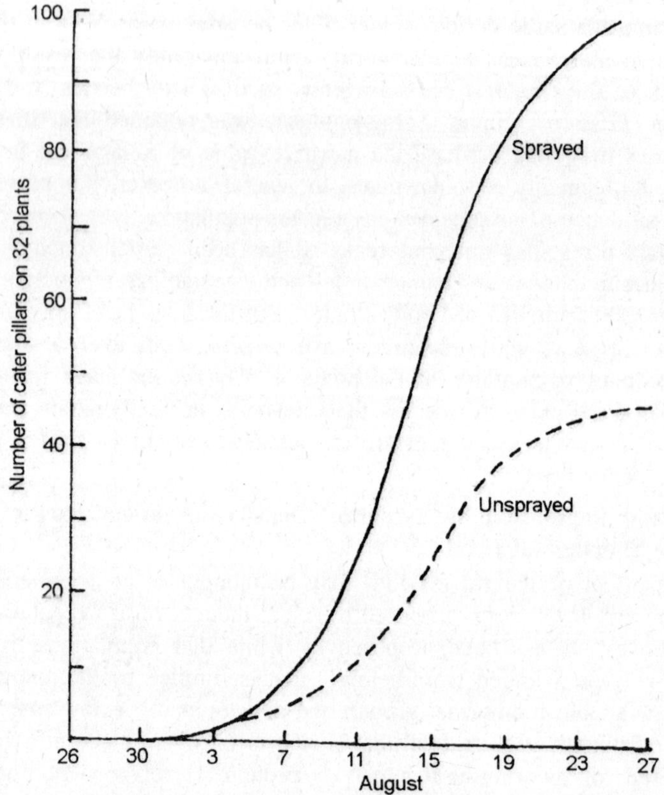

Fig. 11.11. The concept of population regulation "from above" versus that "from below".

less so; any unusual weather extreme at a nondiapausing stage may cause widespread death. Changes in soil characteristics (such as increased salinity) may influence insects directly or via their plants hosts. Similarly, reduced oxygen or increased acidity in a stream may have profound effects on the fauna. Populations suffer most when subjected to a true catastrophe, such as forest fire, flood, unseasonable frost, or sudden change in chemistry of the environment.

In general, density-independent factors operate in one of four ways:

1. By inducing plant stress, resulting in a change in composition of nutrients or defensive chemicals that in turn results in increased or decreased availability of food for herbivoures and ultimately for their predators and parasitoids.
2. By direct destruction of individuals as a result of temperatures, moisture, or chemical concentrations they cannot tolerate.

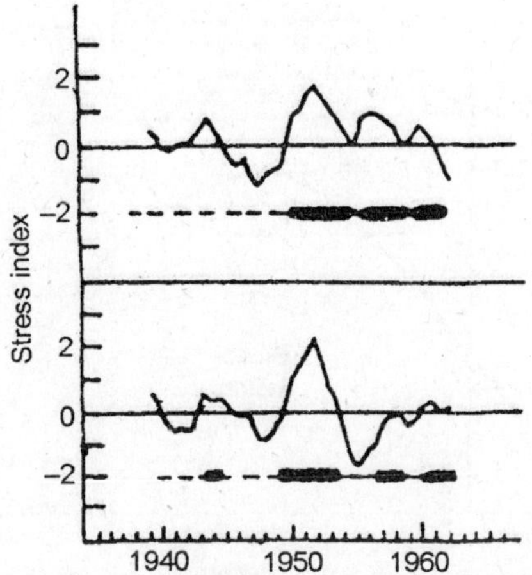

Fig. 11.12. Index of water stress, calculated as varying from +2 (most stressful) to -2 (least stressful) over 25 year period at two localities.

3. By shortening the time of adults for mating and oviposition and thus reducing the number of eggs laid.
4. By slowing of developmental rates such that a diapausing stage is not reached before the onset of a seasonal change.

In many cases population reduction will be most noticeable in subequent generations. Thus a series of unseasonable winter or unusually dry summers may cause a severe depression of numbers. Conversely, a series of favourable years or entry into a new, highly favourable area may permit a buildup in numbers; such a population may be said to have undergone *climatic release* comparable to biotic release, discussed above. It should be remembered also that the effect of climate may be twice or three times revmoved from the population under study. That is, to take a hypothetical example, a predator may become rare because of scarcity of its prey, and the latter may be sparse because the effect of drought has reduced the number of available host plants.

Natural situations are often far more complex than this. Some of the best examples of population regulation by climatic factors have been from fruit fly that formerly bred in small fruits in rain forests. It is now a serious pest of peaches, pears, and other fruits but the severity of its attacks has varied greatly. M.A. Batcman, of the University of Sydney, studied 12 environmental parameters in experimental orchards. Of these, a single factor-summer rainfall, acting mainly by increasing survival of pupae and adults—proved of overriding

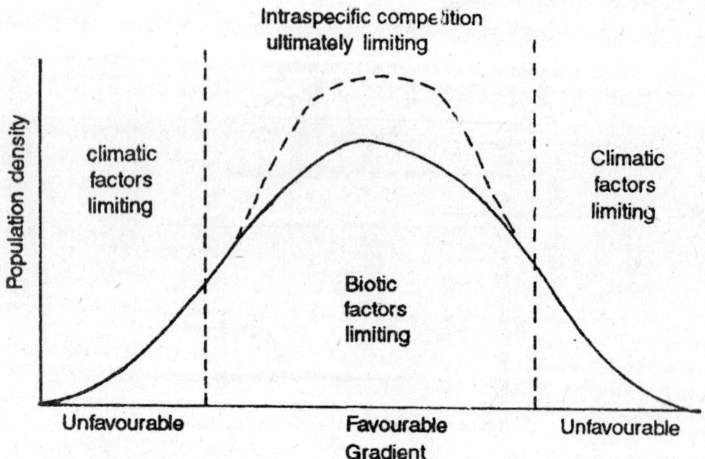

Fig. 11.13. Generalized relationship between the major regulating factors on a species throughout its range.

influence. In favourable years larvae were produced in such numbers that intra-specific competition became severe; but in very dry summers populations approached extinction.

The apple blossom thrips reproduce rapidly in spring and early summer and reach a population peak each year at the time of apple and rose blossoming. Their abundance varies greatly from year to year; in some years over 1000 could be found in a single blossom; in other year, a maximum of only about 200. Andrewartha and his colleagues found that several weather factors working together accounted for most of the variation in population size; winter temperatures affecting time and length of flowering of hosts; spring temperatures influencing rate of development of the thrips; and rainfall in early spring promoting growth of the host plants and pupation and emergence of thrips in the soil. In no case did the thrips populations come close to exhausting their food supply, and influence of natural enemies appeared minimal.

Knowledge of the factors controlling population size obviously requires studies of many factors over a considerable period of time, preferably both in the field and under controlled laboratory conditions. Since each species in unique, we have had only limited success in predicting outbreaks and in preparing to meet them in advance. Each case may require a team of highly qualified persons with long-term financial support for research unlikely to produce immediate and dramatic results. Modern society does not often see fit to direct its affluence toward such goals.

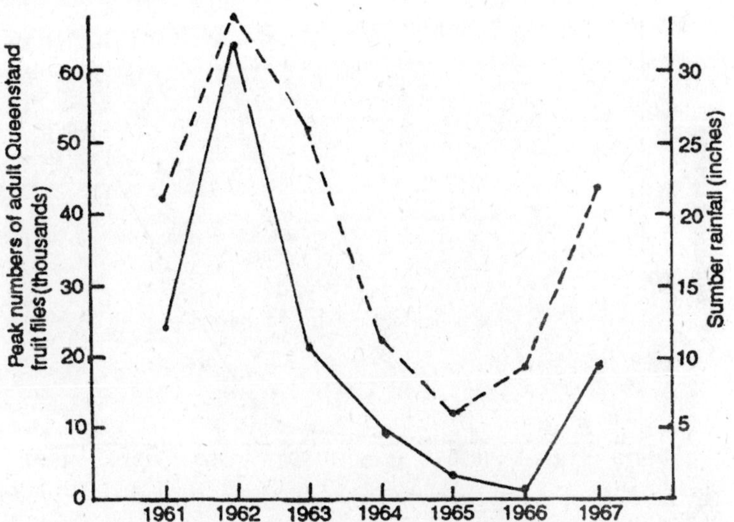

Fig. 11.14. Population of adult Queensland fruit flies (Dacus tryoni, Tephritidae) over seven years (solid line) in relation to summer rainfall (dash line).

Insect Bioeconomics

Prior to the development of modern synthetic insecticides in the mid-1900s, it was generally considered satisfactory to *suppress* insects populations sufficiently to obtain crop yields. With the advent of modern chemical insecticides, agriculturalists found themselves with powerful new weapons with which to reduce the abundance of pest species. The notion of *eradication* became popular; species could be completely eliminated. Why was there such a change in attitude? The new insecticides, such as DDT, were so effective that it was only natural to believe that eradication was possible. However, it was not long before it became apparent that some species would not be easily eradicated. Populations of insects such as the house fly became tolerant or *resistant* to insecticides in as short a time as two years.

The quantity of insecticides applied, and the frequency of application, was often increased, but the insects became more difficult to kill. Modern society's wonderful new weapons, synthetic insecticides, were quickly neutralized by natural selection for insects that could detoxify these potent poisons. Once agriculturalists were exposed to pest-free and damage-free crops, it was only natural to expect such levels of control. The legacy of eradication persists, in part because many species have yet to exhibit significant levels of resistance. Thus, we continue to witness the desire for cosmetically perfect crops,

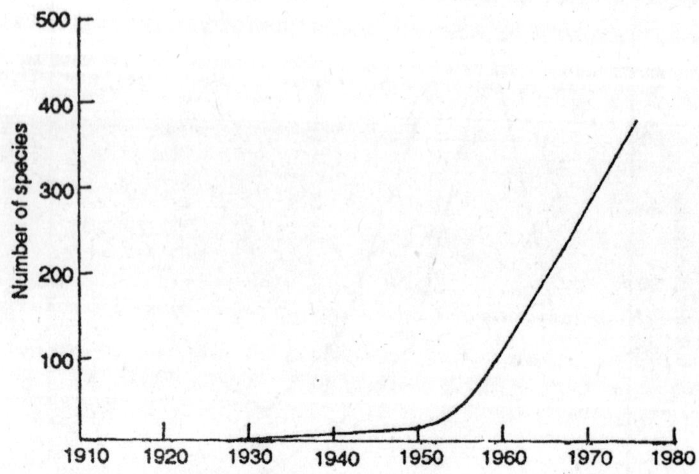

Fig. 11.15. Increase in the number of insect pest species resistant to insecticides.

irrespective to whether or not a few "pests" or a little "injury" really exert an economic effect. It has been observed that, as the number of pests increases, there usually is a linear reduction in yield. Yield stabilizes at a very low level, and additional pests cause little additive reduction in yield. Some studies, however, suggest that plants may be stimulated by insect feeding and that crop yield actually increases when exposed to low levels of damage. No single graphic model adequately describes all yield/loss relationships for all crops and insect pests.

The relationship is characteristic of *indirect pests*. Indirect pets feed on foliage, stems, and plant roots, but not the portion of the crop that is marketed. When, for example, apple foliage is attacked by European red mites, or twigs are attacked by green apple aphids, or roots are attacked by woolly apple aphids, there is no immediate decrease in apple yield associated with a small amount of feeding. Some insects are called *direct pests*, because they attack the marketed produce. Apple maggots, tarnished plant bugs, and plum curculios are examples of direct pests of apple because they attack the apple fruit directly. Damage to even a single apple could be considered a loss because the apple farmer might not be able to market it.

A useful technique for evaluating the relative importance of pests is the *crop life table*. The use of a life was demonstrated various factors were shown to account for mortality of alfalfa weevils. In a crop life table, factors responsible for decreases in crop production are noted similarly. Note that in this study cutworms were responsible for a significant level of cabbage destruction while the plants were seedlings, but that other caterpillar species were more destructive later in the season. Also, the relative importance of disease, hail, or other natural forms of destruction can be documented, and a monetary cost attached to each pest. Thus, the farmer can judge the importance of preventing damage by each type of pest.

Plant Compensation

The amount of damage that occurs is usually directly related to the numerical abundance of pests. How can there sometimes be no loss of yield, or even a gain, although damage occurs? Damaged plants attempt to repair the damage caused by insect and to grow normally, a process known as *compensation*. Plant compensation is due to several factors, including the following:

Removal of apical dominance

The lateral growth of plants is inhibited by plant hormone. Thus plants tend to grow upright. When clipped, the hormonal balance is disrupted, resulting in increased lateral growth and tillering. The net result may be more foliage and increased, growth. Crop yield may by higher under these circumstances.

Removal of less-productive tissue

The photosynthetic ability of plant foliage is related to age. Intermediate-aged foliage usually is more productive than either young or old foliage. When insect herbivores selectively remove the less-productive tissue, the efficiency of the remaining tissue may increase.

Increased penetration by light

The lower leaves on a plant may be shaded by the upper leaves. Shaded leaves are less efficient photosynthetically. Partial defoliation of young, upper foliage may allow penetration of light to lower, shaded foliage and thus increase the rate of photosynthesis.

Reduction in carbohydrate-induced inhibition of photosynthesis

The rate of photosynthesis of a plant is generally less than maximum because carbohydrate accumulation produces an inhibitory feedback. When plants produce new tissue to replace that which was lost by defoliation or because apical dominance has been disrupted, carbohydrates are transolocated to the new tissues. This reduces the carbohydrate-induced inhibition, and photosynthesis is stimulated.

Compensation within a crop can occur even when some plants are killed. The loss of some plants from a field is known as *reduction in stand*. Compensation can occur because plants surviving insect attack experience less competition for light, water, and nutrients; therefore, they are able to grow larger. The yield of surviving plants located near plants that have been killed may be superior to the yield of an "average" plant. If the plants killed by insect herbivores such as cutworms are spaced evenly throughout a field, a significant reduction in stand may be accompanied by no reduction in yield. However, if the mortality is aggregated, with many adjacent plants killed by insects, compensation may not be sufficient, and significant reduction in yield is more likely to occur. Unfortunately, insect distribution is more often aggregated than uniform. Grasshoppers, for example, characteristically attack the margins of fields and are infrequently found evenly distributed through the field. In arid environments reduction in stand may be damaging even where plant compensation is complete, because reduction in plant cover makes fields more susceptible to wing erosion.

Economic Factors

It is not necessarily true that a pest-free crop will be more profitable to farmer. For indirect pests, profits do not increase initially because moderate numbers of indirect pests are usually tolerated by crops, and control of the "pests" may not significantly improve yield. The situation is quite different with respect to direct pests, and control of direct pests often results in a rapid increase in profits, even where moderately expensive control procedures or materials are used. Profits level off as control of both indirect and direct pests increases because it becomes more and more expensive to kill the few ramaining pests. The appropriate level of pest control is determined by economic conditions.

The point at which suppression becomes economically feasible is called the *economic injury level*. The economic injury level (EIL) can be defined as a level of damage, or abundance of insects capable to causing that damage, equal in value to the cost of suppression measures. The position of the EIL is determined principally by the damage potential of the insect and the value of the corp. As suggested earlier, potential insect pests never, or rarely, reach pest status in some crops. The average density of insects, or equilibrium position (EP), is well below the economic injury level. Even when insects cycle to their highest levels, they do not become damaging. Examples include alfalfa webworm in alfafla, flea beetles in potatoes, and rose chafers on apples. Note that the *economic threshold* (ET) is below EIL but above EP.

The economic threshold, or action threshold, is a level of damage or pest abundance that serves to warn the agriculturalist of impending problems and allows the initiation of suppressive measures before the

EIL is surpassed. The pest may regularly exceed the ET and require suppressive action; examples include Colorado potato beetles in potato, corn earworms in corn, and boll weevils in cotton. In the extreme case the EP is above the EIL, and the pest population must be suppressed and maintained at a new, lower EP. Examples of this latter relationship include codling moth in apple, green peach aphid in seed potato, and whiteflies on flori-cultural crops. For many homeowners and gardeners, the value of ornamental and vegetable crops cannot be expressed by economics. Thus, we can say that insects or insect damage sometimes exceed an *emotional threshold* and suppressive action is warranted, even though it may be less expensive to purchase the desired horticultural products rather than protecting them from insects.

Insect Sampling

To estimate the level of insect populations or damage, the agriculturalist must *sample*. Insect sampling is quite sophisticated. Methods of sampling can conveniently be divided into two types : absolute methods and relative methods. Absolute methods are used to estimate the density of insects per unit of area. Thus, we might use absolute methods to determine the number of Colorado potato beetles per acre or Mexican bean beetles per plant. Also we might determine the number of corn seedlings killed by cutworms in a field or the number of tarnished plant bug "stings" per apple. The most frequently used type of absolute sampling method is the *unit of habitat* method. The unit of habitat to be sampled is determined by the biology of the pest insect. Therefore, the abundance of codling moth larvae is determined by sampling fruit, corn earworms by sampling ears of corn, and face flies by sampling the bodies of cattle.

Suction crops, brushing machines, extraction with heat or liquids, vegetation beating, visual searches, and other techniques are used to sample the unit of habitat. Two additional absolute methods sometimes used to estimate insect populations are recapture techniques and removal trapping. *Recapture techniques* involve an initial capture of insects; they are then marked in some manner and released. The area is again sampled, and the proportion of marked individuals in the sample is used to estimate the total population in the area. *Removal trapping* requires repeated collection of individuals from an area. The rate of decline in insect abundance as the population density decreases due to sampling and removal is used to estimate the original population size. Relative methods provide an indication of insect abundance or damage relative to other times or locations.

Visual searches often provide relative estimates because it is difficult to assess insect number accurately. *Traps* are widely employed for relative estimates. Traps are usually baited with sex pheromones or food lures. Light traps disrupt the normal visual orientation of nocturnal species and can be used to capture insects that fly during the evening. Insects that are active during the day can be capture insects that fly during the evening. Insects that are active during the day can be captured by using sticky traps painted with attractive colours. As entomologists learn more about the chemical communication of insects, pheromones become more readily available and pheromone traps will be employed more widely. Pheromone traps are useful because they are effective at detecting low densities of pests, they are quite specific, and they are economical to use.

Plant damage is often used to estimate the relative abundance of insects. The degree of defoliation, number of clipped plants, percentage of bolls infested, and the like are usually hightly correlated with the abundance of insect pests. Plant damage is the most convenient method of population estimation for some insect species because of difficulty or expense associated with sampling the insects directly. This if often the case with subterranean and nocturnal species, those that tunnel or mine foliage of plants, or those that are very numerous.

Absolute sampling methods are desirable because they are accurate and it is easy to convert from density of pests per unit area to damage potential. However, absolute methods are time consuming, they often are difficult to conduct, and they usually are quite expensive compared to relative methods. Relative methods capture an unknown, but consistent, proportion of insects present in an area. Although difficult, it is possible to convert relative estimates to absolute estimates. Relative methods are more economical in terms of time, labor, and equipment. However, to utilize relative estimates effectively, we must know the level of damage associated with a certain estimate. This requires information on yield reduction associated with relative abundance of pests, which must be collected over a period of time or from a number of locations. Various sources of error must be borne in mind when sampling insect populations. What is actually being sampled is the portion of those individuals whose behaviour is such that they are readily captured under the prevailing conditions. It has been observed that codling moths taken in flight traps were largely prereproductive, dispersing moths, while those taken in bait traps were largely mature or postreproductive females.

Wing speed may greatly influence the number of individuals flying or resting high in vegetation, and light intensity may influence the response to light traps (which are much less effective when the moon in full). Why is insect sampling so important for the management of insects pets? The routine use of control procedures (usually insecticides) without regard for pest density and damage potential is economically wasteful and may result in needles destruction of beneficial insect species, contamination of the environment with toxic pesticide residues, and selection for inseticide-resistant pest species. The foundation of pest management rests on the belief that no control measure should be initiated unless a pest is present—and present in damaging, or potentially damaging, numbers. Certain exceptions to this principle exists. For example, the use of pest-resistant varieties and certain cultural practices prevent the development of damaging pest populations. Inecticide use in agriculture could be reduced significantly if agriculturalists adhered to the a fore mentioned principle.

Strategy of Pest Management

The basic strategy behind Insect Pest Management (IPM) is to prevent insect populations from attaining their Economic Injury Level (EIL) while avoiding unfavourable ecological, economic, and sociological consequences. Not all pest populations approach the EIL at the same time. Also, some locations may experience pest outbreaks while others do not. When the Economic Threshold (ET) is reached, however, we must resort to various *tactics*, or methods of pest suppression, to keep the pest population from reaching the EIL. Sometimes, tactics are utilized in advance, in anticipation of pest problems, so that the ET is never reached. Adherents of IPM principles seek to avoid preventive measures unless they are not costly or damaging to the environment; often they are necessary where damaging pest populations occur regularly or where the EIL is very low. The strategy of pest management has several components, including the following:

Identification of the Problem

Plants and animals respond similarly to a variety of problems. For example, plant foliage will become chlorotic in response to attack by piercing-sucking insects, to infection by several plant diseases, to nutrient deficiencies, and to herbicide injury. Diseases are sometimes transmitted by insects, and nutrient-deficient plants are sometimes especially attractive to insects, so it may be difficult to ascribe the primary cause of the problem to the correct causative agent.

Assessment of Damage

As indicated earlier, plants have a remarkable ability to recover from, or compensate for, insect attack. We should not be misled into initiating costly but unnecessary actions. Also, it is quite difficult to estimate accurately the level of damage. For instance, 5% or 10% foliage removal appears much more damaging than it actually is. On the other hand, mites and small insects may escape notice, and it may require thorough examination to locate nocturnal and subterranean insects.

Cost-benefit Analysis

It has been observed that the actual benefits derived from a particular pest suppression activity usually are not calculated. The value associated with the increased crop yield should be equal to, or exceed, the cost of the suppressive action. We often do not know the value of increased yield associated with a management action because EILs have not been calculated. This makes cost-benefit analysis difficult. Another variable that should be considered is the long-term effect of the suppressive action on the pest population. Often we can achieve season-long control by suppressing the first generation of the pest, while if we wait until later in the season that pests may be more numerous and difficult to control. Sometimes a suppressive action reduces the abundance of a pest for more than one season; thus, the cost of control can be amortized over several crop harvest. On the negative side, suppressive actions may have deleterious effects on beneficial insects, which can lead to more frequent pest outbreaks, increased need for suppressive action, and increased cost.

Selection of Management Tactic

The tactics available vary with crops, pest, time of year, and geographic locality. Possibly the most common tactics employed are application of insecticide and planting of pest-resistant crop varieties. These tactics are commonly used because they are effective, available and economical and generally do not require that the user possess a great deal of entomological knowledge. Tactics such as crop rotation, modification of planting time, and release of beneficial organisms may be equally effective, but these latter tactics require more knowledge of pest life history.

Implementation of Management Tactic

A major factor influencing selection of management tactics is the ability to actually implement the chosen tactic. All too often we find a novice who is devoted to biological suppression but is unable to implement effective biological control. We witness dependence on chemical suppression tactics because these materials are readily availability of alternative suppression methods. For example, release of parasites of dung-breeding flies into cattle feedlots is becoming more common because insectaries are making these beneficial parasites more common because insectaries are making these beneficial parasites more available. Similarly, use of the bacterium *Bacillus thuringiensis* for suppression of caterpillars has become widespread because it can be purchased from most pesticide retailers. For many suppressive tactics to be successful, we must plan ahead.

Many cultural controls must be implemented before or during crop planting. For example, once seeds have been planted, it is usually impossible to apply insecticides to protect them. The decision to plant insect-resistant crop varieties obviously must be made well in advance of planting. We should not always plant for the worst possible consequences and resort to preventive measures. Many insect populations can be monitored and damage predicted well in advance. When sufficient pest life history and sampling information is available to predict population trends and resultant damage, we should monitor the crop environment carefully and initiate suppressive actions only when needed.

Efficacy Assessment

The effectiveness of the management tactic selected can be judged only by careful monitoring of insect populations and crop yield. All too often we assume that pest suppression has been achieved because a control tactic has been initiated. We always should check to ascertain that the desired level of suppression has been attained. Again, sampling is required. If, as part of efficacy assessment, yields from pest-infested fields are determined, valuable information on the economic justification for pest suppression can be calculated.

Follow-up Periodic Assessment

Management tractics may result in less than complete suppression of pest population. Also, immigration of pests from unmanaged fields may occur. Crops should be monitored regularly and thoroughly to prevent unexplained losses and unpredicted pest population outbreaks.

Conclusion

The size of population is controlled by the of the interaction of fecundity and mortality. With respect to mortality, ecologists distinguish between factors that are density dependent and those that are density independent. Stability is the ability of a system to absorb disturbance an dreturn to an equilibrium state; resilience is the capacity to adapt to change in the environment. Species of insects likely to become agricultural pests are those that are small, mobile, and able to reproduce rapidly. These are termed r-strategists, in contrast to K-strategists, which tend to have lower reproductive rates and to be less dispersive.

Certain factors intrinsic in populations often prevent them from coming close to exhausting their food supplies. Such selfregulating factors may be genetically controlled and triggered by change in food quality or quantity. In certain bark beetles, behavioural mechanisms controlling density and distribution have been described. Intraspecific competition may also result in a decrease in oviposition rate, a slowing of the rate of development, or an increased tendency to migrate. In controlling population size is the importance of extrinsic density-dependent factors well-demonstrated by cases of biotic release, that is, cases in which a population is suddenly released from its natural enemies and increases greatly in size. The effect of extrinsic, density-independent factors in populations is to produce fluctuations of an irregular nature. Long-term studies of the effect of climate on populations may, however, often permit predictions concerning the occurrence of population outbreaks. Prior to the development of modern synthetic insecticides, it was considered satisfactory to suppress populations of pest species, but more recently the concept of eradication has become popular. However, this has often proved impracticable because of the development of resistance of many of these newer insecticides.

The contemporary approach is in terms of pest management. This involves an assessment of loss of revenue resulting from specific agents, which may well be expressed in terms of a crop life table. It is useful to distinguish between indirect pests, which feed on foliage, stems, or roots that are not marketed, and direct pests, which attack the fruit or whatever part of the plant is marketed. The plants tend to compensate the damage caused by the pests in various ways, so that in fact yield may not decrease and may sometimes increase. Thus, the amount of damage is usually directly related to the numerical abundance of pests abundance of pests. In the case of direct pests, moderate levels of pests abundance cannot usually be tolerated, and even the use of relatively expensive controls may be justified. The appropriate level of control is determined by economic conditions. The point at which pest suppression becomes economically feasible is called the Economic Injury Level (EIL). This differs from and is higher than the Economic Threshold (ET), which is the level of damage or pest abundance that serves to warn the agriculturalist of impending problems.

In order to determine whether insect populations have reached the ET, careful sampling is required. Absolute methods of sampling may involve counting the actual number of individuals per unit area or may involve mark and recapture techniques or removal trapping. Relative methods may involve visual estimates, trapping, or assessments of plant damage. The routine use of control procedures (usually insecticides) without regard to pest density is economically wasteful and may result in needless destruction of beneficial species, contamination of the environment with toxic materials, and selection of insecticide-resistant pest species. The basic strategy behind insect pest management is to prevent insect populations from attaining their EIL. When the ET is reached, we must resort to various methods of suppression to keep the pest populations from reaching the EIL. The strategy involves several components : identifying the problem; assessment of the damage; cost-benefit analysis; selection of management tactic; implementation of this tactic; and finally an assessment of efficacy as well as periodic follow-up assessment.

12

Wood Decay

Biological control may generally be described as the introduced use of organisms (macro or micro) or their products to keep in check the numbers or activities of particular pest species. While this definition is probably the most commonly accepted one, it is nevertheless rather limited and does not include control strategies which involve manipulation of the substrate, environment, or inherent factors in the pest, all of which are considered as biological control methods by many researchers. Common to all definitions however is that biological control is the manipulation by mankind of factors which are fundamental to natural control within ecosystems. As such therefore, biological control has been portrayed as a much more environmentally acceptable approach when compared with control strategies involving chemicals which by definition involve the artificial introduction of toxic chemicals not naturally found in the particular ecosystem. Biological control in agricultural systems is now a well established and accepted technology for the control of a wide range of pests including nematodes, weeds, insects, as well as microbial plant pathogens. The technology is not as advanced, however, for the biological protection of processed wooden products even though successful systems have been studied or commercially used for the protection of growing trees and stumps against basidiomycete fungi including *Heterobasidium annosum*, *Chondostereum purpureum*, *Phellinus weirii*, *Ophiostoma ulmi*, *Phellinus tremulae* and *Armillaria luteobubalina*.

Particular Requirements for Biological Control of Wood Deterioration

The principle reasons for the development of biological control research in the wood preservation field are the same as those which have driven similar developments in agriculture, i.e., the need to develop more environmentally acceptable treatments at a time when the legislation governing the use of toxic chemicals has become increasingly restrictive. The change in focus towards more environmentally safe preservatives in the UK is nicely illustrated in a recent government report on the use of timber in construction which highlights the need to 'develop improved, environmentally benign, protection strategies to enhance the durability of wood components'. The strategies developed and experiences gained from biological control systems in agriculture have undoubtedly provided an excellent database for researchers in the wood preservation field.

In both situations the objective has been to develop efficient, non-toxic control systems which are cost-effective when compared with the currently used preservatives, and have minimal environmental impact. Prevention of wood deterioration however provides a number of particular challenges for the biological control researcher, which are not encountered in the agricultural situation.

Diversity of Target

Wood can be attacked by a range of microbial as well as insect and invertebrate deteriogens and the particular organism responsible for the decay will be dependent on either the wood type or the environmental conditions in which the wood is used. One of the attractive features of biological control agents in agricultural systems is their target specificity which decreases the likelihood of adverse reactions against other members of the ecosystem.

Since most crop species, due to their constitutive and inducible defences, are attacked by a relatively narrow range of pathogens, development of a target specific control system is feasible. Although some wood types contain chemical extractives which will confer resistance against wood decay fungi, most are non-durable and subject to attack by a wide range of fungi, thereby necessitating a broader spectrum biological control agent. In addition, changing environmental conditions will also influence the range of deteriogens which must be controlled, unlike the situation in agriculture where the host plant is the major determinant of pest type.

Length of Protection

Most agricultural crops only need to be protected from disease during their growing season which in many cases will be less than a year. This means that any control agent need only be effective during this time; reapplication on a regular basis is good business for manufacturers as it results in annual sales of the biological control product. Wood, depending on its intended use, may require to be protected for varying lengths of time ranging from a few months to 40 years field exposure.

This has major implications for any biological control system including: formulation considerations, for example whether continued viability of the organisms must be maintained; whether any active metabolites are stable and will be permanently retained in the wood; suitability of delivery systems and/or need for reapplication and continued tolerance by the control agent of fluctuating biotic and abiotic conditions.

Efficacy of the System

Wood is often used as a structural material and therefore an essential prerequisite of any treatment system is that it does not compromise the strength of the timber. This limits the range of potential control agents to those organisms which will only use the non-structural materials, i.e., starches and sugars is the ray parenchyma and other storage tissues of the timber, and not themselves attack any of the structural polymers of the timber.

Additionally the protection they provide must be 100 per cent effective even in the early stages of colonization (for example by brown-rot fungi) significant strength losses can occur due to depolymerization of the cellulose before any substantial weight losses are generated. This is different from agricultural systems where the success of the control agent is measured against the increase or decrease in crop field compared with the use of chemical biocides. It may be justified to use a biological control agent which is marginally less efficient than its chemical counterpart if its use is associated with cost savings or is environmentally more acceptable than the chemical which it replaces.

Formulation and Delivery System Technology

As highlighted above, biological control agents for timber applications may need to be effective over long time periods without damaging the structure of the wood. This may necessitate the development of formulations with sufficient extraneous nutrients to allow survival and growth in a wooden substrate which itself is devoid of nutrients, particularly nitrogen. Similarly isolates must be tolerant of the chemical extractives present in wood. Method and timing of application is generally a critical determinant of the success of any biological control system and in agricultural systems most control agents are delivered as seed dressings, spray inoculation or by drenching, i.e. in a similar manner to traditional chemical biocides. Wood preservatives however are often applied by pressure processes under high temperature conditions.

Treatment technology and development of suitable delivery systems therefore provide an additional challenge to biological control researchers. Biological agents do however, unlike chemicals, have the ability to colonize a substrate by their growth and this may, in suitable systems, be used to advantage. While ingenious surface application systems have been efficient in allowing control agents to colonize freshly felled timber it may be necessary to inoculate finished wooden structures by alternative methods.

Bruce and King (1986a) applied a commercial pelleted product into boreholes to colonize the groundline region of creosoted distribution poles and recent unpublished work undertaken at the Scottish Institute for Wood Technology has shown that *Trichoderma* conidiospores can be successfully applied to wooden stakes in a pressure treatment cylinder. Pressure operating conditions were those which would normally be used for the chemical treatment of spruce and pine lumber.

Target Areas for Biological Control in Wood

Wood is a variable substrate which is used for a variety of purposes such as building construction composites manufacture and pulp and paper products, and a variety of finished materials including furniture, posts, pilings and distribution poles. As such it is often attacked by a wide range of deteriogens at any one time and therefore it is unlikely that a single biological control system will be suitable for all situations just as no one chemical preservative is useful for all applications.

As in agriculture, most biological control treatments are likely to be applied as prophylactic treatments to prevent colonization and subsequent decay by the deteriogens. In some situations however, for example decay in buildings, it may be essential to apply a remedial treatment against established decay. With this in mind Freitag et al. (1991) suggested the terms 'bioprotection' and 'biocontrol' to differentiate between prophylactic and remedial wood treatment systems, respectively. Freitag et al (1991) and Bruce (1992) have reviewed the use of biological control for wood protection against microorganisms and particularly fungi, but as far as the author is aware, no biological control systems have yet been reported for the control of wood deterioration by insects or marine borers. Bacteria, though major contributors to decay of waterlogged wood, are much less important than fungi as agents of wood degradation and as such do not represent a significant target for biological control systems. Most research to date has therefore been targeted against either sapstain/bluestain or decay fungi.

Sapstain Biocontrol

Moulds and staining fungi (including bluestain) cause surface growth and deep sapwood discoloration, respectively, and are among the primary colonizers of freshly felled timber prior to drying. While neither category causes any significant structural damage (they use only non-structural materials in the wood) and only minimal strength losses, they are nevertheless significant biodeteriogens; due to their pigmented mycelia, the aesthetic value of the timber is lost and its usefulness for pulp and paper manufacture significantly reduced.

Bluestain fungi can discolour timber shortly after felling or in service; in the UK however this term is more commonly used to describe colonization and growth of these pigmented fungi in finished wooden structures such as windows and doors. As primary colonizers of freshly felled lumber, sapstain fungi are an ideal target for biological control systems. Lack of previous colonizers means that bioprotectant agents can become readily established in the substrate and generally the wood only requires to be protected for a reasonably short time during storage prior to the wood being seasoned.

A major limitation however is that the control agent itself must not add any colouration to the wood. This has led to a number of researchers examining the use of non-pigmented or hyaline strains of selected fungal isolates. Horvath et al (1995) have reported the development of mutant strains of *Trichoderma* with reduced sporulation and production of non-pigmented spores for general biocontrol uses, while Behrendt et al. (1995a,b) and Croan (1996) have examined the use of non-pigmented strains of *Ophiostoma piliferum* for control of staining in chip samples. Some of the earlier studies on sapstain biocontrol examined bacteria and culture filtrate from species including *Bacillus subtilis* and *Pseudomonas cepacia*. Various authors have continued to examine bacteria. Other workers however have concentrated on the use of fungal species as bioprotectants.

As early as 1973, Klingstrom and Johansson reported the activity of various *Scytalidium* spp. against a wood stain fungus, *Leptographium lundbergii*, on agar and in wood, while Stranks (1976) noted that fungal produced antibiotics such as scytalidin, hyalodendrin and cryptosporiopsin were capable of inhibiting blue-strain in pine sapwood. Since these early studies may authors have reported the use of various other fungal antagonists of bluestain including *Trichoderma* spp.; *Ophiostoma piliferum*; *Talaromyces flavus*; *Stachybotrys cylindrospora*; *Lecythophora hoffmannii*; *Sporomiella similis*; basidiomycetes and/or their products ranges of fungi and yeasts. In most of the above cases the intention is to use the biological agent as a prophylactic treatment to prevent stain.

Croan and Highley (1996) however have recently examined the use of fungal metabolites from *Bjerkandera adusta* and *Talaromyces flavus* to de-stain existing sapstained wood (i.e. as a remedial treatment). An alternative strategy to control sapstain development is to target specific key enzymes of sapstain fungi. Breuil et al. (1995) identified and characterized a specific subtilisin-like serine proteinase enzyme produced by the staining fungus *Ophiostoma piceae*. Characterization of the cleavage specificity of this enzyme, and knowledge of the factors likely to affect the autolysis of such enzymes may lead to more specific control systems for sapstain fungi.

Decay Biocontrol

The protection of wood from decay fungi presents a greater challenge to biological control than that of sapstain biocontrol. While prior colonization and removal of available soluble nutrients may help biocontrol agents to prevent sapstain, basidiomycete fungi are also able to utilize the structural elements of the wood and therefore any control agent cannot be expected successfully to exclude decay fungi solely on the basis of competition for nutrients. Many authors have reported the antagonism of various wood decay fungi by biological control agents in cultural studies using either agar or wood block test methods. Despite this wealth of research effort few workers have reported on field performance of biological control agents.

Processed wood is used in many applications and thereby subjected to varying environmental conditions which will determine the range and variety of decay fungi against which the wood must be protected. This represents a challenge for biological control agents which have been tested most often in pure culture systems against single target fungi. It is perhaps not too surprising therefore that where field testing of biological control agents has taken place it has been directed at particular wooden products such as distribution poles or against specific target organisms such as the dry rot fungus *Serpula lacrymans*.

The earliest field tests of biocontrol agents for wood decay were carried out on birch logs, while in the late 1960s and early 1970s internal decay in wooden distribution poles became the focus of attention for biological control systems. Ricard and Bollen (1968) and Ricard et al (1969) examined *Scytalidium* and *Trichoderma* respectively to control decay in Douglas fir poles and subsequent field work has concentrated on these two fungal genera and particularly *Trichoderma* spp. Further field trials of *Trichoderma* in poles continued with variable levels of control reported. Bruce and King (1986b) reported some decrease in the level of decay of poles artificially inoculated with *Lentinus lepideus* when *Trichoderma* spp. were applied either before or after the decay fungus.

The level of control was found to be variable and was adversely affected by the level of resident fungi already present in pole interiors. This failure of the *Trichoderma* spp. to colonize throughout the groundline regions of the poles did not improve even after subsequent exposure periods. Wood removed from *Trichoderma*-colonized regions of poles 7 years after pole inoculation was however resistant to attack by selected basidiomycete fungi when tested using standard soil block test systems. This result is significant since it indicates that provided control agents can properly colonize throughout a wooden structure, they can biologically protect the material even after extended time periods.

Other authors have considered that *Trichoderma* spp. may be better suited to provide short-term pre-seasoning bioprotection of freshly felled logs from decay and successfully applied *Trichoderma* spores to the wood by incorporating them in the chain-saw oil also examined the use of a *Trichoderma viride* isolate in conjunction with aqueous disodium octoborate and reported good control using this integrated control system.

Scytalidium and *Trichoderma* spp. have received the greatest attention as control agents in field trails since *Scytalidium* had previously been shown to produce diffusible antibiotics with antifungal activity whereas *Trichoderma* isolates have long been recognized for their antagonistic traits. *Trichoderma* spp. are also generally tolerant of other wood preservatives which makes them attractive for use in integrated control strategies with chemicals.

Future Considerations

The future development of biological control systems for wood protection or treatment will ultimately depend on how they measure up against traditional chemical preservatives. New biological systems must perform as well as chemical preservatives under field conditions often over extended periods of service of the treated wood product; be competitive in terms of product cost; be easy to apply, store and handle; and satisfy the same level of stringent testing and regulatory control which is required during the development of any new chemical wood preservative. Only when a biocontrol agent has satisfied all the above will the wood preservative industries happily embrace the technology.

Test Methodologies

Many different approaches have been developed to screen potential biocontrol agents. While agar systems have most commonly been used as a primary screening method various authors have adapted their screening systems to be more reflective of wood as a substrate. Freitag and Morrell (1990) developed a wood sandwich method and Schoeman et al (1994c) combined pine discs and agar media to produce a bilayer assay for screening purposes and also introduced a computer assisted system to aid assessment during screening of large number of isolates. Tucker and Bruce (1995) developed an agar medium containing the carbon : nitrogen balance and major amino acids composition present in Scots pine sapwood and found that isolates selected using this medium gave excellent protection from decay when subsequently assessed in wood.

Ultimately however, a control agent must be tested in solid wood. It would seem reasonable to attempt, if appropriate, to use standard test methods which are currently used for this purpose to evaluate chemical preservatives. Tucker et al (1997) showed that standard American and European test methods designed to establish the concentrations of chemicals required to protect wood could also be successfully used, with only slight modification, to evaluate the efficacy of biocontrol agents for wood protection. Another important consideration that has been addressed by some researchers is that of isolate identity and subsequent product quality assurance.

Since the efficiency of most biological control agents is strain dependent it is essential that the end user has surety with the product. Schlick et al (1994a, 1994b) showed that DNA and PCR (polymerase chain reaction) fingerprinting methods could be used to identify individual strains of *Trichoderma* for biocontrol. In addition to improving consumer confidence, development of specific identification processes also allows product protection for the manufacturer through patenting of identifiable isolates. Further work is however required to provide field performance data and to develop suitable delivery systems before control agents can be accepted as viable alternatives to chemical preservatives.

Modes of Action

Further research is also required to establish the specific mechanisms of action of biocontrol agents against wood decay fungi. Many antagonistic mechanisms have been attributed to the control of plant pathogens by *Trichoderma* spp. and these can be categorized as follows: soluble metabolites; inhibitory volatiles; mycoparasitism via lytic enzymes and production of siderophores. In contrast fewer studies have been undertaken into the specific mechanisms of action of these and other fungi against wood biodeteriogens. Srinivasan et al. (1992) and Srinivasan (1993), however, examined a range of antagonistic mechanisms of *Trichoderma* against wood decay fungi and assessed how each was influenced by media type.

Bruce et al (1995) showed that the presence of the cell walls of wood decay fungi stimulated the production of chitinase and laminarinase by *Trichoderma* isolates and indeed found that the concentration of these enzymes produced was dependent on the species of wood decay fungal cell wall used. Other workers have also examined mycoparasitism and lytic enzymes as a mechanism of biocontrol of wood decay fungi. The inhibitory effect of *Trichoderma* volatiles against wood decay fungi was first reported by Bruce et al. (1984) and recent work has identified some of the volatile organic compounds (VOCs) produced by these organisms.

As with most other antagonistic traits the range of VOCs produced is isolate specific and is dependent on the growing conditions. Recent work has, however, attempted to identify those VOCs which may be responsible for the volatile inhibition of the wood decay fungi. Bruce and Highley (1991) showed that the culture filtrate from *Trichoderma* spp. could significantly reduce the growth of a wide range of wood decay fungi and that white-rot fungi were affected to a lesser extent than brown-rot organisms.

Canessa and Morrell (1996) reported that a *T. harzianum* isolate induced increased laccase production in *Trametes versicolor*; this may account for the greater selective action of *Trichoderma* isolates against brown-rots. Other workers have reported the effect of metabolite production by biocontrol agents on various wood decay fungi. Srinivasan et al. (1993) showed that germination of basidiospores could also be inhibited by soluble metabolites from *Trichoderma* spp.

Little work has been undertaken however to identify the metabolites responsible although Horvath et al. (1995) concluded that Trichorzianines, associated with the process of conidiogenesis, were responsible for the inhibition of wood decay fungi by a *T. harzianum* isolate. It is known that iron plays an important role in the biological degradation of wood both as an essential component of the extracellular haem enzymes involved in white-rot decay and possibly in brown-rot organisms during non-enzymic catalysis of cellulose degradation.

Competition for iron between wood decay fungi and biocontrol agents is therefore likely to be a significant mechanism to prevent wood decay. Srinivasan et al. (1995) showed that *Trichoderma* spp. produced both hydroxymate and phenolate siderophores and that these are implicated in the biological control of wood decay fungi in agar test systems. It is clear from the above that, although some interesting and exciting work is currently being undertaken into the factors which determine the outcome of fungal interactions, more work needs to be undertaken in this area if biological control systems are to be compete with chemical preservatives as bioprotectants or biocontrol agents of wood decay.

13

IDENTIFICATION OF TREES

The following tables are keys to the families and genera of conifers and broadleaves covered in this book. For both groups identification of the family is required before moving on to the keys to genera. Most couplets are dichotomous (e.g. 3, 3 or A, AA) but in cases where there are three or more statements to each couplet a vertical arrow is used to indicate that there is an extra statement to consider (e.g. 4, 4↓, 4 or B, BB↓, BBB).

KEY TO CONIFER FAMILIES

1 Female inflorescence a typical cone comprising a few to many ultimately woody cone-scales and maturing numerous seeds. An important exception *Juniperus* (junipers) in which the 3-8 cone-scales unite, become fleshy and form the well-known juniper berry-like fruit with one or more seeds: 2

1 Female inflorescence, or 'cone,' of relatively few scales (about 10 or fewer) which ultimately are fleshy and mature usually 1, sometimes 2 seeds which may be more or less surrounded by whitish or coloured aril or epimatium. Sometimes the seed is borne on a receptacle composed of a number of fused sterile bracts: 4

2 Mostly dioecious species; leaves mostly lanceolate to ovate with many veins but without midrib; pollen sacs often long (to 20 cm), more than 10; pollen wingless; each cone scale a single structure, not comprising a more or less distinct bract- and ovuliferous-scale; only a single ovule per cone-scale; seeds winged or not: *Araucariaceae*

2 Not this combination of characters; pollen sacs fewer than 10 : 3

3 Typically monoecious species; leaves linear, single, in fascicles of 2-5(8) or clusters of more than so, spirally attached as are the

cone-scales; pollen winged; bract-scales and ovuliferous-scales clearly distinct, each of the latter with 2 inverted ovules; seeds usually winged: *Pinaceae*

3↓ Typically monoecious species; leaves linear or awl-shaped, spirally arranged but pairs of connate leaves in whorls of 10-30(40) in *Sciadopitys* and opposite in *Metasequoia*: bract- and cone-scales more or less fused together, spirally arranged, each fused structure with 2-8(9) erect or inverted ovules; pollen wingless: *Taxodiaceae*

3 Monoecious or dioecious species; leaves typically scale-like and adpressed in decussate pairs, rarely in whorls of 3 or in 3 ranks, rarely linear, but not uncommonly linear in juvenile forms; cone-scales uniform without distinction between bract- and ovuliferous-scales: ovules one or more on each scale; pollen wingless: *Cupressaceae*

4 Monoecious or dioecious species; leaves typically spirally arranged, variable: scale-like, linear, more or less lanceolate, oblong, functionally replaced by phylloclades in *Phyllocladus*; 'cones' with 1 or more sterile fleshy bracts, a few upper fertile scales, each with an inverted ovule more or less enclosed by an epimatium (except *Microstrobos*): 'cone' often borne on a much swollen fleshy receptacle (*Podocarpus*, *Acmopyle*): seed often with basal cup-like aril: pollen sacs 2; pollen with 2-4 wings: *Podocarpaceae*

4↓ Dioecious species with opposite or whorled branches; leaves spirally arranged on vertical shoots, 2-ranked on laterals, linear lanceolate, lower surface with numerous stomatic lines grouped into 2 whitish bands on either side of the midrib; 'cone' of a few decussate pairs of scales each scale with 2 ovules; typically each 'cone' matures a single seed rather like a green olive; pollen sacs 3; pollen wingless: *Cephalotaxaceae*

4 Dioecious species; leaves more or less linear, spirally attached (more or less opposite in *Torreya*, *Amentotaxus*), generally appearing 2-ranked in the same plane; 'cone' (very un-cone-like) of several sterile bracts and a single terminal erect ovule; seed partially or almost wholly enclosed by a whitish, orange or scarlet aril; pollen sacs 2-8(9): pollen wingless: *Taxaceae*

Key to Conifer Genera by Families

Pinaceae

1 Leaves needle-like, arranged at least on short shoots, in clusters, but not in whorls: 2

1 Leaves solitary and not in whorls: 5

2 Needles on short shoots in fascicles of 2-5(8) - a single needle occurs in *Pinus monophylla* - and typically more than 2.5 cm long: *Pinus*

2 Needles on short shoots in clusters of 10-30(40): 3

3 Needles dark green and evergreen mostly less than 2.5(3) cm; cones barrel-shaped 5-12 cm long, the scales falling away at maturity (after 2-3 years) : *Cedrus*

3 Needles pale (yellowish) green and deciduous; cones smaller: 4

4 Bud-scales shortly tapering to a point; male cones in clusters, female cones maturing in one year, the scales then falling away: *Pseudolarix*

4 Bud-scales blunt at the apex; male cones solitary; female cones maturing in one year but the scales not then falling away: *Larix*

5 Cone with prominently exserted bract-scale, trifid at apex; crushed foliage with characteristic pineapple or citronella smell (not typically resinous); leaves virtually sessile, the leaf bases not obviously decurrent, the bare shoot more or less smooth; winter buds characteristically pointed rather like beech (*Fagus* spp) buds: *Pseudotsuga*

5 Not this combination of characters; bract-scales neither exserted nor trifid: 6

6 Shoots more or less smooth, the circular leaf-scars not in relief; leaves mostly flat; cones always erect: 7

6 Shoots rough from inclined leaf-scars or from the persistent more or less decurrent and woody leaf bases of fallen needles: cones always pendulous or at least reflexed: 8

7 Needles grooved on upper surface, the lower surface typically with whitish stomatal bands; cone-scales falling away from axis at maturity: *Abies*

7 Needles keeled on upper surface, the lower surface pale (yellowish) green; cone-scales not falling away at maturity: *Keteleeria*

8 Needles flat with one resin canal, their short (1-2 mm) petioles more or less closely adpressed against the shoot and leaving a more or less semicircular scar; main branches more or less alternating: *Tsuga*

8 Needles mostly quadrangular with 2-4 resin canals, sessile on raised decurrent leaf bases and falling, to leave a more or less diamond-shaped scar; main branches commonly in (false) whorls: *Picea*

Taxodiaceae

1 Needles 5-10-15 cm long, fused in pairs back to back for the whole of their length and with a longitudinal furrow, there being 10-30(40) such pairs arranged in whorls on the shoots: *Sciadopitys*

1 Leaves single, not fused in pairs or arranged in whorls: 2

2 Foliage evergreen, bark fibrous spongy, brown to reddishbrown, ultimately shredding, the leaves dark green: 5

2 Foliage deciduous, but semievergreen in *Taxodium mucronatum* which is rare in cultivation; bark different from above, the leaves typically pale (yellowish) green: 3

3 Leaves and branchlets opposite, the leaves linear and branchlets of one kind only: *Metasequoia*

3 Leaves and branchlets not opposite: 4

4 Branchlets of 2 kinds: the upper ones persisting, with axillary buds and more or less radially arranged subulate leaves, the lower branchlets deciduous, lacking axillary buds, the leaves 2-ranked in one plane: cone globose to ovoid, stalk short, about 3 mm long: *Taxodium*

4 Leaves on upper nonfruiting branches 8-13 mm long in 3 ranks: those on lower or fruiting branches scale-like; cone obovate, stalk 10-18 mm long: *Glyptostrobus*

5 Leaves alternate of two kinds: spirally arranged, scale-like, adpressed to slightly spreading, or linear-lanceolate and 2-ranked in one plane, with petiole; cone-scales peltate, nor more than 20: *Sequoia*

5 Leaves uniform of one kind only: 6

6 Leaves scale-like, spirally arranged, adpressed or slightly spreading; cone-scales peltate, more than 25: *Sequoiadendron*

6 Not this combination of characters; cone-scales flattened imbricate, each scale with 2-5 seeds: 7

7 Leaves awl-shaped, curved toward shoot, 1-3 cm long, apex not spiny, spirally arranged in 5 ranks; bark fibrous spongy: cones globose 1.5-2.5 cm across with 20-30 scales, each scale with a recurved mucro and a 3-5-spined crest on upper margin; ovules erect: *Cryptomeria*

7 Not this combination of characters: 8

8 Leaves *either* scale-like 1-2(3) mm long, more or less adpressed to shoot and very crowded, or up to 10 mm (12) and more or less spreading and less crowded; leaf apex sharp pointed enough to

puncture skin; cone globose with 10-16 scales, each scale with 3-6 inverted ovules: *Athrotaxis*

8↓ Leaves more or less distant, margin serrulate, 1.5-6.0(7) cm long, more or less curved linear-lanceolate, base broad, decurrent, spirally arranged but appearing more or less 2-ranked in one plane; cones more or less globose, the scales each with an eroded margin and bearing 3 inverted ovules on the upper surface below a toothed ridge: *Cunninghantia*

8 General habit of *Cunninghamia*; leaves densely crowded and more or less awl-shaped, margin entire, curved toward shoot, 3-sided, 5-6(7) mm long when adult with stomatal hands on all sides; cones oblong or subglobose, 12-20 mm long with numerous scales, each scale with 2 erect ovules on upper surface: *Taimania*

Araucariaceae

1 Leaves with parallel venation and without conspicuous midrib, spirally arranged, sometimes imbricate, small and scale-like or awl-shaped and then mostly less than 2 cm long, or flat and broad and then up to 5 cm long (to 10 cm in 3 species from New Guinea); terminal bud inconspicuous, male cones up to 20 cm long; female cones large, of numerous woody scales each with apical point; seed solitary on each scale and united with it, mostly wingless; generally monoecious: *Araucaria*

1 Leaves opposite or alternate, but often appearing 2-ranked, flat, lanceolate-elliptic to ovate with numerous more or less obsolete veins without conspicuous midrib; male cones less than 5 cm long; female cones large with numerous woody scales but no apical point; seed solitary on each scale but not united with it, with a single wing but sometimes a rudimentary second; monoecious or dioecious: *Agathis*

Cupressaceae

1 Fruit indehiscent and berry-like of 3-6(8) finally fleshy united scales enclosing 1-12 wingless seeds; leaves either scale-like, crowded, closely adpressed and opposite or needle-like or awl-shaped and spreading in whorls of 3 (always this type on young plants): *Juniperus*

1 Fruit a woody more or less typical cone, the scales finally separating to release the seeds: 2

2 Cone more or less globose of 3-8 pairs of woody, valvate, peltate scales: 3

2 Cone more or less elongated, ovoid to oblong, the scales flat, not peltate: 5

3 Scale leaves in whorls of 4 arising at same level, about 2 mm long: facial leaves narrowly oblanceolate with pointed apex, lateral leaves ovate and somewhat compressed; cones almost globose, 25 × 20 mm, with 12-16 scales; fertile scales with 2 seeds having very unequal wings: *Fokiena*

3 Not this combination; leaves scale-like, opposite and decussate: seeds more or less winged: 4

4 Cones of 6-12 peltate scales and ripening in the second year: each scale with 6-20 ovules: *Cupressus*

4$^{\downarrow}$ Cones typically of (4)6-12 peltate scales and ripening within the year except *Ch. nootkatensis* which mature in the second year; each scale with 2-5 ovules; wings of seed more conspicuous than in *Cupressus*: *Chamaecyparis*

4 A much cultivated quick-growing inter-generic hybrid with the foliage of *Chamaecyparis nootkatensis* and the cones of *Cupressus macrocarpa*. Foliage often in flattened sprays, but not always: × *Cupressocyparis*

5 Leaves in whorls of 3, scale-like to 3 mm long, incurved with pointed tip and borne on shoots more or less round or square in cross section; cone globose 8(10) mm across, of 3 whorls of more or less alternating scales, each whorl having 3 slightly overlapping scales, the upper whorl always fertile, the lower sterile, the middle whorl sometimes fertile; fertile scales with umbo, each scale with 2-6 seeds, each seed with 2-3 wings: *Fitzroya*

5 Not this combination of characters; leaves and cone-scales opposite: 6

6 Scales leaves minute (1 mm long) and adpressed, mostly decussate, sometimes in whorls, more or less keeled and with blunt point; shoots more or less round or square in cross section; sexes on different plants; cone small of 2 pairs of scales on a stout central axis, only the upper pair fertile, each scale with 2 3-winged seeds: *Diselma*

6 Not this combination of characters: 7

7 Cone-scales clearly imbricate; scales not in whorls of 3 or 4:8

7 Cone-scales not imbricate, laterally adpressed and separating from above downward as valves; scales in pairs or whorls of 3 or 4: 11

8 Cone reflexed of 3-5 pairs of scales, each scale with 3-5(6) winged seeds on its lower surface; branchlets much flattened; leaves broadly elliptical, 5-6 mm long: *Thujnpsis*

8 Each cone-scale with not more than 2 unequally winged seeds beneath each scale, wingless in *Thuja orientalis*: 9

9 Cone pendulous of (3)4-10 pairs of scales, 2-3 middle pairs fertile: *Thuja*

9 Cones composed of 2-3 pairs of scales: 10

10 All the leaves of equal length and long decurrent: cones erect, each of 3 pairs of scales with subapical recurved spine, the lowest pair small, recurved, middle pair alone fertile, the upper fused together: *Calocedrus*

10 Facial leaves bluntly diamond-shaped, smaller than laterals, scarcely 1 mm long; laterals incurved awl-shaped 1.5-4.5 mm long: *Austrocedrus*

11 Cones with 6-8 scales arranged in whorls of 3 or 4: 12 11 Cones with 4 scales in 2 pairs: 13

11 Cones with 3 whorls each of 3 scales: *Fitzroya*

12 Scale leaves in ranks of 3; cones with 2 whorls, each of 3 scales; seeds 2-9 on each scale, each with 1-3 broad wings: *Callitris*

12 Scale leaves arranged in 8 vertical rows; cones with 2 whorls, each of 4 scales; seeds virtually unwinged: *Neocallitropsis*

13 Lateral and facial (especially juvenile) leaves different (dimorphic) : 14

13 Adult leaves at least not dimorphic: 16

14 Branchlets flattened (phyllomorphs); the shoots appearing jointed owing to the scale leaves barely overlapping, the lateral leaves the larger and long decurrant; cone terminal and globose, 8-12 mm across, outer surface of scales deeply grooved; seeds with 2 broad wings, widening upward: *Tetraclinis*

14↓ Cone leathery, the upper pair of scales 2-3 times longer than lower pair and all with a triangular basal appendage (below middle); lateral leaves 4-5 mm the facial shorter: *Papuacedrus*

14 Not the respective characters of the above two genera, but foliage in more or less flattened sprays (phyllomorphs) : 15

15 Cone-scales with curved dorsal mucro; only 1 seed per fertile scale; stomata on both sides of leaf: *Libocedrus*

15 Cone-scales with minute dorsal boss; 1 or 2 seeds per fertile scale; facial leaves about one-quarter length of the laterals, the latter to

4.5 mm with longitudinal groove on both sides; stomata virtually confined to lower leaf surface: *Austrocedrus*

16 Fertile scales of cone similar, each with 5 or more ovules; seeds 12 or more per cone, each seed 2-winged: *Widdringtonia*

16 Ovules and seeds 1 or 2 per cone-scale: 17

17 Leaves about 1 mm long, more or less keeled; cone with conspicuous central axis; each upper fertile cone-scale with 2 ovules; seed 2 mm long, a little longer than its scale and with typically 3 wings: *Diselma*

17 Leaves about 2 mm long, with white stomatal bands and more or less keeled; cone with inconspicuous central axis, 1 ovule per fertile cone-scale with 2 very unequal wings: *Pilgerodendron*

Podocarpaceae

1 True leaves scale-like, found only on seedlings; replaced by expanded branchlets (phylloclades) which may be simple and leaf-like and spirally arranged or lobed or pinnate and arranged in whorls, both types up to about 5 × 0.75 cm; cones irregularly more or less globose about 6-13 mm across, of one or more fleshy scales, each scale with a protruding arillate ovule; seeds more or less ellipsoidal, small, about twice as long as its scale; 'cone' often coloured green or red: *Phyllocladus*

1 Branchlets not expanded; leaves not replaced by phylloclades : 2

2 Tree with branchlets opposite or in whorls of 3 or 4; leaves linear, spirally arranged but characteristically twisted and curled 12-18 mm long, tapering to sharp, horny point, and lower surface with a broad, whitish stomatic band on each side of the midrib; 'cone' irregularly globose finally fleshy, 8-13 mm across, of a few pyramidal furrowed scales, the upper scales each with 2 inverted ovules; seeds flattish, ovoid, 3-4 mm long, brown and shiny: *Saxegothea* (cultivated specimens in the absence of fruit are often mistaken for *Podocarpus andinus* and *vice versa*.)

2 Not this combination of characters: 3

3 Bushes or shrubs with overlapping scale-like leaves up to 2.5 mm long; scales of 'cone' fleshy either of 4-8 scales with erect ovule (epimatium absent), seed without aril or more than 8 scales and inverted ovule, the seed with scarlet aril (epimatium present): 4

3 Other character combinations; mostly trees: 5

4 'Cone' 6-9 mm long, of more than 8 scales, each scale finally with an inverted arillate seed (epimatium present): *Microcachrys*

4 'Cone' 2-3 mm long, of 4-8 scales; ovule erect, seed not arillate (epimatium absent): *Microstrobos*

5 Epimatium free from the integument of the ovule; ovule at first inverted, finally more or less erect; 'cone' of 1-8 scales, each scale with a solitary ovule; seed shed with attached short basal cup-like aril: *Dacrydium*

5 Epimatium joined with the integument of the ovule; seed often borne on a fleshy receptacle: 6

6 Foliage like *Taxus* (yews) of sessile linear leaves about 0.5-2 cm × 2-3 mm, appearing 2-ranked in one plane; ovule erect, borne on a fleshy receptacle of 7-9 fused scales, only the upper scale fertile and maturing a single seed; epimatium shorter than seed: *Acmopyle*

6 Leaves very variable in shape and texture, size from small and scale-like up to 30 × 5 cm; 'cone'-scales mostly 2-4, but may be more, only 1 or 2 fertile and bearing a single inverted ovule of which only one matures to a seed; remaining sterile scales often, but not in all species, fused together to form a fleshy, edible, coloured receptacle; the epimatium is well developed and surrounds the whole seed and falls with it: *Podocarpus*

Cephalotaxaceae

Only one genus: *Cephalotaxus*

Taxaceae

1 Leaves opposite, linear-lanceolate, 3-13.5 cm long, with raised midrib on both surfaces, that on lower surface flanked by whitish stomatic band; seed surrounded by more or less orange aril open at the top; male inflorescence pendulous: *Amentotaxus*

1 Not this combination of characters; leaves inserted spirally: 2

2 Leaves linear, 7-15 cm long and up to 3.5 mm wide, spirally arranged; male cones in dense axillary spikes 12-16 mm long; seed 12-16 mm long, ovoid to ellipsoidal, enclosed, except at extreme tip, by a fleshy aril: *Austrotaxus*

2 Not this combination of characters; male inflorescence never in spikes: 3

3 Stalk of male inflorescence with 8 decussate, sterile, more or less ovate scales 2-3 mm long; the ovule-bearing stalk similar but with 16-18 scales, the uppermost 4-5 mm long and surrounding the ovule; aril cup-shaped, white; leaves twisted at base and appearing 2-ranked in same plane, linear 12-25 mm long: *Pseudotaxus*

3 Not this combination of characters: 4

4 Leaves linear, yellowish-green beneath without stomatic bands or lines, rarely exceeding 25 mm long, spirally inserted but often, though not always, appearing 2-ranked; seed surrounded to just above the middle by scarlet aril: *Taxus*

4 Leaves 12-80 mm long, linear to linear-lanceolate, sharply pointed, lower surface with one longitudinal stomatal band in a sunken furrow on either side of a raised midrib; seed mostly broadly ellipsoidal, 25-45 mm long, surrounded by a thin, fleshy aril – whitish, green, reddish-brown, sometimes purple-streaked: *Torreya*

Key to Broadleaved Families and Aberrant Genera

1 Plants with white latex or milky resin (cut petiole, pedicel or branchlet): 2

1 Not so: any juice watery: 4

2 Leaves opposite, lobed; stipules absent: *Aceraceae* (*Acer*) (part)

2 Leaves alternate, rarely opposite (*Broussonetia*) and then with (deciduous) stipules: 3

3 Leaves odd-pinnate (terminal leaflet present) or with just 3 leaflets; flowers with petals: *Anacardiaceae* (*Rhus*)

3 Leaves simple, sometimes lobed, the lobes more or less constricted toward the base; petals absent, the perianth a single whorl, its parts and the stamens typically 4, the latter opposite the perianth lobes: *Moraceae*

4 Flowers with modified calyx and corolla, the sepals and petals being united in the bud stage to form a 'lid' (operculum) which falls off as the flower opens; stamens numerous, exceeding petals, free or united in bundles opposite the petals; ovary with 2-5 chambers. Trees or shrubs (not climbers) with alternate leaves (opposite in very young plants), aromatic when crushed: *Myrtaceae* (*Eucalyptus*)

4 Not this combination of characters : 5

5 Horsetail (*Equisetuin*) like woody plants lacking ordinary leaf-like foliage, with striate jointed stems and branches bearing whorls of small teeth-like scales; perianth absent in female flowers which are clustered in a head; male flowers with a single stamen accompanied by 2 small scales and up to 2 inconspicuous perianth scales; fruiting heads forming woody, more or less globose cone-like structures, the winged nutlets protruding between hard persistent bractlets: *Casuarinaceae* (*Casuarina*)

5↓ Flowers typically with a single distinct perianth whorl or none: petals absent or reduced to inconspicuous scales or glands, the perianth whorl rarely petaloid: 6

5 Flowers typically with two perianth whorls, the calyx mostly green(ish), the corolla coloured; calyx sometimes absent: 23

6 At least the male flowers arranged in catkins: 7

6 No flowers arranged in catkins: 10

7 Male and female flowers in catkins, perianth absent; ovary superior; leaves alternate, simple, lobed or not: 8

7 Typically only flowers of one sex in catkins; at least one sex with perianth: 9

8 Fruit a capsule with many woolly seeds; dioecious plants, the male catkins *either* erect with the exserted stamens subtended by a gland *or* pendulous and the stamens subtended by a fimbriate bract: Salicaceae

8 Fruit a 1-seeded nut or samara; female flowers 2-3 in the axil of a scale, styles 2: catkins mostly pendulous: *Betulaceae*

9 Ovary inferior, styles 2; leaves pinnate: *Juglandaceae*

9 Ovary inferior, styles 3-6: leaves simple: fruit a nut: *Fagaceaſ*

10 Ovaries 2 or more, the carpels free from one another: 11

10 Ovary solitary of 1 carpel or more than 1 carpel fused together: 13

11 Perianth absent, flowers not in heads; leaves opposite and ralmately veined: *Cercidiphyllaceae* (*Cercidiphyllum*)

11 Perianth present: 12

12 Hyrogynous flowers, the perianth of 6 or more pretaloid lobes; carpels numerous, spirally arranged on an elongated receptacle; leaves simple, the stipules falling to leave a circular scar; fruit 1-seeded: *Magnoliaceae*

12↓ Similar to above but stipules absent and ovaries not on an elongated receptacle: *Winteraceae* (*Drimys*)

12 Perigynous flowers; leaves alternate: Rosaceae

13 Perianth absent; flowers in globose heads; ovary inferior, 6-10 celled: *Nyssaceae* (*Davidia*)

13 Perianth present: 14

14 At least the female flowers in globular heads or dense spikes or lining the inside of a hollow receptacle: 15

14 Not so: 16

15 Nodes sheathed by stipules; leaves palmately lobed; fruit a nutlet: *Platanaceae* (*Platanus*)

15↓ Nodes not so sheathed; leaves palmately lobed; fruit a capsule: *Hamamelidaceae* (*Liquidambar*)

15↓ Leaves pinnate or absent and then replaced by flattened petioles; fruit a legume: *Leguminosae* (*Acacia*)

15 Fruit neither a nutlet nor a legume but a fleshy syncarp, the individual fruitlets borne externally or within a hollow receptacle: *Moraceae*

16 Trees or shrubs with superior ovary: 17

16 Trees or shrubs, the ovary inferior or virtually so; leaves alternate, fruit drupe-like: 22

17 Heaves opposite: 18

17 Leaves alternate: 20

18 Fruit dehiscent; leaves simple, entire, unlobed: *Buxaceae* (*Buxus*)

18 Fruit an indehiscent samara: leaves mostly compound or lobed : 19

19 Samara single with one wing: leaves typically pinnate: *Oleaceae* (*Fraxinus*)

19 Samara double with 2 wings: leaves simple, palmately lobed or 3-7 foliolate: *Aceraceae*

20 Anthers opening by hinged flaps; *either* leaves unlobed, evergreen and pleasant or unpleasant smelling when crushed *or* leaves deciduous and the adult leaves at least more or less 3-lobed: *Lauraceae*

20 Not this combination of characters: 21

21 Ovary of 1 chamber, styles 2; flowers bisexual or unisexual; fruit *either* a nutlet surrounded by a more or less broad membranous wing or a more or less oblique drupe: *Ulmaceae*

21 Ovary of 1 chamber, style 1; perianth petaloid, more or less tubular, often narrowly so and splitting as flower opens; stamens 4, more or less sessile on upper part of tube or one on each perianth lobe: flowers solitary, in racemes or large heads: *Proteaceae*

22 Shoots and alternate leaves more or less scurfy with peltate or star-shaped scales; ovary of 1 chamber: *Elaeagnaceae* (*Elaeagnus*)

22 Plants not scaly; *either* ovary with 1(2) chambers and inflorescence without conspicuous bracts *or* ovary with 6-10 chambers and inflorescence with 2 conspicuous white bracts: *Nyssaceae*

23 Petals free to the base, falling off singly (polyretalous): 24 23 Petals more or less united at least toward the base and forming a longer or shorter tube, the corolla falling as a whole (gamoretalous): 46

24 Ovaries 2 or more, the individual carpels free to the base: 25

24 Ovary *either* of one carpel or of several united carpels: 30

25 Stamens numerous (more than to): 26

25 Stamens 10 or fewer: 32

26 Ovary superior and flower *either* hypogynous or prerigynous: 27

26 Ovary inferior, perianth and numerous stamens arising above it; a free calyx tube absent: 29

27 Hyrogynous flower: 28

27 Perigynous flower with differentiated sepals and petals; leaves typically alternate and serrate: Rosaceae

28 Sepals and petals imbricate, the latter large (more than 3.5 cm across), typically more than 5, often in whorls of 3, spirally arranged on an elongated axis: stipules conspicuous and falling to leave a circular scar; fruit a rod or achene: *Magnoliaceae*

28 Not this combination; sepals valvate or shortly united below, 2-4(6), distinct from the small (less than 3.5 cm across) corolla; ovaries not on an elongated axis; stipules absent or minute, not leaving a circular scar; fruit a berry: *Winteraceae* (*Drimys*)

29 Woody not fleshy plants; leaves typically alternate and toothed, stipules typically present: *Rosaceae*

29 Woody not fleshy plants: leaves without stipules, usually evergreen and entire, often gland-dotted (hold against light) and aromatic when bruised: *Myrtaceae* (*Eucalyptus*)

30 Leaves alternate and bipinnate, fruit a 1-chambered legume: *Leguminosae* (*Albizia*)

30 Not this combination: 31

31 Leaves alternate; sepals valvate; ovary of 2 or more chambers; fruit indehiscent: *Tiliaceae* (*Tilia*)

31 Not this combination; leaves opposite, at most only simply pinnate; sepals and petals typically 4; evergreen plants: *Eucryphiaceae*

32 Ovary superior: 33

32 Ovary inferior: 45

33 Perigynous flowers with 2 or more free carpels; leaves not pellucid punctate, typically alternate and toothed with stipules: *Rosaceae*

33 Hypogynous flowers with 2 or more free carpels, the stamens inserted below the ovary: 34

33 Hypogynous flowers as before, but 2 more carpels united to form a 1 to many-chambered ovary: 35

34 Leaves gland-dotted (hold against light); *either* pinnate or 3-foliolate and fruit a samara; *or* apparently simple and the fruit a lemon: *Rutaceae*

34 Leaves not gland-dotted; leaves pinnate with 13-41 leaflets; fruit a samara: *Simaroubaceae* (*Ailanthus*)

35 Ovary of 1 chamber with more than 1 ovule attached to the wall; leaves alternate, typically compound; fruit a legume: *Leguminosae*

35 Not this combination: 36

36 Leaves alternate, odd-pinnate or of 3 leaflets; stamens 5; styles 2-5; fruit a drupe with 1 seed: *Anacardiaceae* (*Rhus*)

36 Style solitary; ovary of 2 or more chambers: 37

37 Flowers clearly irregular: 38

37 Flowers virtually regular: 40

38 Leaves simple; anthers opening by pores: *Ericaceae* (*Rhododendron*)

38 Not so: 39

39 Leaves opposite, digitate: *Hippocastanaceae*

39 Leaves alternate, bipinnate: *Sapindaceae* (*Koelreuteria*)

40 Leaves opposite or in whorls – if alternate, then fruit a lobed capsule: 41

40 Leaves alternate: 42

41 Leaves typically pinnate; fruit always a single samara: *Oleaceae* (*Fraxinus*)

41 Leaves typically simple, often lobed, rarely 3-7-foliolate; fruit always a double samara: *Aceraceae* (*Acer*)

41 Fruit a dehiscent lobed capsule of 4-5 chambers: *Celastraceae* (*Euonymus*)

42 Leaves compound: 43

42 Leaves simple, often spiny; flower parts in 4's or 5's; fruit a berry-like drupe: *Aquifoliaceae* (*Ilex*)

43 Leaves 3-foliolate; fruit dry: *Rutaceae* (*Ptelea*)

43 Leaves pinnate or bipinnate: 44

44 At least some of the leaves bipinnate; flowers in conspicuous panicles before the leaves; stamens 8 or less, free below: *Sapindaceae* (*Koelreuteria*)

44 Leaves pinnate or bipinnate; stamens 5 or to, united below: *Meliaceae*

45 Leaves alternate, more or less serrate, stipules present; stamens more than twice petal number; fruit a pome: *Rosaceae*

45 Not this combination. Plants with no prickles but with star-shaped hairs; styles 2, free to the base; fruit a woody capsule: *Hamamelidaceae*

46 Ovary superior (hypogynous flower): 47

46 Ovary inferior (half inferior in Styracaceae) (epigynous flower) : 53

47 Number of stamens equal to at least twice number of petal lobes: 48

47 Number of stamens not more than the number of petal lobes and alternating with them: 50

48 Stamens arising free from corolla; style solitary; fruit a 5-chambered capsule: *Ericaceae*

48 Stamens united to corolla tube; styles and chambers of ovary 2 or more: 49

49 Stamen filaments more or less united into bundles; fruit a capsule: *Theaceae*

49 Stamen filaments free, not united into bundles; styles 4; fruit a berry: *Ebenaceae*

50 Deciduous trees with opposite large broad leaves (at least 10 × 10 cm); flowers irregular, conspicuous and trumpet shaped with 4 fertile stamens; fruit a capsule opening along midribs of carpels, with numerous ovules on a central axis: *Scrophulariaceae* (*Pauloinnia*)

50 Corolla regular, stamens up to 5; ovary solitary: 51

51 Leaves opposite; stamens less than 5, mostly joined to corolla, but alternating with lobes: *Oleaceae*

51 Leaves typically alternate, sometimes appearing whorled (*Pittosporum*); stamens 5, free from corolla; ovary solitary: 52

52 Anthers opening by apical pores (slightly elongated in *Oxydendrum*), style present; fruit a capsule: *Ericaceae*

52 Anthers opening by longitudinal slits; style present; fruit capsular; seeds resinous: *Pittosporaceae* (*Pittosporum*)

52 Anthers opening by longitudinal slits, but style absent, the stigma virtually sessile; fruit a drupe; seeds not resinous: *Aquifoliaceae* (*Ilex*)

53 Anthers not laterally cohering to form a tube round the style; leaves alternate; stamens twice as many as corolla lobes: 54

53 Anthers as above, but stamens 4-5; leaves opposite: *Caprifoliaceae*

54 Stamens united at base; anthers opening by slits; fruit a dry, winged drupe: *Styracaceae*

54 Stamens free; anthers opening by apical pores; fruit a berry: *Ericaceae*.

Key to Broadleaved Genera by Families

Where only one genus occurs in a family, this is accompanied by a short diagnosis to distinguish it from other related genera not dealt with and the plant under examination must comply with the short diagnosis.

Magnoliaceae

A Leaves entire, acute or tapering at apex; fruit a dehiscent follicle: *Magnolia*

AA Leaves lobed, more or less truncate at apex; fruit a samara (indehiscent): *Liriodendron*

Winteraceae

Sometimes included in Magnoliaceae, but stipules absent and floral axis short: *Drimys*

Lauraceae

A Leaves entire, not lobed, evergreen, faintly pungent but pleasant when crushed; flowers bisexual, typically with 12(8-14) stamens: *Laurus*

AA↓ Leaves entire, not lobed, evergreen, painfully pungent when crushed and sniffed; flowers bisexual; stamens 9: *Umbellularia*

AAA Leaves deciduous, at least some (mainly adult ones) lobed; flowers unisexual : *Sassafras*

Cercidiphyllaceae

Deciduous trees with mostly opposite, broadly ovate leaves; flowers dioecious: stamens numerous; carpels 3·4(5): *Cercidiphyllum*

Platanaceae

Trees with scaling bark; leaves alternate, palmately lobed and veined; petiole base enlarged and enclosing axillary bud: *Platanus*

Hamamelidaceae

A Trees; leaves palmately lobed and veined; flowers unisexual monoecious, in dense clusters; petals absent: *Liquidambar*

AA↓ Trees; leaves with stellate pubescence, sinuate-dentate; flowers bisexual; petals absent: *Parrotia*

AAA Shrubs; leaves penninerved, more or less sinuate-dentate; flowers bisexual; petals conspicuous, strap-like (linear): *Hamanielis*

Fagaceae

A Male flowers solitary or in threes: leaves usually less than 8 cm long, evergreen or deciduous; involucre 2-4 lobed; fruit a 3-angled nut: *Nothofagus*

AA↓ Male flowers numerous in pendulous globose heads; female flowers in 2's; leaves deciduous, usually more than 8 cm long when adult; involucre (cupule) distinctly prickly; fruit a 3-angled nut: *Fagus*

AAA↓ Male flowers numerous in pendulous catkins; female flowers solitary or in 2 to numerous flowered spikes; fruit a subglobose or more or less elongated nut (acorn) without angles, the involucre (cupule) basal or almost enclosing the fruit, its surface rugose or variously scaly to prickly: *Quercus*

AAAA Male flowers in upright spikes and leaves deciduous, dentate; ovary 6-chambered involucre prickly (burr); terminal bud absent: *Castanea*

AAAAA Male flowers in upright spikes; leaves entire or dentate, evergreen: B

B Involucre (cupule) of fruit more or less cup-shaped, virtually smooth; nut ovoid, solitary: *Lithocarpus*

BB Involucre covered with branched spines (burr); nuts 3 in each burr and triangular in cross section: *Chrysolepis*

Betulaceae

A Perianth present in female flowers, absent in male; nut enclosed in more or less leafy involucre formed from united bracteoles: B

AA Perianth present in male flowers, absent in female; nut more or less flat, often winged or with margin; involucre absent: C

B Female flowers few, more or less bud-like; acorn-like (hazel) nut enclosed by leafy, involucre: *Corylus*

BB[↓] Female flowers numerous in short, erect spikes; male flowers appear in the fall; involucre tubular or bladder-like: *Ostrya*

BBB Female flowers in long pendulous catkins; male flowers appear in spring; involucre flat, 3-lobed: *Carpinus*

C Stamens 2, the filaments divided; fruiting catkins with 3-lobed deciduous scales: *Betula*

CC Stamens 4, the filaments not divided; fruits forming a black, woody cone-like structure composed of 5-lobed persistent scales: *Alnus*

Casuarinaceae

Horsetail (*Equisetum*) like plants, the foliage leaves replaced by whorls of minute scales: *Casuarina*

Theaceae

A Leaves evergreen; flowers erect with deciduous sepals; fruit a subglobose capsule with 1-3 large (2 cm) seeds: *Camellia*

AA Leaves deciduous; flowers with evident stalk; seeds numerous, smaller, more or less flat: *Stemartia*

Tiliaceae

Trees with star-shaped hairs; leaves alternate, simple; peduncle with large, oblong, partly adnate bract: *Tilia*

Ulmaceae

A Leaves with 3 more or less prominent basal veins; remaining veins less than 7, virtually pinnate; bark usually smooth without fissures; perianth free to the base; fruit a drupe: *Celtis*

AA Not this combination of characters; pinnate veins of leaves 7 or more: B

B Bark typically fissured; leaves typically oblique and twice serrate; fruit a broadly-winged nut (samara): *Ulmus*

BB Bark typically smooth; leaves simply serrate; perianth joined below; style excentric; fruit an oblique drupe without wing: *Zelkova*

Moraceae

A Leaves entire but may be lobed; stipules large, completely clasping the stem, soon falling to leave circular scar; flowers borne on the inside of a fleshy receptacle (syncarp) which becomes the edible: *Ficus*

AA Not this combination; stipules small: B

B Leaves entire, not lobed; branches spiny; 'fruit' cluster a globose syncarp 10-14 cm across, the individual drupelet fruits borne externally each on a short stalk: *Maclura*

BB Leaves crenate-serrate, possibly lobed; branches not spiny: C

C Flowers borne in small similar catkin-like spikes; ripe fruit red, like a loganberry: *Morus*

CC Male flowers in pendulous catkins; female flowers borne externally in globose heads; 'fruit' cluster a globose syncarp, the individual ripe fruits protruding on a fleshy stalk: *Broussonetia*

Salicaceae

A Catkins pendulous, the scales typically laciniate; leaves mostly broad with long stalk; flowers with basal cup-shaped disk: *Populus*

AA Scales of catkins entire, the male catkins at least typically erect; leaves mostly more or less lanceolate with short stalk; flowers with one or more basal glands: *Salix*

Ericaceae

A Flowers urn-shaped in large terminal panicles; anthers with 2 long reflexed awns; ovary superior; fruit a more or less warty berry; leaves evergreen: *Arbutus*

AA Not so; anthers without awns; fruit a capsule: B

B Fruit a septicidal capsule; corolla more or less funnel-shaped, more than 1 cm long, weakly irregular, the 5-20 stamens typically upturned; leaves typically entire, evergreen or deciduous: *Rhododendron* (incl. *Azalea*)

BB Fruit a loculicidal capsule; leaves deciduous, serrulate; flowers urn-shaped, less than 1 cm long: *Oxydendrum*

Ebenaceae

Deciduous or evergreen trees or shrubs; leaves alternate, simple, entire; flowers dioecious; ovary superior: *Diospyros*

Styracaceae

A Flowers solitary or in racemes; ovary superior or virtually so; fruit neither ribbed nor winged; corolla 5(8)-lobed: *Styrax*

AA Some flowers in axillary clusters; ovary inferior; fruit with 2-4 wings; corolla 4-lobed: *Halesia*

Pittosporaceae

Evergreen trees or shrubs; leaves alternate but sometimes appearing whorled, mostly entire without stipules; flowers not blue, petals less than 15 mm long; fruit a capsule: *Pittosporum*

Eucryphiaceae

Evergreen trees or shrubs; leaves opposite, simple or pinnate, and stipulate; sepals 4, petals 4(5); stamens numerous; fruit a capsule: *Eucryphia*

Rosaceae

A Flowers perigynous with superior ovary; leaves serrate, simple; fruit a drupe typically of 1 carpel; sepals 5, petals conspicuous: *Prunus* (*sensu lato*)

AA Flowers epigynous with an inferior ovary; leaves simple or compound, entire in *Cydonia* and *Mespilus*: fruit a pome of 2-5 more or less united carpels: B

B Leaves pinnate with odd, terminal leaflet: *Sorbus* (part)

BB Leaves simple, unlobed, lobed or variously dissected: C

C Leaves entire or almost so and flowers 2-5 cm across, solitary: D

CC Leaf margins variously toothed, lobed or dissected: E

D Fruit globose, 2-3 cm across, brownish with persistent leafy calyx lobes, open above and with 5 'stones' (endocarp stony): *Mespilus*

DD Fruit 5-7 cm across, more or less pear-shaped, yellowish, without leafy calyx lobes, closed above with many 'pips', the endocarp being papery and not stony: *Cydonia*

E Deciduous trees or shrubs, typically with leafless spines (rarely spines absent); leaves variously toothed or lobed; flowers 12 mm or more across in cymes or panicles; fruit with 1-5 bony nutlets: *Crataegus*

EE Not this combination of characters; fruits with 'pip' seeds only (papery endocarp): F

F Inflorescence corymbose or paniculate; flowers less than 10 mm across; the 5 chambers of the fruit each with 1-2 seeds: *Sorbus* (part)

FF Inflorescence of umbels or racemes or flowers solitary; flowers more than 15 mm across: G

G Each chamber of fruit with numerous 'pips' (more than 4): *Chaenomeles*

GG Each chamber of the fruit with not more than 2 seeds: H

H Ovary and fruit incompletely divided into 6-10 chambers; flowers typically in terminal racemes and styles 5: *Amelanchier*

HH Ovary and fruit with 2-5 chambers, each chamber with 2 seeds; deciduous trees and shrubs with umbel-like inflorescence: J

J Flowers with petals some shade of pink; styles joined below; fruit an 'apple' without grit cells or very few such cells: *Malus*

JJ Flowers typically with pure white petals; styles free below; fruit a 'pear', the grit cells numerous and evident: *Pyrus*

Leguminosae (Fabaceae)

A Flowers regular - not pea-like - petals, valvate, sometimes absent: B

AA Flowers irregular, typically pea-like: G

B Leaves replaced by flattened petioles functioning as leaves; flowers typically yellow in close globose or cylindric spikelike clusters; stamens numerous (more than 10) long exserted, the filament not, or scarcely joined below: *Acacia* (part)

B Leaves 1-2 pinnate: C

C Stamens numerous (more than 10) long exserted; petals 4-5, valvate: D

CC Stamens 10 or fewer; petals imbricate; flowers not in close clusters: E

D Flowers as in B above, the stamens not or scarcely joined at the base; fruit mostly opening by 2 valves: *Acacia* (part)

DD Flowers as in B above but stamen filaments more or less united to form a tube below; pod indehiscent: *Albizia*

E Flowers mostly yellow; leaves 1-pinnate; stamens 5-10, but some often infertile: *Cassia*

EE Flowers greenish to more or less white, not conspicuous; leaves 1- or 2-pinnate: F

F Trees lacking spines; leaves 2-pinnate with entire leaflets; flowers in loose terminal panicles: *Gymnocladus*

FF Trees typically with spines; leaves 1-2-pinnate with more or less toothed leaflets; flowers in spike-like racemes: *Gleditsia*

G Leaves typically simple, with palmate venation, more or less kidney-shaped, 6-12 cm long; flowers light or deep pink, borne on trunk or branches before the leaves: *Cercis*

GG↓ Leaves compound, 3-foliolate; flowers in pendulous racemes, the 10 staminal filaments united below in a tube; calyx 2-lipped; flowers yellow in *Laburnum*; more or less purplish in *Laburnocytisus*

GGG Leaves odd-pinnate with 5 or more leaflets: H

H Trees with white or yellow(ish) flowers, inflorescence pendulous; stamens 10; pod flat, not jointed: I

HH As above, but flowers in upright panicles; pod terete, jointed: *Sophora*

I Inflorescence paniculate; leaflets alternate: *Cladrastis*

II Inflorescence a raceme; leaflets opposite: *Robinia*

Myrtaceae

Evergreen trees, rarely shrubs; leaves alternate in *Eucalyptus* (often opposite in young plants of that genus); calyx lobes and petals unite in a 'lid' (operculum) which falls off as flower opens; stamens numerous; fruit a capsule opening above by 3-6 valves: *Eucalyptus*

Nyssaceae

A Leaves tapering to more or less rounded at base, margin entire or with a few scattered teeth; inflorescence with 2(3) conspicuous, ovate white bracts to 16 cm long: *Davidia*

AA Leaves cordate at base, margin toothed; inflorescence without bracts: *Nyssa*

Cornaceae

Inflorescence axillary or terminal; leaves typically deciduous, entire, opposite (alternate in *C. alternifolia*, and *C. controversa*); flowers white, bisexual in corymbs or umbels: *Cornus*

Proteaceae

A Flowers bisexual, one in the axil of numerous conspicuous, elongated bracts forming a head; upper and lateral lobes of elongated, narrow perianth fused laterally to form a spoon-like structure with 3 more or less sessile stamens with laterally cohering anthers, occupying the 'bowl' of the 'spoon'; leaves alternate, the margins entire; fruit a nut with one seed: *Protea*

AA Flowers bisexual, but two in the axil of each bract; perianth lobes not fused, the surface of each flat and bearing a more or less sessile stamen; leaves entire or variously toothed and dissected; fruit a follicle with (2)4 seeds: B

B Flowers in racemes or axillary clusters; style disc- or cone-like above; follicles thin-walled: *Grevillea*

BB Flowers crowded in large (10-50 × 5-20 cm) cone-like heads; style not obviously enlarged above; follicles hard, woody, enclosed by bracts and bracteoles: *Banksia*

Elaeagnaceae

Deciduous or evergreen trees or shrubs with peltate to star-shaped grayish to brownish scales, especially on lower leaf surface; leaves entire, alternate, without stipules; sepals and petals 4, the corolla tube much exceeding the ovary; fruit drupe-like: *Elaeagnus*

Celastraceae

Deciduous or evergreen trees or shrubs; leaves mostly opposite; fruit a 4-5-chambered capsule mostly lobed or winged: *Euonymus*

Aquifoliaceae

Evergreen or deciduous trees or shrubs; leaves typically alternate, entire, toothed or spiny; petals oblong to obovate, united below; sepals persistent: *Ilex*

Buxaceae

Evergreen trees or shrubs; leaves opposite, entire; fruit a capsule: *Buxus*

Sapindaceae

Deciduous trees; leaves alternate, odd-pinnate or bipinnate, leaflets serrate; flowers yellow, irregular, in large terminal panicles; fruit a bladder-like capsule; seeds black: *Koelreuteria*

Hippocastanaceae

Trees or shrubs; leaves opposite, digitately 3-9-foliolate; stipules absent: *Aesculus*

Aceraceae

Predominantly deciduous trees, rarely shrubs; leaves opposite 3-5(7)-foliolate or simple and then typically palmately lobed: *Acer*

Anacardiaceae

Deciduous or evergreen trees or shrubs, rarely climbers; leaves alternate, 3-foliolate or odd pinnate; flowers with petals; inflorescence a panicle without sterile branches: *Rhus*

Rutaceae

A Leaves apparently simple comprising 1 'leaflet,' but petiole mostly with leaflet-like wings or margins; fruit of an orange, lemon, grapefruit or tangerine type etc: *Citrus*

AA Leaves compound: B

B Leaves trifoliolate, alternate, deciduous; branches without spines: *Ptelea*

BB Leaves pinnate and opposite: C

C Winter buds hidden within petiole base; fruit a drupe: *Phellodendron*

CC Winter buds exposed in leaf axils; fruit a follicle: *Euodia*

Simaroubaceae

Deciduous trees; leaves alternate, odd-pinnate; leaflets 13-41 with 1 or more glandular teeth near the base; inflorescence terminal; fruit separating into 2-5(6) compressed samaras: *Ailanthus*

Meliaceae

A Leaves typically bipinnate; flowers to 2 cm across, tinged purple; fruit a drupe: *Melia*

AA Leaves once-pinnate; flowers smaller; fruit a septicidal capsule: *Cedrela*

Juglandaceae

A Branches with solid continuous pith; perianth absent or inconspicuous; fruit a dehiscent drupe with almost smooth stone: *Carya*

AA Branches with septate-laminate pith; perianth clearly visible: B

B Fruit indehiscent, stone wrinkled, wing absent: *Juglans*

BB Fruit a pendulous catkin of winged nuts: *Pterocarya*

Oleaceae

A Leaves deciduous, typically pinnate, rarely 3-foliolate or simple; fruit a winged achene (samara): *Fraxinus*

AA↓ Leaves deciduous, simple, rarely pinnate (*Syringa*), fruit a drupe or berry: B

AAA Leaves evergreen, simple; corolla-lobes valvate; fruit a drupe or berry: C

B Corolla 4-lobed, never yellow, its tube at least as long as the lobes; fruit a capsule: *Syringa*

BB As B, but flowers white or creamy and fruit a berry-like drupe: *Ligustrum*

C Flowers in axillary clusters; leaves often silvery scaly beneath; fruit a drupe: *Olea*

CC Flowers in terminal panicles; leaves smooth beneath; fruit a berry: *Ligustrum*

Scrophulariaceae

Trees with large broad opposite leaves 12-25-50 cm long; stamens 4; fruit a loculicidal capsule: *Paulownia*

Bignoniaceae

Mostly deciduous trees, leaves opposite or whorled, margin entire, toothed or lobed, ovate; stamens 2; fruit a long, pendulous, pod-like capsule, the seeds tufted at each end: *Catalpa*

Caprifoliaceae

A Corolla typically rotate; leaves pinnate, style very short, 3-5 lobed; no capitate stigmas; fruit berry-like with 3-5 seeds: *Sambucus*

AA Corolla rotate, leaves simple, lobed or not; style very short 3-5 lobed; no capitate stigmas; fruit a drupe with 1 seed: *Viburnum*

Index